CompTIA Network+ N10-005 Authorized Cert Guide

Kevin Wallace, CCIE #7945

800 East 96th Street
Indianapolis, Indiana 46240 USA

CompTIA Network+ N10-005 Authorized Cert Guide

Library of Congress Cataloging-in-Publication Data

Wallace, Kevin, CCNP.

  CompTIA Network+ N10-005 cert guide / Kevin Wallace.

     p. cm.

  Includes index.

  ISBN 978-0-7897-4821-8 (hardcover w/dvd)

  1. Computer networks—Examinations—Study guides. 2. Electronic data processing personnel—Certification. I. Title.

  TK5105.5.W345 2012

  004.6—dc23

                                                            2011037792

ISBN-13: 978-0-7897-4821-8
ISBN-10: 0-7897-4821-5
Printed in the United States of America
First Printing: November 2011

Trademarks

Warning and Disclaimer

Bulk Sales

Pearson IT Certification offers excellent discounts on this book when ordered in quantity for bulk purchases or special sales. For more information, please contact

U.S. Corporate and Government Sales

1-800-382-3419

corpsales@pearsontechgroup.com

For sales outside of the U.S., please contact

International Sales

international@pearson.com

Associate Publisher
David Dusthimer

Executive Editor
Brett Bartow

Senior Development Editor
Christopher Cleveland

Managing Editor
Sandra Schroeder

Project Editor
Mandie Frank

Copy Editor
Sheri Cain

Indexer
Christine Karpeles

Proofreader
Water Crest Publishing

Technical Editors
Michelle Plumb
Theodor Richardson

Publishing Coordinator
Vanessa Evans

Multimedia Developer
Tim Warner

Designer
Gary Adair

Composition
Mark Shirar

Contents at a Glance

Table of Contents

About the Author

Kevin Wallace, CCIE No. 7945, is a certified Cisco instructor, and he holds multiple certifications, including CCNP, CCNP Voice, CCNP Security, and CCDP, in addition to multiple security and voice specializations. With networking experience dating back to 1989 (and computer experience dating back to 1982), Kevin is a senior technical instructor for SkillSoft. Kevin has been a network design specialist for the Walt Disney World Resort and a network manager for Eastern Kentucky University. Kevin holds a bachelor's of science degree in electrical engineering from the University of Kentucky. Also, Kevin has authored multiple books for Cisco Press, including *Implementing Cisco Unified Communications Voice over IP and QoS (CVOICE), TSHOOT Official Certification Guide, Routing Video Mentor*, and *TSHOOT Video Mentor*. Kevin lives in central Kentucky with his wife (Vivian) and two daughters (Sabrina and Stacie). You can follow Kevin online through the following social-media outlets:

Web page: http://1ExamAMonth.com

Facebook fan page: Kevin Wallace Networking

Twitter: http://twitter.com/kwallaceccie

YouTube: http://youtube.com/kwallaceccie

Network World blog: http://nww.com/community/wallace

iTunes podcast: 1ExamAMonth.com

Dedication

This book is dedicated to my beautiful (inside and out) wife, Vivian. As of this writing, we are 17 years along on our way to forever together.

Acknowledgments

Huge thanks go out to my editor, Brett Bartow, and all the other professionals at Pearson IT Certification. It is my great pleasure to have been associated with you for the past eight years, and I look forward to more exciting projects in the future.

My director at SkillSoft, Dan Young, has been super-supportive of my writing efforts, and I extend my gratitude to him.

Thanks to my technical editors, Michelle Plumb and Theodor Richardson. In a book such as this, with all of its terminology, I'm grateful that you guys were looking over my shoulder and pointing out errors.

In the "Dedication" section, I mentioned my wife, Vivian. I once again want to acknowledge her. Being the parents of two teenage daughters can be time-intensive, and she is always willing to take on more than her fair share so that I can immerse myself in writing.

Speaking of our girls, Stacie and Sabrina, I also want to acknowledge you two. I am very proud of the young ladies you are becoming. Your character and your love for God are an inspiration to others.

As I've grown in my own personal faith, I've discovered that my spiritual gift is teaching. The book you now hold in your hands is a manifestation of that gift. My desire is to be a good steward of that God-given gift. So, with His guidance and continued blessings, I plan to continue demystifying complex concepts to my students and readers.

Albert Einstein once said, "If you can't explain it simply, you don't understand it well enough." My goal for you, the reader, is that you will understand the concepts in this book so well, you will be able to explain them simply to others.

About the Reviewers

Michelle Plumb is a full-time Cisco certified instructor for SkillSoft. Michelle has 22+ years of experience in the field as an IT professional and telephony specialist. She maintains a high level of Cisco, Microsoft, and CompTIA certifications, including A+, Network+, and Project+. Michelle has been a technical reviewer for numerous books related to the Cisco CCNP, CCNP Voice, and CompTIA course material tracks. Michelle currently lives in Phoenix, Arizona, with her husband and two dogs.

Theodor D. Richardson is an author, *Choice* magazine book reviewer, Online Program Director, and Assistant Professor for a private university. He has served as an Assistant Professor for five years in the area of security and multimedia/web design. Theodor has authored *Secure Software Design* (Jones and Bartlett Learning, 2012) and *Microsoft Office and Beyond* (Mercury Learning and Information, 2011). Theodor earned his Ph.D. degree in Computer Science and Engineering from the University of South Carolina in 2006 with a concentration in multimedia and image processing (Graduate Student of the Year 2005). Theodor received an NSF Graduate Research Fellowship and an NSF GK-12 Graduate/K-12 Teaching Fellowship during his graduate studies. He has earned the NSA Graduate Certificate in Information Assurance and Security from the University of South Carolina.

We Want to Hear from You!

As the reader of this book, you are our most important critic and commentator. We value your opinion and want to know what we're doing right, what we could do better, what areas you'd like to see us publish in, and any other words of wisdom you're willing to pass our way.

As an Associate Publisher for Pearson Certification, I welcome your comments. You can e-mail or write me directly to let me know what you did or didn't like about this book—as well as what we can do to make our books better. Please note that I cannot help you with technical problems related to the topic of this book. We do have a User Services group, however, where I will forward specific technical questions related to the book.

When you write, please be sure to include this book's title and author as well as your name, e-mail address, and phone number. I will carefully review your comments and share them with the author and editors who worked on the book.

E-mail: feedback@pearsonitcertification.com

Mail: David Dusthimer
Associate Publisher
Pearson
800 East 96th Street
Indianapolis, IN 46240 USA

Reader Services

Visit our website and register this book at www.pearsonitcertification.com/title/9780789748218 for convenient access to any updates, downloads, or errata that might be available for this book.

CompTIA.

CompTIA Network+

The CompTIA Network+ (2009 Edition) certification ensures that the successful candidate has the important knowledge and skills necessary to manage, maintain, troubleshoot, install, operate, and configure basic network infrastructure, describe networking technologies, basic design principles, and adhere to wiring standards and use testing tools.

It Pays to Get Certified

In a digital world, digital literacy is an essential survival skill—Certification proves you have the knowledge and skill to solve business problems in virtually any business environment. Certifications are highly valued credentials that qualify you for jobs, increased compensation, and promotion.

CompTIA Network+ certification held by many IT staff in organizations—21% of IT staff within a random sampling of U.S. organizations within a cross section of industry verticals hold Network+ certification.

- **The CompTIA Network+ credential**—Proves knowledge of networking features and functions and is the leading vendor-neutral certification for networking professionals.

- **Starting Salary**—The average starting salary of network engineers can be up to $70,000.

- **Career Pathway**—CompTIA Network+ is the first step in starting a networking career and is recognized by Microsoft as part of their MS program. Other corporations, such as Novell, Cisco, and HP, also recognize CompTIA Network+ as part of their certification tracks.

- **More than 260,000**—Individuals worldwide are CompTIA Network+ certified.

- **Mandated/recommended by organizations worldwide**—Such as Cisco, HP, Ricoh, the U.S. State Department, and U.S. government contractors such as EDS, General Dynamics, and Northrop Grumman.

How Certification Helps Your Career

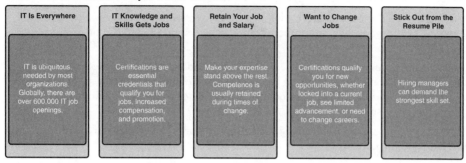

IT Is Everywhere	IT Knowledge and Skills Gets Jobs	Retain Your Job and Salary	Want to Change Jobs	Stick Out from the Resume Pile
IT is ubiquitous, needed by most organizations. Globally, there are over 600,000 IT job openings.	Certifications are essential credentials that qualify you for jobs, increased compensation, and promotion.	Make your expertise stand above the rest. Competence is usually retained during times of change.	Certifications qualify you for new opportunities, whether locked into a current job, see limited advancement, or need to change careers.	Hiring managers can demand the strongest skill set.

CompTIA Career Pathway

CompTIA offers a number of credentials that form a foundation for your career in technology and allow you to pursue specific areas of concentration. Depending on the path you choose to take, CompTIA certifications help you build upon your skills and knowledge, supporting learning throughout your entire career.

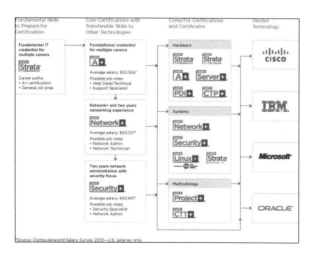

Steps to Getting Certified and Staying Certified	
Review Exam Objectives	Review the certification objectives to make sure you know what is covered in the exam: http://certification.comptia.org/Training/testingcenters/examobjectives.aspx
Practice for the Exam	After you have studied for the certification, take a free assessment and sample test to get an idea of what type of questions might be on the exam: http://certification.comptia.org/Training/testingcenters/samplequestions.aspx
Purchase an Exam Voucher	Purchase your exam voucher on the CompTIA Marketplace, which is located at: http://www.comptiastore.com/
Take the Test!	Select a certification exam provider and schedule a time to take your exam. You can find exam providers at the following link: http://certification.comptia.org/Training/testingcenters.aspx
Stay Certified! Continuing education	Effective January 1, 2011, CompTIA Network+ certifications are valid for three years from the date of certification. There are a number of ways the certification can be renewed. For more information, go to: http://certification.comptia.org/getCertified/steps_to_certification/stayCertified.aspx

Join the Professional Community

Join IT Pro Community http://itpro.comptia.org	The free IT Pro online community provides valuable content to students and professionals.
	Career IT Job Resources:
	■ Where to start in IT ■ Career Assessments ■ Salary Trends ■ U.S. Job Board
	Forums on networking, security, computing, and cutting-edge technologies.
	Access to blogs written by industry experts.
	Current information on cutting-edge technologies.
	Access to various industry resource links and articles related to IT and IT careers.

Content Seal of Quality

This courseware bears the seal of **CompTIA Approved Quality Content.** This seal signifies this content covers 100% of the exam objectives and implements important instructional design principles. CompTIA recommends multiple learning tools to help increase coverage of the learning objectives.

Why CompTIA?

- **Global Recognition**—CompTIA is recognized globally as the leading IT non-profit trade association and has enormous credibility. Plus, CompTIA's certifications are vendor-neutral and offer proof of foundational knowledge that translates across technologies.

- **Valued by Hiring Managers**—Hiring managers value CompTIA certification, because it is vendor- and technology-independent validation of your technical skills.

- **Recommended or Required by Government and Businesses**—Many government organizations and corporations either recommend or require technical staff to be CompTIA certified. (For example, Dell, Sharp, Ricoh, the U.S. Department of Defense, and many more.)

- **Three CompTIA Certifications Ranked in the Top 10**—In a study by DICE of 17,000 technology professionals, certifications helped command higher salaries at all experience levels.

How to Obtain More Information

- **Visit CompTIA online**—www.comptia.org to learn more about getting CompTIA certified.

- **Contact CompTIA**—Call 866-835-8020 ext. 5 or email questions@comptia.org.

- **Join the IT Pro community**—http://itpro.comptia.org to join the IT community to get relevant career information.

- **Connect with us**—

Introduction

The CompTIA Network+ certification is a popular certification for those entering the computer-networking field. Although many vendor-specific networking certifications are popular in the industry, the CompTIA Network+ certification is unique in that it is vendor-neutral. The CompTIA Network+ certification often acts as a stepping-stone to more specialized and vendor-specific certifications, such as those offered by Cisco Systems.

Notice in your CompTIA Network+ study that the topics are mostly generic, in that they can apply to networking equipment regardless of vendor. However, as you grow in your career, I encourage you to seek specialized training for the equipment you work with on a daily basis.

Goals and Methods

The goal of this book is twofold. The #1 goal of this book is a simple one: to help you pass the N10-005 version of the CompTIA Network+ exam.

To aid you in mastering and understanding the Network+ certification objectives, this book uses the following methods:

- **Opening topics list:** This defines the topics that are covered in the chapter.

- **Foundation topics:** At the heart of a chapter, this section explains the topics from a hands-on and a theory-based standpoint. This includes in-depth descriptions, tables, and figures that build your knowledge so that you can pass the N10-005 exam. The chapters are each broken into multiple sections.

- **Key topics:** This indicates important figures, tables, and lists of information that you need to know for the exam. They are sprinkled throughout each chapter and are summarized in table format at the end of each chapter.

- **Memory tables:** These can be found on the DVD within Appendices C and D. Use them to help memorize important information.

- **Key terms:** Key terms without definitions are listed at the end of each chapter. Write down the definition of each term, and check your work against the complete key terms in the Glossary.

For current information about the CompTIA Network+ certification exam, you can visit http://certification.comptia.org/getCertified/certifications/network.aspx.

Who Should Read This Book?

The CompTIA Network+ exam measures the necessary competencies for an entry-level networking professional with the equivalent knowledge of at least 500 hours of hands-on experience in the lab or field. This book was written for people who have that amount of experience working with computer networks. Average readers will have connected a computer to a network, configured IP addressing on that computer, installed software on that computer, used command-line utilities (for example, the **ping** command), and used a browser to connect to the Internet.

Readers will range from people who are attempting to attain a position in the IT field to people who want to keep their skills sharp or perhaps retain their job because of a company policy that mandates they take the new exams.

This book also targets the reader who wants to acquire additional certifications beyond the Network+ certification (for example, the Cisco Certified Network Associate [CCNA] certification and beyond). The book is designed in such a way to offer easy transition to future certification studies.

Strategies for Exam Preparation

Strategies for exam preparation vary, depending on your existing skills, knowledge, and equipment available. Of course, the ideal exam preparation would include building and configuring a computer network from scratch. Preferably, the network would contain both Microsoft Windows® and UNIX hosts, at least two Ethernet switches, and at least two routers.

However, not everyone has access to this equipment, so the next best step you can take is to read the chapters in this book, jotting down notes with key concepts or configurations on a separate notepad. For more visual learners, you might consider the Network+ Video Mentor product by Anthony Sequeira, which is available from Pearson IT Certification, where you get to watch an expert perform multiple configurations.

After you read the book, you can download the current exam objectives by submitting a form on the following web page: http://certification.comptia.org/Training/testingcenters/examobjectives.aspx

If there are any areas shown in the certification exam outline that you still want to study, find those sections in this book and review them.

When you feel confident in your skills, attempt the practice exam, which is included on this book's DVD. As you work through the practice exam, note the areas where you lack confidence and review those concepts or configurations in this book. After you review these areas, work through the practice exam a second time, and rate your skills. Keep in mind that the more you work through the practice exam, the more familiar the questions become, and the practice exam becomes a less accurate judge of your skills.

After you work through the practice exam a second time and feel confident with your skills, schedule the real CompTIA Network+ exam (N10-005). The following website provides information about registering for the exam: http://certification. comptia.org/Training/testingcenters.aspx

To prevent the information from evaporating out of your mind, you should typically take the exam within a week of when you consider yourself ready to take it.

CompTIA Network+ Exam Topics

Table I-1 lists general exam topics (objectives) and specific topics under each general topic (subobjectives) for the CompTIA Network+ N10-005 exam. This table also lists the chapter in which each exam topic is covered. Note that some objectives and subobjectives are addressed in multiple chapters.

Table I-1   CompTIA Network+ Exam Topics

Chapter	N10-005 Exam Objective	N10-005 Exam Subobjective
1 (Introducing Computer Networks)	3.0 Network Media and Topologies	3.5 Describe different network topologies.
2 (Dissecting the OSI Model)	1.0 Network Technologies	1.1 Compare the layers of the OSI and TCP/IP models.
		1.2 Classify how applications, devices, and protocols relate to the OSI layers.
		1.5 Identify common TCP and UDP default ports.
		1.6 Explain the function of common network protocols.

Table I-1 CompTIA Network+ Exam Topics

Chapter	N10-005 Exam Objective	N10-005 Exam Subobjective
3 (Identifying Network Components)	1.0 Network Technologies 2.0 Network Installation and Configuration 3.0 Network Media and Topologies 4.0 Network Management	1.7 Summarize DNS concepts and its components. 1.9 Identify virtual desktop components. 2.3 Explain the purpose and properties of DHCP. 3.1 Categorize standard media types and associated properties. 3.2 Categorize standard connector types based on network media. 3.8 Identify components of wiring distribution. 4.1 Explain the purpose and features of various network appliances.
4 (Understanding Ethernet)	1.0 Network Technologies 2.0 Network Installation and Configuration 3.0 Network Media and Topologies	1.4 Explain the purpose of routing and switching. 2.1 Given a scenario, install and configure routers and switches. 3.7 Compare and contrast different LAN technologies.
5 (Working with IP Addresses)	1.0 Network Technologies	1.3 Explain the purpose and properties of IP addressing.
6 (Routing Traffic)	1.0 Network Technologies 2.0 Network Installation and Configuration	1.4 Explain the purpose and properties of routing and switching. 2.1 Given a scenario, install and configure routers and switches.
7 (Introducing Wide-Area Networks)	3.0 Network Media and Topologies	3.4 Categorize WAN technology types and properties.
8 (Connecting Wirelessly)	2.0 Network Installation and Configuration 3.0 Network Media and Topologies 5.0 Network Security	2.2 Given a scenario, install and configure a wireless network. 2.4 Given a scenario, troubleshoot common wireless problems. 3.3 Compare and contrast different wireless standards. 5.1 Given a scenario, implement appropriate wireless security measures. 5.4 Explain common threats, vulnerabilities, and mitigation techniques.

Table I-1   CompTIA Network+ Exam Topics

Chapter	N10-005 Exam Objective	N10-005 Exam Subobjective
9 (Optimizing Network Performance)	2.0 Network Installation and Configuration	2.6 Given a set of requirements, plan and implement a basic SOHO network.
	4.0 Network Management	4.6 Explain different methods and rationales for network performance optimization.
10 (Using Command-Line Utilities)	4.0 Network Management	4.3 Given a scenario, use appropriate software tools to troubleshoot connectivity issues.
11 (Managing a Network)	4.0 Network Management	4.2 Given a scenario, use appropriate hardware tools to troubleshoot connectivity issues.
		4.3 Given a scenario, use appropriate software tools to troubleshoot connectivity issues.
		4.4 Given a scenario, use the appropriate network resource to analyze traffic.
		4.5 Describe the purpose of configuration management documentation.
12 (Securing a Network)	4.0 Network Management 5.0 Network Security	4.1 Explain the purpose and features of various network appliances.
		5.2 Explain the methods of network access security.
		5.3 Explain methods of user authentication.
		5.4 Explain common threats, vulnerabilities, and mitigation techniques.
		5.5 Given a scenario, install and configure a basic firewall.
		5.6 Categorize different types of network security appliances and methods.
13 (Troubleshooting Network Issues)	1.0 Network Technologies 2.0 Network Installation and Configuration 3.0 Network Media and Topologies	1.8 Given a scenario, implement a given troubleshooting methodology.
		2.4 Given a scenario, troubleshoot common wireless problems.
		2.5 Given a scenario, troubleshoot common router and switch problems.
		3.6 Given a scenario, troubleshoot common physical connectivity problems.

How This Book Is Organized

Although this book could be read cover-to-cover, it is designed to be flexible and allow you to easily move between chapters and sections of chapters to cover just the material that you need more work with. However, if you do intend to read all the chapters, the order in the book is an excellent sequence to use:

- **Chapter 1, "Introducing Computer Networks,"** introduces the purpose of computer networks and their constituent components. Additionally, networks are categorized by their geography, topology, and resource location.

- **Chapter 2, "Dissecting the OSI Model,"** presents the two network models: the OSI model and the TCP/IP stack. These models categorize various network components from a network cable up to and including an application, such as e-mail. These models are contrasted, and you are given a listing of well-known TCP and UDP port numbers used for specific applications.

- **Chapter 3, "Identifying Network Components."** A variety of network components are introduced in this chapter. You are given an explanation of various media types, the roles of specific infrastructure components, and the features provided by specialized network devices (for example, a firewall or content switch).

- **Chapter 4, "Understanding Ethernet."** The most widely deployed LAN technology is Ethernet, and this chapter describes the characteristics of Ethernet networks. Topics include media access, collision domains, broadcast domains, and distance/speed limitations for popular Ethernet standards. Additionally, you are introduced to some of the features available on Ethernet switches, such as VLANs, trunks, STP, link aggregation, PoE, port monitoring, and user authentication.

- **Chapter 5, "Working with IP Addresses."** One of the most challenging concepts for many CompTIA Network+ students is IP subnetting. This chapter demystifies IP subnetting by reviewing the basics of binary numbering, before delving into basic subnetting and then advanced subnetting. Although most of the focus of this chapter is on IP version 4 (IPv4) addressing, the chapter concludes with an introduction to IP version 6 (IPv6).

- **Chapter 6, "Routing Traffic."** A primary job of a computer network is to route traffic between subnets. This chapter reviews the operation of routing IP traffic and discusses how a router obtains routing information. One way a router can populate its routing table is through the use of dynamic routing protocols, several of which are discussed in this chapter. Many environments (such as a home network connecting to the Internet via a cable modem) use NAT to convert between private IP addresses inside a network and public IP addresses outside a network. This chapter discusses DNAT, SNAT, and PAT.

Although the primary focus on this chapter is on unicast routing, the chapter concludes with a discussion of multicast routing.

- **Chapter 7, "Introducing Wide-Area Networks."** Many corporate networks need to interconnect multiple sites separated by large distances. Connections between such geographically dispersed sites make up a WAN. This chapter discusses three categories of WAN connections and contrasts various WAN connection types, based on supported data rates and media types. Finally, this chapter lists characteristics for multiple WAN technologies.

- **Chapter 8, "Connecting Wirelessly."** In this increasingly mobile world, wireless technologies are exploding in popularity. This chapter discusses the basic operation of WLANs. Additionally, WLAN design and security considerations are addressed.

- **Chapter 9, "Optimizing Network Performance."** This chapter explains the importance of high availability for a network and what mechanisms help provide a high level of availability. Network performance optimization strategies are addressed, including a section on QoS. Finally, this chapter allows you to use what you have learned in this and preceding chapters to design a SOHO network.

- **Chapter 10, "Using Command-Line Utilities."** In your daily administration and troubleshooting of computer networks, you need familiarity with various command-line utilities available on the operating systems present in your network. This chapter presents a collection of popular command-line utilities for both Microsoft Windows® and UNIX platforms.

- **Chapter 11, "Managing a Network,"** reviews some of the more common tools used to physically maintain a network. The components of configuration management are also presented. Finally, this chapter discusses some of the network-monitoring tools available to network administrators and what types of information are included in various logs.

- **Chapter 12, "Securing a Network."** Network security is an issue for most any network, and this chapter covers a variety of network security technologies. You begin by understanding the goals of network security and the types of attacks you must defend against. Then, you review a collection of security best practices. Next, the chapter discusses specific security technologies, including firewalls, VPNs, IDSs, and IPSs.

- **Chapter 13, "Troubleshooting Network Issues."** Troubleshooting network issues in an inherent part of network administration, and this chapter presents a structured approach to troubleshooting various network technologies. Specifically, you learn how to troubleshoot common Layer 2, Layer 3, and wireless network issues.

- **Chapter 14, "Final Preparation,"** reviews the exam-preparation tools available in this book and the enclosed DVD. For example, the enclosed DVD contains a practice exam engine and a collection of ten training videos presented by the author. Finally, a suggested study plan is presented to assist you in preparing for the CompTIA Network+ exam (N10-005).

In addition to the 13 main chapters, this book includes tools to help you verify that you are prepared to take the exam. The DVD includes a practice test and memory tables that you can work through to verify your knowledge of the subject matter. The DVD also contains ten training videos that cover some of the most fundamental and misunderstood content in the CompTIA Network+ curriculum, specifically the OSI model and IP addressing.

After completion of this chapter, you will be able to answer the following questions:

- What is the purpose of a network?

- What are some examples of network components?

- How are networks defined by geography?

- How are networks defined by topology?

- How are networks defined by resource location?

CHAPTER 1

Introducing Computer Networks

What comes to mind when you think of a computer network? Is it the Internet? Is it e-mail? Is it the wireless connection that lets you print to your printer from your laptop?

Whatever your current perception of a computer network, this chapter and book, as a whole, helps you gain deep appreciation and understanding of networked computing. Be aware that although we commonly think of computer networks as interconnecting computers, today, computer networks interconnect a variety of devices in addition to just computers. Examples include game consoles, video-surveillance devices, and IP-based telephones. Therefore, throughout this book, you can think of the term *computer network* as being synonymous with the more generic term *network*, as these terms will be used interchangeably.

In this chapter, the goal is to acquaint you with the purpose of a network and help you categorize a given network based on criteria such as geography, topology, and the location of a network's resources. An implied goal of this and all other chapters in this book is to prepare you to successfully pass the CompTIA Network+ exam, which is considered to be a cornerstone exam in the *information technology* (IT) industry.

Foundation Topics

Defining a Network

It was in the movie *A Field of Dreams* where they said, "If you build it, they will come." That phrase most certainly applies to the evolution of network-based services seen in modern-day networks. Computer networks are no longer relegated to allowing a group of computers to access a common set of files stored on a computer designated as a *file server*. Instead, with the building of high-speed, highly redundant networks, network architects are seeing the wisdom of placing a variety of traffic types on a single network. Examples include voice and video, in addition to data.

One could argue that a network is the sum of its parts. So, as you begin your study of networking, you should grasp a basic understanding of fundamental networking components. These components include such entities as a client, server, hub, switch, router, and the media used to interconnect these devices.

The Purpose of Networks

At its essence, a network's purpose is to make connections. These connections might be between a PC and a printer or between a laptop and the Internet, as just a couple of examples. However, the true value of a network comes from the traffic flowing over those connections. Consider a sampling of applications that can travel over a network's connections:

- File sharing between two computers
- Video chatting between computers located in different parts of the world
- Surfing the web (for example, to use social media sites, watch streaming video, listen to an Internet radio station, or do research for a school term paper)
- Instant messaging (IM) between computers with IM software installed
- E-mail
- Voice over IP (VoIP), to replace traditional telephony systems

A term commonly given to a network transporting multiple types of traffic (for example, voice, video, and data) is a *converged network*. A converged network might offer significant cost savings to organizations that previously supported separate network infrastructures for voice, data, and video traffic. This convergence can also potentially reduce staffing costs, because only a single network needs to be maintained, rather than separate networks for separate traffic types.

Overview of Network Components

Designing, installing, administering, and troubleshooting a network requires the ability to recognize various network components and their functions. Although this is the focus of Chapter 3, "Identifying Network Components," before we can proceed much further, we need a basic working knowledge of how individual components come together to form a functioning network.

The components to consider for now are client, server, hub, switch, router, media, and wide-area network (WAN) link. As a reference for this discussion, consider Figure 1-1.

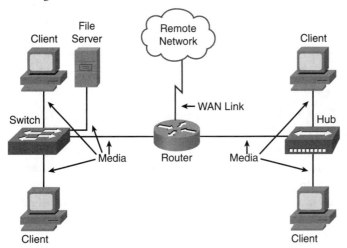

Figure 1-1   Sample Computer Network

The following list describes the network components depicted in Figure 1-1 and the functions they serve:

- **Client:** The term *client* defines the device an end user uses to access a network. This device might be a workstation, laptop, smartphone with wireless capabilities, or a variety of other end-user terminal devices.

- **Server:** A *server*, as the name suggests, serves up resources to a network. These resources might include e-mail access as provided by an e-mail server, web pages as provided by a web server, or files available on a file server.

- **Hub:** A *hub* is an older technology that interconnects network components, such as clients and servers. Hubs vary in their number of available ports. However, for scalability, hubs can be interconnected, up to a point. If too many hubs are chained together, network errors can result. As discussed further in Chapter 3, a hub does not perform any inspection of the traffic it passes.

Rather, a hub simply receives traffic in a port (that is, a receptacle to which a network cable connects) and repeats that traffic out all of the other ports.

- **Switch:** Like a hub, a *switch* interconnects network components, and they are available with a variety of port densities. However, unlike a hub, a switch does not simply take traffic in on one port and blast that traffic out all other ports. Rather, a switch learns which devices reside off of which ports. As a result, when traffic comes in a switch port, the switch interrogates the traffic to see where it is destined. Then, based on what the switch has learned, the switch forwards the traffic out of the appropriate port, and not out all of the other ports. This dramatically cuts down on the volume of traffic coursing through your network. A switch is considered a *Layer 2* device, which means that it makes its forwarding decisions based on addresses that are physically burned into a network interface card (NIC) installed in a *host* (that is, any device that transmits or receives traffic on a network). This burned-in address is a *Media Access Control* (MAC) address.

- **Router:** As discussed in Chapter 3, a *router* is considered to be a *Layer 3* device, which means that it makes its forwarding decisions based on logical network addresses. Most modern networks use *Internet Protocol* (IP) addressing. Therefore, most routers know what logical IP networks reside off of which router interfaces. Then, when traffic comes into a router, the router examines the destination IP address of the traffic and, based on the router's database of networks (that is, the routing table), the router intelligently forwards the traffic out the appropriate interface.

- **Media:** The previously mentioned devices need to be interconnected via some sort of *media*. This media could be copper cabling. It could be a fiber-optic cable. Media might not even be a cable, as is the case with wireless networks, where radio waves travel through the media of air. Chapter 3 expands on this discussion of media. For now, realize that media varies in its cost, bandwidth capacity, and distance limitation. For example, although fiber-optic cabling is more expensive than unshielded twisted-pair cabling, it can typically carry traffic over longer distances and has a greater bandwidth capacity (that is, the capacity to carry a higher data rate).

- **WAN link:** Today, most networks connect to one or more other networks. For example, if your company has two locations, and those two locations are interconnected (perhaps via a Frame Relay or Multiprotocol Label Switching [MPLS] network), the link that interconnects those networks is typically referred to as a *wide-area network* (WAN) link. WANs, and technologies supporting WANs, are covered in Chapter 7, "Introducing Wide-Area Networks."

Networks Defined by Geography

As you might be sensing at this point, not all networks look the same. They vary in numerous ways. One criterion by which we can classify networks is how geographically dispersed the networks components are. For example, a network might interconnect devices within an office, or a network might interconnect a database at a corporate headquarters location with a remote sales office located on the opposite side of the globe.

Based on the geographical dispersion of network components, networks can be classified into various categories, including the following:

- Local-area network (LAN)

- Wide-area network (WAN)

- Campus-area network (CAN)

- Metropolitan-area network (MAN)

- Personal-area network (PAN)

The following sections describe these different classifications of networks in more detail.

LAN

A LAN interconnects network components within a local region (for example, within a building). Examples of common LAN technologies you're likely to encounter include Ethernet (that is, IEEE 802.3) and wireless networks (that is, IEEE 802.11). Figure 1-2 illustrates an example of a LAN.

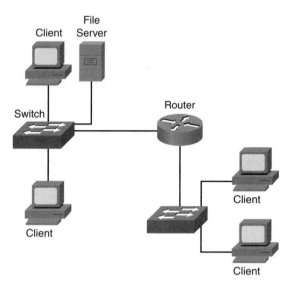

Figure 1-2   Sample LAN Topology

NOTE   *IEEE* stands for the *Institute of Electrical and Electronics Engineers*, and it is an internationally recognized standards body.

WAN

A WAN interconnects network components that are geographically separated. For example, a corporate headquarters might have multiple WAN connections to remote office sites. Multiprotocol Label Switching (MPLS), Asynchronous Transfer Mode (ATM), and Frame Relay are examples of WAN technologies. Figure 1-3 depicts a simple WAN topology, which interconnects two geographically dispersed locations.

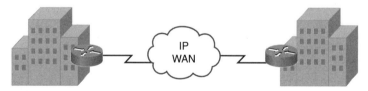

Figure 1-3   Sample WAN Topology

Other Categories of Networks

Although LANs and WANs are the most common terms used to categorize computer networks based on geography, other categories include campus-area network (CAN), metropolitan-area network (MAN), and personal-area network (PAN).

CAN

Years ago, I was a network manager for a university. The university covered several square miles and had several dozen buildings. Within many of these buildings was a LAN. However, those building-centric LANs were interconnected. By interconnecting these LANs, another network type was created, a CAN. Besides an actual university campus, a CAN might also be found in an industrial park or business park.

MAN

More widespread than a CAN and less widespread than a WAN, a MAN interconnects locations scattered throughout a metropolitan area. Imagine, for example, that a business in Chicago had a location near O'Hare Airport, another location near the Navy Pier, and another location in the Sears Tower. If a service provider could interconnect those locations using a high-speed network, such as a 10-Gbps (that is, 10 billion bits per second) network, the interconnection of those locations would constitute a MAN. One example of a MAN technology is Metro Ethernet.

PAN

A PAN is a network whose scale is even smaller than a LAN. As an example, a connection between a PC and a digital camera via a *universal serial bus* (USB) cable could be considered a PAN. Another example is a PC connected to an external hard drive via a FireWire connection. A PAN, however, is not necessarily a wired connection. A Bluetooth connection between your cell phone and your car's audio system is considered a wireless PAN (WPAN). The main distinction of a PAN, however, is that its range is typically limited to just a few meters.

Networks Defined by Topology

In addition to classifying networks based on the geographical placement of their components, another approach to classifying a network is to use the network's topology. Looks can be deceiving, however. You need to be able to distinguish between a physical topology and a logical topology.

Physical Versus Logical Topology

Just because a network appears to be a star topology (that is, where the network components all connect back to a centralized device, such as a switch), the traffic might be flowing in a circular pattern through all the network components attached to the centralized device. The actual traffic flow determines the *logical topology*, while how components are physically interconnected determines the *physical topology*.

As an example, consider Figure 1-4. The figure shows a collection of computers connected to a Token Ring Media Access Unit (MAU). From a quick inspection of Figure 1-4, you can conclude that the devices are physically connected in a star topology, where the connected devices radiate out from a centralized aggregation point (that is, the MAU in this example).

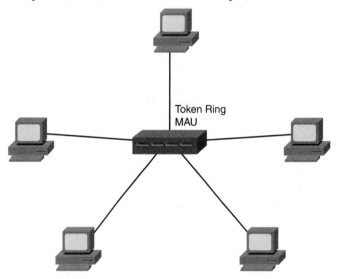

Figure 1-4   Physical Star Topology

Next, contrast the physical topology in Figure 1-4 with the logical topology illustrated in Figure 1-5. Although the computers physically connect to a centralized MAU, when you examine the flow of traffic through (or in this case, around) the network, you see that the traffic flow actually loops round-and-round the network. The traffic flow dictates how to classify a network's logical topology. In this instance, the logical topology is a *ring topology*, because the traffic circulates around the network as if circulating around a ring.

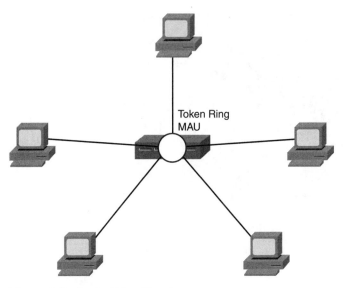

Figure 1-5   Logical Ring Topology

Although Token Ring, as used in this example, is rarely seen in modern networks, it illustrates how a network's physical and logical topologies can be quite different.

Bus Topology

A bus topology, as depicted in Figure 1-6, typically uses a cable running through the area requiring connectivity. Devices that need to connect to the network then tap into this nearby cable. Early Ethernet networks commonly relied on bus topologies.

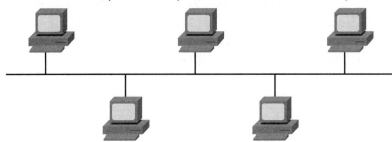

Figure 1-6   Bus Topology

A network tap might be in the form of a T connector (commonly used in older 10BASE2 networks) or a vampire tap (commonly used in older 10BASE5 networks). Figure 1-7 shows an example of a T connector.

Figure 1-7   T Connector

NOTE   The Ethernet standards mentioned here (that is, 10BASE2 and 10BASE5), in addition to many other Ethernet standards, are discussed in detail in Chapter 4, "Understanding Ethernet."

A bus and all devices connected to that bus make up a *network segment*. As discussed in Chapter 4, a single network segment is a single collision domain, which means that all devices connected to the bus might try to gain access to the bus at the same time, resulting in an error condition known as a *collision*. Table 1-1 identifies some of the primary characteristics, benefits, and drawbacks of a bus topology.

Table 1-1   Characteristics, Benefits, and Drawbacks of a Bus Topology

Characteristics	Benefits	Drawbacks
One cable is used per network segment.	Less cable is required to install a bus topology, as compared with other topologies.	Because a single cable is used per network segment, the cable becomes a potential single point of failure.

Table 1-1 Characteristics, Benefits, and Drawbacks of a Bus Topology

Characteristics	Benefits	Drawbacks
To maintain appropriate electrical characteristics of the cable, the cable requires a terminator (of a specific resistance) at each end of the cable.	Depending on the media used by the bus, a bus topology can be less expensive.	Troubleshooting a bus topology can be difficult because problem isolation might necessitate an inspection of multiple network taps to make sure they either have a device connected or they are properly terminated.
Bus topologies were popular in early Ethernet networks.	Installation of a network based on a bus topology is easier than some other topologies, which might require extra wiring to be installed.	Adding devices to a bus might cause an outage for other users on the bus.
Network components tap directly into the cable via a connector such as a T connector or a vampire tap.		An error condition existing on one device on the bus can impact performance of other devices on the bus.
		A bus topology does not scale well, because all devices share the bandwidth available on the bus. Also, if two devices on the bus simultaneously request access to the bus, an error condition results.

Ring Topology

Figure 1-8 offers an example of a ring topology, where traffic flows in a circular fashion around a closed network loop (that is, a ring). Typically, a ring topology sends data, in a single direction, to each connected device in turn, until the intended destination receives the data. Token Ring networks typically relied on a ring topology, although the ring might have been the logical topology, while physically, the topology was a star topology.

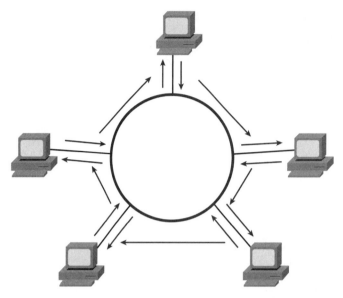

Figure 1-8   Ring Topology

Token Ring, however, was not the only popular ring-based topology popular in networks back in the 1990s. Fiber Distributed Data Interface (FDDI) was another variant of a ring-based topology. Most FDDI networks (which, as the name suggests, have fiber optics as the media) used not just one ring, but two. These two rings sent data in opposite directions, resulting in *counter-rotating rings*. One benefit of counter-rotating rings was that if a fiber broke, the stations on each side of the break could interconnect their two rings, resulting in a single ring capable of reaching all stations on the ring.

Because a ring topology allows devices on the ring to take turns transmitting on the ring, contention for media access was not a problem, as it was for a bus topology. If a network had a single ring, however, the ring became a single point of failure. If the ring were broken at any point, data would stop flowing. Table 1-2 identifies some of the primary characteristics, benefits, and drawbacks of a ring topology.

Table 1-2   Characteristics, Benefits, and Drawbacks of a Ring Topology

Characteristics	Benefits	Drawbacks
Devices are interconnected by connecting to a single ring, or in some cases (for example, FDDI), a dual ring.	A dual ring topology adds a layer of fault tolerance. Therefore, if a cable break occurred, connectivity to all devices could be restored.	A break in a ring when a single ring topology is used results in a network outage for all devices connected to the ring.

Table 1-2 Characteristics, Benefits, and Drawbacks of a Ring Topology

Characteristics	Benefits	Drawbacks
Each device on a ring includes both a receiver (for the incoming cable) and a transmitter (for the outgoing cable)	Troubleshooting is simplified in the event of a cable break, because each device on a ring contains a repeater. When the repeater on the far side of a cable break doesn't receive any data within a certain amount of time, it reports an error condition (typically in the form of an indicator light on a network interface card [NIC]).	Rings have scalability limitations. Specifically, a ring has a maximum length and a maximum number of attached stations. Once either of these limits is exceeded, a single ring might need to be divided into two interconnected rings. A network maintenance window might need to be scheduled to perform this ring division.
Each device on the ring repeats the signal it receives.		Because a ring must be a complete loop, the amount of cable required for a ring is usually higher than the amount of cable required for a bus topology serving the same number of devices.

Star Topology

Figure 1-9 shows a sample star topology with a hub at the center of the topology and a collection of clients individually connected to the hub. Notice that a star topology has a central point from which all attached devices radiate. In LANs, that centralized device was typically a hub back in the early 1990s. Modern networks, however, usually have a switch located at the center of the star.

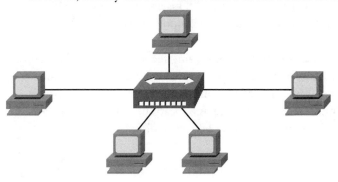

Figure 1-9 Star Topology

> **NOTE**   Chapter 3 discusses UTP and other types of cabling.

The star topology is the most popular physical LAN topology in use today, with an Ethernet switch at the center of the star and unshielded twisted-pair cable (UTP) used to connect from the switch ports to clients.

Table 1-3 identifies some of the primary characteristics, benefits, and drawbacks of a star topology.

Table 1-3   Characteristics, Benefits, and Drawbacks of a Star Topology

Characteristics	Benefits	Drawbacks
Devices have independent connections back to a central device (for example, a hub or a switch).	A cable break only impacts the device connected via the broken cable, and not the entire topology.	More cable is required for a star topology, as opposed to bus or ring topologies, because each device requires its own cable to connect back to the central device.
Star topologies are commonly used with Ethernet technologies (described in Chapter 4).	Troubleshooting is relatively simple, because a central device in the star topology acts as the aggregation point of all the connected devices.	Installation can take longer for a star topology, as opposed to a bus or ring topology, because more cable runs that must be installed.

Hub-and-Spoke Topology

When interconnecting multiple sites (for example, multiple corporate locations) via WAN links, a hub-and-spoke topology has a WAN link from each remote site (that is, a *spoke site*) to the main site (that is, the *hub site*). This approach, an example of which is shown in Figure 1-10, is similar to the star topology used in LANs.

With WAN links, a service provider is paid a recurring fee for each link. Therefore, a hub-and-spoke topology helps minimize WAN expenses by not directly connecting any two spoke locations. If two spoke locations need to communicate between themselves, their communication is sent via the hub location. Table 1-4 contrasts the benefits and drawbacks of a hub-and-spoke WAN topology.

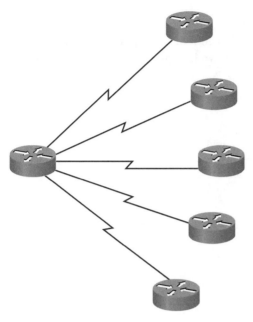

Figure 1-10   Hub-and-Spoke Topology

Table 1-4   Characteristics, Benefits, and Drawbacks of a Hub-and-Spoke WAN Topology

Characteristics	Benefits	Drawbacks
Each remote site (that is, a spoke) connects back to a main site (that is, the hub) via a WAN link.	Costs are reduced (as compared to a full-mesh or partial-mesh topology) because a minimal number of links are used.	Suboptimal routes must be used between remote sites, because all intersite communication must travel via the main site.
Communication between two remote sites travels through the hub site.	Adding one or more additional sites is easy (as compared to a full-mesh or partial-mesh topology) because only one link needs to be added per site.	Because all remote sites converge on the main site, this hub site potentially becomes a single point of failure.
		Because each remote site is reachable by only a single WAN link, the hub-and-spoke topology lacks redundancy.

Full-Mesh Topology

Although a hub-and-spoke WAN topology lacked redundancy and suffered from suboptimal routes, a full-mesh topology, as shown in Figure 1-11, directly connects every site to every other site.

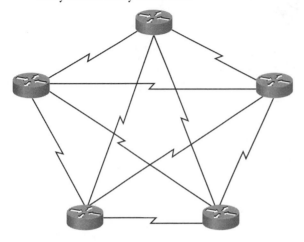

Figure 1-11   Full-Mesh Topology

Because each site connects directly to every other site, an optimal path can be selected, as opposed to relaying traffic via another site. Also, a full-mesh topology is highly fault tolerant. By inspecting Figure 1-11, you can see that multiple links in the topology could be lost, and every site might still be able to connect to every other site. Table 1-5 summarizes the characteristics of a full-mesh topology.

Table 1-5   Characteristics, Benefits, and Drawbacks of a Full-Mesh WAN Topology

Characteristics	Benefits	Drawbacks
Every site has a direct WAN connection to every other site.	An optimal route exists between any two sites.	A full-mesh network can be difficult and expensive to scale, because the addition of one new site requires a new WAN link between the new site and every other existing site.

Table 1-5   Characteristics, Benefits, and Drawbacks of a Full-Mesh WAN Topology

Characteristics	Benefits	Drawbacks
The number of required WAN connections can be calculated with the formula $w = n * (n\text{-}1) / 2$, where w = the number of WAN links and n = the number of sites. For example, a network with 10 sites would require 45 WAN connections to form a fully meshed network: $45 = 10 * (10\text{-}1) / 2$.	A full-mesh network is fault tolerant, because one or more links can be lost, and reachability between all sites might still be maintained.	
	Troubleshooting a full-mesh network is relatively easy, because each link is independent of the other links.	

Partial-Mesh Topology

A partial-mesh WAN topology, as depicted in Figure 1-12, is a hybrid of the previously described hub-and-spoke topology and full-mesh topology. Specifically, a partial-mesh topology can be designed to provide an optimal route between selected sites, while avoiding the expense of interconnecting every site to every other site.

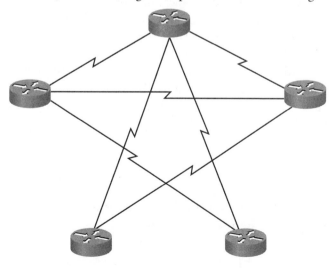

Figure 1-12   Partial-Mesh Topology

When designing a partial-mesh topology, a network designer must consider network traffic patterns and strategically add links interconnecting sites that have higher volumes of traffic between themselves. Table 1-6 highlights the characteristics, benefits, and drawbacks of a partial-mesh topology.

Table 1-6   Characteristics, Benefits, and Drawbacks of a Partial-Mesh Topology

Characteristics	Benefits	Drawbacks
Selected sites (that is, sites with frequent intersite communication) are interconnected via direct links, while sites that have less frequent communication can communicate via another site.	A partial-mesh topology provides optimal routes between selected sites with higher intersite traffic volumes, while avoiding the expense of interconnecting every site to every other site.	A partial-mesh topology is less fault tolerance than a full-mesh topology.
A partial-mesh topology uses fewer links than a full-mesh topology and more links than a hub-and-spoke topology for interconnecting the same number of sites.	A partial-mesh topology is more redundant than a hub-and-spoke topology.	A partial-mesh topology is more expensive than a hub-and-spoke topology.

Networks Defined by Resource Location

Yet another way to categorize networks is based on where network resources reside. An example of a *client-server network* is a collection of PCs all sharing files located on a centralized server. However, if those PCs had their operating system (OS) (for example, Microsoft Windows 7 or Mac OS X) configured for file sharing, they could share files from one another's hard drives. Such an arrangement would be referred to as a *peer-to-peer network*, because the peers (that is, the PCs in this example) make resources available to other peers. The following sections describe client-server and peer-to-peer networks in more detail.

Client-Server Networks

Figure 1-13 illustrates an example of a client-server network, where a dedicated file server provides shared access to files, and a networked printer is available as a resource to the network's clients. Client-server networks are commonly used by businesses. Because resources are located on one or more servers, administration is simpler than trying to administer network resources on multiple peer devices.

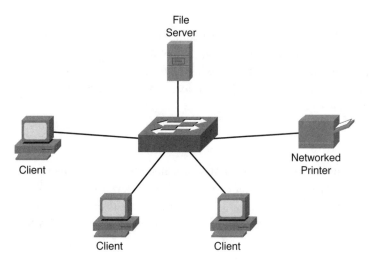

Figure 1-13   Client-Server Network Example

Performance of a client-server network can be better than that of a peer-to-peer network, because resources can be located on dedicated servers, rather than on a PC running a variety of end-user applications. Backups can be simplified, since fewer locations must be backed up. However, client-server networks come with the extra expense of dedicated server resources. Table 1-7 contrasts the benefits and drawbacks of client-server networks.

Table 1-7   Characteristics, Benefits, and Drawbacks of a Client-Server Network

Characteristics	Benefits	Drawbacks
Client devices (for example, PCs) share a common set of resources (for example, file or print resources) located on one or more dedicated servers.	Client-server networks can easily scale, which might require the purchase of additional client licenses.	Because multiple clients might rely on a single server for their resources, the single server can become a single point of failure in the network.
Resource sharing is made possible via dedicated server hardware and network OSs.	Administration is simplified, because parameters, such as file sharing permissions and other security settings, can be administered on a server as opposed to multiple clients.	Client-server networks can cost more than peer-to-peer networks. For example, client-server networks might require the purchase of dedicated server hardware and a network OS with an appropriate number of licenses.

NOTE A server in a client-server network could be a computer running a *network operating system* (NOS), such as *Novell NetWare* or a variety of *Microsoft Windows Server* OSs. Alternately, a server might be a host making its file system available to remote clients via the *Network File System* (NFS) service, which was originally developed by Sun Microsystems.

NOTE A variant of the traditional server in a client-server network, where the server provides shared file access, is *network-attached storage* (NAS). A NAS device is a mass storage device that attaches directly to a network. Rather than running an advanced NOS, a NAS device typically makes files available to network clients via a service such as NFS.

Peer-to-Peer Networks

Peer-to-peer networks allow interconnected devices (for example, PCs) to share their resources with one another. Those resources could be, for example, files or printers. As an example of a peer-to-peer network, consider Figure 1-14, where each of the peers can share files on their own hard drives, and one of the peers has a directly attached printer that can be shared with the other peers in the network.

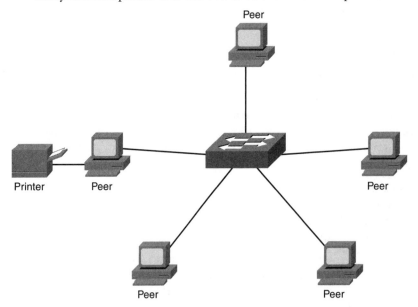

Figure 1-14   Peer-to-Peer Network Example

Peer-to-peer networks are commonly seen in smaller businesses and in homes. The popularity of these peer-to-peer networks is fueled in part by client operating systems which support file and print sharing. Scalability for peer-to-peer networks is a concern, however. Specifically, as the number of devices (that is, peers) increases, the administration burden increases. For example, a network administrator might have to manage file permissions on multiple devices, as opposed to a single server. Consider the characteristics of peer-to-peer networks as presented in Table 1-8.

Table 1-8   Characteristics, Benefits, and Drawbacks of a Peer-to-Peer Network

Characteristics	Benefits	Drawbacks
Client devices (for example, PCs) share their resources (for example, file and printer resources) with other client devices.	Peer-to-peer networks can be installed easily because resource sharing is made possible by the clients' OSs, and knowledge of advanced NOSs is not required.	Scalability is limited because of the increased administration burden of managing multiple clients.
Resource sharing is made available through the clients' OSs.	Peer-to-peer networks typically cost less than client-server networks because there is no requirement for dedicated server resources or advanced NOS software.	Performance might be less than that seen in a client-server network because the devices providing network resources might be performing other tasks not related to resource sharing (for example, word processing).

NOTE   Some networks have characteristics of both peer-to-peer and client-server networks. For example, PCs in a company might all point to a centralized server for accessing a shared database in a client-server topology. However, these PCs might simultaneously share files and printers between one another in a peer-to-peer topology. Such a network, which has a mixture of client-server and peer-to-peer characteristics, is called a *hybrid* network.

Summary

The main topics covered in this chapter are the following:

- You were introduced to various network components, including client, server, hub, switch, router, media, and WAN link.

- One way to classify networks is by their geographical dispersion. Specifically, these network types were identified: LAN, WAN, CAN, MAN, and PAN.

- Another approach to classifying networks is based on a network's topology. Examples of network types, based on topology, include bus, ring, start, partial mesh, full mesh, and hub and spoke.

- This chapter contrasted client-server and peer-to-peer networks.

Exam Preparation Tasks

Review All the Key Topics

Review the most important topics from inside the chapter, noted with the Key Topic icon in the outer margin of the page. Table 1-9 lists these key topics and the page numbers where each is found.

Table 1-9 Key Topics for Chapter 1

Key Topic Element	Description	Page Number
List	Network types, as defined by geography	7
Table 1-1	Characteristics, benefits, and drawbacks of a bus topology	12–13
Table 1-2	Characteristics, benefits, and drawbacks of a ring topology	14–15
Table 1-3	Characteristics, benefits, and drawbacks of a star topology	16
Table 1-4	Characteristics, benefits, and drawbacks of a hub-and-spoke topology	17
Table 1-5	Characteristics, benefits, and drawbacks of a full-mesh topology	18–19
Table 1-6	Characteristics, benefits, and drawbacks of a partial-mesh topology	20
Table 1-7	Characteristics, benefits, and drawbacks of a client-server network	21
Table 1-8	Characteristics, benefits, and drawbacks of a peer-to-peer network	23

Complete Tables and Lists from Memory

Print a copy of Appendix C, "Memory Tables" (found on the DVD), or at least the section for this chapter, and complete as much of the tables as possible from memory. Appendix D, "Memory Tables Answer Key," also on the DVD, includes the completed tables and lists so you can check your work.

Define Key Terms

Define the following key terms from this chapter, and check your answers in the Glossary:

client, server, hub, switch, router, media, WAN link, local-area network (LAN), wide-area network (WAN), campus-area network (CAN), metropolitan-area network (MAN), personal-area network (PAN), logical topology, physical topology, bus topology, ring topology, star topology, hub-and-spoke topology, full-mesh topology, partial-mesh topology, client-server network, peer-to-peer network

Review Questions

The answers to these review questions appear in Appendix A, "Answers to Review Questions."

1. Which of the following is a device directly used by an end user to access a network?

    a. Server

    b. LAN

    c. Client

    d. Router

2. Which device makes traffic-forwarding decisions based on MAC addresses?

    a. Hub

    b. Router

    c. Switch

    d. Multiplexer

3. A company has various locations in a city interconnected using Metro Ethernet connections. This is an example of what type of network?

    a. WAN

    b. CAN

    c. PAN

    d. MAN

4. A network formed by interconnecting a PC to a digital camera via a USB cable is considered what type of network?

    a. WAN

    b. CAN

    c. PAN

    d. MAN

5. Which of the following LAN topologies requires the most cabling?

    a. Bus

    b. Ring

    c. Star

    d. WLAN

6. Which of the following topologies offers the highest level of redundancy?

   a. Full mesh

   b. Hub and spoke

   c. Bus

   d. Partial mesh

7. How many WAN links are required to create a full mesh of connections between five remote sites?

   a. 5

   b. 10

   c. 15

   d. 20

8. Identify two advantages of a hub-and-spoke WAN topology as compared to a full-mesh WAN topology. (Choose two.)

   a. Lower cost

   b. Optimal routes

   c. More scalable

   d. More redundancy

9. Which type of network is based on network clients sharing resources with one another?

   a. Client-server

   b. Client-peer

   c. Peer-to-peer

   d. Peer-to-server

10. Which of the following is an advantage of a peer-to-peer network, as compared with a client-server network?

   a. More scalable

   b. Less expensive

   c. Better performance

   d. Simplified administration

After completion of this chapter, you will be able to answer the following questions:

- What is the purpose of a network model?
- What are the layers of the OSI model?
- What are the characteristics of each layer of the OSI model?
- How does the TCP/IP stack compare to the OSI model?
- What are the well-known TCP and/or UDP port numbers for a given collection of common applications?

CHAPTER 2

Dissecting the OSI Model

Way back in 1977, the International Organization for Standardization (ISO) developed a subcommittee to focus on the interoperability of multivendor communications systems. What sprang from this subcommittee was the *Open Systems Interconnection* (OSI) *reference model* (commonly referred to as the *OSI model* or the *OSI stack*). With this model, you can take just about any networking technology and categorize that technology as residing at one or more of the seven layers of the model.

This chapter defines those seven layers and provides examples of what you might find at each layer. Finally, this chapter contrasts the OSI model with another model (the *TCP/IP stack*, also known as the *Department of Defense* [DoD] *model*), which focuses on Internet Protocol (IP) communications.

Foundation Topics

The Purpose of Reference Models

Throughout your networking career, and throughout this book, you will encounter various protocols and devices that play a role in your network. To better understand how a particular technology fits in, however, it helps to have a common point of reference against which various technologies from various vendors can be compared.

One of the most common ways of categorizing the function of a network technology is to state at what layer (or layers) of the OSI model that technology operates. Based on how that technology performs a certain function at a certain layer of the OSI model, you can better determine if one device is going to be able to communicate with another device, which might or might not be using a similar technology at that layer of the OSI reference model.

For example, when your laptop connects to a web server on the Internet, your laptop has been assigned an IP address. Similarly, the web server to which you are communicating has an IP address. As you see in this chapter, an IP address lives at Layer 3 (the network layer) of the OSI model. Because both your laptop and the web server use a common protocol (that is, IP) at Layer 3, they can communicate with one another.

Personally, I've been in the computer-networking industry since 1989, and I have had the OSI model explained in many classes I've attended and books I've read. From this, I've taken away a collection of metaphors to help describe the operation of the different layers of the OSI model. Some of the metaphors involve sending a letter from one location to another or placing a message in a series of envelopes. However, my favorite (and the most accurate) way to describe the OSI model is to simply think of it as being analogous to a bookshelf, such as the one shown in Figure 2-1.

Figure 2-1   A Bookshelf Is Analogous to the OSI Model

If you were to look at a bookshelf in my home, you'd see that I organized different types of books on different shelves. One shelf contains my collection of Star Wars books, another shelf contains the books I wrote for Cisco Press, another shelf contains my audio books, and so on. I grouped similar books together on a shelf, just as the OSI model groups similar protocols and functions together in a layer.

A common pitfall my students and readers encounter when studying the OSI model is to try to neatly fit all the devices and protocols in their network into one of the OSI model's seven layers. However, not every technology is a perfect fit into these layers. In fact, some networks might not have any technologies operating at one or more of these layers. This reminds me of my favorite statement regarding the OSI model. It comes from Rich Seifert's book *The Switch Book*. In that book, Rich reminds us that the OSI model is a *reference* model, not a *reverence* model. That is, there is no cosmic law stating that all technologies must cleanly plug into the model. So, as you discover the characteristics of the OSI model layers throughout this chapter, remember that these layers are like shelves for organizing similar protocols and functions, not immutable laws.

The OSI Model

As previously stated, the OSI model is comprised of seven layers:

- **Layer 1:** The physical layer

- **Layer 2:** The data link layer

- **Layer 3:** The network layer

- **Layer 4:** The transport layer

- **Layer 5:** The session layer

- **Layer 6:** The presentation layer

- **Layer 7:** The application layer

Graphically, these layers are usually depicted with Layer 1 at the bottom of the stack, as shown in Figure 2-2.

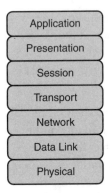

Figure 2-2   OSI "Stack"

Various mnemonics are available to help memorize these layers in their proper order. A top-down (that is, starting at the top of the stack with Layer 7 and working your way down to Layer 1) acrostic is *All People Seem To Need Data Processing*. As a couple of examples, using this acrostic, the *A* in *A*ll reminds us of the *A* in *A*pplication, and the *P* in *P*eople reminds us of the *P* in *P*resentation.

At the physical layer, binary expressions (that is, a series of 1s and 0s) represent data. A binary expression is made up of bits, where a bit is a single 1 or a single 0. At upper layers, however, bits are grouped together, into what is known as a *protocol data unit* (PDU) or a *data service unit*.

The term *packet* is used fairly generically to refer to these PDUs. However, PDUs might have an additional name, depending on their OSI layer. Figure 2-3 illustrates these PDU names. A common memory aid for these PDUs is the acrostic *Some People Fear Birthdays*, where the *S* in *S*ome reminds us of the *S* in *S*egments. The *P* in *P*eople reminds us of the *P* in *P*ackets, and the *F* in *F*ear reflects the *F* in *F*rames. Finally, the *B* in *B*irthdays reminds us of the *B* in *B*its.

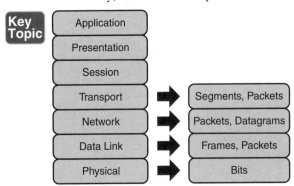

Figure 2-3   PDU Names

Layer 1: The Physical Layer

The physical layer, as shown in Figure 2-4, is concerned with the transmission of data on the network.

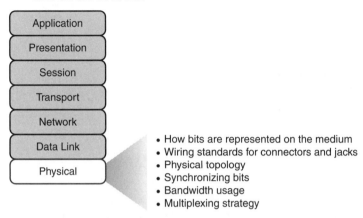

Figure 2-4   Layer 1: The Physical Layer

As a few examples, the physical layer defines

- **How bits are represented on the medium:** Data on a computer network is represented as a binary expression. Chapter 5, "Working with IP Addresses," discusses binary in much more detail. Electrical voltage (on copper wiring) or light (carried via fiber-optic cabling) can represent these 1s and 0s.

  For example, the presence or the absence of voltage on a wire can represent a binary 1 or a binary 0, respectively, as illustrated in Figure 2-5. Similarly, the presence or absence of light on a fiber-optic cable can represent a 1 or 0 in binary. This type of approach is called *current state modulation*.

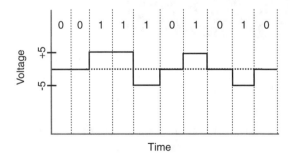

Figure 2-5   Current State Modulation

An alternate approach to representing binary data is *state transition modulation*, as shown in Figure 2-6, where the transition between voltages or the presence of light indicates a binary value.

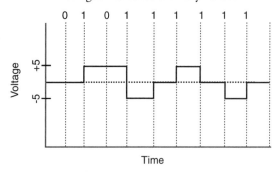

Figure 2-6 Transition Modulation

NOTE Other modulation types you might be familiar with from radio include amplitude modulation (AM) and frequency modulation (FM). AM uses a variation in a waveform's amplitude (that is, signal strength) to represent the original signal. However, FM uses a variation in frequency to represent the original signal.

- **Wiring standards for connectors and jacks:** Several standards for network connectors are addressed in Chapter 3, "Identifying Network Components." As an example, however, the TIA/EIA-568-B standard describes how an RJ-45 connector should be wired for use on a 100BASE-TX Ethernet network, as shown in Figure 2-7.

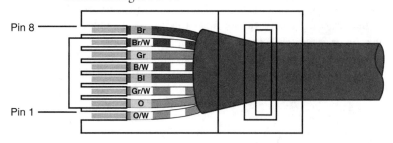

Figure 2-7 TIA/EIA-568-B Wiring Standard for an RJ-45 Connector

- **Physical topology:** Layer 1 devices view a network as a physical topology (as opposed to a logical topology). Examples of a physical topology include bus, ring, and star topologies, as described in Chapter 1, "Introducing Computer Networks."

- **Synchronizing bits:** For two networked devices to successfully communicate at the physical layer, they must agree on when one bit stops and another bit starts. Specifically, what is needed is a method to synchronize the bits. Two basic approaches to bit synchronization include *asynchronous* and *synchronous* synchronization:

  - **Asynchronous:** With this approach, a sender indicates that it's about to start transmitting by sending a start bit to the receiver. When the receiver sees this, it starts its own internal clock to measure the subsequent bits. After the sender transmits its data, it sends a stop bit to indicate that is has finished its transmission.

  - **Synchronous:** This approach synchronizes the internal clocks of both the sender and receiver to ensure that they agree on when bits begin and end. A common approach to make this synchronization happen is to use an external clock (for example, a clock provided by a service provider), which is referenced by both the sender and receiver.

- **Bandwidth usage:** The two fundamental approaches to bandwidth usage on a network are *broadband* and *baseband*:

  - **Broadband:** Broadband technologies divide the bandwidth available on a medium (for example, copper or fiber-optic cabling) into different channels. Different communication streams are then transmitted over the various channels. As an example, consider *Frequency-Division Multiplexing* (FDM) used by a cable modem. Specifically, a cable modem uses certain ranges of frequencies on the cable coming into your home from the local cable company to carry incoming data, another range of frequencies for outgoing data, and several other frequency ranges for various TV stations.

  - **Baseband:** Baseband technologies, in contrast, use all the available frequencies on a medium to transmit data. Ethernet is an example of a networking technology that uses baseband.

- **Multiplexing strategy:** Multiplexing allows multiple communications sessions to share the same physical medium. Cable TV, as previously mentioned, allows you to receive multiple channels over a single physical medium (for example, a coaxial cable plugged into the back of your television). Here are some of the more common approaches to multiplexing:

  - **Time-division multiplexing (TDM):** TDM supports different communication sessions (for example, different telephone conversations in a telephony network) on the same physical medium by causing the sessions to take turns. For a brief period of time, defined as a *time slot*, data from the first session will be sent, followed by data from the second sessions. This continues until all sessions have had a turn, and the process repeats itself.

- **Statistical time-division multiplexing (StatTDM):** A downside to TDM is that each communication session receives its own time slot, even if one of the sessions does not have any data to transmit at the moment. To make a more efficient use of available bandwidth, StatTDM dynamically assigns time slots to communications sessions on an as-needed basis.

- **Frequency-division multiplexing (FDM):** FDM divides a medium's frequency range into channels, and different communication sessions transmit their data over different channels. As previously described, this approach to bandwidth usage is called broadband.

Examples of devices defined by physical layer standards include hubs, wireless access points, and network cabling.

> **NOTE**   A hub can interconnect PCs in a LAN. However, it is considered to be a physical layer device, because a hub takes bits coming in on one port and retransmits those bits out all other hub ports. At no point does the hub interrogate any addressing information in the data.

Layer 2: The Data Link Layer

The data link layer, as shown in Figure 2-8, is concerned with packaging data into frames and transmitting those frames on the network, performing error detection/ correction, uniquely identifying network devices with an address, and handling flow control. These processes are collectively referred to as *data link control* (DLC).

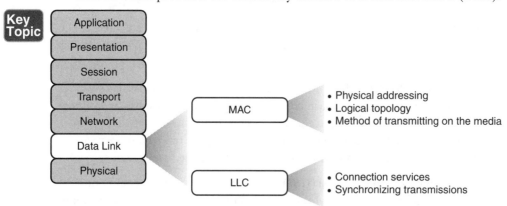

Figure 2-8   Layer 2: The Data Link Layer

In fact, the data link layer is unique from the other layers in that it has two sublayers of its own: MAC and LLC.

Media Access Control

Characteristics of the Media Access Control (MAC) sublayer include the following:

- **Physical addressing:** A common example of a Layer 2 address is a MAC address, which is a 48-bit address assigned to a device's network interface card (NIC). The address is commonly written in hexadecimal notation (for example, 58:55:ca:eb:27:83). The first 24 bits of the 48-bit address are collectively referred to as the *vendor code*. Vendors of networking equipment are assigned one or more unique vendor codes. You can use the list of vendor codes at `http://standards.ieee.org/develop/regauth/oui/oui.txt` to determine the manufacturer of a networking device, based on the first half of the device's MAC address. Because each vendor is responsible for using unique values in the last 24 bits of a MAC address, and because each vendor has a unique vendor code, no two MAC addresses in the world should have the same value.

- **Logical topology:** Layer 2 devices view a network as a logical topology. Examples of a logical topology include bus and ring topologies, as described in Chapter 1.

- **Method of transmitting on the media:** With several devices connected to a network, there needs to be some strategy for determining when a device is allowed to transmit on the media. Otherwise, multiple devices might transmit at the same time, and interfere with one another's transmissions.

Logical Link Control

Characteristics of the Logical Link Control (LLC) sublayer include the following:

- **Connection services:** When a device on a network receives a message from another device on the network, that recipient device can provide feedback to the sender in the form of an acknowledgment message. The two main functions provided by these acknowledgment messages are as follows:

  - **Flow control:** Limits the amount of data a sender can send at one time; this prevents the receiver from being overwhelmed with too much information.

  - **Error control:** Allows the recipient of data to let the sender know if the expected data frame was not received or if it was received, but is corrupted. The recipient determines if the data frame is corrupted by mathematically calculating a checksum of the data received. If the calculated checksum does not match the checksum received with the data frame, the recipient of the data draws the conclusion that the data frame is corrupted and can then notify the sender via an acknowledgment message.

- **Synchronizing transmissions:** Senders and receivers of data frames need to co-ordinate when a data frame is being transmitted and should be received. Three methods of performing this synchronization are as follows:

  - **Isochronous:** With isochronous transmission, network devices look to a common device in the network as a clock source, which creates fixed-length time slots. Network devices can determine how much free space, if any, is available within a time slot and insert data into an available time slot. A time slot can accommodate more than one data frame. Isochronous transmission does not need to provide clocking at the beginning of a data string (as does synchronous transmission) or for every data frame (as does asynchronous transmission). As a result, isochronous transmission uses little overhead when compared to asynchronous or synchronous transmission methods.

  - **Asynchronous:** With asynchronous transmission, network devices reference their own internal clocks, and network devices do not need to synchronize their clocks. Instead, the sender places a start bit at the beginning of each data frame and a stop bit at the end of each data frame. These start and stop bits tell the receiver when to monitor the medium for the presence of bits.

    An additional bit, called the parity bit, might also be added to the end of each byte in a frame to detect an error in the frame. For example, if even parity error detection (as opposed to odd parity error detection) is used, the parity bit (with a value of either 0 or 1) would be added to the end of a byte, causing the total number of 1s in the data frame to be an even number. If the receiver of a byte is configured for even parity error detection and receives a byte where the total number of bits (including the parity bit) is even, the receiver can conclude that the byte was not corrupted during transmission.

NOTE   Using a parity bit to detect errors might not be effective if a byte has more than one error (that is, more than one bit that has been changed from its original value).

  - **Synchronous:** With synchronous transmission, two network devices that want to communicate between themselves must agree on a clocking method to indicate the beginning and ending of data frames. One approach to providing this clocking is to use a separate communications channel over which a clock signal is sent. Another approach relies on specific bit combinations or control characters to indicate the beginning of a frame or a byte of data.

Like asynchronous transmissions, synchronous transmissions can perform error detection. However, rather than using parity bits, synchronous communication runs a mathematical algorithm on the data to create a *cyclic redundancy check* (CRC). If both the sender and receiver calculate the same CRC value for the same chunk of data, the receiver can conclude that the data was not corrupted during transmission.

Examples of devices defined by data link layer standards include switches, bridges, and network interface cards (NIC).

NOTE   NICs are not entirely defined at the data link layer, because they are partially based on physical layer standards, such as a NIC's network connector.

Layer 3: The Network Layer

The network layer, as shown in Figure 2-9, is primarily concerned with forwarding data based on logical addresses.

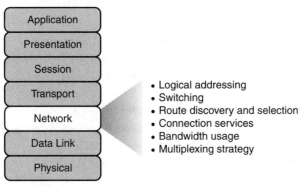

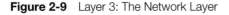

Figure 2-9   Layer 3: The Network Layer

Although many network administrators immediately think of routing and IP addressing when they hear about the network layer, this layer is actually responsible for a variety of tasks:

- **Logical addressing:** Although the data link layer uses physical addresses to make forwarding decisions, the network layer uses logical addressing to make forwarding decisions. A variety of routed protocols (for example, AppleTalk and IPX) have their own logical addressing schemes, but by far, the most widely deployed routed protocol is Internet Protocol (IP). IP addressing is discussed in detail in Chapter 5, "Working with IP Addresses."

- **Switching:** The term *switching* is often associated with Layer 2 technologies; however, the concept of switching also exists at Layer 3. Switching, at its essence, is making decisions about how data should be forwarded. At Layer 3, three common switching techniques exist:

  - **Packet switching:** With packet switching, a data stream is divided into packets. Each packet has a Layer 3 header, which includes a source and destination Layer 3 address. Another term for packet switching is *routing*, which is discussed in more detail in Chapter 6, "Routing Traffic."

  - **Circuit switching:** Circuit switching dynamically brings up a dedicated communication link between two parties in order for those parties to communicate.

    As a simple example of circuit switching, think of making a phone call from your home to a business. Assuming you have a traditional landline servicing your phone, the telephone company's switching equipment interconnects your home phone with the phone system of the business you're calling. This interconnection (that is, *circuit*) only exists for the duration of the phone call.

  - **Message switching:** Unlike packet switching and circuit switching technologies, message switching is usually not well-suited for real-time applications, because of the delay involved. Specifically, with message switching, a data stream is divided into messages. Each message is tagged with a destination address, and the messages travel from one network device to another network device on the way to their destination. Because these devices might briefly store the messages before forwarding them, a network using message switching is sometimes called a *store-and-forward* network. Metaphorically, you could visualize message switching like routing an e-mail message, where the e-mail message might be briefly stored on an e-mail server before being forwarded to the recipient.

- **Route discovery and selection:** Because Layer 3 devices make forwarding decisions based on logical network addresses, a Layer 3 device might need to know how to reach various network addresses. For example, a common Layer 3 device is a router. A router can maintain a routing table indicating how to forward a packet based on the packet's destination network address.

A router can have its routing table populated via manual configuration (that is, by entering static routes), via a dynamic routing protocol (for example, RIP, OSPF, or EIGRP), or simply by the fact that the router is directly connected to certain networks.

NOTE   Routing protocols are discussed in Chapter 6.

- **Connection services:** Just as the data link layer provided connection services for flow control and error control, connection services also exist at the network layer. Connection services at the network layer can improve the communication reliability, in the event that the data link's LLC sublayer is not performing connection services.

  The following functions are performed by connection services at the network layer:

  - **Flow control (also known as congestion control):** Helps prevent a sender from sending data more rapidly that the receiver is capable is receiving the data.
  - **Packet reordering:** Allows packets to be placed in the appropriate sequence as they are sent to the receiver. This might be necessary, because some networks support load-balancing, where multiple links are used to send packets between two devices. Because multiple links are used, packets might arrive out of order.

Examples of devices found at the network layer include routers and multilayer switches. The most common Layer 3 protocol in use today, and the protocol on which the Internet is based, is IP.

A less popular Layer 3 protocol is Novell's *Internetwork Packet Exchange* (IPX), which has its own format for Layer 3 addressing. Although IPX is a Novell-developed protocol, most modern Novell networks use IP as their Layer 3 protocol.

NOTE   Routers and multilayer switches are discussed in Chapter 3.

Layer 4: The Transport Layer

The transport layer, as shown in Figure 2-10, acts as a dividing line between the upper layers and lower layers of the OSI model. Specifically, messages are taken from upper layers (Layers 5–7) and are encapsulated into segments for transmission to the lower layers (Layers 1–3). Similarly, data streams coming from lower layers are decapsulated and sent to Layer 5 (the session layer), or some other upper layer, depending on the protocol.

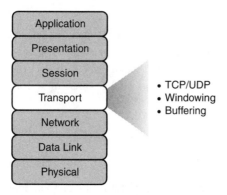

Figure 2-10   Layer 4: The Transport Layer

Two common transport layer protocols include *Transmission Control Protocol* (TCP) and *User Datagram Protocol* (UDP):

- **Transmission Control Protocol (TCP):** A connection-oriented transport protocol. Connection-oriented transport protocols provide reliable transport, in that if a segment is dropped, the sender can detect that drop and retransmit that dropped segment. Specifically, a receiver acknowledges segments that it receives. Based on those acknowledgments, a sender can determine which segments were successfully received and which segments need to be transmitted again.

- **User Datagram Protocol (UDP):** A connectionless transport protocol. Connectionless transport protocols provide unreliable transport, in that if a segment is dropped, the sender is unaware of the drop, and no retransmission occurs.

A less popular Layer 4 protocol is Novell's *Sequenced Packet Exchange* (SPX). Similar to the TCP/IP stack of protocols, Novell's solution (much more popular in the mid 1990s) was the IPX/SPX stack of protocols. However, most modern Novell networks rely on TCP/IP rather than IPX/SPX.

NOTE   Microsoft introduced its own implementation of Novell's IPX/SPX, which was named *NWLink IPX/SPX*.

Just as Layer 2 and Layer 3 each offer flow control services, flow control services also exist at Layer 4. Two common flow control approaches at Layer 4 are as follows:

- **Windowing:** TCP communication uses windowing, in that one or more segments are sent at one time, and a receiver can acknowledge the receipt of all the segments in a window with a single acknowledgment. In some cases, as illustrated in Figure 2-11, TCP uses a sliding window, where the window size begins with one segment. If there is a successful acknowledgment of that one segment (that is, the receiver sends an acknowledgment asking for the next segment), the window size doubles to two segments. Upon successful receipt of those two segments, the next window contains four segments. This exponential increase in window size continues until the receiver does not acknowledge successful receipt of all segments within a certain time period (known as the round trip time [RTT], which is sometimes called real transfer time), or until a configured maximum window size is reached.

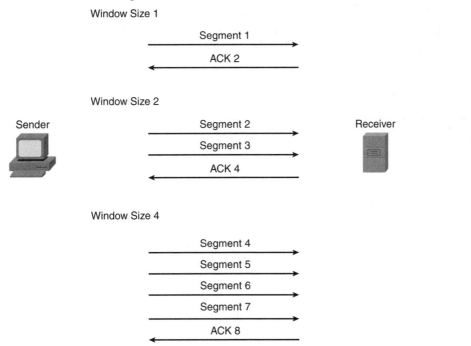

Figure 2-11 TCP Sliding Window

- **Buffering:** With buffering, a device (for example, a router) allocates a chunk of memory (sometimes called a buffer or a queue) to store segments if bandwidth is not currently available to transmit those segments. A queue has a finite capacity, however, and can overflow (that is, drop segments) in the event of sustained network congestion.

In addition to TCP and UDP, *Internet Control Message Protocol* (ICMP) is another transport layer protocol you are likely to encounter. ICMP is used by utilities such as ping and traceroute, which are discussed in Chapter 10, "Using Command-Line Utilities."

Layer 5: The Session Layer

The session layer, as shown in Figure 2-12, is responsible for setting up, maintaining, and tearing down sessions. A session can be thought of as a conversation that needs to be treated separately from other sessions to avoid intermingling of data from different conversations.

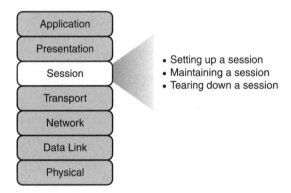

Figure 2-12   Layer 5: The Session Layer

- **Setting up a session:** Examples of the procedures involved in setting up a session include:

  - Checking user credentials (for example, username and password)

  - Assigning numbers to a session's communications flows to uniquely identify each flow

  - Negotiating services required during the session

  - Negotiating which device begins sending data

- **Maintaining a session:** Examples of the procedures involved in maintaining a session include:

  - Transferring data

  - Reestablishing a disconnected session

  - Acknowledging receipt of data

■ **Tearing down a session:** A session can be disconnected based on mutual agreement of the devices in the session. Alternately, a session might be torn down because one party disconnects (either intentionally or because of an error condition). In the event that one party disconnects, the other party can detect a loss of communication with that party and tear down its side of the session.

H.323 is an example of a session layer protocol, which can help set up, maintain, and tear down a voice or video connection. Keep in mind, however, that not every network application neatly maps directly into all seven layers of the OSI model. The session layer is one of those layers where it might not be possible to identify what protocol in a given scenario is operating at this layer. *Network Basic Input/Output System* (NetBIOS) is one example of a session layer protocol.

NOTE NetBIOS is an *application programming interface* (API) that was developed in the early 1980s to allow computer-to-computer communication on a small LAN (specifically, *PC-Network*, which was IBM's LAN technology at the time). Later, IBM needed to support computer-to-computer communication over larger Token Ring networks. As a result, IBM enhanced the scalability and features of NetBIOS with a NetBIOS emulator named *NetBIOS Extended User Interface* (NetBEUI).

Layer 6: The Presentation Layer

The presentation layer, as shown in Figure 2-13, is responsible for the formatting of data being exchanged and securing that data with encryption.

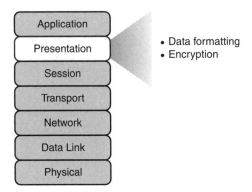

• Data formatting
• Encryption

Figure 2-13 Layer 6: The Presentation Layer

The following describes the function of data formatting and encryption in more detail:

- **Data formatting:** As an example of how the presentation layer handles data formatting, consider how text is formatted. Some applications might format text using American Standard Code for Information Interchange (ASCII), while other applications might format text using Extended Binary Coded Decimal Interchange Code (EBCDIC). The presentation layer is responsible for formatting the text (or other types of data, such as multimedia or graphics files) in a format that allows compatibility between the communicating devices.

- **Encryption:** Imagine that you are sending sensitive information over a network (for example, your credit-card number or bank password). If a malicious user were to intercept your transmission, he might be able to obtain this sensitive information. To add a layer of security for such transmissions, encryption can be used to scramble up (encrypt) the data in such a way that if the data were intercepted, a third party would not be able to unscramble it (decrypt). However, the intended recipient would be able to decrypt the transmission.

Encryption is discussed in detail in Chapter 12, "Securing a Network."

Layer 7: The Application Layer

The application layer, as shown in Figure 2-14, provides application services to a network. An important, and often-misunderstood, concept is that end-user applications (for example, Microsoft Word) do not reside at the application layer. Instead, the application layer supports services used by end-user applications. For example, e-mail is an application layer service that does reside at the application layer, while Microsoft Outlook (an example of an e-mail client) is an end-user application that does not live at the application layer. Another function of the application layer is advertising available services.

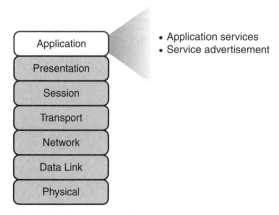

Figure 2-14   Layer 7: The Application Layer

The following describes the functions of the application layer in more detail:

- **Application services:** Examples of the application services residing at the application layer include file sharing and e-mail.

- **Service advertisement:** Some applications' services (for example, some net-worked printers) periodically send out advertisements, making the availability of their service known to other devices on the network. Other services, how-ever, register themselves and their services with a centralized directory (for example, Microsoft Active Directory), which can be queried by other network devices seeking such services.

Recall that even though the application layer is numbered as Layer 7, it is consid-ered to be at the top of the OSI stack, because its functions are closest to the end user.

The TCP/IP Stack

The ISO developed the OSI reference model to be generic, in terms of what proto-cols and technologies could be categorized by the model. However, the vast majority of traffic on the Internet (and traffic on corporate networks) is based on the TCP/IP protocol suite. Therefore, a more relevant model for many network designers and administrators to reference is a model developed by the United States Department of Defense (DoD). This model is known as the *DoD model* or the *TCP/IP stack*.

NOTE   An older protocol, which is similar to the TCP/IP protocol suite, you might come across in networking literature is *Network Control Protocol* (NCP). NCP was a protocol used on *ARPANET* (the predecessor to the Internet), and it provided fea-tures similar to (although not as robust) those provided by the TCP/IP suite of proto-cols on the Internet.

Layers of the TCP/IP Stack

The TCP/IP stack has only four defined layers, as opposed to the seven layers of the OSI model. Figure 2-15 contrasts these two models for an illustrative understanding.

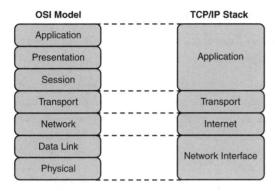

Figure 2-15 TCP/IP Stack

The TCP/IP stack is comprised of the following layers:

- **Network interface:** The TCP/IP stack's network interface layer encompasses the technologies addressed by Layers 1 and 2 (physical and data link layers) of the OSI model.

NOTE Some literature refers to the network interface layer as the *network access layer*.

- **Internet:** The Internet layer of the TCP/IP stack maps to Layer 3 (the network layer) of the OSI model. Although multiple routed protocols (for example, IP, IPX, and AppleTalk) reside at the OSI model's network layer, the Internet layer of the TCP/IP stack focuses on IP as the protocol to be routed through a network. Figure 2-16 shows the format of an IP version 4 packet.

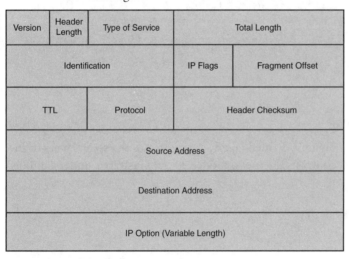

Figure 2-16 IP Version 4 Packet Format

Notice that there are fields in the IP packet header for both a source and a destination IP address. The Protocol field identifies the transport layer protocol from which the packet was sent or to which the packet should be sent. Also of note is the *Time-to-Live* (TTL) field. The value in this field is decremented by one every time this packet is routed from one IP network to another (that is, passes through a router). If the TTL value ever reaches 0, the packet is discarded from the network. This behavior helps prevent routing loops.

- **Transport:** The transport layer of the TCP/IP stack maps to Layer 4 (the transport layer) of the OSI model. The two primary protocols found at the TCP/IP stack's transport layer are TCP and UDP.

Figure 2-17 details the structure of a TCP segment. Notice the fields for source and destination ports. As described later in this chapter, these ports identify to which upper-layer protocol data should be forwarded, or from which upper-layer protocol the data is being sent.

Key Topic

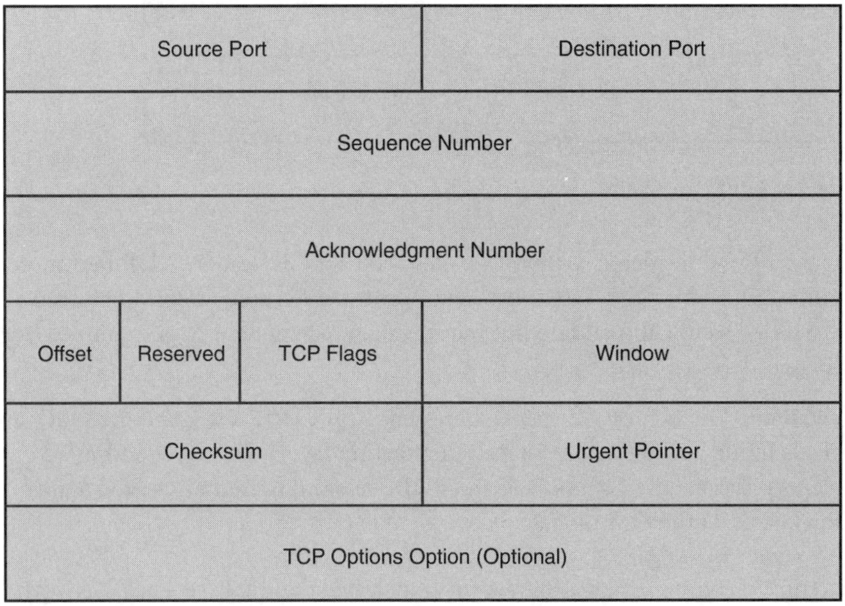

Source Port			Destination Port	
Sequence Number				
Acknowledgment Number				
Offset	Reserved	TCP Flags	Window	
Checksum			Urgent Pointer	
TCP Options Option (Optional)				

Figure 2-17   TCP Segment Format

Also notice the field for window size. The value in this field determines how many bytes a device can receive before expecting an acknowledgment. As previously described, this feature offers flow control.

The header of a TCP segment also contains sequence numbers for segments. With sequence numbering, if segments arrive out of order, the recipient can put them back in the appropriate order based on these sequence numbers.

The acknowledgment number in the header indicates the next sequence number the receiver expects to receive. This is a way for the receiver to let the sender know that all segments up to and including that point have been received.

Figure 2-18 presents the structure of a UDP segment. Because UDP is considered to be a connectionless, unreliable protocol, it lacks the sequence numbering, window size, and acknowledgment numbering present in the header of a TCP segment. Rather, the UDP segment's header only contains source and destination port numbers, a UDP checksum (which is an optional field used to detect transmission errors), and the segment length (measured in bytes).

Source Port	Destination Port
UDP Length	UDP Checksum

Figure 2-18   UDP Segment Format

Because a UDP header is so much smaller than a TCP header, UDP becomes a good candidate for the Transport Layer protocol for applications that need to maximize bandwidth and do not require acknowledgments (for example, audio or video streams).

- **Application:** The biggest difference between the TCP/IP stack and the OSI model is found at the TCP/IP stack's application layer. This layer addresses concepts described by Layers 5, 6, and 7 (the session, presentation, and application layers) of the OSI model.

With the reduced complexity of a four-layer model, like the TCP/IP stack, network designers and administrators can more easily categorize a given networking technology into a specific layer. For example, although H.323 was identified earlier as a session layer protocol within the OSI model, you would have to know more about the behavior of H.323 to properly categorize it. However, with the TCP/IP stack, you could quickly determine that H.323 is a higher-level protocol that gets encapsulated inside of TCP, and thus classify H.323 in the application layer of the TCP/IP stack.

Common Application Protocols in the TCP/IP Stack

Application layer protocols in the TCP/IP stack are identifiable by unique *port numbers*. For example, when you enter a web address in an Internet browser, you are (by default) communicating with that remote web address using TCP port 80. Specifically, Hypertext Transfer Protocol (HTTP), which is the protocol commonly used by web servers, uses a TCP port of 80. Therefore, the data you send to that remote web server has a target port number of 80. That data is then encapsulated into a TCP segment at the transport layer. That segment is then encapsulated into a packet at the Internet layer, and sent out on the network using an underlying network interface layer technology (for example, Ethernet).

Continuing with the example depicted in Figure 2-19, when you send traffic to that remote website, the packet you send out to the network needs not only the destination IP address (that is, 172.16.1.2 in this example) of the web server and the port number for HTTP (that is, 80), it also needs the IP address of your computer (that is, 10.1.1.1 in this example). Because your computer is not acting as a web server, its port is not 80. Instead, your computer selects a port number greater than 1023. In this example, let's imagine that the client PC selected a port number of 1248.

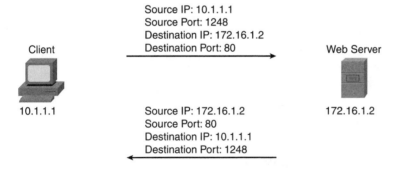

Figure 2-19   Example: Port Numbers and IP Addresses

Notice that when the web server sends content back to the PC, the data is destined for the PC's IP address and for the port number the PC associated with this session (1248 in this example). With both source and destination port numbers, along with source and destination IP addresses, two-way communication becomes possible.

NOTE   Ports numbered 1023 and below are called *well-known* ports, while ports numbered above 1023 are called *ephemeral ports*. The maximum value of a port is 65,535. Well-known port number assignments can be found at www.iana.org/assignments/port-numbers.

Table 2-1 serves as a reference for some of the more popular application layer protocols and applications found in the TCP/IP stack. Some protocols or applications (for example, DNS) can use either TCP or UDP for their transport.

Key Topic

Table 2-1 Application Layer Protocols/Applications

Protocol	Description	TCP Port	UDP Port
FTP	**File Transfer Protocol**: Transfers files with a remote host (typically requires authentication of user credentials)	20 and 21	
SSH	**Secure Shell**: Securely connect to a remote host (typically via a terminal emulator)	22	
SFTP	**Secure FTP**: Provides FTP file-transfer service over a SSH connection	22	
SCP	**Secure Copy**: Provides a secure file-transfer service over a SSH connection and offers a file's original date and time information, which is not available with FTP	22	
Telnet	**Telnet**: Used to connect to a remote host (typically via a terminal emulator)	23	
SMTP	**Simple Mail Transfer Protocol**: Used for sending e-mail	25	
DNS	**Domain Name System**: Resolves domain names to corresponding IP addresses	53	53
TFTP	**Trivial File Transfer Protocol**: Transfers files with a remote host (does not require authentication of user credentials)		69
DHCP	**Dynamic Host Configuration Protocol**: Dynamically assigns IP address information (for example, IP address, subnet mask, DNS server's IP address, and default gateway's IP address) to a network device		67
HTTP	**Hypertext Transfer Protocol**: Retrieves content from a web server	80	
POP3	**Post Office Protocol version 3**: Retrieves e-mail from an e-mail server	110	
NNTP	**Network News Transport Protocol**: Supports the posting and reading of articles on Usenet news servers	119	
NTP	**Network Time Protocol**: Used by a network device to synchronize its clock with a time server (NTP server)		123

Table 2-1   Application Layer Protocols/Applications

Protocol	Description	TCP Port	UDP Port
SNTP	**Simple Network Time Protocol**: Supports time synchronization among network devices, similar to Network Time Protocol (NTP), although SNTP uses a less complex algorithm in its calculation and is slightly less accurate than NTP		123
IMAP4	**Internet Message Access Protocol version 4**: Retrieves e-mail from an e-mail server	143	
LDAP	**Lightweight Directory Access Protocol**: Provides directory services (for example, a user directory—including username, password, e-mail, and phone number information) to network clients	389	
HTTPS	**Hypertext Transfer Protocol Secure**: Used to securely retrieve content from a web server	443	
rsh	**Remote Shell:** Allows commands to be executed on a computer from a remote user	514	
RTSP	**Real Time Streaming Protocol:** Communicates with a media server (for example, a video server) and controls the playback of the server's media files	554	554
RDP	**Remote Desktop Protocol:** A Microsoft protocol that allows a user to view and control the desktop of a remote computer	3389	

Summary

The main topics covered in this chapter are the following:

- The ISO's OSI reference model consists of seven layers: physical (Layer 1), data link (Layer 2), network (Layer 3), transport (Layer 4), session (Layer 5), presentation (Layer 6), and application (Layer 7). The purpose of each layer was presented, along with examples of technologies residing at the various layers.

- The TCP/IP stack was presented as an alternate model to the OSI reference model. The TCP/IP stack consists of four layers: network interface, Internet, transport, and application. These layers were compared and contrasted with the seven layers of the OSI model.

- This chapter discussed how port numbers are used to associate data at the transport layer with an appropriate application layer protocol. Examples of common application layer protocols in the TCP/IP suite were presented, along with their port numbers.

Exam Preparation Tasks

Review All the Key Topics

Review the most important topics from inside the chapter, noted with the Key Topic icon in the outer margin of the page. Table 2-2 lists these key topics and the page numbers where each is found.

Table 2-2 Key Topics for Chapter 2

Key Topic Element	Description	Page Number
List	Layers of the OSI model	31
Figure 2-3	Protocol data unit names	32
Figure 2-4	Layer 1: The physical layer	33
Figure 2-8	Layer 2: The data link layer	36
Figure 2-9	Layer 3: The network layer	39
Figure 2-10	Layer 4: The transport layer	42
Figure 2-11	TCP sliding window	43
Figure 2-12	Layer 5: The session layer	44
Figure 2-13	Layer 6: The presentation layer	45
Figure 2-14	Layer 7: The application layer	46
Figure 2-15	TCP/IP stack	48
Figure 2-16	IP version 4 packet format	48
Figure 2-17	TCP segment format	49
Figure 2-18	UDP segment format	50
Figure 2-19	Example: Port numbers and IP addresses	51
Table 2-1	Application layer protocols/applications	52

Complete Tables and Lists from Memory

Print a copy of Appendix C, "Memory Tables" (found on the DVD), or at least the section for this chapter, and complete the tables and lists from memory. Appendix D, "Memory Tables Answer Key," also on the DVD, includes the completed tables and lists so you can check your work.

Define Key Terms

Define the following key terms from this chapter, and check your answers in the Glossary:

Open Systems Interconnection (OSI) reference model, protocol data unit (PDU), current state modulation, state transition modulation, cyclic redundancy check (CRC), physical layer, data link layer, network layer, transport layer (OSI model), session layer, presentation layer, application layer (OSI model), network interface layer, Internet layer, transport layer (TCP/IP stack), application layer (TCP/IP stack), time-division multiplexing (TDM), Transmission Control Protocol (TCP), User Datagram Protocol (UDP), TCP/IP stack

Review Questions

The answers to these review questions appear in Appendix A, "Answers to Review Questions."

1. Which layer of the OSI reference model contains the MAC and LLC sublayers?

   a. Network layer

   b. Transport layer

   c. Physical layer

   d. Data link layer

2. Which approach to bandwidth usage consumes all the available frequencies on a medium to transmit data?

   a. Broadband

   b. Baseband

   c. Time-division multiplexing

   d. Simplex

3. Windowing is provided at what layer of the OSI reference model?

   a. Data link layer

   b. Network layer

   c. Transport layer

   d. Physical layer

4. IP addresses reside at which layer of the OSI reference model?

    a. Network layer

    b. Session layer

    c. Data link layer

    d. Transport layer

5. Which of the following is a connectionless transport layer protocol?

    a. IP

    b. TCP

    c. UDP

    d. H.323

6. Identify the four layers of the TCP/IP stack. (Choose four.)

    a. Session layer

    b. Transport layer

    c. Internet layer

    d. Data link layer

    e. Network layer

    f. Application layer

    g. Network control layer

7. What is the range of well-known TCP and UDP ports?

    a. Below 2048

    b. Below 1024

    c. 16,384–32,768

    d. Above 8192

8. Which protocol supports a secure connection to a remote host via terminal emulation software?

   a. Telnet

   b. SSH

   c. FTP

   d. SFTP

9. Identify the well-known port number for NTP.

   a. 53

   b. 69

   c. 123

   d. 143

10. Identify three e-mail protocols. (Choose three.)

   a. SNMP

   b. SMTP

   c. POP3

   d. IMAP4

After completion of this chapter, you will be able to
answer the following questions:

- What are the characteristics of various media types?

- What is the role of a given network infrastructure component?

- What features are provided by specified specialized network devices?

- How are virtualization technologies impacting traditional corporate data
  center designs?

- What are some of the primary protocols and hardware components found
  in a Voice over IP (VoIP) network?

CHAPTER 3

Identifying Network Components

Many modern networks contain a daunting number of devices, and it's your job to understand the function of each device and how they work with one another. To create a network, these devices obviously need some sort of interconnection. That interconnection uses one of a variety of media types. Therefore, this chapter begins by delving into the characteristics of media types, such as coaxial cable, twisted-pair cable, fiber-optic cable, and wireless technologies.

Next, infrastructure components (for example, hubs, bridges, switches, multilayer switches, and routers) are identified, along with their purpose. Special attention is given to switches, because they make up a significant part of a local-area network's (LAN) infrastructure.

Finally, this chapter introduces you to a collection of specialized network devices. These include a VPN concentrator, a firewall, a DNS server, a DHCP server, a proxy server, a caching engine, and a content switch.

Foundation Topics

Media

By definition, a network is an interconnection of devices. Those interconnections occur over some type of media. The media might be physical, such as a copper or fiber-optic cable. Alternately, the media might be the air, through which radio waves propagate (as is the case with wireless networking technologies).

This section contrasts various media types, including physical and wireless media. Although wireless technologies are introduced, be aware that wireless technologies are examined more thoroughly in Chapter 8, "Connecting Wirelessly."

Coaxial Cable

Coaxial cable (commonly referred to as *coax*) is composed of two conductors. As illustrated in Figure 3-1, one of the conductors is an inner insulated conductor. This inner conductor is surrounded by another conductor. This second conductor is sometimes made of a metallic foil or woven wire.

Figure 3-1   Coaxial Cable

Because the inner conductor is shielded by the metallic outer conductor, coaxial cable is resistant to *electromagnetic interference* (EMI). For example, EMI occurs when an external signal is received on a wire and might result in a corrupted data transmission. As another example, EMI occurs when a wire acts as an antenna and radiates electromagnetic waves, which might interfere with data transmission on another cable. Coaxial cables have an associated *characteristic impedance*, which needs to be balance with the device (or terminator) with which the cable connects.

NOTE   The term *electromagnetic interference* (EMI) is sometimes used interchangeably with the term *radio frequency interference* (RFI).

Three of the most common types of coaxial cables include the following:

- **RG-59:** Typically used for short-distance applications, such as carrying composite video between two nearby devices. This cable type has loss characteristics such that it is not appropriate for long-distance applications. RG-59 cable has a characteristic impedance of 75 Ohms.

- **RG-6:** Commonly used by local cable companies to connect individual homes to the cable company's distribution network. Like RG-59 cable, RG-6 cable has a characteristic impedance of 75 Ohms.

- **RG-58:** Has loss characteristics and distance limitations similar to those of RG-59. However, the characteristic impedance of RG-58 is 50 Ohms, and this type of coax was popular with early 10BASE2 Ethernet networks (which are discussed in Chapter 4, "Understanding Ethernet").

Although RG-58 coaxial cable was commonplace in early computer networks (in 10BASE2 networks), coaxial cable's role in modern computer networks is as the media used by cable modems. Cable modems are commonly installed in residences to provide high-speed Internet access over the same connection used to receive multiple television stations.

NOTE The *RG* prefix used in coaxial cable types stands for *radio guide*.

Common connectors used on coaxial cables are as follows:

- **BNC:** A *Bayonet Neill-Concelman* (BNC) (also referred to as *British Naval Connector* in some literature) connector can be used for a variety of applications, including being used as a connector in a 10BASE2 Ethernet network.

- **F-connector:** An F-connector is frequently used for cable TV (including cable modem) connections.

Figure 3-2 shows what both of these connectors look like.

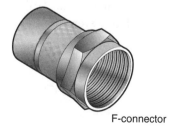

BNC

F-connector

Figure 3-2 Coaxial Cable Connectors

Twisted-Pair Cable

Today's most popular LAN media type is twisted-pair cable, where individually insulated copper strands are intertwined into a *twisted-pair* cable. Two categories of twisted-pair cable include *shielded twisted pair* (STP) and *unshielded twisted pair* (UTP). Also, for adherence to fire codes, you might need to select *plenum* cable versus *non-plenum* cable.

To define industry-standard pinouts and color coding for twisted-pair cabling, the TIA/EIA-568 standard was developed. The first iteration of the TIA/EIA-568 standard has come to be known as the *TIA/EIA-568-A* standard, which was released in 1991.

NOTE   The TIA/EIA acronym comes from *Telecommunications Industry Association/ Electronic Industries Alliance.*

In 2001, an updated standard was released, which became known as *TIA/EIA-568-B.* Interestingly, the pinout of these two standards is the same. However, the color coding of the wiring is different.

Shielded Twisted Pair

If wires in a cable are not twisted or shielded, that cable can act as an antenna, which might receive or transmit EMI. To help prevent this type of behavior, the wires (which are individually insulated) can be twisted together in pairs.

If the distance between the twists is less than a quarter of the wavelength of an electromagnetic waveform, the twisted pair of wires will not radiate that wavelength or receive EMI from that wavelength (in theory, if the wires were perfect conductors). However, as frequencies increase, wavelengths decrease.

One option of supporting higher frequencies is to surround a twisted pair in a metallic shielding, similar to the outer conductor in a coaxial cable. This type of cable is referred to as a *shielded twisted-pair (STP) cable.*

Figure 3-3 shows an example of STP cable. This outer conductors shield the copper strands from EMI; however, the addition of the metallic shielding adds to the expense of STP.

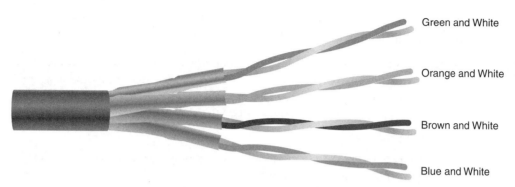

Green and White

Orange and White

Brown and White

Blue and White

Figure 3-3 Shielded Twisted Pair

Unshielded Twisted Pair

Another way to block EMI from the copper strands making up a twisted-pair cable is to twist the strands more tightly (that is, more twists per centimeters [cm]). By wrapping these strands around each other, the wires insulate each other from EMI.

Figure 3-4 illustrates an example of UTP cable. Because UTP is less expensive than STP, it has grown in popularity since the mid 1990s to become the media of choice for most LANs.

Blue/Blue and White

Brown/Brown and White

Orange/Orange and White

Green/Green and White

Figure 3-4 Unshielded Twisted Pair

UTP cable types vary in their data carrying capacity. Common categories of UTP cabling include the following:

- **Category 3:** Category 3 (Cat 3) cable is commonly used in Ethernet 10BASE-T networks, which carry data at a rate of 10 Mbps (where *Mbps* stands for *megabits per second*, meaning millions of bits per second). However, Cat 3 cable can carry data at a maximum rate of 16 Mbps, as seen in some Token Ring networks.

- **Category 5:** Category 5 (Cat 5) cable is commonly used in Ethernet 100BASE-TX networks, which carry data at a rate of 100 Mbps. However, Cat 5 cable can carry ATM traffic at a rate of 155 Mbps. Most Cat 5 cables consist of four pairs of 24 gauge wires. Each pair is twisted, with a different number of twists per meter. However, on average, one pair of wires has a twist every 5 cm.

- **Category 5e:** Category 5e (Cat 5e) cable is an updated version of Cat 5 and is commonly used for 1000BASE-T networks, which carry data at a rate of 1 Gbps. Cat 5e cable offers reduced crosstalk, as compared to Cat 5 cable.

- **Category 6:** Like Cat 5e cable, Category 6 (Cat 6) cable is commonly used for 1000BASE-T Ethernet networks. Some Cat 6 cable is made of thicker conductors (for example, 22 gauge or 23 gauge wire), although some Cat 6 cable is made from the same 24 gauge wire used by Cat 5 and Cat 5e. Cat 6 cable has thicker insulation and offers reduced crosstalk, as compared with Cat 5e.

- **Category 6a:** Category 6a (Cat 6a), or *augmented Cat 6*, supports twice as many frequencies as Cat 6 and can be used for 10GBASE-T networks, which can transmit data at a rate of 10 billion bits per second (10 Gbps).

Although other wiring categories exist, those presented in the previous list are the categories most commonly seen in modern networks.

Most UTP cabling used in today's networks is considered to be *straight-through*, meaning that the RJ-45 jacks at each end of a cable have matching pinouts. For example, pin 1 in an RJ-45 jack at one end of a cable uses the same copper conductor as pin 1 in the RJ-45 jack at the other end of a cable.

However, some network devices cannot be interconnected with a straight-through cable. As an example, consider two PCs interconnected with a straight-through cable. Because the network interface cards (NIC) in these PCs use the same pair of wires for transmission and reception, when one PC sends data to the other PC, the receiving PC would receive the data on its transmission wires, rather than its reception wires. For such a scenario, you can use a *crossover cable*, which swaps the transmit and receive wire pairs between the two ends of a cable.

NOTE A crossover cable for Ethernet devices is different than a crossover cable used for a digital T1 circuit (as discussed in Chapter 7, "Introducing Wide-Area Networks"). Specifically, an Ethernet crossover cable has a pin mapping of 1 -> 3, 2 -> 6, 3 -> 1, and 6 -> 2, while a *T1 crossover* cable has a pin mapping of 1 -> 4, 2 ->5, 4 -> 1, and 5 ->2.

NOTE A traditional port found in a PC's NIC is called a *media-dependent interface* (MDI). If a straight-through cable connects a PC's MDI port to an Ethernet switch port, the Ethernet switch port needs to swap the transmit pair of wires (that is, the wires connected to pins 1 and 2) with the receive pair of wires (that is, the wires connected to pins 3 and 6).

Therefore, a traditional port found on an Ethernet switch is called a *media-dependent interface crossover* (MDIX), which reverses the transmit and receive pairs. However, if you want to interconnect two switches, where both switch ports used for the interconnection were MDIX ports, the cable would need to be a crossover cable.

Fortunately, most modern Ethernet switches have ports that can automatically detect if they need to act as MDI ports or MDIX ports and make the appropriate adjustments. This eliminates the necessity of using straight-through cables for some Ethernet switch connections and crossover cables for other connections. With this *Auto-MDIX* feature, you can use either straight-through cables or crossover cables.

Common connectors used on twisted-pair cables are as follows:

- **RJ-45:** A *type 45 registered jack* (RJ-45) is an eight-pin connector found in most Ethernet networks. However, most Ethernet implementations only use four of the eight pins.

- **RJ-11:** A type 11 registered jack (RJ-11) has the capacity to be a six-pin connector. However, most RJ-11 connectors have only two or four conductors. An RJ-11 connector is found in most home telephone networks. However, most home phones only use two of the six pins.

- **DB-9 (RS-232):** A 9-pin D-subminiature (DB-9) connector is commonly used as a connector for asynchronous serial communications. One of the more popular uses of a DB-9 connector is to connect the serial port on a computer with an external modem.

Figure 3-5 shows what these connectors look like.

Figure 3-5   Twisted-Pair Cable Connectors

Plenum Versus Non-Plenum Cable

If a twisted-pair cable is to be installed under raised flooring or in an open-air return, fire codes must be considered. For example, imagine that there was a fire in a building. If the outer insulation of a twisted-pair cable caught on fire or started to melt, it could release toxic fumes. If those toxic fumes were released in a location such as an open-air return, those fumes could be spread throughout a building, posing a huge health risk.

To mitigate the concern of pumping poisonous gas throughout a buildings heating, ventilation, and air conditioning (HVAC) system, *plenum* cabling can be used. The outer insulator of a plenum twisted-pair cable is not only fire retardant; some plenum cabling uses a fluorinated ethylene polymer (FEP) or a low-smoke polyvinyl chloride (PVC) to minimize dangerous fumes.

NOTE   Check with your local fire codes before installing network cabling.

Fiber-Optic Cable

An alternative to copper cabling is fiber-optic cabling, which sends light (instead of electricity) through an optical fiber (typically made of glass). Using light instead of electricity makes fiber optics immune to EMI. Also, depending on the Layer 1 technology being used, fiber-optic cables typically have greater range (that is, a greater maximum distance between networked devices) and greater data-carrying capacity.

Lasers are often used to inject light pulses into a fiber-optic cable. However, lower-cost light emitting diodes (LED) are also on the market. Fiber-optic cables are generally classified according to their diameter and fall into one of two categories: *multimode fiber* (MMF) and *single-mode fiber* (SMF).

The wavelengths of light also vary between MMF and SMF cables. Usually, wavelengths of light in a MMF cable are in the range of 850–1300 nm, where *nm* stands for *nanometers*. A nanometer is one billionth of a meter. Conversely, the wavelengths of light in a SMF cable use usually in the range of 1310–1550 nm.

Multimode Fiber

When a light source, such as a laser, sends light pulses into a fiber-optic cable, what keeps the light from simply passing through the glass and being dispersed into the surrounding air? The trick is that fiber-optic cables use two different types of glass. There is an inner strand of glass (that is, a *core*) surrounded by an outer *cladding* of glass, similar to the construction of the previously mentioned coaxial cable.

The light injected by a laser (or LED) enters the core, and the light is prevented from leaving that inner strand and going into the outer cladding of glass. Specifically, the indices of refraction of these two different types of glass are so different that if the light attempts to leave the inner strand, it hits the outer cladding and bends back on itself.

To better understand this concept, consider a straw in a glass of water, as shown in Figure 3-6. Because air and water have different indices of refraction (that is, light travels at a slightly different speed in air and water), the light that bounces off of the straw and travels to our eyes is bent by the water's index of refraction. When a fiber-optic cable is manufactured, dopants are injected into the two types of glasses, making up the core and cladding to give them significantly different indices of refraction, thus causing any light attempting to escape to be bent back into the core.

Figure 3-6   Example: Refractive Index

The path that light travels through a fiber-optic cable is called a *mode of propagation*. The diameter of the core in a multimode fiber is large enough to permit light to enter the core at different angles, as depicted in Figure 3-7. If light enters at a steep angle, it bounces back and forth much more frequently on its way to the far end of the cable as opposed to light that enters the cable perpendicularly. If pulses of light representing different bits might travel down the cable using different modes of propagation, it's possible that the bits (that is, the pulses of light representing the bits) will arrive out of order at the far end (where the pulses of light, or absence of light, are interpreted as binary data by a photoelectric sensors).

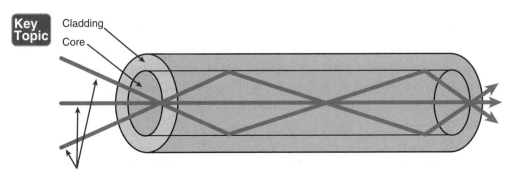

Figure 3-7   Light Propagation in Multimode Fiber

For example, perhaps the pulse of light representing the first bit intersected the core at a steep angle and bounced back and forth many times on its way to the far end of the cable, while the light pulse representing the second bit intersected the core perpendicularly and did not bound back and forth very much. With all of its bouncing, the first bit has to travel further than the second bit, which might cause the bits to arrive out of order. Such a condition is known as *multimode delay distortion*. To mitigate the issue of multimode delay distortion, MMF typically has shorter distance limitations, as opposed to SMF.

Single-Mode Fiber

SMF eliminates the issue of multimode delay distortion by having a core with a diameter so small that it only permits one mode (that is, one path) of propagation, as shown in Figure 3-8. With the issue of multimode delay distortion mitigated, SMF typically has longer distance limitations than MMF.

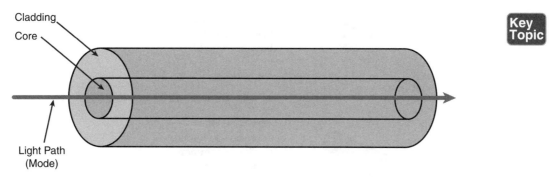

Cladding

Core

Light Path
(Mode)

Figure 3-8   Light Propagation in Single-Mode Fiber

A potential downside to SMF, however, is cost. Because SMF has to be manufactured to very exacting tolerances, you usually pay more for a given length of fiber-optic cabling. However, for some implementations, where greater distances are required, the cost is an acceptable trade-off to reach greater distances.

Some common connectors used on fiber-optic cables are as follows:

- **ST:** A *straight tip* (ST) connector is sometimes referred to as a *bayonet connector*, because of the long tip extending from the connector. ST connectors are most commonly used with MMF. An ST connector connects to a terminating device by pushing the connector into the terminating equipment and then twisting the connector housing to lock it in place.

- **SC:** Different literature defines an SC connector as *subscriber connector*, *standard connector*, or *square connector*. The SC connector is connected by pushing the connector into the terminating device, and it can be removed by pulling the connector from the terminating device.

- **LC:** A *Lucent connector* (LC) connects to a terminating device by pushing the connector into the terminating device, and it can be removed by pressing the tab on the connector and pulling it out of the terminating device.

- **MTRJ:** The most unique characteristics of a *media termination recommended jack* (MTRJ) connector is that two fiber strands (a transmit strand and a receive strand) are included in a single connector. An MTRJ connector is connected by pushing the connector into the terminating device, and it can be removed by pulling the connector from the terminating device.

Figure 3-9 shows what these connectors look like.

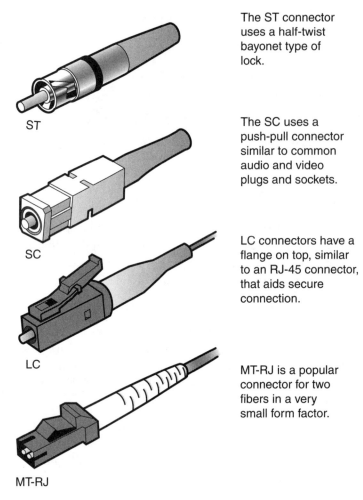

The ST connector uses a half-twist bayonet type of lock.

ST

The SC uses a push-pull connector similar to common audio and video plugs and sockets.

SC

LC connectors have a flange on top, similar to an RJ-45 connector, that aids secure connection.

LC

MT-RJ is a popular connector for two fibers in a very small form factor.

MT-RJ

Figure 3-9   Common Fiber-Optic Connectors

Cable Distribution

After deciding on what type of media you are going to use in your network (for example, UTP, STP, MMF, or SMF), that media should be installed as part of an organized cable distribution system. Typically, cable distribution systems are hierarchical in nature.

Consider the example profiled in Figure 3-10. In this example, cable from end-user offices run back to common locations within the building. These locations are sometimes referred to as *wiring closets*. Cables in these locations might terminate in a *patch panel*. This patch panel might consist of some sort of cross-connect block wired into a series of ports (for example, RJ-45 ports), which can be used to quickly interconnect cables coming from end-user offices with a network device, such as an Ethernet switch. A building might have multiple patch panels (for example, on different floors of a building). These common locations, where cables from nearby offices terminate, are often called *intermediate distribution frames* (IDF).

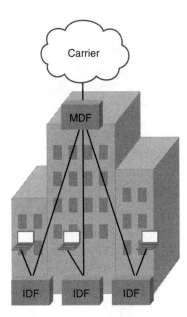

Figure 3-10   Example: Cable Distribution System

The two most popular types of cross-connect blocks found in an IDF are as follows:

- **66 block:** A 66 block, as shown in Figure 3-11, was traditionally used in corporate environments for cross-connecting phone system cabling. As 10-Mbps LANs grew in popularity, in the late 1980s and early 1990s, these termination blocks were used to cross-connect Cat 3 UTP cabling. The electrical characteristics (specifically, crosstalk) of a 66 block, however, do not support higher-speed LAN technologies, such as 100-Mbps Ethernet networks.

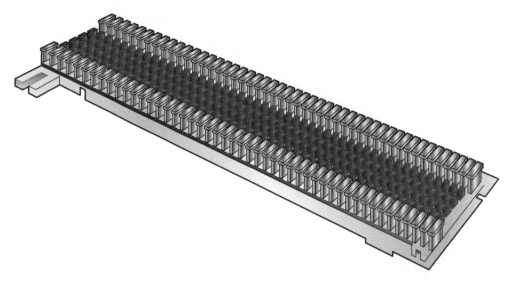

Figure 3-11   66 Block

- **110 block:** Because 66 blocks are subject to too much crosstalk (that is, inter-ference between different pairs of wires) for higher-speed LAN connections, 110 blocks, an example of which is provided in Figure 3-12, can terminate a cable (for example, a Cat 5 cable) being used for those higher-speed LANs.

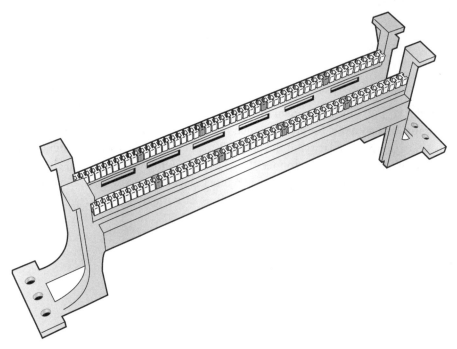

Figure 3-12   110 Block

This centralized distribution frame, which connects out to multiple IDFs, is called the *main distribution frame* (MDF).

With such a wide variety of copper and fiber cabling used by different network devices, you might need one or more *media converters*. Examples of media converters include the following:

- Fiber (MMF or SMF) to Ethernet

- Fiber to coaxial

- SMF to MMF

Wireless Technologies

Not all media is physical, as is the case of wireless network technologies. This book dedicates Chapter 8 to these technologies. However, for now, you just need to understand the basics.

Consider the sample wireless topology presented in Figure 3-13. Notice that wireless clients gain access to a wired network by communicating via radio waves with a wireless access point (AP). The AP is then hardwired to a LAN.

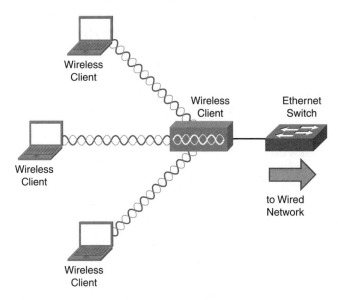

Figure 3-13 Example: Wireless Network Topology

As will be discussed in Chapter 8, wireless technologies include multiple standards that support various transmission speeds and security features. However, you need to understand, at this point, that all wireless devices connecting to the same AP are considered to be on the same *shared network segment*, which means that only one device can send data to and receive data from an AP at any one time.

Network Infrastructure Devices

The devices used in a network infrastructure can vary based on the Layer 1 technology used. For example, a Token Ring network (which is rare today) might use a *multistation access unit* (MAU), while an Ethernet network might use a switch.

Because Ethernet-based networks are dominant in today's LANs, however, the infrastructure devices presented here lend themselves to networks using Ethernet as the Layer 1 transport. Some devices (such as a router, for example) function basically the same regardless of the Layer 1 transport being used.

Hubs

As mentioned in Chapter 2, "Dissecting the OSI Model," a hub (specifically, an Ethernet hub in this discussion) lives at Layer 1 of the OSI model. As a result, a hub does not make forwarding decisions. Instead, a hub receives bits in on one port and then retransmits those bits out all other ports (that is, all ports on the hub other than the port on which the bits were received). This basic function of a hub has caused it to gain the nickname of a *bit spitter*.

Hubs most often use UTP cabling to connect to other network devices; however, some early versions of Ethernet hubs (prior to the popularization of Ethernet switches) supported fiber-optic connections.

Three basic types of Ethernet hubs exist:

- **Passive hub:** Does not amplify (that is, electrically regenerate) received bits.

- **Active hub:** Regenerates incoming bits as they are sent out all the ports on a hub, other than the port on which the bits were received.

- **Smart hub:** The term *smart hub* usually implies an active hub with enhanced features, such as Simple Network Management Protocol (SNMP) support.

A significant downside to hubs, and the main reason they have largely been replaced with switches, is that all ports on a hub belong to the same *collision domain*. As will be discussed in Chapter 4, a collision domain represents an area on a LAN on which there can be only one transmission at a time. Because multiple devices can reside in the same collision domain, as is the case with multiple PCs connected to a hub, if two devices transmit at the same time, those transmissions *collide* and have to be retransmitted.

Because of the collision-domain issue, and the inefficient use of bandwidth (that is, bits being sent out all ports rather than only the port needing the bits), hubs are rarely seen in modern LANs. However, hubs are an important piece of the tapestry that makes up the history of Ethernet networks and represent characteristics found in different areas of modern Ethernet networks. For example, a wireless AP is much like a hub, in that all the wireless devices associated with the AP belong to the same collision domain.

Consider Figure 3-14. Notice that the PCs depicted are interconnected using an Ethernet hub, but they are all in the same collision domain. As a result, only one of the connected PCs can transmit at any one time. This characteristic of hubs can limit scalability of hub-based LANs.

Also notice that all devices on a hub belong to the same broadcast domain, which means that a broadcast sent into the hub will be propagated out all of the ports on the hub (other than the port on which the broadcast was received).

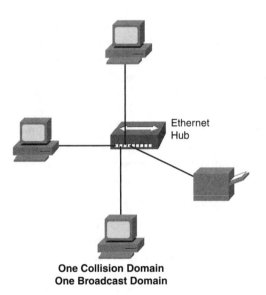

One Collision Domain
One Broadcast Domain

Figure 3-14   Ethernet Hub

Bridges

A bridge joins together two or more LAN segments, typically two Ethernet LAN segments. Each LAN segment is in separate collision domains, as shown in Figure 3-15. As a result, an Ethernet bridge can be used to scale Ethernet networks to a larger number of attached devices.

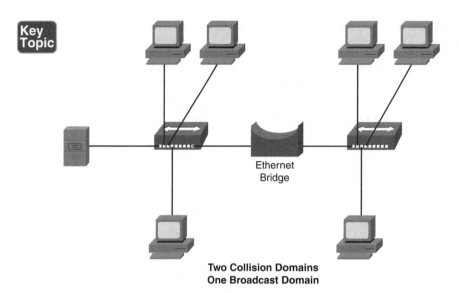

Two Collision Domains
One Broadcast Domain

Figure 3-15 Ethernet Bridge

Unlike a hub, which blindly forwards received bits, a bridge (specifically, an Ethernet bridge in this discussion) makes intelligent forwarding decisions based on the destination MAC address present in a frame. Specifically, a bridge analyzes source MAC address information on frames entering the bridge and populates an internal MAC address table based on the learned information. Then, when a frame enters the bridge destined for a MAC address known by the bridge's MAC address table to reside off of a specific port, the bridge can intelligently forward the frame out the appropriate port. Because this operation is logically the same as switch operation, a more detailed description is presented in the upcoming discussion on switches. Because a bridge makes forwarding decisions based on Layer 2 information (that is, MAC addresses), a bridge is considered to be a Layer 2 device.

Although a bridge segments a LAN into multiple collision domains (that is, one collision domain per bridge port), all ports on a bridge belong to the same broadcast domain. To understand this concept, think about the destination MAC address found in a broadcast frame. At Layer 2, the destination MAC address of a broadcast frame is FFFF.FFFF.FFFF in hexadecimal notation. Also, recall that a bridge filters frames (that is, sends frames only out necessary ports) if the bridge has previously learned the destination MAC address in its MAC address table. Because no device on a network will have a MAC address of FFFF.FFFF.FFFF, a bridge will never enter that MAC address in its MAC address table. As a result, broadcast frames are *flooded* out all bridge ports other than the port which received the frame.

Popular in the mid-to-late 1980s and early 1990s, bridges have largely been replaced with switches, for reasons including price, performance, and features. From a performance perspective, a bridge makes its forwarding decisions in software, while a switch makes its forwarding decisions in hardware, using *application-specific integrated circuits* (ASIC). Also, not only do these ASICs help reduce the cost of switches, they enable switches to offer a wider array of features. For example, Chapter 4 discusses a variety of switch features, including VLANs, trunks, port mirroring, Power over Ethernet (PoE), and 802.1x authentication.

Switches

Like a bridge, a switch (specifically, a Layer 2 Ethernet switch in this discussion) can dynamically learn the MAC addresses attached to various ports by looking at the source MAC address on frames coming into a port. For example, if switch port Gigabit Ethernet 1/1 received a frame with a source MAC address of DDDD. DDDD.DDDD, the switch could conclude that MAC address DDDD.DDDD. DDDD resided off of port Gigabit Ethernet 1/1. In the future, if the switch received a frame destined for a MAC address of DDDD.DDDD.DDDD, the switch would only send that frame out of port Gigabit Ethernet 1/1.

Initially, however, a switch is unaware of what MAC addresses reside off of which ports (unless MAC addresses have been statically configured). Therefore, when a switch receives a frame destined for a MAC address not yet present in the switch's MAC address table, the switch floods that frame out of all of the switch ports, other than the port on which the frame was received. Similarly, broadcast frames (that is, frames with a destination MAC address of FFFF.FFFF.FFFF) are always flooded out all switch ports, other than the port on which the frame was received. As mentioned in the discussion on bridges, the reason broadcast frames are always flooded is that no endpoint will have a MAC address of FFFF.FFFF.FFFF, meaning that the FFFF.FFFF.FFFF MAC address will never be learned in a switch's MAC address table.

To illustrate how a switch's MAC address table becomes populated, consider an endpoint named PC1 that wants to form a Telnet connection with a server. Also, assume that PC1 and its server both reside on the same subnet (that is, no routing is required to get traffic between PC1 and its server). Before PC1 can send a Telnet session to its server, PC1 needs to know the IP address (that is, the Layer 3 address) and the MAC address (Layer 2 address) of the server. The IP address of the server is typically known or is resolved via a Domain Name System (DNS) lookup. In this example, assume the server's IP address is known. To properly form a Telnet segment, however, PC1 needs to know the server's Layer 2 MAC address. If PC1 does not already have the server's MAC address in its ARP cache, PC1 can send an *address resolution protocol* (ARP) request in an attempt to learn the server's MAC address, as shown in Figure 3-16.

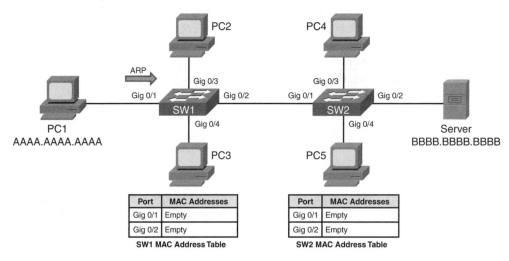

Figure 3-16   Endpoint Sending an ARP Request

When switch SW1 sees PC1's ARP request enter port Gigabit 0/1, PC1's MAC address of AAAA.AAAA.AAAA is added to switch SW1's MAC address table. Also, because the ARP request is a broadcast, its destination MAC address is FFFF.FFFF. FFFF. Because the MAC address of FFFF.FFFF.FFFF is not known to switch SW1's MAC address table, switch SW1 floods a copy of the incoming frame out all switch ports, other than the port on which the frame was received, as shown in Figure 3-17.

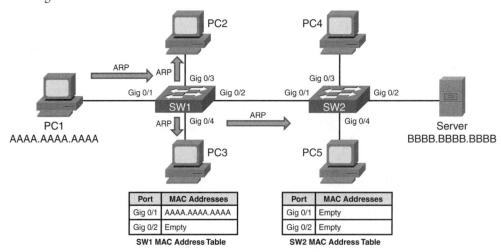

Figure 3-17   Switch SW1 Flooding the ARP Request

When switch SW2 receives the ARP request over its Gig 0/1 trunk port, the source MAC address of AAAA.AAAA.AAAA is added to switch SW2's MAC address table, as illustrated in Figure 3-18. Also, similar to the behavior of switch SW1, switch SW2 floods the broadcast.

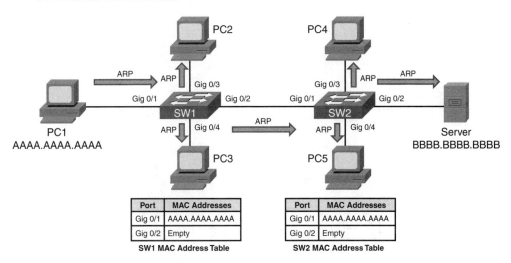

Figure 3-18   Switch SW2 Flooding the ARP Request

The server receives the ARP request and responds with an ARP reply, as shown in Figure 3-19. Unlike the ARP request, however, the ARP reply frame is not a broadcast frame. The ARP reply, in this example, has a destination MAC address of AAAA.AAAA.AAAA.

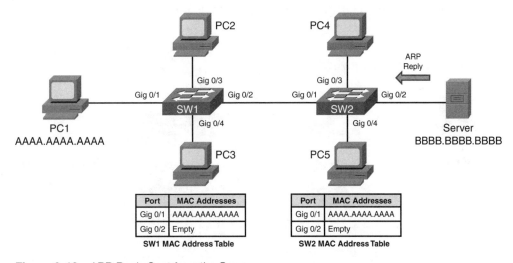

Figure 3-19   ARP Reply Sent from the Server

Upon receiving the ARP reply from the server, switch SW2 adds the server's MAC address of BBBB.BBBB.BBBB to its MAC address table, as shown in Figure 3-20. Also, the ARP reply is only sent out port Gig 0/1, because switch SW1 knows that the destination MAC address of AAAA.AAAA.AAAA is available off of port Gig 0/1.

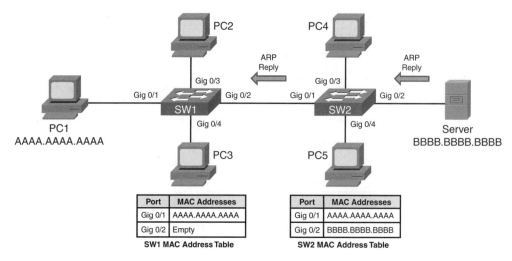

Figure 3-20 Switch SW2 Forwarding the ARP Reply

When receiving the ARP reply in its Gig 0/2 port, switch SW1 adds the server's MAC address of BBBB.BBBB.BBBB to its MAC address table. Also, like switch SW2, switch SW1 now has an entry in its MAC address table for the frame's destination MAC address of AAAA.AAAA.AAAA. Therefore, switch SW1 forwards the ARP reply out port Gig 0/1 to the endpoint of PC1, as illustrated in Figure 3-21.

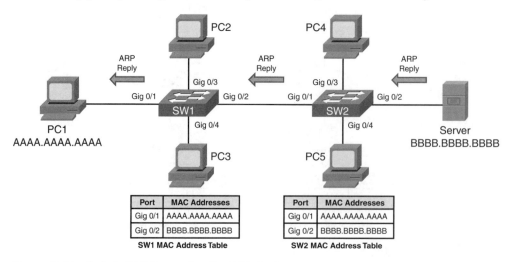

Figure 3-21 Switch SW1 Forwarding the ARP Reply

After receiving the server's ARP reply, PC1 now knows the MAC address of the server. Therefore, PC1 can now send a properly construct a Telnet segment destined for the server, as depicted in Figure 3-22.

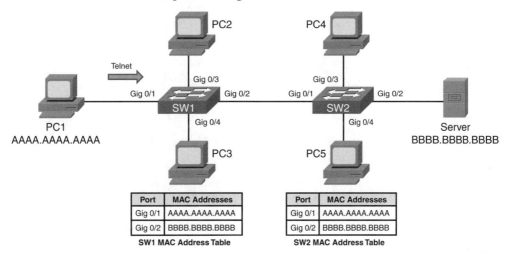

Figure 3-22   PC1 Sending a Telnet Segment

Switch SW1 has the server's MAC address of BBBB.BBBB.BBBB in its MAC address table. Therefore, when switch SW1 receives the Telnet segment from PC1, that segment is forwarded out of switch SW1's Gig 0/2 port, as shown in Figure 3-23.

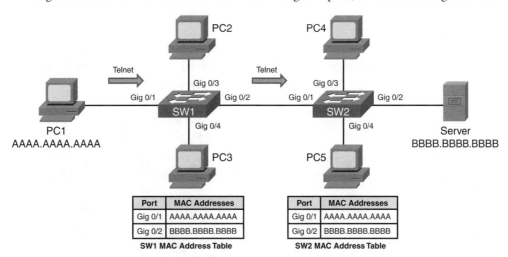

Figure 3-23   Switch SW1 Forwarding the Telnet Segment

Similar to the behavior of switch SW1, switch SW2 forwards the Telnet segment out of its Gig 0/2 port. This forwarding, shown in Figure 3-24, is possible, because

switch SW2 has an entry for the segment's destination MAC address of BBBB.
BBBB.BBBB in its MAC address table.

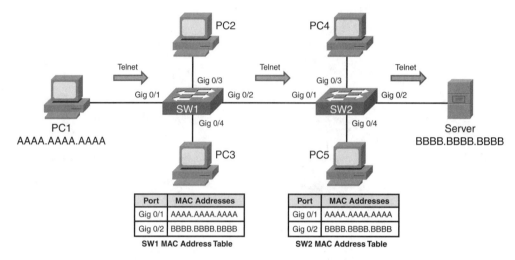

Figure 3-24   Switch SW2 Forwarding the Telnet Segment

Finally, the server responds to PC1, and a bidirectional Telnet session is established
between PC and the server, as illustrated in Figure 3-25. Because PC1 learned the server's MAC address as a result of its earlier ARP request and stored that result in its local
ARP cache, the transmission of subsequent Telnet segments does not require additional
ARP requests. However, if unused for a period of time, entries in a PC's ARP cache can
timeout. Therefore, the PC would have to broadcast another ARP frame if it needs to
send traffic the same destination IP address. The sending of the additional ARP adds
a small amount of delay when reestablishing a session with that destination IP address.

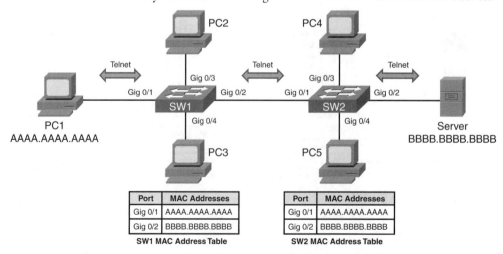

Figure 3-25   Bidirectional Telnet Session Between PC1 and the Server

As seen in Figure 3-26, like a bridge, each port on a switch represents a separate collision domain. Also, all ports on a switch belong to the same broadcast domain, with one exception.

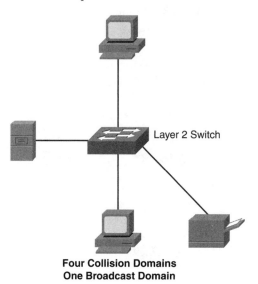

Figure 3-26   Switch Collision and Broadcast Domains

The exception is when the ports on a switch have been divided up into separate virtual LANs (VLAN). As will be discussed in Chapter 5, each VLAN represents a separate broadcast domain, and for traffic to travel from one VLAN to another, that traffic must be routed by a Layer 3 device.

Multilayer Switches

Although a Layer 2 switch, as previously described, makes forwarding decisions based on MAC address information, a multilayer switch can make forwarding decisions based on upper-layer information. For example, a multilayer switch could function as a router and make forwarding decisions based on destination IP address information.

Some literature refers to a multilayer switch as a *Layer 3 switch*, because of the switch's capability to make forwarding decisions like a router. The term *multilayer switch* is more accurate, however, because many multilayer switches have policy-based routing features that allow upper-layer information (for example, application port numbers) to be used in making forwarding decisions.

Figure 3-27 makes the point that a multilayer switch can be used to interconnect not just network segments, but entire networks. Specifically, Chapter 6, "Routing

Traffic," explains how logical Layer 3 IP addresses are used to assign network devices to different logical networks. For traffic to travel between two networked devices that belong to different networks, that traffic must be *routed* (that is, a device, such as a multilayer switch, has to make a forwarding decision based on Layer 3 information).

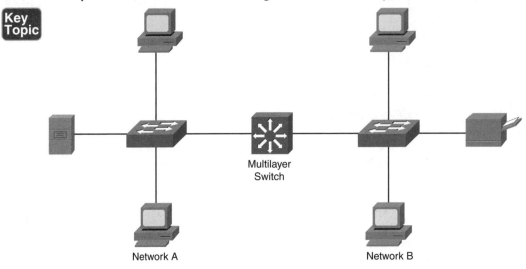

Eight Collision Domains
Two Broadcast Domain

Figure 3-27   Multilayer Ethernet Switch

Like a Layer 2 switch, each port on a multilayer switch represents a separate collision domain; however, a characteristic of a multilayer switch (and a router) is that it can become a boundary of a broadcast domain. Although all ports on a Layer 2 switch belonged to the same broadcast domain, if configured as such, all ports on a multilayer switch can belong to different broadcast domains.

Routers

A router is a Layer 3 device, meaning that it makes forwarding decisions based on logical network address (for example, IP address) information. Although a router is considered to be a Layer 3 device, like a multilayer switch, a router has the capability to consider high-layer traffic parameters (for example, quality of service [QoS] settings) in making its forwarding decisions.

As shown in Figure 3-28, each port on a router is a separate collision domain and a separate broadcast domain. At this point in the discussion, routers are beginning to sound much like a multilayer switch. So, why would a network designer select a router rather than a multilayer switch in his design?

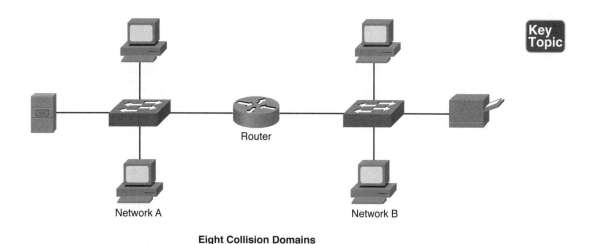

Eight Collision Domains
Two Broadcast Domain

Figure 3-28   Router Broadcast and Collision Domains

One reason a router is preferable to a multilayer switch, in some cases, is that rout-ers are typically more feature-rich and support a broader range of interface types. For example, if you need to connect a Layer 3 device out to your Internet service provider (ISP) using a serial port, you will be more likely to find a serial port expan-sion module for your router, rather than your multilayer switch.

Infrastructure Device Summary

Table 3-1 summarizes the characteristics of the network infrastructure devices dis-cussed in this section.

Table 3-1   Network Infrastructure Device Characteristics

Device	Number of Collision Domains Possible	Number of Broadcast Domains Possible	OSI Layer of Operation
Hub	1	1	1
Bridge	1 per port	1	2
Switch	1 per port	1	2
Multilayer switch	1 per port	1 per port	3+
Router	1 per port	1 per port	3+

Specialized Network Devices

Although network infrastructure devices make up the backbone of a network, for added end-user functionality, many networks integrate various specialized network devices, such as VPN concentrators, firewalls, DNS servers, DHCP servers, proxy servers, caching engines, and content switches.

VPN Concentrators

Companies with locations spread across multiple sites often require secure communications between those sites. One option is to purchase multiple WAN connections interconnecting those sites. Sometimes, however, a more cost-effective option is to create secure connections through an untrusted network, such as the Internet. Such a secure tunnel is called a *virtual private network* (VPN). Depending on the VPN technology being used, the devices that terminate the ends of a VPN tunnel might be required to perform heavy processing. For example, consider a company headquarters location with VPN connections to each of 100 remote sites. The device at the headquarters terminating these VPN tunnels might have to perform encryption and authentication for each tunnel, resulting in a heavy processor burden on that device.

Although several router models can terminate a VPN circuit, a dedicated device, called a *VPN concentrator*, can be used instead. A VPN concentrator performs the processor-intensive process required to terminate multiple VPN tunnels. Figure 3-29 shows a sample VPN topology, with a VPN concentrator located at each corporate location.

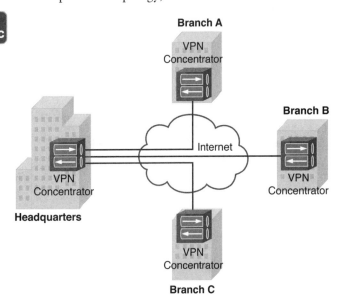

Figure 3-29   VPN Concentrator

The term *encryption* refers to the capability of a device to scramble data from a sender in such a way that the data can be unscrambled by the receiver, but not by any other party who might intercept the data. With a VPN concentrator's capability to encrypt data, it is considered to belong to a class of devices called *encryption devices*, which are devices (for example, routers, firewalls, and VPN concentrators) capable of participating in an encrypted session.

Firewalls

A firewall is primarily a network security appliance, and it is discussed in Chapter 12, "Securing a Network." As depicted in Figure 3-30, a firewall stands guard at the door of your network, protecting it from malicious Internet traffic.

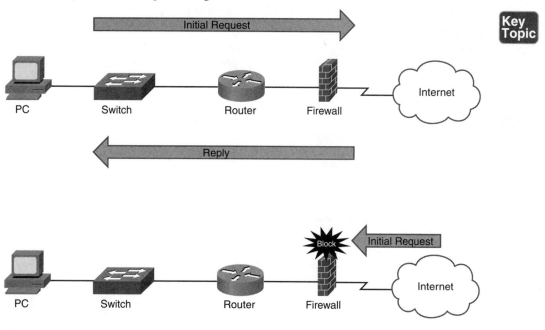

Figure 3-30   Firewall

For example, a *stateful firewall* allows traffic to originate from an inside network (that is, a trusted network) and go out to the Internet (an untrusted network). Likewise, return traffic coming back from the Internet to the inside network is allowed by the firewall. However, if traffic were originated from a device on the Internet (that is, not returning traffic), the firewall blocks that traffic.

DNS Servers

A Domain Name System (DNS) server performs the task of taking a domain name (for example, www.ciscopress.com) and resolving that name into a corresponding IP address (for example, 10.1.2.3). Because routers (or multilayer switches) make their forwarding decisions based on Layer 3 information (for example, IP addresses), an IP packet needs to contain IP address information, not DNS names. However, as humans, we more readily recall meaningful names rather than 32-bit numbers.

As shown in Figure 3-31, an end user who wants to navigate to the www.cisco press.com website enters that *fully-qualified domain name* (FQDN) into her web browser; however, the browser cannot immediately send a packet destined for www.ciscopress.com. First, the end user's computer needs to take the FQDN of www.ciscopress.com and resolve it into a corresponding IP address, which can be inserted as the destination IP address in an IP packet. This resolution is made possible by a DNS server, which maintains a database of local FQDNs and their corresponding IP addresses, in addition to pointers to other servers that can resolve IP addresses for other domains.

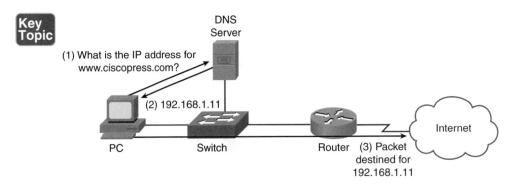

Figure 3-31   DNS Server

An FQDN is a series of strings delimited by a period (as in the previous example, www.ciscopress.com). The right-most string represents the root domain. Examples of root domains include .com, .mil, .gov, and .edu. Although many other root domains exist, these are among some of the more common domains seen in the United States.

Lower-level domains can point upward, to higher-level DNS servers to resolve non-local FQDNs, as illustrated in Figure 3-32.

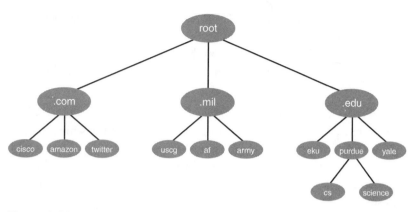

Figure 3-32   Hierarchical Domain Name Structure

A DNS server's database contains not only FQDNs and corresponding IP addresses, but also contains *DNS record types*. For example, a Mail Exchange (MX) record would be the record type for an e-mail server. As a few examples, Table 3-2 lists a collection of common DNS record types.

Table 3-2   Common DNS Record Types

Record Type	Description
A	An *address record* (that is, A record) maps a hostname to an IPv4 address.
AAAA	An *IPv6 address record* (that is, AAAA record) maps a hostname to an IPv6 address.
CNAME	A *canonical name record* (that is, CNAME record) is an alias of an existing record, thus allowing multiple DNS records to map to the same IP address.
MX	A *mail exchange record* (that is, MX record) maps a domain name to an e-mail (or *message transfer agent*) server for that domain.
PTR	A *pointer record* (that is, PTR record) points to a canonical name. A PTR record is commonly used when performing a *reverse DNS lookup*, which is a process used to determine what domain name is associated with a known IP address.
SOA	A *start of authority* record (that is, SOA record) provides authoritative information about a DNS zone, such as e-mail contact information for the zone's administrator, the zone's primary name server, and various refresh timers.

A potential challenge when setting up DNS records is when you want to point to the IP address of a device, which might change its IP address. For example, if you have a cable modem or DSL modem in your home, that device might obtain its

IP address from your service provider via DHCP (as discussed in the next section, "DHCP Servers"). As a result, if you add the IP address of your cable modem or DSL modem to a DNS record (to allow users on the Internet to access one or more devices inside your network), that record could be incorrect if your device obtains a new IP address from your service provider.

To overcome such a challenge, you can turn to *dynamic DNS* (DDNS). A DDNS provider provides you with software that you run on one of your PCs, which monitors the IP address of the device referenced in the DNS record (that is, your cable modem or DSL modem in this example). If the software detects a change in the monitored IP address, that change is reported to your service provider, which is also providing DNS service.

Yet another DNS variant is *Extension Mechanisms for DNS* (EDNS). The original specification for DNS had size limitations that prevented the addition of certain features, such as security features. EDNS supports these additional features, while maintaining backwards compatibility with the original DNS implementation. Rather than using new flags in the DNS header, which would negate backwards compatibility, EDNS sends optional *pseudo-resource-records* between devices supporting EDNS. These records support 16 new DNS flags. If a legacy DNS server were to receive one of these optional records, the record would simply be ignored. Therefore, backwards compatibility is maintained, while new features can be added for newer DNS servers.

When you enter a web address into your browser in the form of http://*FQDN* (for example, http://www.1ExamAMonth.com), notice that you not only indicate the FQDN of your web address, you also specify that you want to access this location using the HTTP protocol. Such a string, which indicates both an address (for example, www.1ExamAMonth.com) and a method for accessing that address (for example, http://), is called a *uniform resource locator* (URL).

DHCP Servers

Most modern networks have IP addresses assigned to network devices, and those logical Layer 3 addresses are used to route traffic between different networks. However, how does a network device receive its initial IP address assignment?

One option is to manually configure an IP address on a device; however, such a process is time consuming and error prone. A far more efficient method of IP address assignment is to dynamically assign IP addresses to network devices. The most common approach for this auto assignment of IP addresses is Dynamic Host Configuration Protocol (DHCP). Not only does DHCP assign an IP address to a network device, it can assign a wide variety of other IP parameters, such as a subnet mask, a default gateway, and the IP address of a DNS server.

If you have a cable modem or DSL connection in your home, your cable modem or DSL router might obtain its IP address from your service provider via DHCP. In many corporate networks, when a PC boots up, that PC receives its IP address configuration information from a corporate DHCP server.

Figure 3-33 illustrates the exchange of messages that occur as a DHCP client obtains IP address information from a DHCP server. The following list describes each step in further detail.

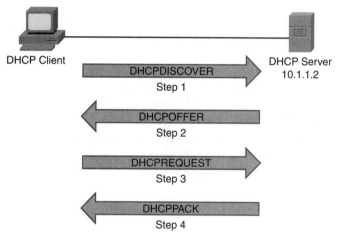

Figure 3-33 Obtaining IP Address Information from a DHCP Server

1. When a DHCP client initially boots, it has no IP address, default gateway, or other such configuration information. Therefore, the way a DHCP client initially communicates is by sending a broadcast message (that is, a DHCPDISCOVER message to a destination address of 255.255.255.255) in an attempt to discover a DHCP server.

2. When a DHCP server receives a DHCPDISCOVER message, it can respond with a unicast DHCPOFFER message. Because the DHCPDISCOVER message is sent as a broadcast, more than one DHCP server might respond to this discover request. However, the client typically selects the server that sent the first DHCPOFFER response received by the client.

3. The DHCP client communicates with this selected server by sending a unicast DHCPREQUEST message asking the DHCP server to provide IP configuration parameters.

4. The DHCP server responds to the client with a unicast DHCPACK message. This DHCPACK message contains a collection of IP configuration parameters.

Notice that in Step 1, the DHCPDISCOVER message was sent as a broadcast. By default, a broadcast cannot cross a router boundary. Therefore, if a client resides on a different network than the DHCP server, the client's next-hop router should be configured as a DHCP relay agent, which allows a router to relay DHCP requests to either a unicast IP address or a directed broadcast address for a network.

A DHCP server can be configured to assign IP addresses to devices belonging to different subnets. Specifically, the DHCP server can determine the source subnet of the DHCP request and select an appropriate address pool from which to assign an address. One of these address pools (which typically corresponds to a single subnet) is called a *scope*.

When a network device is assigned an IP address from an appropriate DHCP scope, that assignment is not permanent. Rather, it is a temporary assignment referred to as a *lease*. Although most client devices on a network work well with this *dynamic addressing*, some devices (for example, servers) might need to be assigned a specific IP address. Fortunately, you can configure a DHCP reservation, where a specific MAC address is mapped to a specific IP address, which will not be assigned to any other network device. This *static addressing* approach is referred to as a DHCP *reservation*.

Proxy Servers

Some clients are configured to forward their packets, which are seemingly destined for the Internet, to a *proxy server*. This proxy server receives the client's request, and on behalf of that client (that is, as that client's proxy), the proxy server sends the request out to the Internet. When a reply is received from the Internet, the proxy server forwards the response on to the client. Figure 3-34 illustrates the operation of a proxy server.

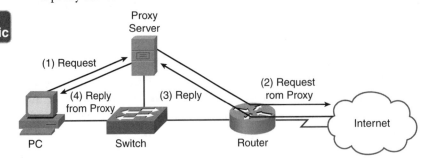

Figure 3-34 Proxy Server Operation

What possible benefit could come from such an arrangement? Security is one benefit. Specifically, because all requests going out to the Internet are sourced from the proxy server, the IP addresses of network devices inside the trusted network are hidden from the Internet.

Yet another benefit could come in the form of bandwidth savings, because many proxy servers perform *content caching*. For example, without a proxy server, if multiple clients all visited the same website, the same graphics from the home page of the website would be downloaded multiple times (one time for each client visiting the website). However, with a proxy server performing content caching, when the first client navigates to a website on the Internet, and the Internet-based web server returns its content, the proxy server not only forwards this content to the client requesting the web page but stores a copy of the content on its hard drive. Then, when a subsequent client points its web browser to the same website, after the proxy server determines that the page hasn't changed, the proxy server can locally serve up the content to the client, without having to once again consume Internet bandwidth to download all the graphic elements from the Internet-based website.

As a final example of a proxy server benefit, some proxy servers can perform content filtering. Content filtering restricts clients from accessing certain URLs. For example, many companies use content filtering to prevent their employees from accessing popular social networking sites, in an attempt to prevent a loss of productivity.

Content Engines

As previously described, many proxy servers are capable of performing content caching; however, some networks used dedicated appliances to perform this content caching. These appliances are commonly referred to as *caching engines* or *content engines*.

Figure 3-35 demonstrates how a corporate branch office can locally cache information from a server located at the corporate headquarters location. Multiple requests from branch office clients for the content can then be serviced from the content engine at the branch office, thus eliminating the repetitive transfer of the same data. Depending on traffic patterns, such an arrangement might provide significant WAN bandwidth savings.

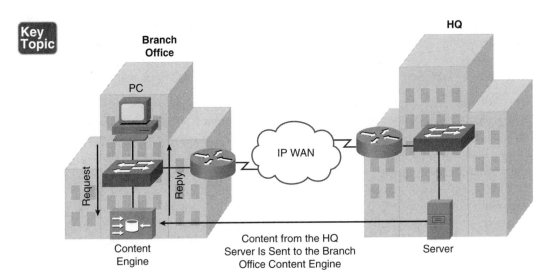

Figure 3-35 Content Engine Operation

Content Switches

Consider the server farm presented in Figure 3-36. The servers making up this server farm house the same data. For companies with a large Internet presence (for example, a search engine company, an online book store, or a social networking site), a single server could be overwhelmed with the glut of requests flooding in from the Internet. To alleviate the burden placed on a single server, a *content switch* (also known as a *load balancer*) distributes incoming requests across the various servers in the server farm, each of which maintain an identical copy of data and applications.

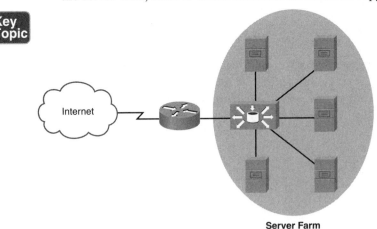

Figure 3-36 Content Switching Operation

A major benefit of content switching is that it allows a server farm to scale. Specifically, as demand increases, new servers can be added to the group of servers across which requests are load balanced. Also, if maintenance (for example, applying an operating system patch) needs to be performed on a server, a server can simply be taken out of the load-balancing rotation, with the remaining servers picking up the slack. Then, after the maintenance is complete, the server can once again be added back to the defined server group.

Virtual Network Devices

A major data center paradigm shift is underway. This shift is away from a company having its own data center (with its raised flooring and large air conditioning system) containing multiple physical servers, each of which offered a specific service (for example, e-mail, DNS services, or Microsoft Active Directory).

Virtual Servers

The computing power available in a single high-end server is often sufficient to handle the tasks of multiple independent servers. With the advent of *virtualization*, multiple servers (which might be running different operating systems) can run in *virtual server* instances on one physical device. For example, a single high-end server might be running an instance of a Microsoft Windows Server providing Microsoft Active Directory (AD) services to an enterprise, while simultaneously running an instance of a Linux server acting as a corporate web server, and at the same time acting as a Sun Solaris UNIX server providing corporate DNS services. Figure 3-37 illustrates this concept of a virtual server. Although the virtual server in the figure uses a single network interface card (NIC) to connect out to an Ethernet switch, many virtual server platforms support multiple NICs. Having multiple NICs offers increased throughput and load balancing.

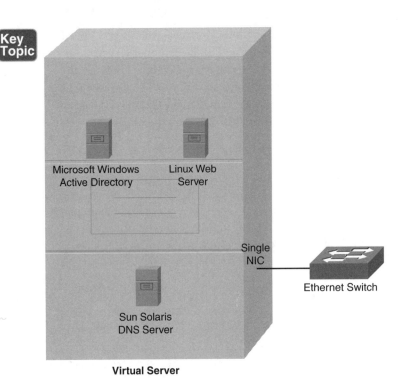

Virtual Server

Figure 3-37   Virtual Server

> **NOTE**   Although the previous example used a Linux-based web server, be aware that web servers can run on a variety of *operating system* (OS) platforms. As one example, Microsoft Windows servers support a web server application called *Internet Information Services* (IIS), which was previously known as Internet Information Server.

Virtual Switches

One potential tradeoff you make with the previously described virtual server scenario is that all servers belong to the same IP subnet, which could have QoS and security implications. If these server instances ran on separate physical devices, they could be attached to different ports on an Ethernet switch. These switch ports could belong to different VLANs, which could place each server in a different broadcast domain.

Fortunately, some virtual servers allow you to still have Layer 2 control (for example, VLAN separation and filtering). This Layer 2 control is made possible by the virtual server not only virtualizing instances of servers, but also virtualizing a Layer 2 switch.

Figure 3-38 depicts a *virtual switch*. Notice that the servers logically reside on separate VLANs, and frames from those servers are appropriately tagged when traveling over a trunk to the attached Ethernet switch.

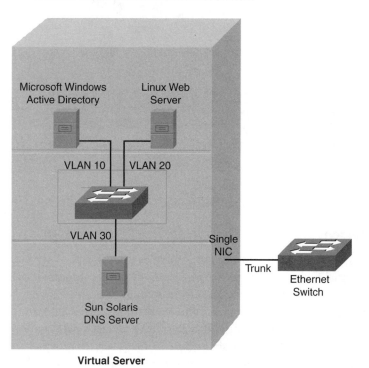

Virtual Server

Figure 3-38 Virtual Server with a Virtual Switch

Virtual Desktops

Another emerging virtualization technology is *virtual desktops*. With today's users being more mobile than ever, they need access to information traditionally stored on their office computers' hard drives from a variety of other locations. For example, a user might be at an airport using his smart phone, and she needs access to a document she created on her office computer. With virtual desktops, a user's data is stored in a data center rather than on an office computer's hard drive. By providing authentication credentials, a secure connection can be established between the centralized repository of user data and that user's device, as shown in Figure 3-39, thus allowing the user to remotely access her document.

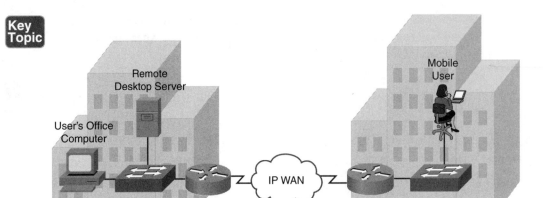

Figure 3-39   Virtual Desktop Topology

Other Virtualization Solutions

Although the previously discussed virtualization technologies (that is, virtual servers, virtual switches, and virtual desktops) were described as residing at a corporate location (that is, *on-site*), some service providers offer *off-site* options. Specifically, if a service provider's customer did not want to house and maintain his own data center, these virtualization technologies could be located at a service provider's data center, and the customer could be billed based on usage patterns. Such a service provider offering is called *Network as a Service* (NaaS), implying that network features can be provided by a service provider, just as a telephony service provider offers access to the *Public Switched Telephone Network* (PSTN), and an ISP offers access to the public Internet.

> **NOTE**   An *application service provider* (ASP) provides application software access to subscribers. This service is sometimes called *Software as a Service* (SaaS).

Similar to outsourcing the features of a data network with NaaS, a corporate telephony solution might also be outsourced. Many companies own and maintain their own *Private Branch Exchange* (PBX), which is a privately owned telephone system. One option for companies who want to outsource their telephony service is to use a service provider's *virtual PBX*. A virtual PBX is usually a *Voice over IP* (VoIP) solution, where voice is encapsulated inside data packets for transmission across a data network. Typically, a service provider provides all necessary IP telephony gateways to convert between a customer's existing telephony system and the service provider's virtual PBX.

NOTE A virtual PBX is different than a *hosted PBX*, which is usually a traditional (that is, not VoIP) PBX that is hosted by a service provider.

Voice over IP Protocols and Components

As previously mentioned, a *Voice over IP* (VoIP) network digitizes the spoken voice into packets and transmits those packets across a data network. This allows voice, data, and even video to share the same medium. Figure 3-40 shows a sample VoIP network topology. Not only can a VoIP network provide significant cost savings over a traditional PBX solution, many VoIP networks offer enhanced services (for example, integration with video conferencing applications and calendaring software to determine availability) not found in traditional corporate telephony environments.

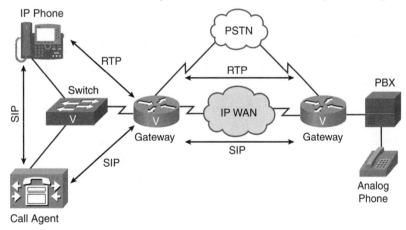

Figure 3-40 Sample VoIP Network Topology

Table 3-3 defines the VoIP devices and protocols shown in Figure 3-40.

Table 3-3   VoIP Network Elements

Protocol/ Device	Description
IP phone	An *IP phone* is a telephone with an integrated Ethernet connection. Although users speak into a traditional analog handset (or headset) on the IP phone, the IP phone digitizes the spoken voice, packetizes it, and sends it out over a data network (via the IP phone's Ethernet port).
Call agent	A *call agent* is a repository for a VoIP network's dial plan. For example, when a user dials a number from an IP phone, the call agent analyzes the dialed digits and determines how to route the call toward the destination.
Gateway	A *gateway* in a VoIP network acts as a translator between two different telephony signaling environments. In the figure, both gateways interconnect a VoIP network with the PSTN. Also, the gateway on the right interconnects a traditional PBX with a VoIP network.
PBX	A *Private Branch Exchange* (PBX) is a privately owned telephone switch traditionally used in corporate telephony systems. Although a PBX is not typically considered a VoIP device, it can connect into a VoIP network through a gateway, as shown in the figure.
Analog phone	An *analog phone* is a traditional telephone, like you might have in your home. Even though an analog phone is not typically considered a VoIP device, it can connect into a VoIP network via a VoIP or, as shown in the figure, via a PBX, which is connected to a VoIP network.
SIP	*Session Initiation Protocol* (SIP) is a VoIP signaling protocol used to set up, maintain, and tear down VoIP phone calls. Notice in the figure that SIP is spoken between the IP phone and the call agent to establish a call. The call agent then uses SIP to signal a local gateway to route the call, and that gateway uses SIP (across an IP WAN) to signal the remote gateway (on the right) about the incoming call.
RTP	*Real-time Transport Protocol* (RTP) is a Layer 4 protocol that carries voice (and interactive video). Notice in the figure that the bidirectional RTP stream does not flow through the call agent.

Summary

The main topics covered in this chapter are the following:

- This chapter contrasted various media types, including coaxial cable, shielded twisted pair, unshielded twisted pair, fiber-optic cable, and wireless technologies.

- The roles of various network infrastructure components were contrasted. These components include hubs, bridges, switches, multilayer switches, and routers.

- This chapter provided examples of specialized network devices and explained how they could add network enhancements. These devices include VPN concentrators, firewalls, DNS servers, DHCP servers, proxy servers, content engines, and content switches.

- Virtual networking components were described. These components include virtual server, virtual switch, virtual desktop, and virtual PBX technologies.

- This chapter introduced VoIP, along with a description of some of the protocols and hardware components that make up a VoIP network.

Exam Preparation Tasks

Review All the Key Topics

Review the most important topics from inside the chapter, noted with the Key Topic icon in the outer margin of the page. Table 3-4 lists these key topics and the page numbers where each is found.

Table 3-4 Key Topics for Chapter 3

Key Topic Element	Description	Page Number
List, Figure 3-2	Common coaxial connectors	61
List	Categories of UTP cabling	64
List, Figure 3-5	Common twisted-pair connectors	65–66
Figure 3-7	Light propagation in multimode fiber	68
Figure 3-8	Light propagation in single-mode fiber	69
List, Figure 3-9	Common fiber-optic connectors	69–70
Figure 3-10	Example: Cable distribution system	71
List	Three types of Ethernet hubs	74
Figure 3-14	Ethernet hub	75
Figure 3-15	Ethernet bridge	76
Figure 3-26	Layer 2 Ethernet switch	83
Figure 3-27	Multilayer Ethernet switch	84
Figure 3-28	Router	85
Table 3-1	Network infrastructure device characteristics	85
Figure 3-29	VPN concentrator	86
Figure 3-30	Firewall	87
Figure 3-31	DNS server	88
Figure 3-32	Hierarchical domain name structure	89
Table 3-2	Common DNS record types	89
Step list	Obtaining IP address information from a DHCP server	91
Figure 3-34	Proxy server operation	92
Figure 3-35	Content engine operation	94

Table 3-4 Key Topics for Chapter 3

Key Topic Element	Description	Page Number
Figure 3-36	Content switching operation	94
Figure 3-37	Virtual server	96
Figure 3-38	Virtual server with a virtual switch	97
Figure 3-39	Virtual desktop topology	98
Figure 3-40	Sample VoIP network topology	99
Table 3-3	VoIP network elements	100

Complete Tables and Lists from Memory

Print a copy of Appendix C, "Memory Tables" (found on the CD), or at least the section for this chapter, and complete the tables and lists from memory. Appendix D, "Memory Table Answer Key," also on the CD, includes completed tables and lists so you can check your work.

Define Key Terms

Define the following key terms from this chapter, and check your answers in the Glossary:

coaxial cable, twisted-pair cable, shielded twisted-pair cable, unshielded twisted-pair cable, electromagnetic interference (EMI), plenum, multimode fiber (MMF), single-mode fiber (SMF), 66 block, 110 block, hub, switch, router, multilayer switch, firewall, Domain Name System (DNS) server, Dynamic Host Configuration Protocol (DHCP), proxy server, content engine, content switch, virtual server, virtual switch, virtual desktop, on-site, off-site, Network as a Service (NaaS), virtual PBX, Session Initiation Protocol (SIP), Real-time Transport Protocol (RTP)

Review Questions

The answers to these review questions appear in Appendix A, "Answers to Review Questions."

1. What type of coaxial cable was often used for 10BASE2 Ethernet networks?

   a. RG-6

   b. RG-45

   c. RG-58

   d. RG=59

2. Which of the following categories of UTP cabling are commonly used for 1000BASE-T networks? (Choose two.)

   a. Cat 5

   b. Cat 5e

   c. Cat 6

   d. Cat 6e

3. Which type of cable might be required for installation in a drop ceiling, which is used as an open air return duct?

   a. Riser

   b. Plenum

   c. Multimode

   d. Twin-axial

4. Which network infrastructure device primarily makes forwarding decisions based on MAC addresses?

   a. Router

   b. Switch

   c. Hub

   d. Multilayer switch

5. A router primarily makes its forwarding decisions based on what address?

   a. Destination MAC address

   b. Source IP address

   c. Source MAC address

   d. Destination IP address

6. Identify two differences between an Ethernet bridge and an Ethernet switch. (Choose two.)

   a. Switches use ASICs to make forwarding decisions, while bridges make their forwarding decisions in software.

   b. Bridges typically operate faster than switches.

   c. Switches typically have higher port densities than bridges.

   d. Bridges can base their forwarding decisions on logical network layer addresses.

7. A router has 12 ports. How many broadcast domains does the router have?

   a. None

   b. One

   c. Two

   d. Twelve

8. A switch has 12 ports. How many collision domains does the switch have?

   a. None

   b. One

   c. Two

   d. Twelve

9. What is the first DHCP message sent by a client attempting to obtain IP address information from a DHCP server?

   a. DHCPOFFER

   b. DHCPACK

   c. DHCPDISCOVER

   d. DHCPREQUEST

10. What specialized network device is commonly used to load balance traffic across multiple servers in a group?

   a. Content switch

   b. Proxy server

   c. DNS server

   d. Content engine

After completion of this chapter, you will be able to
answer the following questions:

- What are the characteristics of Ethernet networks, in terms of media
  access, collisions domains, broadcast domains, and distance/speed limitations of various Ethernet standards?

- What functions are performed by Ethernet switch features, such as
  VLANs, trunks, Spanning Tree Protocol, link aggregation, Power over
  Ethernet, port monitoring, user authentication, and first-hop redundancy?

CHAPTER 4

Understanding Ethernet

Odds are, when you are working with local-area networks (LAN), you are working with Ethernet as the Layer 1 technology. Back in the mid 1990s, there was tremendous competition between technologies such as Ethernet, Token Ring, and Fiber Distributed Data Interface (FDDI). Today, however, we can see that Ethernet is the clear winner of those Layer 1 wars.

Of course, over the years, Ethernet has evolved. Several Ethernet standards exist in modern LANs, with a variety of distance and speed limitations. This chapter begins by reviewing the fundamentals of Ethernet networks, including a collection of Ethernet speeds and feeds.

Chapter 3, "Identifying Network Components," introduced you to Ethernet switches. Because these switches are such an integral part of LANs, this chapter delves into many of the features offered by some Ethernet switches.

Foundation Topics

Principles of Ethernet

The genesis of Ethernet was 1972, when this technology was developed by Xerox Corporation. The original intent was to create a technology to allow computers to connect with laser printers. A quick survey of most any corporate network reveals that Ethernet rose well beyond its humble beginnings, with Ethernet being used to interconnect such devices as computers, printers, wireless access points, servers, switches, routers, video-game systems, and more. This section discusses early Ethernet implementations and limitations, along with a reference of up-to-date Ethernet throughput and distance specifications.

Ethernet Origins

In the network-industry literature, you might come upon the term *IEEE 802.3* (where *IEEE* refers to the *Institute of Electrical and Electronics Engineers* standards body). In general, you can use the term IEEE 802.3 interchangeably with the term *Ethernet*. However, be aware that these technologies have some subtle distinctions. For example, an Ethernet frame is a fixed-length frame, while an 802.3 frame length can vary.

A popular implementation of Ethernet, in the early days, was called *10BASE5*. The *10* in 10BASE5 referred to network throughput, specifically 10 Mbps (that is, 10 million (mega) bits per second). The *BASE* in 10BASE5 referred to baseband, as opposed to broadband, as discussed in Chapter 2, "Dissecting the OSI Model." Finally, the *5* in 10BASE5 indicated the distance limitation of 500 meters. The cable used in 10BASE5 networks, as shown in Figure 4-1, was a larger diameter than most types of media. In fact, this network type became known as *thicknet*.

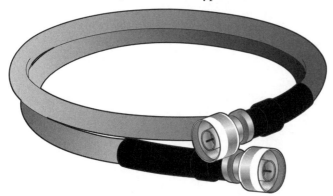

Figure 4-1   10BASE5 Cable

Another early Ethernet implementation was *10BASE2*. From the previous analysis of 10BASE5, you might conclude that 10BASE2 was a 10-Mbps baseband technology with a distance limitation of 200 meters. That is almost correct. However, 10BASE2's actual distance limitation was 185 meters. The cabling used in 10BASE2 networks was significantly thinner and therefore less expensive than 10BASE5 cabling. As a result, 10BASE2 cabling, as shown in Figure 4-2, was known as *thinnet* or *cheapernet*.

Figure 4-2   10BASE2 Cable

10BASE5 and 10BASE2 networks are rarely, if ever, seen today. Other than their 10-Mbps bandwidth limitation, the cabling used by these legacy technologies quickly faded in popularity with the advent of unshielded twisted-pair cabling (UTP), as discussed in Chapter 2. The 10-Mbps version of Ethernet that relied on UTP cabling, an example of which is provided in Figure 4-3, is known as *10BASE-T*, where the *T* in 10BASE-T refers to twisted-pair cabling.

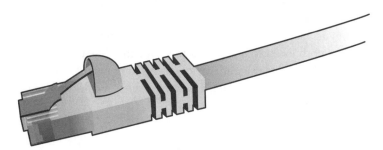

Figure 4-3   10BASE-T Cable

Carrier Sense Multiple Access Collision Detect

Ethernet was based on the philosophy that all networked devices should be eligible, at any time, to transmit on a network. This school of thought is in direct opposition to technologies such as Token Ring, which boasted a *deterministic* media access approach. Specifically, Token Ring networks passed a token around a network in a circular fashion, from one networked device to the next. Only when a networked device was in possession of that token was it eligible to transmit on the network.

Recall from Chapter 1, "Introducing Computer Networks," the concept of a bus topology. An example of a bus topology is a long cable (such as thicknet or thinnet) running the length of a building, with various networked devices tapping into that cable to gain access to the network.

Consider Figure 4-4, which depicts an Ethernet network using a shared bus topology.

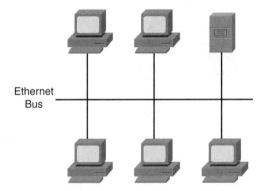

Figure 4-4 Ethernet Network Using a Shared Bus Topology

In this topology, all devices are directly connected to the network and are free to transmit at any time, if they have reason to believe no other transmission currently exists on the wire. Ethernet permits only a single frame to be on a network segment at any one time. So, before a device in this network transmits, it listens to the wire to see if there is currently any traffic being transmitted. If no traffic is detected, the networked device transmits its data. However, what if two devices simultaneously had data to transmit? If they both listen to the wire at the same time, they could simultaneously, and erroneously, conclude that it is safe to send their data. However, when both devices simultaneously send their data, a *collision* occurs. A collision, as depicted in Figure 4-5, results in data corruption.

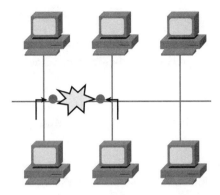

Figure 4-5 Collision on an Ethernet Segment

Fortunately, Ethernet was designed with a mechanism to detect collisions and allow the devices whose transmissions collided to retransmit their data at different times. Specifically, after the devices notice that a collision occurred, they independently set a random *back off timer*. Each device waits for this random amount of time to elapse before again attempting to transmit. Here's the logic: Because each device almost certainly picked a different amount of time to back off from transmitting, their transmissions should not collide the next time these devices transmit, as illustrated in Figure 4-6.

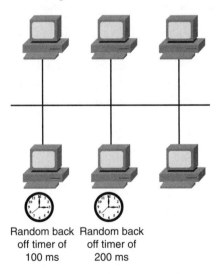

Random back   Random back
off timer of   off timer of
100 ms   200 ms

Figure 4-6 Recovering from a Collision with Random Back Off Timers

The procedure used by Ethernet to determine if it is safe to transmit, detect collisions, and retransmit if necessary is called carrier sense multiple access collision detect (CSMA/CD).

Let's break CSMA/CD down into its constituent components:

- **Carrier sense:** A device attached to an Ethernet network can listen to the wire, prior to transmitting, to make sure a frame is not currently being transmitted on the network segment.

- **Multiple access:** Unlike a deterministic method of network access (for example, the method used by Token Ring), all Ethernet devices simultaneously have access to an Ethernet segment.

- **Collision detect:** If a collision occurs (perhaps because two devices were simultaneously listening to the network and simultaneously concluded that it was safe to transmit), Ethernet devices can detect that collision and set random back off timers. After each device's random timer expires, each device again attempts to transmit its data.

Even with Ethernet's CSMA/CD feature, Ethernet segments still suffer from scalability limitations. Specifically, the likelihood of collisions increases as the number of devices on a shared Ethernet segment increases.

All devices on a shared Ethernet segment are said to belong to the same *collision domain*. One example of a shared Ethernet segment is a 10BASE5 or 10BASE2 network with multiple devices attaching to the same cable. On that cable, only one device can transmit at any one time. Therefore, all devices attached to the thicknet or thinnet cable are in the same collision domain.

Similarly, devices connected to an Ethernet hub are, as shown in Figure 4-7, in the same collision domain. As described in Chapter 3, a hub is considered to be a Layer 1 device and does not make forwarding decisions. Instead, a hub takes bits in on one port and sends them out all the other hub ports, other than the port on which the bits were received.

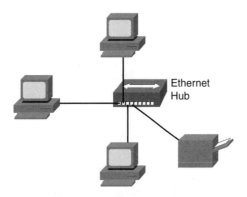

One Collision Domain

Figure 4-7   Shared Ethernet Hub—One Collision Domain

Ethernet switches, an example of which is presented in Figure 4-8, dramatically increase the scalability of Ethernet networks by creating multiple collision domains. In fact, every port on an Ethernet switch is in its own collision domain.

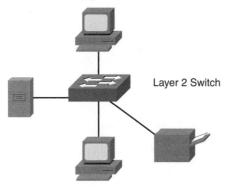

Layer 2 Switch

Four Collision Domains

Figure 4-8   Ethernet Switch—One Collision Domain per Port

A less obvious, but powerful, benefit also accompanies Ethernet switches. Because a switch port is connecting to a single device, there is no chance of having a collision. With no chance of collision, CSMA/CD is no longer needed. Without CSMA/CD, network devices can operate in *full-duplex* mode rather than *half-duplex* mode.

When multiple devices are connected to the same shared Ethernet segment, CSMA/CD must be enabled. As a result, the network must be operating in a half-duplex mode, which means that a networked device can only transmit or receive at any one time. In other words, a networked device cannot simultaneously transmit and receive, which is an inefficient use of a network's bandwidth. However, by having networked devices connected to a switch, and with each switch port connected to a single device and residing in its own collision domain, CSMA/CD can be turned off. The benefit of turning off CSMA/CD is that networked devices can then operate in full-duplex mode, where they can transmit and receive traffic at the same time (because different wires within a cable are used for transmitting and receiving), which is a far more efficient use of network bandwidth, as opposed to half-duplex communication.

Distance and Speed Limitations

To understand the bandwidth available on networks, we need to define a few terms. You should already know that a *bit* refers to one of two possible values. These values are represented using binary math, which uses only the numbers of 0 and 1. On a cable such as twisted-pair cable, a bit could be represented by the absence or presence of voltage. Fiber-optic cables, however, might represent a bit with the absence or presence of light.

The bandwidth of a network is measured in terms of how many bits the network can transmit during a 1-second period of time. For example, if a network has the capacity to transmit 10,000,000 (that is, 10 million) bits in a 1-second period of time, the bandwidth capacity is said to be 10 *Mbps*, where Mbps refers to megabits (that is, millions of bits) per second. Table 4-1 defines common bandwidths supported on various types of Ethernet networks.

Table 4-1   Ethernet Bandwidth Capacities

Ethernet Type	Bandwidth Capacity
Standard Ethernet	10 Mbps: 10 million bits per second (that is, 10 megabits per second)
FastEthernet	100 Mbps: 100 million bits per second (that is, 100 megabits per second)
Gigabit Ethernet	1 Gbps: 1 billion bits per second (that is, 1 gigabit per second)
10-Gigabit Ethernet	10 Gbps: 10 billion bits per second (that is, 10 gigabits per second)
100-Gigabit Ethernet	100 Gbps: 100 billion bits per second (that is, 100 gigabits per second)

The type of cabling used in your Ethernet network influences the bandwidth capacity and the distance limitation of your network. For example, fiber-optic cabling often has a higher bandwidth capacity and a longer distance limitation than twisted-pair cabling.

Recall Chapter 3's contrasting of single-mode fiber (SMF) with multimode fiber (MMF). Because of the issue of multimode delay distortion, SMF usually has a longer distance limitation than MMF.

When you want to uplink one Ethernet switch to another, you might need different connectors (for example, MMF, SMF, or UTP) for different installations. Fortunately, some Ethernet switches have one or more empty slots in which you can insert a *Gigabit Interface Converter* (GBIC). GBICs are interfaces that have a bandwidth capacity of 1 Gbps and are available with MMF, SMF, or UDP connectors. This allows you to have flexibility in the uplink technology you use in an Ethernet switch.

NOTE   A variant of a regular GBIC, which is smaller, is the *small form-factor pluggable* (SFP), which is sometimes called a *mini-GBIC*.

Although not comprehensive, Table 4-2 offers a listing of multiple Ethernet standards, along with their media type, bandwidth capacity, and distance limitation.

Table 4-2   Types of Ethernet

Ethernet Standard	Media Type	Bandwidth Capacity	Distance Limitation
10BASE5	Coax (thicknet)	10 Mbps	500 m
10BASE2	Coax (thinnet)	10 Mbps	185 m
10BASE-T	Cat 3 (or higher) UTP	10 Mbps	100 m
100BASE-TX	Cat 5 (or higher) UTP	100 Mbps	100 m
100BASE-FX	MMF	100 Mbps	2 km
1000BASE-T	Cat 5e (or higher) UTP	1 Gbps	100 m
1000BASE-TX	Cat 6 (or higher) UTP	1 Gbps	100 m
1000BASE-LX	MMF/SMF	1 Gbps/1 Gbps	5 km
1000BASE-LH	SMF	1 Gbps	10 km
1000BASE-ZX	SMF	1 Gbps	70 km
10GBASE-SR	MMF	10 Gbps	26–82 m
10GBASE-LR	SMF	10 Gbps	25 km
10GBASE-ER	SMF	10 Gbps	40 km
10GBASE-SW	MMF	10 Gbps	300 m
10GBASE-LW	SMF	10 Gbps	10 km
10GBASE-EW	SMF	10 Gbps	40 km
10GBASE-T	Cat 6a (or higher)	10 Gbps	100 m
100GBASE-SR10	MMF	100 Gbps	125 m
100GBASE-LR4	SMF	100 Gbps	10 km
100GBASE-ER4	SMF	100 Gbps	40 km

NOTE   Two often-confused terms are *100BASE-T* and *100BASE-TX*. 100BASE-T itself is not a specific standard. Rather, 100BASE-T is a category of standards and includes 100BASE-T2 (which uses two pairs of wires in a Cat 3 cable), 100BASE-T4 (which uses four pairs of wires in a Cat 3 cable), and 100BASE-TX. 100BASE-T2 and 100BASE-T4 were early implementations of 100-Mbps Ethernet and are no longer used. Therefore, you can generally use the 100BASE-T and 100BASE-TX terms interchangeably.

Similarly, the term *1000BASE-X* is not a specific standard. Rather, 1000BASE-X refers to all Ethernet technologies that transmit data at a rate of 1 Gbps over fiber-optic cabling.

Ethernet Switch Features

Chapter 3 delved into the operation of Layer 2 Ethernet switches (which we generically refer to as *switches*). You read an explanation of how a switch learns which Media Access Control (MAC) addresses reside off of which ports and an explanation of how a switch makes forwarding decisions based on destination MAC addresses.

Beyond basic frame forwarding, however, many Layer 2 Ethernet switches offer a variety of other features to enhance such things as network performance, redundancy, security, management, flexibility, and scalability. Although the specific features offered by a switch vary, this section introduces you to some of the more common features found on switches.

Virtual LANs

In a basic switch configuration, all ports on a switch belong to the same *broadcast domain*, as explained in Chapter 3. In such an arrangement, a broadcast received on one port gets forwarded out all other ports.

Also, from a Layer 3 perspective, all devices connected in a broadcast domain have the same *network address*. Chapter 5, "Working with IP Addresses," gets into the binary math behind the scenes of how networked devices can be assigned an IP address (that is, a logical Layer 3 address). A portion of that address is the address of the network to which that device is attached. The remaining portion of that address is the address of the device itself. Devices that have the same network address are said to belong to the same network, or *subnet*.

Imagine that you decide to place PCs from different departments within a company into their own subnet. One reason you might want to do this is for security purposes. For example, by having the Accounting department in a separate subnet (that is, a separate broadcast domain) than the Sales department, devices in one subnet will not see the broadcasts being sent on the other subnet.

A design challenge might be that PCs belonging to these departments might be scattered across multiple floors in a building. Consider Figure 4-9 as an example. The Accounting and Sales departments each have a PC on both floors of a building. Because the wiring for each floor runs back to a wiring closet on that floor, to support these two subnets using a switch's default configuration, you would have to install two switches on each floor. For traffic to travel from one subnet to another subnet, that traffic has to be routed, meaning that a device such as a multilayer switch or a router forwards traffic based on a packet's destination network addresses.

So, in this example, the Accounting switches are interconnected and then connect to a router, and the Sales switches are connected similarly.

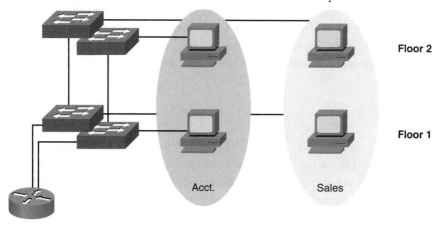

Figure 4-9   Example: All Ports on a Switch Belonging to the Same Subnet

The design presented lacks efficiency, in that you have to install at least one switch per subnet. A more efficient design would be to logically separate a switch's ports into different broadcast domains. Then, in the example, an Accounting department PC and a Sales department PC could connect to the same switch, even though those PCs belong to different subnets. Fortunately, *virtual LANs* (VLAN) make this possible.

With VLANs, as illustrated in Figure 4-10, a switch can have its ports logically divided into more than one broadcast domain (that is, more than one subnet or VLAN). Then, devices that need to connect to those VLANs can connect to the same physical switch, yet logically be separate from one another.

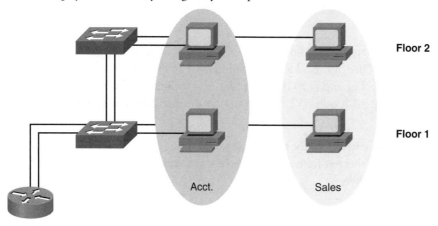

Figure 4-10   Example: Ports on a Switch Belonging to Different VLANs

One challenge with VLAN configuration in large environments is the need to configure identical VLAN information on all switches. Manually performing this configuration is time consuming and error prone. However, switches from Cisco Systems support *VLAN Trunking Protocol* (VTP), which allows a VLAN created on one switch to be propagated to other switches in a group of switches (that is, a *VTP domain*). VTP information is carried over a *trunk* connection, which is discussed next.

Trunks

One challenge with carving a switch up into multiple VLANs is that several switch ports (that is, one port per VLAN) could be consumed to connect a switch back to a router. A more efficient approach is to allow traffic for multiple VLANs to travel over a single connection, as shown in Figure 4-11. This type of connection is called a *trunk*.

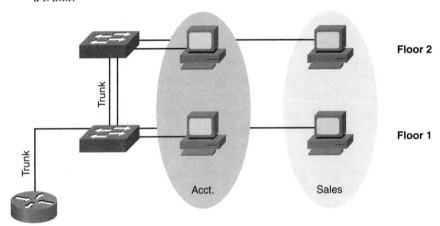

Figure 4-11 Example: Trunking Between Switches

The most popular trunking standard today is *IEEE 802.1Q*, which is frequently referred to as *dot1q*. One of the VLANs traveling over an 802.1Q trunk is called a *native VLAN*. Frames belonging to the native VLAN are sent unaltered over the trunk. However, to distinguish other VLANs from one another, the remaining VLANs are tagged.

Specifically, a non-native VLAN has four tag bytes (where a *byte* is a collection of 8 bits) added to the Ethernet frame. Figure 4-12 shows the format an IEEE 802.1Q header with these 4 bytes.

Preamble 7 Bytes	Start-of-Frame Delimiter 7 Bytes	Destination Address 6 Bytes	Source Address 6 Bytes	Tag Protocol Identifier 2 Bytes	Tag Control Identifier 2 Bytes	Type 2 Bytes	Data 48-1500 Bytes	Type 4 Bytes

4 Bytes Added by IEEE 802.1Q

Figure 4-12   IEEE 802.1Q Header

One of these bytes contains a VLAN field. That field indicates to which VLAN a frame belongs. The devices (for example, a switch, a multilayer switch, or a router) at each end of a trunk interrogate that field to determine to which VLAN an incoming frame is associated. As you can see by comparing Figures 4-9, 4-10, and 4-11, VLAN and trunking features allow switch ports to be used far more efficiently than merely relying on a default switch configuration.

Spanning Tree Protocol

Administrators of corporate telephone networks often boast about their telephone system (that is, a private branch exchange [PBX] system) having the *five nines* of availability. If a system has five nines of availability, it is up and functioning 99.999 percent of the time, which translates to only about 5 minutes of downtime per year.

Traditionally, corporate data networks struggled to compete with corporate voice networks, in terms of availability. Today, however, many networks that traditionally carried only data now carry voice, video, and data. Therefore, availability becomes an even more important design consideration.

To improve network availability at Layer 2, many networks have redundant links between switches. However, unlike Layer 3 packets, Layer 2 frames lack a *Time-to-Live* (TTL) field. As a result, a Layer 2 frame can circulate endlessly through a looped Layer 2 topology. Fortunately, *IEEE 802.1D Spanning Tree Protocol* (STP) allows a network to physically have Layer 2 loops while strategically blocking data from flowing over one or more switch ports to prevent the looping of traffic.

Before considering the operation of STP, let's think about what could happen in the absence of STP or what could happen if the STP process on a switch failed. Two significant symptoms include corruption of a switch's MAC address table and broadcast storms.

Corruption of a Switch's MAC Address Table

As described in Chapter 3, a switch's MAC address table can dynamically learn what MAC addresses are available off of its ports. However, in the event of an STP failure, a switch's MAC address table can become corrupted. To illustrate, consider Figure 4-13.

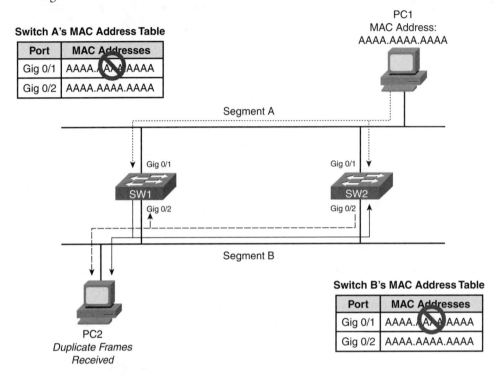

Figure 4-13   MAC Address Table Corruption

PC1 is transmitting traffic to PC2. When the frame sent from PC1 is transmitted on segment A, the frame is seen on the Gig 0/1 ports of switches SW1 and SW2, causing both switches to add an entry to their MAC address tables associating a MAC address of AAAA.AAAA.AAAA with port Gig 0/1. Because STP is not functioning, both switches then forward the frame out on segment B. As a result, PC2 receives two copies of the frame. Also, switch SW1 sees the frame forwarded out of switch SW2's Gig 0/2 port. Because the frame has a source MAC address of AAAA. AAAA.AAAA, switch SW1 incorrectly updates its MAC address table, indicating that a MAC address of AAAA.AAAA.AAAA resides off of port Gig 0/2. Similarly, switch SW2 sees the frame forwarded onto segment B by switch SW1 on its Gig 0/2 port. Therefore, switch SW2 also incorrectly updates its MAC address table.

Broadcast Storms

As previously mentioned, when a switch receives a broadcast frame (that is, a frame destined for a MAC address of FFFF.FFFF.FFFF), the switch floods the frame out of all switch ports, other than the port on which the frame was received. Because a Layer 2 frame does not have a TTL field, a broadcast frame endlessly circulates through the Layer 2 topology, consuming resources on both switches and attached devices (for example, user PCs).

Figure 4-14 and the following list illustrate how a broadcast storm can form in a Layer 2 topology when STP is not functioning correctly.

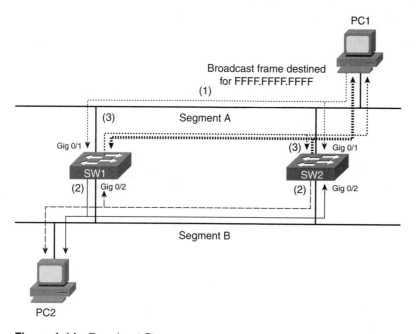

Figure 4-14 Broadcast Storm

1. PC1 sends a broadcast frame onto segment A, and the frame enters each switch on port Gig 0/1.

2. Both switches flood a copy of the broadcast frame out of their Gig 0/2 ports (that is, onto segment B), causing PC2 to receive two copies of the broadcast frame.

3. Both switches receive a copy of the broadcast frame on their Gig 0/2 ports (that is, from segment B) and flood the frame out of their Gig 0/1 ports (that is, onto segment A), causing PC1 to receive two copies of the broadcast frame.

This behavior continues, as the broadcast frame copies continue to loop through the network. The performance of PC1 and PC2 are impacted, because they also continue to receive copies of the broadcast frame.

STP Operation

STP prevents Layer 2 loops from occurring in a network, because such an occurrence might result in a broadcast storm or corruption of a switch's MAC address table. Switches in an STP topology are classified as one of the following:

- **Root bridge:** A switch elected to act as a reference point for a spanning tree. The switch with the lowest bridge ID (BID) is elected as the root bridge. The BID is made up of a priority value and a MAC address.

- **Non-root bridge:** All other switches in the STP topology are considered to be non-root bridges.

Figure 4-15 illustrates the root bridge election in a network. Notice that because the bridge priorities are both 32768, the switch with the lowest MAC address (that is, SW1) is elected as the root bridge.

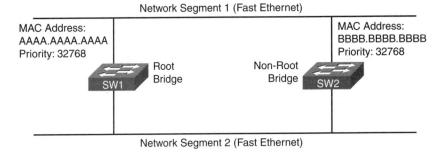

Figure 4-15   Root Bridge Election

Ports that interconnect switches in an STP topology are categorized as one of the port types described in Table 4-3.

Table 4-3   STP Port Types

Port Type	Description
Root port	Every non-root bridge has a single root port, which is the port on that switch that is closest to the root bridge, in terms of cost.
Designated port	Every network segment has a single designated port, which is the port on that segment that is closest to the root bridge, in terms of cost. Therefore, all ports on a root bridge are designated ports.
Non-designated port	Non-designated ports block traffic to create a loop-free topology.

Figure 4-16 illustrates these port types. Notice the root port for switch SW2 is selected based on the lowest port ID, because the costs of both links are equal. Specifically, each link has a cost of 19, because the links are both Fast Ethernet links.

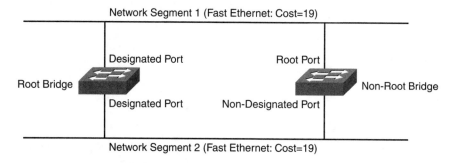

Figure 4-16   Identifying STP Port Roles

Figure 4-17 shows a similar topology to Figure 4-16. In Figure 4-17, however, the top link is running at a speed of 10 Mbps while the bottom link is running at a speed of 100 Mbps. Because switch SW2 seeks to get back to the root bridge (that is, switch SW1) with the least cost, port Gig 0/2 on switch SW2 is selected as the root port.

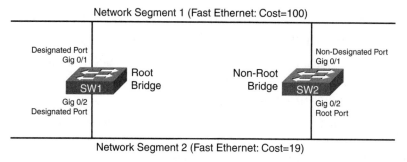

Figure 4-17   STP with Different Port Costs

Specifically, port Gig 0/1 has a cost of 100, and Gig 0/2 has a cost of 19. Table 4-4 shows the port costs for various link speeds.

Table 4-4   STP Port Cost

Link Speed	STP Port Cost
10 Mbps (Ethernet)	100
100 Mbps (Fast Ethernet)	19
1 Gbps (Gigabit Ethernet)	4
10 Gbps (Ten Gig Ethernet)	2

NOTE   A new standard for STP port costs, called *long STP*, will be increasingly adopted over the coming years because of link speeds exceeding 10 Gbps. Long STP values range from 2,000,000 for 10-Mbps Ethernet to as little as 2 for 10 Tbps (that is, 10 trillion (tera) bits per second).

Non-designated ports do not forward traffic during normal operation but do receive bridge protocol data units (BPDU). If a link in the topology goes down, the non-designated port detects the link failure and determines if it needs to transition to the forwarding state.

If a non-designated port needs to transition to the forwarding state, it does not do so immediately. Rather, it transitions through the following states:

- **Blocking:** The port remains in the blocking state for 20 seconds by default. During this time, the non-designated port evaluates BPDUs in an attempt to determine its role in the spanning tree.

- **Listening:** The port moves from the blocking state to the listening state and remains in this state for 15 seconds by default. During this time, the port sources BPDUs, which inform adjacent switches of the port's intent to forward data.

- **Learning:** The port moves from the listening state to the learning state and remains in this state for 15 seconds by default. During this time, the port begins to add entries to its MAC address table.

- **Forwarding:** The port moves from the learning state to the forwarding state and begins to forward frames.

Link Aggregation

If all ports on a switch are operating at the same speed (for example, 1 Gbps), the most likely port(s) to experience congestion is a port(s) connecting to another switch or router. For example, imagine a wiring closet switch connected (via FastEthernet ports) to multiple PCs. That wiring closet switch has an uplink to the main switch for a building. Because this uplink port aggregates multiple 100-Mbps connections and the uplink port is also operating at 100 Mbps, it can quickly become congested if multiple PCs were transmitting traffic that needed to be sent over that uplink, as shown in Figure 4-18.

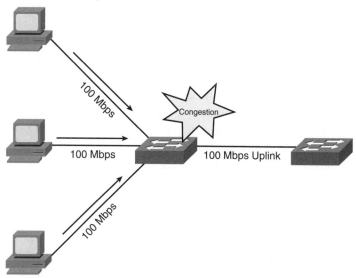

Figure 4-18   Uplink Congestion

To help alleviate congested links between switches, you can (on some switch models) logically combine multiple physical connections into a single logical connection, over which traffic can be sent. This feature, as illustrated in Figure 4-19, is called *link aggregation*.

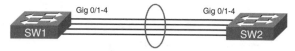

Figure 4-19   Link Aggregation

Although vendor-proprietary solutions for link aggregation have existed for some time, a couple of common issues with some solutions included the following:

- Each link in the logical bundle was a potential single point of failure.

- Each end of the logical bundle had to be manually configured.

In 2000, the IEEE ratified the 802.3ad standard for link aggregation. The IEEE 802.3ad standard supports *Link Aggregation Control Protocol* (LACP). Unlike some of the older vendor-proprietary solutions, LACP supports automatic configuration and prevents an individual link from becoming a single point of failure. Specifically, with LACP, if a link fails, that link's traffic is forwarded over a different link.

Power over Ethernet

Some switches not only transmit data over a connected UTP cable, but they use that cable to provide power to an attached device. For example, imagine that you want to install a wireless access point (AP) mounted to a ceiling. Although no electrical outlet is available near the AP's location, you can, as an example, run a Cat 5 UTP plenum cable above the drop ceiling and connect it to the AP. Some APs allow the switch at the other end of the UTP cable to provide power over the same wires that carry data. Examples of other devices that might benefit by receiving power from an Ethernet switch include security cameras and IP phones.

The switch feature that provides power to attached devices is called *Power over Ethernet* (PoE), and it is defined by the *IEEE 802.3af* standard. As shown in Figure 4-20, the PoE feature of a switch checks for 25k Ohms (25,000 Ohms) of resistance in the attached device. To check the resistance, the switch applies as much as 10 V of direct current (DC) across specific pairs of wires (that is, pins 1 and 2 combine to form one side of the circuit, and pins 3 and 6 combine to form the other side of the circuit) connecting back to the attached device and checks to see how much current flows over those wires. For example, if the switch applied 10 V DC across those wires and noticed 0.4 mA (milliamps) of current, the switch concludes the attached device had 25k Ohms of resistance across those wires (based on the formula E=IR, where E represents current, I represents current, and R represents resistance). The switch could then apply power across those wires.

Switch applies 2.8 – 10 V DC to two pairs of leads to detect a 25K Ohm resistor in the attached device

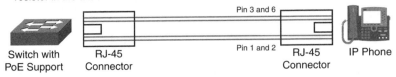

Pin 3 and 6

Pin 1 and 2

Switch with PoE Support   RJ-45 Connector   RJ-45 Connector   IP Phone

Figure 4-20   PoE

The next thing the switch must determine is how much power the attached device needs. The switch makes this determination by applying 15.5 – 20.5 V DC (making sure that the current never exceeds 100 mA) to the attached device, for a brief period of time (less than one-tenth of a second). The amount of current flowing to the attached device tells the switch the *power class* of the attached device. The switch then knows how much power should be made available on the port connecting to the device requiring power, and it begins supplying an appropriate amount of voltage (in the range 44–57 V) to the attached device.

The IEEE 802.af standard can supply a maximum of 15.4 W (Watts) of power. However, a more recent standard, IEEE 802.3at, offers as much as 32.4 W of power, enabling PoE to support a wider range of devices.

Port Monitoring

For troubleshooting purposes, you might want to analyze packets flowing over the network. To capture packets (that is, store a copy of packets on a local hard drive) for analysis, you could attach a *network sniffer* to a hub. Because a hub sends bits received on one port out all other ports, the attached network sniffer sees all traffic entering the hub.

Although several standalone network sniffers are on the market, a low-cost way to perform packet capture and analysis is to use software such as Wireshark (www. wireshark.org), as shown in Figure 4-21.

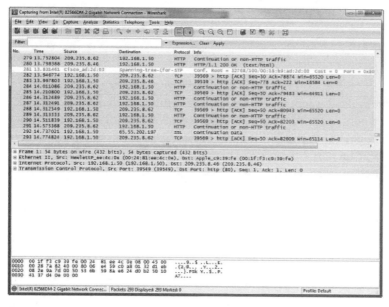

Figure 4-21   Example: Wireshark Packet-Capture Software

A challenge arises, however, if you connect your network sniffer (for example, a laptop running the Wireshark software) to a switch port rather than a hub port. Because a switch, by design, forwards frames out ports containing the frames' destination addresses, a network sniffer attached to one port would not see traffic destined for a device connected to a different port.

Consider Figure 4-22. Traffic enters a switch on port 1 and, based on the destination MAC addresses, exits via port 2. However, a network sniffer is connected to port 3 and is unable to see (and therefore capture) the traffic flowing between ports 1 and 2.

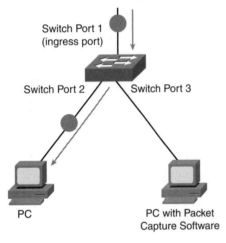

Figure 4-22 Example: Network Sniffer Unable to Capture Traffic

Fortunately, some switches support a *port mirroring* feature, which makes a copy of traffic seen on one port and sends that duplicated traffic out another port (to which a network sniffer could be attached). As shown in Figure 4-23, the switch is configured to mirror traffic on port 2 to port 3. This allows a network sniffer to capture the packets that need to be analyzed.

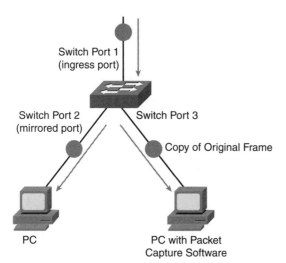

Figure 4-23   Example: Network Sniffer with Port Mirroring Configured on the Switch

User Authentication

For security purposes, some switches might require users to authenticate themselves (that is, provide credentials, such as a username and password, to prove who they are) before gaining access to the rest of the network. A standards-based method of enforcing user authentication is IEEE 802.1X.

With 802.1X enabled, a switch requires a client to authenticate before communicating on the network. After the authentication occurs, a key is generated that is shared between the client and the device to which it attaches (for example, a wireless LAN controller or a Layer 2 switch). The key then encrypts traffic coming from and being sent to the client.

In Figure 4-24, you see the three primary components of an 802.1X network, which are described in the following list.

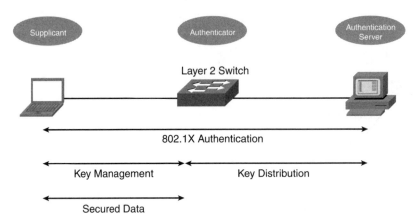

Figure 4-24 802.1X User Authentication

- **Supplicant:** The device that wants to gain access to the network.

- **Authenticator:** The authenticator forwards the supplicant's authentication request on to an authentication server. After the authentication server authenticates the supplicant, the authenticator receives a key that is used to communicate securely during a session with the supplicant.

- **Authentication server:** The authentication server (for example, a RADIUS server) checks a supplicant's credentials. If the credentials are acceptable, the authentication server notifies the authenticator that the supplicant is allowed to communicate on the network. The authentication server also gives the authenticator a key that can be used to securely transmit data during the authenticator's session with the supplicant.

An even more sophisticated approach to admission control is the *Network Admission Control* (NAC) feature offered by some authentication servers. Beyond just checking credentials, NAC can check characteristics of the device seeking admission to the network. The client's operating system (OS) and version of antivirus software are examples of these characteristics.

First-Hop Redundancy

Many devices, such as PCs, are configured with a default gateway. The *default gateway* parameter identifies the IP address of a next-hop router. As a result, if that router were to become unavailable, devices that relied on the default gateway's IP address would be unable to send traffic off their local subnet.

Fortunately, a variety of technologies are available for providing first-hop redundancy. One such technology is *Hot Standby Router Protocol* (HSRP), which is a Cisco proprietary protocol. HSRP can run on routers or multilayer switches.

HSRP uses virtual IP and MAC addresses. One router, known as the *active router*, services requests destined for the virtual IP and MAC addresses. Another router, known as the *standby router*, can service such requests in the event the active router becomes unavailable. Figure 4-25 illustrates a sample HSRP topology.

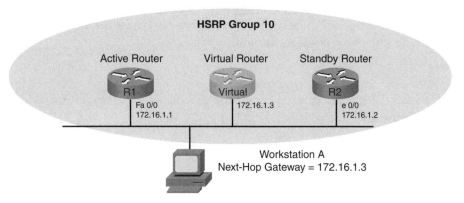

Figure 4-25   Sample HSRP Topology

Notice that router R1 is acting as the active router, and router R2 is acting as the standby router. When workstation A sends traffic destined for a remote network, it sends traffic to its default gateway of 172.16.1.3, which is the IP address being serviced by HSRP. Because router R1 is currently the active router, R1 does the work of forwarding the traffic off the local network. However, router R2 notices if router R1 becomes unavailable, because Hello messages are no longer received from router R1. At that point, router R2 transitions to an active router role. With default timer settings, the time required to fail over to router R2 is approximately 10 seconds. However, timers can be adjusted such that the failover time is as little as 1 second.

NOTE   Although HSRP is a Cisco proprietary solution, *Common Address Redundancy Protocol* (CARP) is an open standard variation of HSRP.

Other Switch Features

Although switch features, such as those previously described, vary widely by manufacturer, some switches offer a variety of security features. For example, *MAC filtering* might be supported, which allows traffic to be permitted or denied based on a device's MAC address. Other types of traffic filtering might also be supported, based on criteria such as IP address information (for multilayer switches).

For monitoring and troubleshooting purposes, interface *diagnostics* might be accessible. This diagnostic information might contain information including various error conditions (for example, late collisions or CRC errors, which might indicate a duplex mismatch).

Some switches also support *quality of service* (QoS) settings. QoS can forward traffic based on the traffic's priority markings. Also, some switches have the ability to perform marking and remarking of traffic priority values.

NOTE   QoS technologies are covered in more detail in Chapter 9, "Optimizing Network Performance."

Summary

The main topics covered in this chapter are the following:

- The origins of Ethernet, which included a discussion of Ethernet's CSMA/CD features.

- A variety of Ethernet standards were contrasted in terms of media type, network bandwidth, and distance limitation.

- Various features that might be available on modern Ethernet switches. These features include VLANs, trunking, STP, link aggregation, PoE, port monitoring, user authentication, and first-hop redundancy.

Exam Preparation Tasks

Review All the Key Topics

Review the most important topics from inside the chapter, noted with the Key Topic icon in the outer margin of the page. Table 4-5 lists these key topics and the page numbers where each is found.

Table 4-5   Key Topics for Chapter 4

Key Topic Element	Description	Page Number
List	Components of CSMA/CD	112
Table 4-1	Ethernet bandwidth capacities	114
Table 4-2	Types of Ethernet	115
Figure 4-12	IEEE 802.1Q tag bytes	119
Step List	Broadcast storm	121
List	STP switch classification	122
Table 4-3	STP port types	122
Table 4-4	STP port cost	124
List	STP port states	124
Figure 4-20	Power over Ethernet	126
Figure 4-23	Example: Network sniffer with port mirroring configured on the switch	129
List	IEEE 802.1X network components	130

Complete Tables and Lists from Memory

Print a copy of Appendix C, "Memory Tables" (found on the DVD), or at least the section for this chapter, and complete the tables and lists from memory. Appendix D, "Memory Table Answer Key," also on the DVD, includes the completed tables and lists so you can check your work.

Define Key Terms

Define the following key terms from this chapter, and check your answers in the Glossary:

Ethernet, collision, carrier sense multiple access collision detect (CSMA/CD), full-duplex, half-duplex, virtual LAN (VLAN), trunk, Spanning Tree Protocol (STP), root port, designated port, non-designated port, link aggregation, Power over Ethernet (PoE), supplicant, authenticator, authentication server

Review Questions

The answers to these review questions are in Appendix A, "Answers to Review Questions."

1. Identify the distance limitation of a 10BASE5 Ethernet network.

   a. 100 m

   b. 185 m

   c. 500 m

   d. 2 km

2. If two devices simultaneously transmit data on an Ethernet network and a collision occurs, what does each station do in an attempt to resend the data and avoid another collision?

   a. Each device compares the other device's priority value (determined by IP address) with its own, and the device with the highest priority value transmits first.

   b. Each device waits for a clear to send (CTS) signal from the switch.

   c. Each device randomly picks a priority value, and the device with the highest value transmits first.

   d. Each device sets a random back off timer, and the device will attempt retransmission after the timer expires.

3. What kind of media is used by 100GBASE-SR10 Ethernet?

   a. UTP

   b. MMF

   c. STP

   d. SMF

4. Which of the following statements are true regarding VLANs? (Choose two.)

   a. A VLAN has a single broadcast domain.

   b. For traffic to pass between two VLANs, that traffic must be routed.

   c. Because of a switch's MAC address table, traffic does not need to be routed to pass between two VLANs.

   d. A VLAN has a single collision domain.

5. What name is given to a VLAN on an IEEE 802.1Q trunk whose frames are not tagged?

   a. Native VLAN

   b. Default VLAN

   c. Management VLAN

   d. VLAN 0

6. In a topology running STP, every network segment has a single _____ port, which is the port on that segment that is closest to the root bridge, in terms of cost.

   a. Root

   b. Designated

   c. Non-designated

   d. Non-root

7. What is the IEEE standard for link aggregation?

   a. 802.1Q

   b. 802.3ad

   c. 802.1d

   d. 802.3af

8. What is the maximum amount of power a switch is allowed to provide per port according to the IEEE 802.3af standard?

   a. 7.7 W

   b. 15.4 W

   c. 26.4 W

   d. 32.4 W

9. What switch feature allows you to connect a network sniffer to a switch port and tells the switch to send a copy of frames seen on one port out the port to which your network sniffer is connected?

   a. Port interception

   b. Port duplexing

   c. Port mirroring

   d. Port redirect

10. Which IEEE 802.1X component checks the credentials of a device wanting to gain access to the network?

   a. Supplicant

   b. Authentication server

   c. Access point

   d. Authenticator

After completion of this chapter, you will be able to
answer the following questions:

- How are decimal numbers represented in binary format?

- What is the format of an IP version 4 (IPv4) address, and what are the
  distinctions between unicast, broadcast, and multicast addresses?

- Which options are available for assigning IP addresses to networked
  devices?

- Given a subnet design requirement (for example, a number of required
  subnets and a number of required hosts per subnet), how do you determine the appropriate subnet mask for a network?

- What are the primary characteristics of IPv6?

CHAPTER 5

Working with IP Addresses

When two devices on a network want to communicate, they need logical addresses (that is, Layer 3 addresses as described in Chapter 2, "Dissecting the OSI Model"). Most modern networks use Internet Protocol (IP) addressing, as opposed to other Layer 3 addressing schemes (for example, Apple's AppleTalk or Novell's Internetwork Packet Exchange [IPX]). Therefore, the focus of this chapter is IP.

Two versions of IP are addressed. First, this chapter discusses how IP concepts apply to *IP version 4* (IPv4). This discussion introduces you to how IP addresses are represented in binary notation. You examine the structure of an IPv4 address and distinguish between different categories of IPv4 addresses.

Next, various options for assigning IP addresses to end stations are contrasted. Also, one of the benefits of IP addressing is that you have flexibility in how you can take a network address and subdivide that address into multiple subnets. This discussion of subnetting tends to get a bit mathematical. So, you are provided with multiple practice exercises to help solidify these concepts in your mind.

Although IPv4 is the most widely deployed Layer 3 addressing scheme in today's networks, its scalability limitation is causing available IPv4 addresses to quickly become depleted. Fortunately, a newer version of IP, *IP version 6* (IPv6), is scalable beyond anything we will need in our lifetimes. So, after focusing on the foundation of IP addressing laid by IPv4, this chapter concludes by introducing you to the fundamental characteristics of IPv6 addressing.

Foundation Topics

Binary Numbering

Chapter 2 described how a network transmitted data as a series of binary 1s and 0s. Similarly, IP addresses can be represented as a series of binary digits (that is, *bits*). IPv4 is comprised of 32 bits, while IPv6 contains a whopping 128 bits.

Later in this chapter, you need to be able to convert between the decimal representation of a number and that number's binary equivalent. This skill is needed for things such as subnet mask calculations. This section describes this mathematical procedure and provides you with practice exercises.

Principles of Binary Numbering

We're accustomed to using Base-10 numbering in our daily lives. In a Base-10 numbering system, there are ten digits, in the range of 0–9, at our disposal. Binary numbering, however, uses a Base-2 numbering system, where there are only two digits: zero (0) and one (1).

Because 32-bit IPv4 addresses are divided into four 8-bit octets, this discussion focuses on converting between 8-bit binary numbers and decimal numbers. To convert a binary number to decimal, you can create a table similar to Table 5-1.

Table 5-1 Binary Conversion Table

128	64	32	16	8	4	2	1

Note the structure of the table. There are eight columns, representing the 8 bits in an octet. The column headings are the powers of 2 (the powers of 0–7), beginning with the right-most column. Specifically, 2 raised to the power of 0 (2^0) is 1 (in fact, any number raised to the 0 power is 1). If you raise a 2 to the first power (2^1), that equals 2. A 2 raised to the second power (that is, 2 * 2, or 2^2) is 4. This continues through 2 raised to power of 7 (that is, 2 * 2 * 2 * 2 * 2 * 2 * 2, or 2^7), which equals 128. This table can be used for converting binary numbers to decimal and decimal numbers to binary. The skill of binary-to-decimal and decimal-to-binary conversion is critical for working with subnet masks, as discussed later in this chapter.

Converting a Binary Number to a Decimal Number

To convert a binary number to a decimal number, you populate the previously described binary table with the given binary digits. Then, you add up the column-heading values for those columns containing a 1.

For example, consider Table 5-2. Only the 128, 16, 4, and 2 columns contain a 1, while all the other columns contain a 0. If you add all the column headings containing a 1 in their column (that is, 128 + 16 + 4 + 2), you get a result of 150. Therefore, you can conclude that the binary number of 10010110 equates to a decimal value of 150.

Table 5-2   Binary Conversion Example #1

128	64	32	16	8	4	2	1
1	0	0	1	0	1	1	0

Converting a Decimal Number to a Binary Number

To convert numbers from decimal to binary, staring with the left-most column, ask the question, "Is this number equal to or greater than the column heading?" If the answer to that question is, "No," place a 0 in that column and move to the next column. If the answer is, "Yes," place a 1 in that column and subtract the value of the column heading from the number you're converting. When you then move to the next column (to your right), again ask yourself the question, "Is this number (which is the result of your previous subtraction) equal to or greater than the column heading?" This process continues (to the right) for all the remaining column headings.

As an example, imagine that you want to convert the number 167 to binary. The following steps walk you through the process:

1. Ask the question, "Is 167 equal to or greater than 128?" Because the answer is, "Yes," you place a 1 in the 128 column, as shown in Table 5-3, and subtract 128 from 167, which yields a result of 39.

Table 5-3   Binary Conversion Example #2: Step 1

128	64	32	16	8	4	2	1
1							

2. Now that you're done with the 128 column, move (to the right) to the 64 column. Ask the question, "Is 39 equal to or greater than 64?" Because the answer is, "No," you place a 0 in the 128 column, as shown in Table 5-4, and continue to the next column (the 32 column).

Table 5-4 Binary Conversion Example #2: Step 2

128	64	32	16	8	4	2	1
1	0						

3. Under the 32 column, ask the question, "Is 39 equal to or greater than 32?" Because the answer is, "Yes," you place a 0 in the 32 column, as shown in Table 5-5, and subtract 32 from 39, which yields a result of 7.

Table 5-5 Binary Conversion Example #2: Step 3

128	64	32	16	8	4	2	1
1	0	1					

4. Now you're under the 16 column and ask, "Is 7 equal to or greater than 16?" Because the answer is, "No," you place a 0 in the 16 column, as shown in Table 5-6, and move to the 8 column.

Table 5-6 Binary Conversion Example #2: Step 4

128	64	32	16	8	4	2	1
1	0	1	0				

5. Similar to the 16 column, the number 7 is not equal to or greater than an 8. So, a 0 is placed in the 8 column, as shown in Table 5-7.

Table 5-7 Binary Conversion Example #2: Step 5

128	64	32	16	8	4	2	1
1	0	1	0	0			

6. Because 7 is greater than or equal to 4, a 1 is placed in the 4 column, as shown in Table 5-8, and 4 is subtracted from 7, yielding 3 as the result.

Table 5-8 Binary Conversion Example #2: Step 6

128	64	32	16	8	4	2	1
1	0	1	0	0	1		

7. Now under the 2 column, you ask the question, "Is 3 greater than or equal to 2?" Because the answer is, "Yes," you place a 1 in the 2 column, as shown in Table 5-9, and subtract 2 from 3.

Table 5-9   Binary Conversion Example #2: Step 7

128	64	32	16	8	4	2	1
1	0	1	0	0	1	1	

8. Finally, in the right-most column (that is, the 1 column) you ask if the number 1 is greater than or equal to 1. Because it is, you place a 1 in the 1 column, as shown in Table 5-10.

Table 5-10   Binary Conversion Example #2: Step 8

128	64	32	16	8	4	2	1
1	0	1	0	0	1	1	1

You can now conclude that a decimal number of 167 equates to a binary value of 10100111. In fact, you can check your work by adding up the values for the column headings that contain a 1 in their column. In this example, the 128, 32, 4, 2, and 1 columns contain a 1. If you add these values, the result is 167 (that is, 128 + 32 + 4 +2 + 1 = 167).

Binary Numbering Practice

Because binary number conversion is a skill developed through practice, you are now challenged with a few conversion exercises. The first two exercises ask you to convert a binary number to a decimal number, and the last two exercises ask you to convert a decimal number to a binary number.

Binary Conversion Exercise #1

Using Table 5-11 as a reference, convert the number binary number *01101011* to a decimal number.

Table 5-11   Binary Conversion Exercise #1: Base Table

128	64	32	16	8	4	2	1

Write your answer here: _____

Binary Conversion Exercise #1: Solution

Given a binary number of 01101011 and filling in a binary conversion table, as shown in Table 5-12, we notice that the 64, 32, 8, 2, and 1 columns contain a 1. Each of the other columns contains a 0. By adding up the value of these column headings (that is, 64 + 32 + 8 + 2 + 1), you get a decimal value of *107*.

Table 5-12   Binary Conversion Exercise #1: Solution Table

128	**64**	**32**	16	**8**	4	**2**	**1**
0	1	1	0	1	0	1	1

Binary Conversion Exercise #2

Using Table 5-13 as a reference, convert the number binary number *10010100* to a decimal number.

Table 5-13   Binary Conversion Exercise #2: Base Table

128	64	32	16	8	4	2	1

Write your answer here: _____

Binary Conversion Exercise #2: Solution

Given a binary number of 10010100 and filling in a binary conversion table, as shown in Table 5-14, we notice that the 128, 16, and 4 columns contain a 1. Each of the other columns contains a 0. By adding up the value of these column headings (that is, 128 + 16 + 4), you get a decimal value of *148*.

Table 5-14   Binary Conversion Exercise #2: Solution Table

128	64	32	**16**	8	**4**	2	1
1	0	0	1	0	1	0	0

Binary Conversion Exercise #3

Using Table 5-15 as a reference, convert the number decimal number *49* to a binary number.

Table 5-15   Binary Conversion Exercise #3: Base Table

128	64	32	16	8	4	2	1

Write your answer here: _____

Binary Conversion Exercise #3: Solution

You can begin your conversion of the decimal number 49 to a binary number by asking the following questions and performing the following calculations:

1. Is 49 greater than or equal to 128? => No => Put a 0 in the 128 column.

2. Is 49 greater than or equal to 64? => No => Put a 0 in the 64 column.

3. Is 49 greater than or equal to 32? => Yes => Put a 1 in the 32 column, and subtract 32 from 49. => 49 - 32 = 17.

4. Is 17 greater than or equal to 16? => Yes => Put a 1 in the 16 column, and subtract 16 from 17. => 17 - 16 = 1.

5. Is 1 greater than or equal to 8? => No => Put a 0 in the 8 column.

6. Is 1 greater than or equal to 4? => No => Put a 0 in the 4 column.

7. Is 1 greater than or equal to 2? => No => Put a 0 in the 2 column.

8. Is 1 greater than or equal to 1? => Yes => Put a 1 in the 1 column.

Combining these eight binary digits forms a binary number of *00110001*, as shown in Table 5-16. Verify your work by adding the values of the column headings whose columns contain a 1. In this case, columns 32, 16, and 1 each have a 1 in their column. By adding these values (that is, 32 + 16 + 1), you get a value of 49.

Table 5-16   Binary Conversion Exercise #3: Solution Table

128	64	32	16	8	4	2	1
0	0	1	1	0	0	0	1

Binary Conversion Exercise #4

Using Table 5-17, as a reference, convert the number decimal number *236* to a binary number.

Table 5-17   Binary Conversion Exercise #4: Base Table

128	64	32	16	8	4	2	1

Write your answer here: _____

Binary Conversion Exercise #4: Solution

You can begin your conversion of the decimal number *236* to a binary number by asking the following questions and performing the following calculations:

1. Is 236 greater than or equal to 128? => Yes => Put a 1 in the 128 column, and subtract 128 from 236. => 236 - 128 = 108.

2. Is 108 greater than or equal to 64? => Yes => Put a 1 in the 64 column, and subtract 64 from 108. => 108 - 64 = 44.

3. Is 44 greater than or equal to 32? => Yes => Put a 1 in the 32 column, and subtract 32 from 44. => 44 - 32 = 12.

4. Is 12 greater than or equal to 16? => No => Put a 0 in the 16 column.

5. Is 12 greater than or equal to 8? => Yes => Put a 1 in the 8 column, and subtract 8 from 12. => 12 - 8 = 4.

6. Is 4 greater than or equal to 4? => Yes => Put a 1 in the 4 column, and subtract 4 from 4. 4 - 4 = 0.

7. Is 0 greater than or equal to 2? => No => Put a 0 in the 2 column.

8. Is 0 greater than or equal to 1? => No => Put a 0 in the 1 column.

Combining these eight binary digits forms a binary number of *11101100*, as shown in Table 5-18. You can verify your work by adding the values of the column headings whose columns contain a 1. In this case, columns 128, 64, 32, 8, and 4 each have a 1 in their column. By adding these values (that is, 128 + 64 + 32 + 8 + 4), you get a value of *236*.

Table 5-18 Binary Conversion Exercise #4: Solution Table

128	64	32	16	8	4	2	1
1	1	1	0	1	1	0	0

IPv4 Addressing

Although IPv6 is increasingly being adopted in corporate networks, IPv4 is by far the most popular Layer 3 addressing scheme in today's networks. For brevity in this section, the term *IPv4 address* will be used interchangeably with the more generic term *IP address*.

Devices on an IPv4 network use unique IP addresses to communicate with one another. Metaphorically, you can relate this to sending a letter through the postal service. You place a destination address on an envelope containing the letter, and in the upper-left corner of the envelope, you place your return address. Similarly, when an IPv4 network device sends data on a network, it places both a destination IP address and a source IP address in the packet's IPv4 header.

IPv4 Address Structure

An IPv4 address is a 32-bit address. However, rather than writing out each individual bit value, the address is typically written in *dotted-decimal* notation. Consider the IP address of 10.1.2.3. This address is written in dotted-decimal notation. Notice that the IP address is divided into four separate numbers, separated by periods. Each number represents one fourth of the IP address. Specifically, each number represents an 8-bit portion of the 32 bits in the address. Because each of these four divisions of an IP address represent 8 bits, these divisions are called *octets*. As an example, Figure 5-1 shows the binary representation of the 10.1.2.3 IP address. In Figure 5-1, notice that the eight left-most bits of 00001010 equate to a decimal value of 10 (the calculation for which was described in the previous section). Similarly, 00000001 in binary equates to a 1 in decimal. A 00000010 in binary equals 2 in decimal, and finally, 00000011 yields a decimal value of 3.

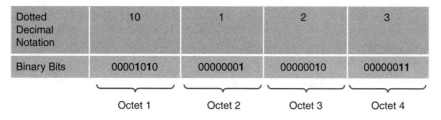

Figure 5-1 Binary Representation of Dotted Decimal IP Address

Interestingly, an IP address is composed of two types of addresses: (1) a network address and (2) a host address. Specifically, a group of contiguous left-justified bits represent the network address, and the remaining bits (that is, a group of contiguous right-justified bits) represent the address of a host on a network. The IP address component that determines which bits refer to the network and which bits refer to the host is called the *subnet mask*. You can think of the subnet mask as a dividing line separating an IP address' 32 bits into a group of network bits (on the left) and a group of host bits (on the right).

A subnet mask typically consists of a series of contiguous 1s followed by a set of continuous 0s. In total, a subnet mask contains 32 bits, which correspond to the 32 bits found in an IPv4 address. The 1s in a subnet mask correspond to network bits in an IPv4 address, while 0s in a subnet mask correspond to host bits in an IPv4 address.

As an example, consider Figure 5-2. The eight left-most bits of the subnet mask are 1s, while the remaining 24 bits are 0s. As a result, the eight left-most bits of the IP address represent the network address, and the remaining 24 bits represent the host address.

Dotted Decimal Notation	10	1	2	3
IP Address (in Binary)	00001010	00000001	00000010	00000011
Subnet Mask	11111111	00000000	00000000	00000000

Network Bits   Host Bits

Figure 5-2   Dividing an IP Address into a Network Portion and a Host Portion

When you write a network address, all host bits are set to 0s. Once again, consider the example shown in Figure 5-2. The subnet mask in this example is an *8-bit subnet mask*, meaning that the eight left-most bits in the subnet mask are 1s. If the remaining bits were set to 0, as shown in Figure 5-3, the network address of 10.0.0.0 can be seen.

Network Address (in Dotted Decimal)	10	0	0	0
Network Address (in Binary)	00001010	00000000	00000000	00000000
Subnet Mask	11111111	00000000	00000000	00000000

Network Bits ⏜   Host Bits ⏜

Figure 5-3 Network Address Calculation

When writing a network address, or an IP address for that matter, more detail needs to be provided than just a dotted-decimal representation of an IP address' 32 bits. For example, just being told that a device has an IP address of 10.1.2.3 does not tell you the network on which the IP address resides. To know the network address, you need to know the subnet mask, which could be written in dotted-decimal notation or in *prefix notation* (also known as *slash notation*). In the example, where we have an IP address of 10.1.2.3 and an 8-bit subnet mask, the IP address could be written as *10.1.2.3 255.0.0.0* or *10.1.2.3 /8*. Similarly, the network address could be written as *10.0.0.0 255.0.0.0* or *10.0.0.0 /8*.

Classes of Addresses

Although an IP address (or a network address) needs subnet mask information to determine which bits represent the network portion of the address, there are default subnet masks with which you should be familiar. The default subnet mask for a given IP address is solely determined by the value in the IP address' first octet. Table 5-19 shows the default subnet masks for various ranges of IP addresses.

Table 5-19 IP Address Classes

Address Class	Value in First Octet	Classful Mask (Dotted Decimal)	Classful Mask (Prefix Notation)
Class A	1–126	255.0.0.0	/8
Class B	128–191	255.255.0.0	/16
Class C	192–223	255.255.255.0	/24
Class D	224–239	N/A	N/A
Class E	240–255	N/A	N/A

These ranges of IP address, which you should memorize, are referred to as different *classes* of addresses. Classes A, B, and C are those ranges of addresses assigned to network devices. Class D addresses are used as destination IP addresses (that is, not assigned to devices sourcing traffic) for multicast networks, and Class E addresses are reserved for experimental use. The default subnet masks associated with address classes A, B, and C are called *classful masks*.

As an example, consider an IP address of 172.16.40.56. If you were told that this IP address used its classful mask, you should know that it has a subnet mask of 255.255.0.0, which is the classful mask for a Class B IP address. You should know that 172.16.40.56 is a Class B IP address, based on the value of the first octet (172), which falls in the Class B range of 128–191.

NOTE You might have noticed that in the ranges of values in the first octet, the number 127 seems to have been skipped. The reason is that 127 is used as a *loopback* IP address, meaning a locally significant IP address representing the device itself. For example, if you were working on a network device and wanted to verify that device had a TCP/IP stack loaded, you could attempt to ping an IP address of 127.1.1.1. If you received ping responses, you could conclude that the device is running a TCP/IP stack. The ping function is discussed in Chapter 10, "Using Command-Line Utilities."

Publicly routable IP addresses are globally managed by the *Internet Corporation for Assigned Names and Numbers* (ICANN) non-profit corporation. ICANN does not directly assign a block of IP addresses to your Internet service provider (ISP), but assigns a block of IP addresses to a regional Internet registry. One example of a regional Internet registry is the *American Registry for Internet Numbers* (ARIN), which acts as an Internet registry for North America.

The *Internet Assigned Numbers Authority* (IANA) is yet another entity responsible for IP address assignment. IANA is operated by ICANN and is responsible for IP address assignment outside of North America.

NOTE Some literature might make reference to the *Internet Network Information Center* (InterNIC). InterNIC was the predecessor to ICANN (until September 18, 1998).

When an organization is assigned one or more publicly routable IP addresses by its service provider, that organization often needs more IP addresses to accommodate all of its devices. One solution is to use *private IP addressing* within an organization, in combination with *Network Address Translation* (NAT). Specific Class A, B, and C networks have been designed for private use. Although these networks are routable (with the exception of the 169.254.0.0–169.254.255.255 address range), within the organization, ISPs do not route these private networks over the public Internet. Table 5-20 shows these IP networks reserved for internal use.

Table 5-20   Private IP Networks

Address Class	Address Range	Default Subnet Mask
Class A	10.0.0.0–10.255.255.255	255.0.0.0
Class B	172.16.0.0–172.31.255.255	255.255.0.0
Class B	169.254.0.0–169.254.255.255	255.255.0.0
Class C	192.168.0.0–192.168.255.255	255.255.255.0

NOTE   The 169.254.0.0–169.254.255.255 address range is not routable. Addresses in this range are only usable on their local subnet and are dynamically assigned to network hosts using the Automatic IP Address Assignment (APIPA) feature, which is discussed later in this section.

NAT is a feature available on routers that allows private IP addresses used within an organization to be translated into a pool of one or more publicly routable IP addresses. Chapter 6, "Routing Traffic," describes the operation of NAT.

Types of Addresses

For the real world, and for the Network+ exam, you need to be familiar with the following three categories of IPv4 addresses: unicast, broadcast, and multicast. The following sections describe these in detail.

Unicast

Most network traffic is unicast in nature, meaning that traffic travels from a single source device to a single destination device. Figure 5-4 illustrates an example of a unicast transmission.

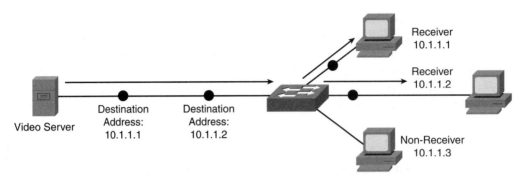

Figure 5-4 Sample Unicast Transmission

Broadcast

Broadcast traffic travels from a single source to all destinations on a network (that is, a broadcast domain). A broadcast address of 255.255.255.255 might seem that it would reach all hosts on all interconnected network. However, 255.255.255.255 targets all devices on a single network, specifically the network local to the device sending a packet destined for 255.255.255.255. Another type of broadcast address is a *directed broadcast address*, which targets all devices in a remote network. For example, the address 172.16.255.255 /16 is a directed broadcast targeting all devices in the 172.16.0.0 /16 network. Figure 5-5 illustrates an example of a broadcast transmission.

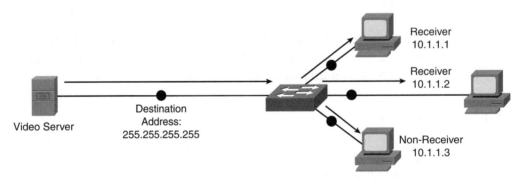

Figure 5-5 Sample Broadcast Transmission

Multicast

Multicast technology provides an efficient mechanism for a single host to send traffic to multiple, yet specific, destinations. For example, imagine a network with 100 users. Twenty of those users want to receive a video stream from a video server. With a unicast solution, the video server would have to send 20 individual streams, one stream for each recipient. Such a solution could consume a significant amount of network bandwidth and put a heavy processor burden on the video server.

With a broadcast solution, the video server would only have to send the video stream once; however, it would be received by every device on the local subnet, even devices not wanting to receive the video stream. Even though those devices do not want to receive the video stream, they still have to pause what they are doing and take time to check each of these unwanted packets.

As shown in Figure 5-6, multicast offers a compromise, allowing the video server to send the video stream only once, and only sending the video stream to devices on the network that wants to receive the stream. What makes this possible is the use of a Class D address. A Class D address, such as 239.1.2.3, represents the address of a *multicast group*. The video server could, in this example, send a single copy of each video stream packet destined for 239.1.2.3. Devices wanting to receive the video stream can join the multicast group. Based on the device request, switches and routers in the topology can then dynamically determine out of which ports the video stream should be forwarded.

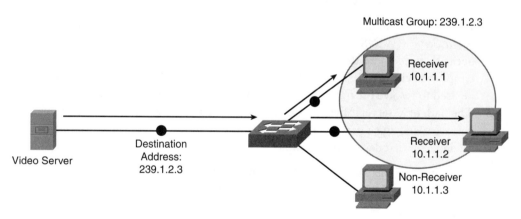

Figure 5-6   Sample Multicast Transmission

Assigning IPv4 Addresses

At this point in the discussion, you should understand that networked devices need an IP address. However, beyond just an IP address, what extra IP address-related information needs to be provided, and how does an IP address get assigned to one of those devices?

This section begins by discussing various parameters that might be assigned to a networked device, followed by discussions addressing various approaches to assign IP addresses to devices.

IP Addressing Components

As discussed in the previous section, an IP address has two portions: a network portion and a host portion. A subnet mask is required to delineate between these two portions.

Additionally, if traffic is destined for a different subnet than the subnet on which the traffic originates, a *default gateway* needs to be defined. A default gateway routes traffic from the sender's subnet towards the destination subnet. The concept of routing is addressed in Chapter 6.

Another consideration is that end users typically do not type in the IP address of the destination device with which they want to connect (for example, a web server on the Internet). Instead, end users typically type in fully qualified domain names (FQDN), such as www.1ExamAMonth.com. When connecting to devices on the public Internet, a *Domain Name System* (DNS) server takes a FQDN and translates it into a corresponding IP address.

In a company's internal network (that is, an *intranet*), a Microsoft *Windows Internet Name Service* (WINS) server might be used, as an example, to convert the names of network devices into their corresponding IP addresses. For example, you might attempt to navigate to a shared folder of *server1**hrdocs*. A WINS server could then be used to resolve the network device name of *server1* to a corresponding IP address. The path of \\server1\hrdocs is in *universal naming convention* (UNC) form, where you are specifying a network device name (for example, server1) and a resource available on that device (for example, hrdocs).

To summarize, network devices (for example, an end-user PC) can benefit from a variety of IP address parameters, such as the following:

- IP address
- Subnet mask
- Default gateway
- Server addresses

Static Configuration

A simple way of configuring a PC, for example, with IP address parameters is to statically configure that information. For example, on a PC running Microsoft

Windows 7 as the operating system, you can navigate to the **Control Panel** as shown in Figure 5-7, and click **Network and Internet**.

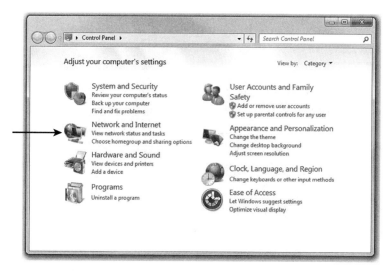

Figure 5-7   Windows 7 Control Panel

From the Network and Internet control panel, click **Network and Sharing Center**, as shown in Figure 5-8.

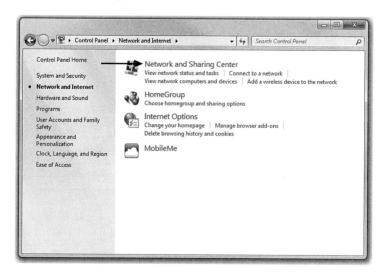

Figure 5-8   Network and Internet Control Panel

You can then click the **Change adapter settings** link, as shown in Figure 5-9.

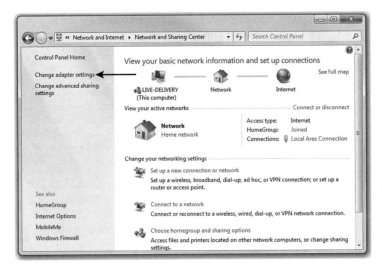

Figure 5-9 Network and Sharing Center

From the **Network Connections** window, double-click the network adapter whose settings you want to change, as shown in Figure 5-10.

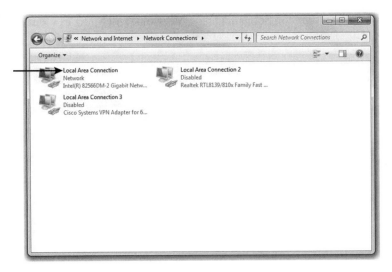

Figure 5-10 Network Connections Window

You are then taken to the **Local Area Connection Status** window, as shown in Figure 5-11. From here, you can click the **Properties** button.

Figure 5-11   Local Area Connection Status Window

As shown in Figure 5-12, you can highlight **Internet Protocol Version 4 (TCP/IPv4)** and click the **Properties** button.

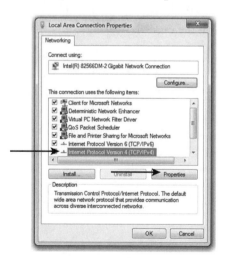

Figure 5-12   Local Area Connection Properties

An IP address, subnet mask, default gateway, and DNS server information can be entered into the **Internet Protocol Version 4 (TCP/IPv4) Properties** window, as depicted in Figure 5-13. Although DNS server information can be entered in this window, more advanced DNS options, and WINS options, are available by clicking the **Advanced...** button.

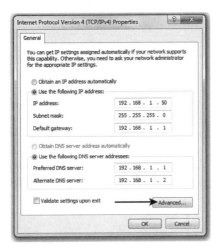

Figure 5-13   Internet Protocol Version 4 (TCP/IPv4) Properties

By clicking the **DNS** tab in the **Advanced TCP/IP Settings**, as shown in Figure 5-14, you can add, remove, or reorder DNS servers, in addition to adjusting various other DNS parameters. Recall that a DNS server converts a FQDN to an IP address. Also, although Figure 5-13 shows the same IP address for the default gateway and a DNS server, these are not always located on the same device.

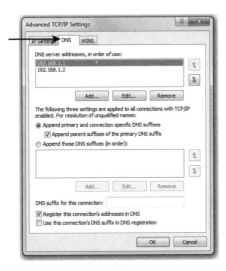

Figure 5-14   Advanced TCP/IP Settings: DNS Tab

Similarly, Windows Internet Name Service (WINS) servers can be configured in the **WINS** tab of **the Advanced TCP/IP Settings** window, as shown in Figure 5-15. Similar to a DNS server, a WINS server converts a NetBIOS computer name to a corresponding IP address.

Figure 5-15   Advanced TCP/IP Settings: WINS Tab

Dynamic Configuration

Statically assigning IP address information to individual networked devices can be time consuming, error-prone, and lacking in scalability. Instead of static IP address assignments, many corporate networks dynamically assign IP address parameters to their devices. An early option for performing this automatic assignment of IP addresses was called *Bootstrap Protocol* (*BOOTP*) for short. Currently, however, the most popular approach for dynamic IP address assignment is *Dynamic Host Configuration Protocol* (DHCP).

BOOTP

BOOTP was developed as a method of assigning IP address, subnet mask, and default gateway information to diskless workstations. In the early days of Microsoft Windows (for example, Microsoft Windows 3.1), Microsoft Windows did not natively support TCP/IP. To add TCP/IP support, an add-on TCP/IP application (for example, Trumpet Winsock) could be run. Such an application would typically support BOOTP.

When a device needed to obtain IP address information, a BOOTP broadcast would be sent out from the device needing an IP address. If a BOOTP server (BOOTPS) received the broadcast, it could match the source MAC address in the received frame (the MAC address from the device wanting to obtain an IP address) with a corresponding IP address, in a database stored on the BOOTP server. The BOOTPS would then respond to the requesting client with IP address information. Because BOOTP requests were based on broadcasts, by default, a BOOTP request could not propagate beyond a device's local subnet. However, most enterprise-class routers can be configured to forward selected broadcast types, including BOOTP broadcasts.

DHCP

DHCP offers a more robust solution to IP address assignment than the solution offered by BOOTP. DHCP does not require a statically configured database of MAC address to IP address mappings. Also, DHCP has a wide variety of options beyond basic IP address, subnet mask, and default gateway parameters. For example, a DHCP server can educate a DHCP client about the IP address of a WINS server, or even an administrator-defined parameter (for example, the IP address of a TFTP server from which a configuration file could be downloaded).

Refer to Chapter 3, "Identifying Network Components," for more information about the operation of DHCP. However, realize that, like BOOTP, DHCP's initial request is a broadcast, requiring a client's local router be configured to appropriately forward DHCP requests to a DHCP server if that DHCP server is not on the local subnet of the requesting client.

As an example of DHCP client configuration, in Microsoft Windows 7, you can select the **Obtain an IP address automatically** and **Obtain DNS server address automatically** options in the **Internet Protocol Version 4 (TCP/IPv4) Properties** window, as shown in Figure 5-16.

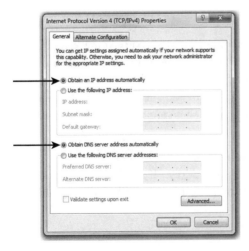

Figure 5-16   Configuring Microsoft Windows 7 to Obtain IP Address Information via DHCP

NOTE   A protocol rendered obsolete by BOOTP and DHCP is *Reverse Address Reso-lution Protocol* (RARP). Although *Address Resolution Protocol* (ARP) requests a MAC address that corresponds to a known IP address, RARP requested an IP address (from a preconfigured host) that corresponded to a station's MAC address. Although RARP did allow a station to dynamically obtain an IP address, both BOOTP and DHCP offer additional features.

Automatic Private IP Addressing

If a networked device does not have a statically configured IP address and is unable to contact a DHCP server, it still might be able to communicate on an IP network thanks to *Automatic Private IP Addressing* (APIPA). The APIPA feature allows a net-worked device to self-assign an IP address from the 169.254.0.0/16 network. Note that this address is usable only on the device's local subnet (the IP address is not routable).

As shown in Figure 5-17, Microsoft Windows 7 defaults to APIPA if a client is con-figured to automatically obtain IP address information, and that client fails to obtain IP address information from a DHCP server.

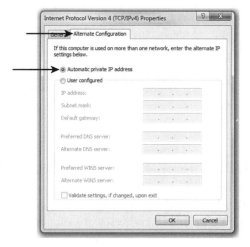

Figure 5-17   APIPA Configuration Enabled by Default

APIPA seems to be a great solution for quickly setting up a localized network with-out the need to configure a DHCP server or the need to statically assign IP address information. However, there remains a need for devices on this localized network to perform name resolution and discover network services. Fortunately, these needs are addressed by *Zero Configuration* (Zeroconf). Zeroconf is a technology supported on most modern operating systems and performs three basic functions:

- **Assigning link-local IP addresses:** A *link-local IP address* is a non-routable IP address usable only on a local subnet. APIPA is an example of a technology that assigns link-local IP addresses.

- **Resolving computer names to IP addresses:** *Multicast Domain Name Service* (mDNS) is an example of a technology that can resolve computer names to their corresponding IP address on a local subnet, without the aid of a DNS server or a WINS server.

- **Locating network services:** Examples of service discovery protocols include the standards-based *Service Location Protocol* (SLP), Microsoft's *Simple Service Discovery Protocol* (SSDP), and Apple's *DNS based Service Discovery* (DNS-SD).

If devices supporting these three Zeroconf features are interconnected on a local subnet, they can dynamically obtain link-local IP addresses, resolve one another's names to IP addresses, and discover services available on a network.

Subnetting

Earlier in this chapter, you were introduced to the purpose of a subnet mask and the default subnet masks for the various IP addresses classes. Default subnet masks (that is, classful subnet masks) are not always the most efficient choice. Fortunately, you can add additional network bits to a subnet masks (thereby extending the subnet mask) to create subnets within a classful network. This section explains why you might want to perform this process and describes how you mathematically perform subnet calculations.

Purpose of Subnetting

Consider the number of assignable IP addresses in the various classes of IP addresses shown in Table 5-21. Recall that the host bits of an IP address cannot be all 0s (which represents the network address) or all 1s (which represents the directed broadcast address). Therefore, the number of assignable IP addresses in a subnet can be determined by the following formula:

Number of assignable IP address in a subnet = $2^h - 2$,

where *h* is the number of host bits in a subnet mask

Table 5-21 Assignable IP Addresses

Address Class	Assignable IP Addresses
Class A	$16,777,214$ (2^{24} - 2)
Class B	$65,534$ (2^{16} - 2)
Class C	254 (2^8 - 2)

Suppose that you decide to use a private Class B IP address (for example, 172.16.0.0/16) for your internal IP addressing. For performance reasons, you probably would not want to support as many as 65,534 hosts in a single broadcast domain. Therefore, a best practice is to take such a network address and subnet the network (thereby extending the number of network bits in the network's subnet mask) into additional subnetworks.

Subnet Mask Notation

As previously mentioned, the number of bits in a subnet mask can be represented in dotted-decimal notation (for example, 255.255.255.0) or in prefix notation (for example, /24). As a reference, Table 5-22 shows valid subnet masks in dotted-decimal notation and the corresponding prefix notation.

Table 5-22 Dotted-Decimal and Prefix-Notation Representations for IPv4 Subnets

Dotted-Decimal Notation	Prefix Notation
255.0.0.0	/8 (Classful subnet mask for Class A networks)
255.128.0.0	/9
255.192.0.0	/10
255.224.0.0	/11
255.240.0.0	/12
255.248.0.0	/13
255.252.0.0	/14
255.254.0.0	/15
255.255.0.0	/16 (Classful subnet mask for Class B networks)
255.255.128.0	/17
255.255.192.0	/18
255.255.224.0	/19
255.255.240.0	/20

Dotted-Decimal Notation	Prefix Notation
255.255.248.0	/21
255.255.252.0	/22
255.255.254.0	/23
255.255.255.0	/24 (Classful subnet mask for Class C networks)
255.255.255.128	/25
255.255.255.192	/26
255.255.255.224	/27
255.255.255.240	/28
255.255.255.248	/29
255.255.255.252	/30

Recall that any octet with a value of 255 contains eight 1s. Also, you should memorize valid octet values for an octet and the corresponding number of 1s (that is, continuous, left-justified 1s) in that octet, as shown in Table 5-23. Based on this information, you should be able to see the dotted-decimal notation of a subnet mask and quickly determine the corresponding prefix notation.

Table 5-23   Subnet Octet Values

Subnet Octet Value	Number of Contiguous Left-Justified Ones
0	0
128	1
192	2
224	3
240	4
248	5
252	6
254	7
255	8

As an example, consider the subnet mask of 255.255.192.0. Because each of the first two octets has a value of 255, you know that you have 16 1s from the first two octets. You then recall that a value of 192 in the third octet requires two 1s from that octet. By adding the 16 ones from the first two octets to the two 1s from the third octet, you can determine that the subnet mask of 255.255.192.0 has a corresponding prefix notation of /18.

To help you develop the skill of making these calculations quickly, work through the following two exercises.

Subnet Notation: Practice Exercise #1

Given a subnet mask of 255.255.255.248, what is the corresponding prefix notation?

_____

Subnet Notation: Practice Exercise #1 Solution

Given a subnet mask of 255.255.255.248, you should recognize that the first three octets, each containing a value of 255, represent 24 1s. To those 24 1s, you add five additional 1s, based on your memorization of how many contiguous, left-justified 1s in an octet are required to produce various octet values. The sum of 24 bits (from the first three octets) and the 5 bits (from the fourth octet) give you a total of 29 bits. Therefore, you can conclude that a subnet mask with a dotted-decimal notation of 255.255.255.248 has an equivalent prefix notation of **/29**.

Subnet Notation: Practice Exercise #2

Given a subnet mask of /17, what is the corresponding dotted-decimal notation?

_____

Subnet Notation: Practice Exercise #2 Solution

You know that each octet contains 8 bits. So, given a subnet mask of /17, you can count by 8s to determine that there are eight 1s in the first octet, eight 1s in the second octet, and one 1 in the third octet. You already knew that an octet containing all 1s has a decimal value of 255. From that knowledge, you conclude that each of the first two octets have a value of 255. Also, based on your memorization of Table 5-23, you know that one 1 (that is, a left-justified 1) in an octet has a decimal equivalent value of 128. Therefore, you can conclude that a subnet mask with a prefix notation of /17 can be represented in dotted-decimal notation as **255.255.128.0**.

Extending a Classful Mask

The way to take a classful network (that is, a network using a classful subnet mask) and divide that network into multiple subnets is by adding 1s to the network's classful subnet mask. However, the class of the IP address does not change, regardless of the new subnet mask. For example, if you took the 172.16.0.0/16 network and subnetted it into multiple networks using a 24-bit subnet mask (172.16.0.0/24, 172.16.1.0/23, 172.16.2.0/24, ...), those networks would still be Class B networks. Specifically, the class of a network is entirely determined by the value of the first octet. The class of a network has nothing to do with the number of bits in a subnet, making this an often-misunderstood concept.

As another example, the network 10.2.3.0/24 has the classful subnet mask of a Class C network (that is, a 24-bit subnet mask). However, the 10.2.3.0/24 network is a Class A network, because the value of the first octet is 10. It's simply a Class A network that happens to have a 24-bit subnet mask.

Borrowed Bits

When you add bits to a classful mask, the bits you add are referred to as *borrowed bits*. The number of borrowed bits you use determines how many subnets are created and the number of usable hosts per subnet.

Calculating the Number of Created Subnets

To determine the number of subnets created when adding bits to a classful mask, you can use the following formula:

Key Topic

Number of created subnets = 2^s,

where s is the number of borrowed bits

As an example, let's say you subnetted the 192.168.1.0 network with a 28-bit subnet mask, and you want to determine how many subnets were created. First, you determine how many borrowed bits you have. Recall that the number of borrowed bits is the number of bits in a subnet mask beyond the classful mask. In this case, because the first octet in the network address has a value of 192, you can conclude that this is a Class C network. You also recall that a Class C network has 24 bits in its classful (that is, its default) subnet mask. Because you now have a 28-bit subnet mask, the number of borrowed bits can be calculated as follows:

Number of borrowed bits = Bits in custom subnet mask - Bits in classful subnet mask

Number of borrowed bits = 28 - 24 = 4

Now that you know you have 4 borrowed bits, you can raise 2 to the power of 4 (2^4, or 2 * 2 * 2 * 2), which equals 16. From this calculation, you conclude that subnetting the 192.168.1.0/24 with a 28-bit subnet mask yields 16 subnets.

Calculating the Number of Available Hosts

Earlier in this section, you were exposed to the formula for calculating the number of available (that is, assignable) host IP addresses, based on the number of host bits in a subnet mask. The formula was

Number of assignable IP address in a subnet = 2^h - 2,

where h is the number of host bits in the subnet mask

Using the previous example, let's say you want to determine the number of available host IP addresses in one of the 192.168.1.0/28 subnets. First, you need to determine the number of host bits in the subnet mask. Because you know that an IPv4 address is comprised of 32 bits, you can subtract the number of bits in the subnet mask (28, in this example) from 32 to determine the number of host bits:

Number of host bits = 32 - Number of bits in subnet mask

Number of host bits = 32 - 28 = 4

Now that you know the number of host bits, you can apply it to the previously presented formula:

Number of assignable IP addresses in a subnet = 2^h - 2,

where h is the number of host bits in the subnet mask

Number of assignable IP addresses in a subnet = 2^4 - 2 = 16 - 2 = 14

From this calculation, you can conclude that each of the 192.168.1.0/28 subnets have 14 usable IP addresses.

To reinforce your skill with these calculations, you are now challenged with a few practice exercises.

Basic Subnetting Practice: Exercise #1

Using a separate sheet of paper, solve the following scenario:

Your company has been assigned the 172.20.0.0/16 network for use at one of its sites. You need to use a subnet mask that will accommodate 47 subnets while simultaneously accommodating the maximum number of hosts per subnet. What subnet mask will you use?

Basic Subnetting Practice: Exercise #1 Solution

To determine how many borrowed bits are required to accommodate 47 subnets, you can write out a table that shows the powers of 2, as shown in Table 5-24. In fact, you might want to sketch out a similar table on the dry-erase card you are given when you take the Network+ exam.

Table 5-24   Number of Subnets Created by a Specified Number of Borrowed Bits

Borrowed Bits	Number of Subnets Created (2s, Where s Is the Number of Borrowed Bits)
0	1
1	2
2	4
3	8
4	16
5	32
6	64
7	128
8	256
9	512
10	1024
11	2048
12	4096

In this example, where you want to support 47 subnets, 5 borrowed bits are not enough, and 6 borrowed bits are more than enough. Because 5 borrowed bits are not enough, you round up and use 6 borrowed bits.

The first octet in the network address 172.20.0.0 has a value of 172, meaning that you are dealing with a Class B address. Because a Class B address has 16 bits in its classful mask, you can add the 6 borrowed bits to the 16-bit classful mask, which results in a 22-bit subnet mask.

One might argue that although a 22-bit subnet mask would accommodate 47 subnets, so would a 23-bit subnet mask or a 24-bit subnet mask. Although that is true, recall that the scenario said you should have the maximum number of hosts per subnet. This suggests that you should not use more borrowed bits than necessary. Therefore, you can conclude that to meet the scenario's requirements, you should use a subnet mask of **/22**, which could also be written as **255.255.252.0**.

Basic Subnetting Practice: Exercise #2

Using a separate sheet of paper, solve the following scenario:

Your company has been assigned the 172.20.0.0/16 network for use at one of its sites. You need to calculate a subnet mask that will accommodate 100 hosts per subnet while maximizing the number of available subnets. What subnet mask will you use?

Basic Subnetting Practice: Exercise #2 Solution

To determine how many host bits are required to accommodate 100 hosts, you can write out a table that shows the number of hosts supported by a specific number of hosts bits, as shown in Table 5-25. Like the previous table, you might want to sketch out a similar table on the dry-erase card you are given when taking the Network+ exam.

Table 5-25   Number of Supported Hosts Given a Specified Number of Host Bits

Host Bits	Number of Supported Hosts (2h - 2, Where h Is the Number of Borrowed Bits)
2	2
3	6
4	14
5	30
6	62
7	126
8	254
9	510
10	1022
11	2046
12	4094

In this example, where you want to support 100 subnets, 6 host bits are not enough, and 7 host bits are more than enough. Because 6 host bits are not enough, you round up and use 7 host bits.

Because an IPv4 address has 32 bits, and you need 7 host bits, you can calculate the number of subnet bits by subtracting the 7 host bits from 32 (that is, the total number of bits in an IPv4 address). This results in a 25-bit subnet mask (that is, 32 total bits - 7 host bits = 25 subnet mask bits). Therefore, you can conclude that to meet the scenario's requirements, you should use a subnet mask of **/25**, which could also be written as **255.255.255.128**.

Calculating New IP Address Ranges

Now that you can calculate the number of subnets created based on a given number of borrowed bits, the next logical step is to calculate the IP address ranges making up those subnets. As an example, if you took the 172.25.0.0/16 and subnetted it with a 24-bit subnet mask, the resulting subnets would be as follows:

172.25.0.0/24

172.25.1.0/24

172.25.2.0/24

...

172.25.255.0/24

Let's consider how such a calculation is performed. Notice in the previous example that you count by 1 in the third octet to calculate the new networks. To determine in what octet you start counting and by want increment you count, a new term needs to be defined. The *interesting octet* is the octet containing the last 1 in the subnet mask.

In this example, the subnet mask was a 24-bit subnet mask, which has a dotted-decimal equivalent of 255.255.255.0, and a binary equivalent of 11111111.11111111.11111111.00000000. From any of these subnet mask representations, you can determine that the third octet is the octet to contain the last 1 in the subnet mask. Therefore, you will be changing the value of the third octet to calculate the new networks.

Now that you know the third octet is the interesting octet, you next need to know by what increment you will be counting in that octet. This increment is known as the *block size*. The block size can be calculated by subtracting the subnet mask value in the interesting octet from 256. In this example, the subnet mask had a value of 255 in the interesting octet (that is, the third octet). If you subtract 255 from 256, you get a result of 1 (that is, 256 - 255 = 1). The first subnet will be the original network address, with all of the borrowed bits set to 0. After this first subnet, you start counting by the block size (1, in this example) in the interesting octet to calculate the remainder of the subnets.

The preceding steps for calculating subnets can be summarized as follows:

1. Determine the interesting octet by determining the last octet in the subnet mask to contain a 1.

2. Determine the block size by subtracting the decimal value in the subnet's interesting octet from 256.

3. Determine the first subnet by setting all the borrowed bits (which are bits in the subnet mask beyond the bits in the classful subnet mask) to 0.

4. Determine additional subnets by taking the first subnet and counting by the block size increment in the interesting octet.

To reinforce this procedure, consider another example. A 27-bit subnet mask is applied to a network address of 192.168.10.0/24. To calculate the created subnets, you can perform the following steps:

1. The subnet mask (in binary) is 11111111.11111111.11111111.11100000. The interesting octet is the fourth octet, because the fourth octet contains the last 1 in the subnet mask.

2. The decimal value of the fourth octet in the subnet mask is 224 (11100000 in decimal). Therefore, the block size is 32 (256 - 224 = 32).

3. The first subnet is 192.168.10.0/27 (the value of the original 192.168.10.0 network with the borrowed bits [the first three bits in the fourth octet] set to 0).

4. Counting by 32 (the block size) in the interesting octet (the fourth octet) allows you to calculate the remaining subnets:

   192.168.10.0

   192.168.10.32

   192.168.10.64

   192.168.10.96

   192.168.10.128

   192.168.10.160

   192.168.10.192

   192.168.10.224

Now that you know the subnets created from a classful network given a subnet mask, the next logical step is to determine the usable addresses within those subnets. Recall that you cannot assign an IP address to a device if all of the host bits in the IP address are set to 0, because an IP address with all host bits set to 0 is the address of the subnet itself.

Similarly, you cannot assign an IP address to a device if all the host bits in the IP address are set to 1, because an IP address with all host bits set to 1 is the directed broadcast address of a subnet.

By excluding the network and directed broadcast addresses from the 192.168.10.0/27 subnets (as previously calculated), the usable addresses shown in Table 5-26 can be determined.

Table 5-26   Usable IP Address Ranges for the 192.168.10.0/27 Subnets

Subnet Address	Directed Broadcast Address	Usable IP Addresses
192.168.10.0	192.168.10.31	192.168.10.1–192.168.10.30
192.168.10.32	192.168.10.63	192.168.10.33–192.168.10.62
192.168.10.64	192.168.10.95	192.168.10.65–192.168.10.94
192.168.10.96	192.168.10.127	192.168.10.97–192.168.10.126
192.168.10.128	192.168.10.159	192.168.10.129–192.168.10.158
192.168.10.160	192.168.10.191	192.168.10.161–192.168.10.190
192.168.10.192	192.168.10.223	192.168.10.193–192.168.10.222
192.168.10.224	192.168.10.255	192.168.10.225–192.168.10.254

To help develop your subnet-calculation skills, you are now challenged with a few practice subnetting exercises.

Advanced Subnetting Practice: Exercise #1

Using a separate sheet of paper, solve the following scenario:

Based on your network design requirements, you determine that you should use a 26-bit subnet mask applied to your 192.168.0.0/24 network. You now need to calculate each of the created subnets. Additionally, you want to know the broadcast address and the range of usable addresses for each of the created subnets.

Advanced Subnetting Practice: Exercise #1 Solution

As described earlier, you can go through the following four-step process to determine the subnet address:

1. The subnet mask (in binary) is 11111111.11111111.11111111.11000000. The interesting octet is the fourth octet, because the fourth octet contains the last 1 in the subnet mask.

2. The decimal value of the fourth octet in the subnet mask is 192 (11000000 in decimal). Therefore, the block size is 64 (256 - 192 = 64).

3. The first subnet is 192.168.0.0/26 (the value of the original 192.168.0.0 network with the borrowed bits [the first two bits in the last octet] set to 0).

4. Counting by 64 (the block size) in the interesting octet (the fourth octet) allows you to calculate the remaining subnets, resulting in the following subnets:

    192.168.0.0

    192.168.0.64

    192.168.0.128

    192.168.0.192

The directed broadcast addresses for each of the preceding subnets can be calculated by adding 63 (that is, one less than the block size) to the interesting octet for each subnet address. Excluding the subnet addresses and directed broadcast addresses, a range of usable addresses can be calculated, the results of which are seen in Table 5-27.

Table 5-27 Usable IP Address Ranges for the 192.168.0.0/26 Subnets

Subnet Address	Directed Broadcast Address	Usable IP Addresses
192.168.0.0	192.168.0.63	192.168.0.1–192.168.0.62
192.168.0.64	192.168.0.127	192.168.0.65–192.168.0.126
192.168.0.128	192.168.0.191	192.168.0.129–192.168.0.190
192.168.0.192	192.168.0.255	192.168.0.193–192.168.0.254

Advanced Subnetting Practice: Exercise #2

Using a separate sheet of paper, solve the following scenario:

The network shown in Figure 5-18 has subnetted the 172.16.0.0/16 network by using a 20-bit subnet mask. Notice that two VLANs (two subnets) are currently configured; however, one of the client PCs is assigned an IP address that is not in that PC's VLAN. Which client PC is assigned an incorrect IP address?

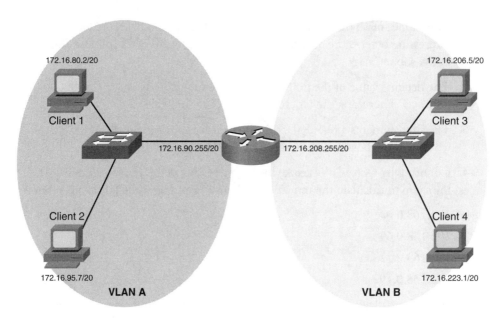

Figure 5-18   Topology for Advanced Subnetting Practice: Exercise #2

Advanced Subnetting Practice: Exercise #2 Solution

To determine which client PC is assigned an IP address outside of its local VLAN, you need to determine the subnets created by the 20-bit subnet mask applied to the 172.16.0.0/16 network:

1. The interesting octet for a 20-bit subnet mask is the third octet, because the third octet is the last octet to contain a 1 in the 20-bit subnet mask (11111111. 11111111.11110000.00000000, which could also be written as 255.255.240.0).

2. The decimal value of the third octet in the subnet mask is 240. Therefore, the block size is 16 (256 - 240 = 16).

3. The first 172.16.0.0/20 subnet is 172.16.0.0 (172.16.0.0/20 with the four borrowed bits in the third octet set to 0).

4. Beginning with the first subnet of 172.16.0.0/20 and counting by the block size of 16 in the interesting octet yields the following subnets:

172.16.0.0/20

172.16.16.0/20

172.16.32.0/20

172.16.48.0/20

172.16.64.0/20

172.16.80.0/20

172.16.96.0/20

172.16.112.0/20

172.16.128.0/20

172.16.144.0/20

172.16.160.0/20

172.16.176.0/20

172.16.192.0/20

172.16.208.0/20

172.16.224.0/20

172.16.240.0/20

Based on the IP addresses of the router interfaces, you can determine the subnets for VLAN A and VLAN B. Specifically, the router interface in VLAN A has an IP address of 172.16.90.255/20. Based on the previous listing of subnets, you can determine that this interface resides in the 172.16.80.0/20 network, whose range of usable addresses is 172.16.80.1–172.16.95.254. Then, you can examine the IP addresses of Client 1 and Client 2 to determine if their IP addresses reside in that range of usable addresses.

Similarly, for VLAN B, the router's interface has an IP address of 172.16.208.255/20. Based on the previous subnet listing, you notice that this interface has an IP address that is part of the 172.16.208.0/20 subnet. As you did for VLAN A, you can check the IP address of Client 3 and Client 4 to determine if their IP addresses reside in VLAN B's range of usable IP addresses (that is, 172.16.208.1–172.16.223.254).

These comparisons are shown in Table 5-28.

Table 5-28 IP Address Comparison for Advanced Subnetting Practice: Exercise 2

Client	VLAN	Range of Usable Addresses	Client IP Address	Is Client in Range of Usable Addresses?
Client 1	A	172.16.80.1–172.16.95.254	172.16.80.2	Yes
Client 2	A	172.16.80.1–172.16.95.254	172.16.95.7	Yes
Client 3	B	172.16.208.1–172.16.223.254	172.16.206.5	No
Client 4	B	172.16.208.1–172.16.223.254	172.16.223.1	Yes

The comparison in Table 5-28 reveals that Client 3 (with an IP address of 172.16.206.5) does not have an IP address in VLAN B's subnet (with a usable address range of 172.16.208.1–172.16.223.254).

Additional Practice

If you want to continue practicing these concepts, make up your own subnet mask and apply it to a classful network of your choosing. Then, you can calculate the created subnets, the directed broadcast IP address for each subnet, and the range of usable IP addresses for each subnet.

To check your work, you can use a subnet calculator. An example of such a calculator is the free subnet calculator available for download from www.solarwinds. com/downloads, as shown in Figure 5-19.

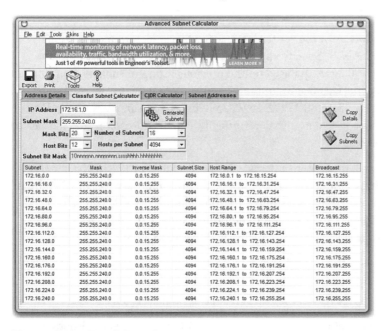

Figure 5-19   Free Subnet Calculator

NOTE   As you read through different networking literature, you might come across other approaches to performing subnetting. Various shortcuts exist (including the one presented in this chapter), and some approaches involve much more binary math. The purpose of this section was not to be an exhaustive treatment of all available subnetting methods, but to provide a quick and easy approach to performing subnet calculations in the real world and in the Network+ certification exam.

Classless Inter-Domain Routing

Although subnetting is the process of extending a classful subnet mask (that is, adding 1s to a classful mask), *Classless Inter-Domain Routing* (CIDR) does just the opposite. Specifically, CIDR shortens a classful subnet mask by removing 1s from the classful mask. As a result, CIDR allows contiguous classful networks to be aggregated. This process is sometimes called *route aggregation*.

A typical use of CIDR is a service provider summarizing multiple Class C networks, assigned to their various customers. For example, imagine that a service provider is responsible for advertizing the following Class C networks:

> 192.168.32.0/24
>
> 192.168.33.0/24
>
> 192.168.34.0/24
>
> 192.168.35.0/24

The service provider could advertise all four networks with a single route advertisement of 192.168.32.0/22. To calculate this advertisement, convert the values in the third octet (that is, the octet where the values start to differ) to binary, as shown in Figure 5-20. Then, determine how many bits the networks have in common. The number of common bits then becomes the number of bits in the CIDR mask.

Network Address	1st Octet	2nd Octet	3rd Octet	4th Octet
192.168.32.0	11000000	10101000	001000|00	00000000
192.168.33.0	11000000	10101000	001000|01	00000000
192.168.34.0	11000000	10101000	001000|10	00000000
192.168.35.0	11000000	10101000	001000|11	00000000

All Networks Have 22 Bits in Common

Figure 5-20 CIDR Calculation Example

Because all four of the network addresses have the first 22 bits in common, and because setting the remaining bits to 0 (11000000.10101000.00100000.0000000 0) creates a network address of 192.168.32.0, these networks can be summarized as 192.168.32.0/22.

IP Version 6

With the global proliferation of IP-based networks, available IPv4 addresses are rapidly becoming extinct. Fortunately, IPv6 provides enough IP addresses for many generations to come. This section introduces IPv6's address structure and discusses some of its unique characteristics.

Need for IPv6

With the worldwide depletion of IP versions 4 (IPv4) addresses, many organizations have migrated, are in the process of migrating, or are considering migrating their IPv4 addresses to IPv6 addresses. IPv6 dramatically increases the number of available IP addresses. In fact, IPv6 offers approximately $5 * 10^{28}$ IP addresses for each person on the planet.

Beyond the increased address space, IPv6 offers many other features:

- Simplified header

  - IPv4 header uses 12 fields
  - IPv6 header uses five fields

- No broadcasts

- No fragmentation (performs MTU discovery for each session)

- Can coexist with IPv4 during a transition

  - Dual stack (running IPv4 and IPv6 simultaneously)
  - IPv6 over IPv4 (tunneling IPv6 over an IPv4 tunnel)

Even if you are designing a network based on IPv4 addressing, a good practice is to consider how readily an IPv6 addressing scheme could be overlaid on that network at some point in the future.

IPv6 Address Structure

An IPv6 address has the following address format, where X = a hexadecimal digit in the range of 0 – F:

XXXX:XXXX:XXXX:XXXX:XXXX:XXXX:XXXX:XXXX

A hexadecimal digit is 4 bits in size (4 binary bits can represent 16 values). Notice that an IPv6 address has eight fields, and each field contains four hexadecimal digits. The following formula reveals why an IPv6 address is a 128-bit address:

4 bits per digit * 4 digits per field * 8 fields = 128 bits in an IPv6 address

IPv6 addresses can be difficult to work with because of their size. Fortunately, the following rules exist for abbreviating these addresses:

- Leading 0s in a field can be omitted.

- Contiguous fields containing all 0s can be represented with a double colon. (Note: This can be done only once for a single IPv6 address.)

As an example, consider the following IPv6 address:

ABCD:0123:4040:0000:0000:0000:000A:000B

Using the rules for abbreviation, the IPv6 address can be rewritten as follows:

ABCD:123:4040::A:B

Also, the *Extended Unique Identifier* (EUI-64) format can be used to cause a router to automatically populate the low-order 64 bits of an IPv6 address based on an interface's MAC address.

IPv6 Data Flows

IPv6 has three types of data flows:

- Unicast

- Multicast

- Anycast

The following sections summarize the characteristics of each address type.

Unicast

With unicast, a single IPv6 address is applied to a single interface, as illustrated in Figure 5-21. The communication flow can be thought of as a one-to-one communication flow.

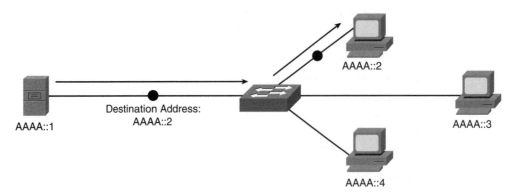

Figure 5-21   IPv6 Unicast Example

In Figure 5-21, a server (AAAA::1) is sending traffic to a single client (AAAA::2).

Multicast

With multicast, a single IPv6 address (a multicast group) can represent multiple devices on a network, as shown in Figure 5-22. The communication flow is one-to-many.

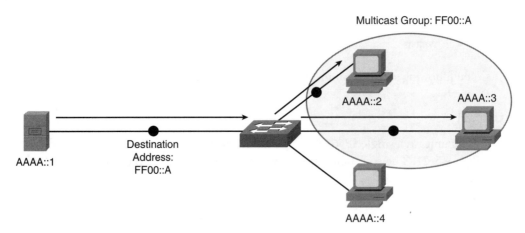

Figure 5-22   IPv6 Multicast Example

In Figure 5-22, a server (AAAA::1) is sending traffic to a multicast group (FF00::A). Two clients (AAAA::2 and AAAA::3) have joined this group. Those clients receive the traffic from the server, while any client that did not join the group (for example, AAAA::4) does not receive the traffic.

Anycast

With anycast, a single IPv6 address is assigned to multiple devices, as depicted in Figure 5-23. The communication flow is one-to-nearest (from the perspective of a router's routing table).

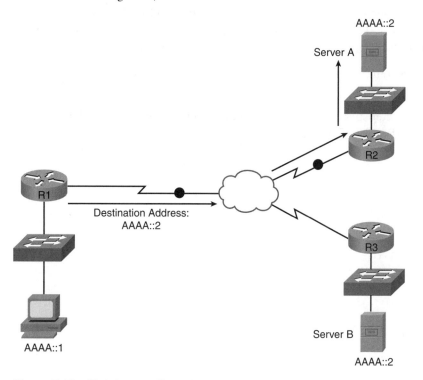

Figure 5-23   IPv6 Anycast Example

In Figure 5-23, a client with an IPv6 address of AAAA::1 wants to send traffic to a destination IPv6 address of AAAA::2. Notice that two servers (server A and server B) have an IPv6 address of AAAA::2. In the figure, the traffic destined for AAAA::2 is sent to server A, via router R2, because the network on which server A resides appears to be closer than the network on which server B resides, from the perspective of router R1's IPv6 routing table.

Summary

The main topics covered in this chapter are the following:

- The binary math tutorial gave you a basic understanding of why binary math is necessary for working with subnet masks.

- The characteristics of IPv4 were presented, including IPv4's address format and a contrast of unicast, broadcast, and multicast data flows.

- You examined various approaches for assigning IP address information to network devices. These approaches included static assignment, dynamic assignment (BOOTP and DHCP), and APIPA (a Zeroconf component).

- Multiple examples and practice exercises were provided for various subnet calculations.

- The characteristics of IPv6 were highlighted, including the IPv6 address format and IPv6 data flows (unicast, multicast, and anycast).

Exam Preparation Tasks

Review All the Key Topics

Review the most important topics from inside the chapter, noted with the Key Topic icon in the outer margin of the page. Table 5-29 lists these key topics and the page numbers where each is found.

Table 5-29   Key Topics for Chapter 5

Key Topic Element	Description	Page Number
Table 5-1	Binary conversion table	140
Section	Converting a decimal number to a binary number	141
Figure 5-2	Dividing an IP address into a network portion and a host portion	148
Table 5-19	IP address classes	149
Table 5-20	Private IP networks	151
List	Basic functions of Zeroconf	162
Formula	Number of assignable IP addresses in a subnet	162
Table 5-22	Dotted-decimal and prefix-notation representations for IPv4 subnets	163
Table 5-23	Subnet octet values	164
Formula	Number of created subnets	166
Formula	Number of borrowed bits	167
Formula	Number of host bits	167
Table 5-25	Number of subnets created by a specified number of borrowed bits	169
Step list	Steps for calculating subnets	171
Table 5-26	Number of supported hosts given a specified number of host bits	172
Figure 5-20	CIDR calculation example	177
List	Rules for abbreviating IPv6 addresses	179
List	Types of IPv6 data flows	179

Complete Tables and Lists from Memory

Print a copy of Appendix C, "Memory Tables" (found on the CD), or at least the section for this chapter, and complete the tables and lists from memory. Appendix D, "Memory Table Answer Key," also on the CD, includes the completed tables and lists so you can check your work.

Define Key Terms

Define the following key terms from this chapter, and check your answers in the Glossary:

classful masks, private IP addresses, octet, prefix notation, slash notation, dotted-decimal notation, classful mask, default gateway, Bootstrap Protocol, Dynamic Host Configuration Protocol (DHCP), Zeroconf, link-local IP address, Automatic Private IP Addressing, borrowed bits, block size, Classless Inter-Domain Routing (CIDR), unicast, multicast, anycast

Review Questions

The answers to these review questions are in Appendix A, "Answers to Review Questions."

1. What is the binary representation of the decimal number 117?

   a. 10110101

   b. 01110101

   c. 10110110

   d. 01101001

2. The binary number 10110100 has what decimal equivalent?

   a. 114

   b. 190

   c. 172

   d. 180

3. What is the class of IP address 10.1.2.3/24?

   a. Class A

   b. Class B

   c. Class C

   d. Class D

4. Which of the following statements are true regarding VLANs? (Choose two.)

    a. A VLAN is a single broadcast domain.

    b. For traffic to pass between two VLANs, that traffic must be routed.

    c. Because of a switch's MAC address table, traffic does not need to be routed in order to pass between two VLANs.

    d. A VLAN is a single collision domain.

5. Which of the following are dynamic approaches to assigning routable IP addresses to networked devices? (Choose two.)

    a. BOOTP

    b. APIPA

    c. Zeroconf

    d. DHCP

6. How many assignable IP addresses exist in the 172.16.1.10/27 network?

    a. 30

    b. 32

    c. 14

    d. 64

7. What is the prefix notation for a subnet mask of 255.255.255.240?

    a. /20

    b. /24

    c. /28

    d. /29

8. Your company has been assigned the 192.168.30.0/24 network for use at one of its sites. You need to use a subnet mask that will accommodate 7 subnets while simultaneously accommodating the maximum number of hosts per subnet. What subnet mask should you use?

    a. /24

    b. /26

    c. /27

    d. /28

9. A client with an IP address of 172.16.18.5/18 belongs to what network?

   a. 172.16.0.0/18

   b. 172.16.4.0/18

   c. 172.16.8.0/18

   d. 172.16.16.0/18

10. How can the following IPv6 address be condensed?

   0AA0:0123:4040:0000:0000:000:000A:100B

   a. AA0::123:404:A:100B

   b. AA::123:404:A:1B

   c. AA0:123:4040::A:100B

   d. 0AA0:0123:4040::0::000A:100BSection

After completion of this chapter, you will be able to
answer the following questions:

- How are source and destination IP addresses used to route traffic through a network?

- What are sources for routing information used to populate a router's routing table?

- How do routed protocols differ from routing protocols?

- When multiple routing protocols know how to reach a destination network, which route is chosen?

- When a single routing protocol knows of multiple routes to reach a destination network, how is the preferred path (or paths) chosen?

- What is the distinction between IGP and EGP?

- What are the primary differences between distance-vector and link-state routing protocols?

- What are the characteristics of the following routing protocols: RIP, OSPF, IS-IS, EIGRP, and BGP?

- How does NAT perform IP address translation, and how do the PAT, SNAT, and DNAT approaches to NAT differ?

- What protocols are used to route multicast traffic?

CHAPTER 6

Routing Traffic

In Chapter 5, "Working with IP Addresses," you learned how Internet Protocol (IP) networks could be divided into subnets. Each subnet is its own broadcast domain, and the device that separates broadcast domains is a router (which is considered to be synonymous with a multilayer switch in this chapter).

For traffic to flow between subnets, that traffic has to be routed, which is a router's primary job. This chapter discusses how routing occurs and introduces you to a variety of approaches of performing address translation. Finally, this chapter concludes with a discussion of how multicast traffic is routed.

Foundation Topics

Basic Routing Processes

To understand basic routing processes, consider Figure 6-1. In this topology, PC1 needs to send traffic to Server1. Notice that these devices are on different networks. So, the question becomes, "How does a packet from a source IP address of 192.168.1.2 get routed to a destination IP address of 192.168.3.2?"

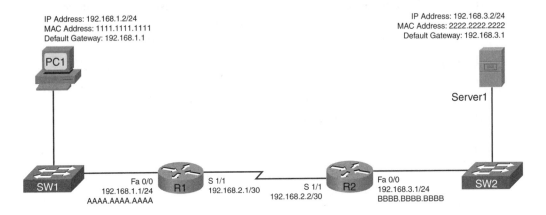

Figure 6-1   Basic Routing Topology

It might help to walk through this process step by step:

1. PC1 compares its IP address and subnet mask of 192.168.1.2/24 with the destination IP address and subnet mask of 192.168.3.2/24. PC1 concludes that the destination IP address resides on a remote subnet. Therefore, PC1 needs to send the packet to its default gateway, which could have been manually configured on PC1 or dynamically learned via Dynamic Host Configuration Protocol (DHCP). In this example, PC1 has a default gateway of 192.168.1.1 (router R1). However, to construct a Layer 2 frame, PC1 also needs the MAC address of its default gateway. PC1 sends an *Address Resolution Protocol* (ARP) request for router R1's MAC address. After PC1 receives an ARP reply from router R1, PC1 adds router R1's MAC address to its ARP cache. PC1 now sends its data in a frame destined for Server1, as shown in Figure 6-2.

NOTE   ARP is a broadcast-based protocol and, therefore, does not travel beyond the local subnet of the sender.

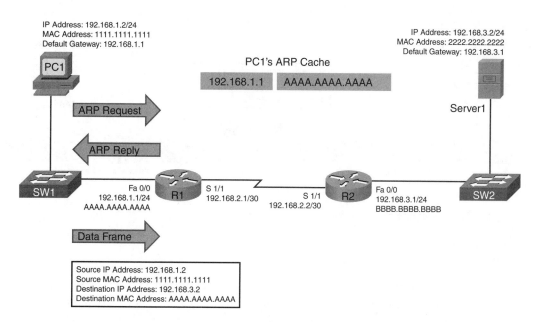

Figure 6-2 Basic Routing: Step 1

2. Router R1 receives the frame sent from PC1 and interrogates the IP header. An IP header contains a *Time to Live* (TTL) field, which is decremented once for each router hop. Therefore, router R1 decrements the packet's TTL field. If the value in the TTL field is reduced to 0, the router discards the frame and sends a *time exceeded Internet Control Message Protocol* (ICMP) message back to the source. Assuming the TTL is not decremented to 0, router R1 checks its routing table to determine the best path to reach network 192.168.3.0/24. In this example, router R1's routing table has an entry stating that network 192.168.3.0/24 is accessible via interface Serial 1/1. Note that ARPs are not required for serial interfaces, because these interface types do not have MAC addresses. Router R1, therefore, forwards the frame out of its Serial 1/1 interface, as shown in Figure 6-3.

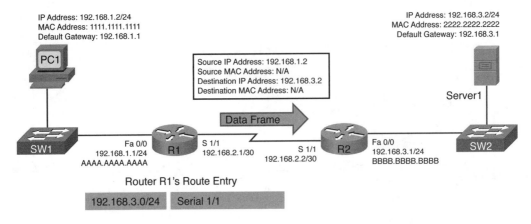

Figure 6-3   Basic Routing: Step 2

3. When router R2 receives the frame, it decrements the TTL in the IP header, just as router R1 did. Again, assuming the TTL did not get decremented to 0, router R2 interrogates the IP header to determine the destination network. In this case, the destination network of 192.168.3.0/24 is directly attached to router R2's Fast Ethernet 0/0 interface. Similar to how PC1 sent out an ARP request to determine the MAC address of its default gateway, router R2 sends an ARP request to determine the MAC address of Server1. After an ARP Reply is received from Server1, router R2 forwards the frame out of its Fast Ethernet 0/0 interface to Server1, as illustrated in Figure 6-4.

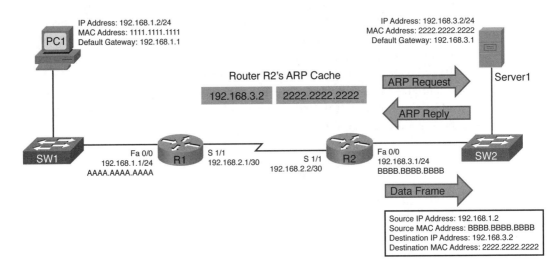

Figure 6-4   Basic Routing: Step 3

The previous steps identified two router data structures:

- **IP routing table:** When a router needed to route an IP packet, it consulted its IP routing table to find the best match. The best match is the route that has the longest prefix. Specifically, a route entry with the longest prefix is the most specific network. For example, imagine that a router has an entry for network 10.0.0.0/8 and for network 10.1.1.0/24. Also, imagine the router is seeking the best match for a destination address of 10.1.1.1/24. The router would select the 10.1.1.0/24 route entry as the best entry, because that route entry has the longest prefix.

- **Layer 3 to Layer 2 mapping:** In the previous example, router R2's ARP cache contained Layer 3 to Layer 2 mapping information. Specifically, the ARP cache had a mapping that said a MAC address of 2222.2222.2222 corresponded to an IP address of 192.168.3.2.

As shown in the preceding example, routers rely on their internal routing table to make packet forwarding decisions. Therefore, at this point, a logical question is, "How does a router's routing table become populated with entries?" This is the focus of the next section.

Sources of Routing Information

A router's routing table can be populated from various sources. As an administrator, you could statically configure a route entry. A route could be learned via a dynamic routing protocol (for example, OSPF or EIGRP), or a router could know how to get to a specific network, because the router is physically attached to that network.

Directly Connected Routes

One way for a router to know how to reach a specific destination network is by virtue of the fact that the router has an interface directly participating in that network. For example, consider Figure 6-5.

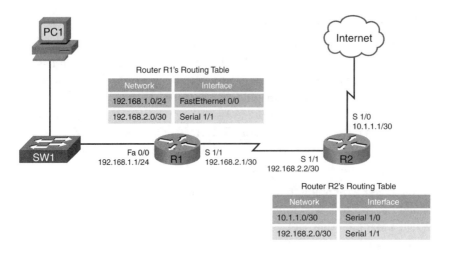

Figure 6-5   Directly Connected Routes

In Figure 6-5, router R1's routing table knows how to reach the 192.168.1.0/24 and 192.168.2.0/30 networks, because router R1 has an interface physically attached to each network. Similarly, router R2 has interfaces participating in the 10.1.1.0/30 and 192.168.2.0/30 networks, and therefore knows how to reach those networks. The entries currently shown to be in the routing tables of routers R1 and R2 are called *directly connected routes*.

Static Routes

Routes can also be statically configured in a router's routing table. Continuing to expand on the previous example, consider router R1. As shown in Figure 6-6, router R1 does not need knowledge of each individual route on the Internet. Specifically, router R1 already knows how to reach devices on its locally attached networks. All router R1 really needs to know at this point is how to get out to the rest of the world. As you can see from Figure 6-6, any traffic destined for a non-local network (for example, any of the networks available on the public Internet) can simply be sent to router R2. Because R2 is the next router hop along the path to reach all those other networks, router R1 could be configured with a *default static route*, which says, "If traffic is destined for a network not currently in the routing table, send that traffic out of interface Serial 1/1."

> **NOTE** A static route does not always reference a local interface. Instead, a static route might point to a *next-hop* IP address (an interface's IP address on the next router to which traffic should be forwarded). The network address of a default route is 0.0.0.0/0.

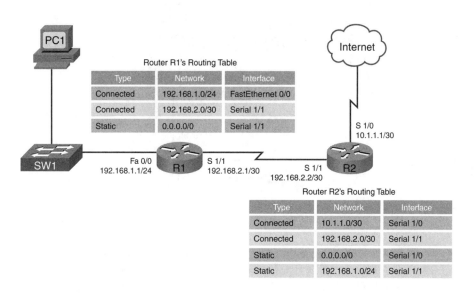

Figure 6-6 Static Routes

Similarly, router R2 can reach the Internet by sending traffic out of its Serial 1/0 interface. However, router R2 does need information about how to reach the 192.168.1.0/24 network available off of router R1. To educate router R2 as to how this network can be reached, a static route, pointing to 192.168.1.0/24, can be statically added to router R2's routing table.

Dynamic Routing Protocols

If you want to add routing information to routers in more complex networks, such as the topology shown in Figure 6-7, static routing does not scale well. Fortunately, a variety of dynamic routing protocols are available that allow a router's routing table to be updated as network conditions change.

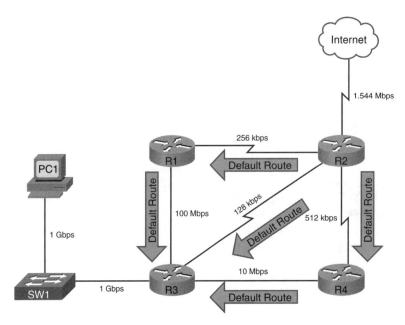

Figure 6-7 Dynamic Routes

In Figure 6-7, router R2 is advertising a default route to its neighbors (routers R1, R3, and R4). What happens if PC1 wants to send traffic to the Internet? PC1's default gateway is router R3, and router R3 has received three default routes. Which one does it use?

Router R3's path selection depends on the dynamic routing protocol being used. As you see later in this chapter, a routing protocol such as *Routing Information Protocol* (RIP) would make the path selection based on the number of routers that must be transited to reach the Internet (that is, *hop count*). Based on the topology presented, router R3 would select the 128-kbps link (where *kbps* stands for *kilobits per second*, meaning thousands of bits per second) connecting to router R2, because the Internet would be only one hop away. If router R3 had instead selected a path pointing to either router R1 or R4, the Internet would be two hops away.

However, based on the link bandwidths, you can see that the path from router R3 to router R2 is a suboptimal path. Unfortunately, RIP does not consider available bandwidth when making its route selection. Some other protocols (for example, *Open Shortest Path First* [OSPF]), can consider available bandwidth when making their routing decisions.

Dynamic routes also allow a router to reroute around a failed link. For example, in Figure 6-8, router R3 had preferred to reach the Internet via router R4. However, the link between routers R3 and R4 went down. Thanks to a dynamic routing protocol, router R3 knows of two other paths to reach the Internet, and it selects the next-best path, which is via router R1 in this example. The process of failing over from one route to a backup route is called *convergence*.

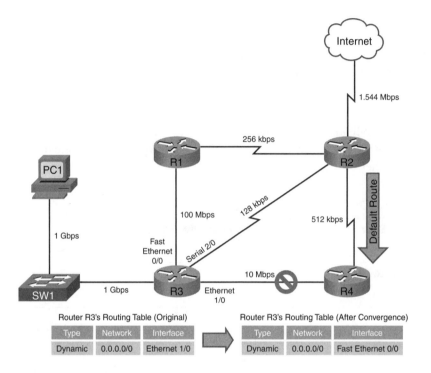

Figure 6-8 Route Redundancy

Routing Protocol Characteristics

Before examining the characteristics of routing protocols, an important distinction to make is the difference between a *routing* protocol and a *routed* protocol. A routing protocol (for example, RIP, OSPF, or EIGRP) is a protocol that advertises route information between routers.

Conversely, a *routed* protocol is a protocol with an addressing scheme (for example, IP) that defines different network addresses. Traffic can then be routed between defined networks, perhaps with the assistance of a routing protocol.

This section looks at routing protocol characteristics, such as how believable a routing protocol is versus other routing protocols. Also, in the presence of multiple routes, different routing protocols use different metrics to determine the best path. A distinction is made between Interior Gateway Protocols (IGP) and Exterior

Gateway Protocols (EGP). Finally, this section discusses different approaches to making route advertisements.

Believability of a Route

If a network is running more than one routing protocol (maybe as a result of a corporate merger), and a router receives two route advertisements from different routing protocols for the same network, which route advertisement does the router believe? Interestingly, some routing protocols are considered to be more believable that others.

The index of believability is called *administrative distance* (AD). Table 6-1 shows the AD for various sources of routing information. Note that lower AD values are more believable than higher AD values.

Table 6-1   Administrative Distance

Routing Information Source	Administrative Distance
Directly connected network	0
Statically configured network	1
EIGRP	90
OSPF	110
RIP	120
External EIGRP	170
Unknown of unbelievable	255 (considered to be unreachable)

Metrics

Some networks might be reachable via more than one path. If a routing protocol knows of multiple paths to reach such a network, which route (or routes) does the routing protocol select? Actually, it varies on the routing protocol and what that routing protocol uses as a *metric*. A metric is a value assigned to a route, and lower metrics are preferred over higher metrics.

If a routing protocol knows of more than one route to reach a destination network and those routes have equal metrics, some routing protocols support load balancing across equal-cost paths. EIGRP can even be configured to load balance across unequal-cost paths.

Different routing protocols can use different parameters in their calculation of a metric. The specific parameters used for a variety of routing protocols are presented later in this chapter.

Interior Versus Exterior Gateway Protocols

Routing protocols can also be categorized based on the scope of their operation. *Interior Gateway Protocols* (IGP) operate within an autonomous system (AS), where an AS is a network under a single administrative control. Conversely, *Exterior Gateway Protocols* (EGP) operate between autonomous systems.

Consider Figure 6-9. Routers R1 and R2 are in one AS (AS 65002), and routers R3 and R4 are in another AS (AS 65003). Within those autonomous systems, an IGP is used to exchange routing information. However, router ISP1 is a router in a separate autonomous system (AS 65001) run by a service provider. EGP (typically, Border Gateway Protocol [BGP]) is used to exchange routing information between the service provider's AS and each of the other autonomous systems.

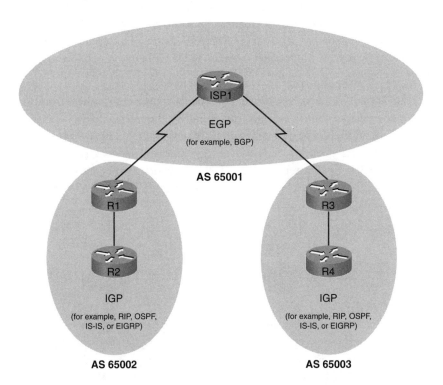

Figure 6-9 IGPs Versus EGPs

Route Advertisement Method

Another characteristic of a routing protocol is how it receives, advertises, and stores routing information. The two fundamental approaches are *distance vector* and *link state*.

Distance Vector

A distance-vector routing protocol sends a full copy of its routing table to its directly attached neighbors. This is a periodic advertisement, meaning that even if there have been no topological changes, a distance-vector routing protocol will, at regular intervals, re-advertise its full routing table to its neighbors.

Obviously, this periodic advertisement of redundant information is inefficient. Ideally, you want a full exchange of route information to occur only once and subsequent updates to be triggered by topological changes.

Another drawback to distance-vector routing protocols is the time they take to converge, which is the time required for all routers to update their routing table in response to a topological change in a network. *Hold-down* timers can speed the convergence process. After a router makes a change to a route entry, a hold-down timer prevents any subsequent updates for a specified period of time. This approach helps stop flapping routes (which are routes that oscillate between being available and unavailable) from preventing convergence.

Yet another issue with distance-vector routing protocols is the potential of a routing loop. To illustrate, consider Figure 6-10. In this topology, the metric being used is *hop count*, which is the number of routers that must be crossed to reach a network. As one example, router R3's routing table has a route entry for network 10.1.1.0/24 available off of router R1. For router R3 to reach that network, two routers must be transited (routers R2 and R1). As a result, network 10.1.1.0/24 appears in router R3's routing table with a metric (hop count) of 2.

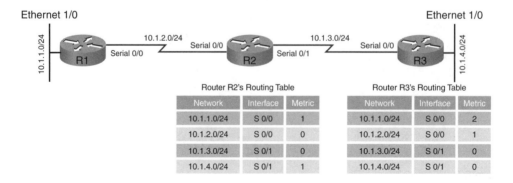

Figure 6-10   Routing Loop: Before Link Failure

Continuing with the example, imagine that interface Ethernet 1/0 on router R3 goes down. As shown in Figure 6-11, router R3 loses its directly connected route (with a metric of 0) to network 10.1.4.0/24. However, router R2 had a route to 10.1.4.0/24 in its routing table (with a metric of 1), and this route was advertised to router R3. Router R3 adds this entry for 10.1.4 to its routing table and increments the metric by 1.

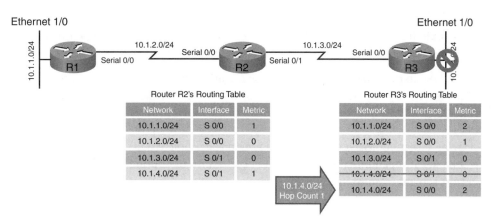

Figure 6-11 Routing Loop: After Link Failure

The problem with this scenario is that the 10.1.4.0/24 entry in router R2's routing table was due to an advertisement router R2 received from router R3. Now, router R3 is relying on that route, which is no longer valid. The routing loop continues as router R3 advertises its newly learned route of 10.1.4.0/24 with a metric of 2 to its neighbor, router R2. Because router R2 originally learned the 10.1.4.0/24 network from router R3, when it sees router R2 advertising that same route with a metric of 2, the network gets updated in router R2's routing table to have a metric of 3, as shown in Figure 6-12.

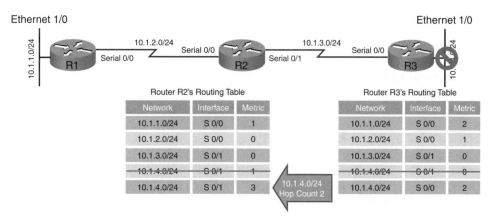

Figure 6-12 Routing Loop: Routers R2 and R3 Incrementing the Metric for 10.1.4.0/24

The metric for the 10.1.4.0/24 network continues to increment in the routing tables for both routers R2 and R3, until the metric reaches a value considered to be an unreachable value (for example, 16 in the case of RIP). This process is referred to as a *routing loop*.

Distance-vector routing protocols typically use one of two approaches for preventing routing loops:

- **Split horizon:** The split horizon feature prevents a route learned on one interface from being advertised back out of that same interface.

- **Poison reverse:** The poison reverse feature causes a route received on one interface to be advertised back out of that same interface with a metric considered to be infinite.

Having either approach applied to the previous example would have prevented router R3 from adding the 10.1.4.0/24 network into its routing table based on an advertisement from router R2.

Link State

Rather than having neighboring routers exchange their full routing tables with one another, a link-state routing protocol allows routers to build a topological map of the network. Then, similar to a global positioning system (GPS) in a car, a router can execute an algorithm to calculate an optimal path (or paths) to a destination network.

Routers send *link-state advertisements* (LSA) to advertise the networks they know how to reach. Routers then use those LSAs to construct the topological map of a network. The algorithm run against this topological map is *Dijkstra's Shortest Path First* algorithm.

Unlike distance-vector routing protocols, link-state routing protocols exchange full routing information only when two routers initially form their adjacency. Then, routing updates are sent in response to changes in the network, as opposed to being sent periodically. Also, link-state routing protocols benefit from shorter convergence times, as compared to distance-vector routing protocols.

Routing Protocol Examples

Now that you understand some of the characteristics that distinguish one routing protocol from another, this section contrasts some of the most popular routing protocols found in modern networks:

- **Routing Information Protocol (RIP):** A distance-vector routing protocol that uses a metric of *hop count*. The maximum number of hops between two routers in an RIP-based network is 15. Therefore, a hop count of 16 is considered to be infinite. Also, RIP is an IGP.

- **Open Shortest Path First (OSPF):** A link-state routing protocol that uses a metric of *cost*, which is based on the link speed between two routers. OSPF is a popular IGP, because of its scalability, fast convergence, and vendor-interoperability.

- **Intermediate System to Intermediate System (IS-IS):** This link-state routing protocol is similar in its operation to OSPF. It uses a configurable, yet dimensionless, metric associated with an interface and runs Dijkstra's Shortest Path First algorithm. Although IS-IS as an IGP offers the scalability, fast convergence, and vendor-interoperability benefits of OSPF, it has not been as widely deployed as OSPF.

- **Enhanced Interior Gateway Routing Protocol (EIGRP):** A Cisco-proprietary protocol. So, although EIGRP is popular in Cisco-only networks, it is less popular in mixed vendor environments. Like OSPF, EIGRP is an IGP with fast convergence and is very scalable. EIGRP is more challenging to classify as a distance-vector or a link-state routing protocol.

  By default, EIGRP uses bandwidth and delay in its metric calculation; however, other parameters can be considered. These optional parameters include reliability, load, and maximum transmission unit (MTU) size.

  Some literature calls EIGRP an *advanced distance-vector* routing protocol, while some literature calls EIGRP a *hybrid* routing protocol (mixing characteristics of both distance-vector and link-state routing protocols). EIGRP uses information from its neighbors to help it select an optimal route (like distance-vector routing protocols). However, EIGRP also maintains a database of topological information (like a link-state routing protocol). The algorithm EIGRP uses for its route selection is not Dijkstra's Shortest Path First algorithm. Instead, EIGRP uses Diffusing-Update Algorithm (*DUAL*).

- **Border Gateway Protocol (BGP):** The only EGP in widespread use today. In fact, BGP is considered to be the routing protocol that runs the Internet, which is an interconnection of multiple autonomous systems. Although some literature classifies BGP as a distance-vector routing protocol, it can more accurately be described as a *path-vector* routing protocol, meaning that it can use as its metric the number of AS hops that must be transited to reach a destination network, as opposed to a number of required router hops. BGPs path selection is not solely based on AS hops, however. BGP has a variety of other parameters that it can consider. Interestingly, none of those parameters are based on link speed. Also, although BGP is incredibly scalable, it does not quickly converge in the event of a topological change.

A network can simultaneously support more than one routing protocol through the process of *route redistribution*. For example, a router could have one of its interfaces participating in an OSPF area of the network and have another interface participating in an EIGRP area of the network. This router could then take routes learned via OSPF and inject those routes into the EIGRP routing process. Similarly, EIGRP-learned routes could be redistributed into the OSPF routing process.

Address Translation

As described in Chapter 5, some IP addresses are routable through the public Internet, while other IP addresses are considered private, and are intended for use within an organization. *Network Address Translation* (NAT) allows private IP addresses (as defined in RFC 1918) to be translated into Internet-routable IP addresses (public IP addresses). This section examines the operation of basic NAT and a variant called *Port Address Translation* (PAT).

NAT

Consider Figure 6-13, which shows a basic NAT topology. Note that, even though the IP networks of 172.16.1.0/24 and 192.168.1.0/24 are actually private IP networks, for this discussion, assume that they are publicly routable IP addresses. The reason for the use of these private IP addresses to represent public IP addresses is to avoid using an entity's registered IP addresses in the example.

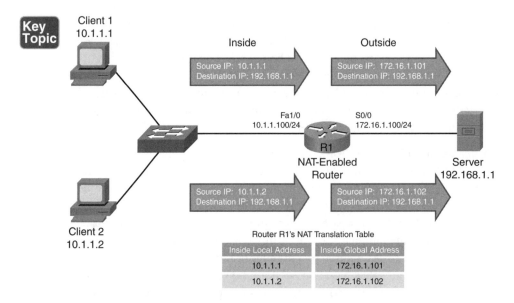

Figure 6-13   Basic NAT Topology

In Figure 6-13's topology, two clients with private IP addresses of 10.1.1.1 and 10.1.1.2, want to communicate with a web server on the public Internet. The server's IP address is 192.168.1.1. Router R1 is configured for NAT. As an example, router R1 takes packets coming from 10.1.1.1 destined for 192.168.1.1 and changes the source IP address in the packets' headers to 172.16.1.101 (which we assume is a publicly routable IP address for the purposes of this discussion). When the server at IP address 192.168.1.1 receives traffic from the client, the server's return traffic is sent to a destination address of 172.16.1.101. When router R1 receives traffic from the outside network destined for 172.16.1.101, the router translates the destination IP address to 10.1.1.1 and forwards the traffic to the inside network, where client 1 receives the traffic. Similarly, client 2's IP address of 10.1.1.2 is translated into an IP address of 172.16.1.102.

Table 6-2 introduces the terminology used when describing the various IP addresses involved in a translation.

Table 6-2 Names of NAT IP Addresses

NAT IP Address	Definition
Inside local	A private IP address referencing an inside device
Inside global	A public IP address referencing an inside device
Outside local	A private IP address referencing an outside device
Outside global	A public IP address referencing an outside device

As a memory aid, remember that *inside* always refers to an inside device, while *outside* always refers to an outside device. Also, think of the word *local* being similar to the Spanish word *loco*, meaning crazy. That is what a local address could be thought of. It is a crazy, made-up address (a private IP address that is not routable on the Internet). Finally, let the g in *global* remind you of the g in *good*, because a global address is a good (routable on the Internet) IP address.

Based on these definitions, Table 6-3 categorizes the IP addresses previously shown in Figure 6-13.

Table 6-3   Classifying the NAT IP Addresses in Figure 6-13

NAT IP Address	NAT IP Address Type
Inside local	10.1.1.101
Inside local	10.1.1.102
Inside global	172.16.1.101
Inside global	172.16.1.102
Outside local	None
Outside global	192.168.1.1

Whether an inside local address is randomly assigned an inside global address from a pool of available addresses or is assigned an address from a static configuration determines the type of NAT you are using. These two approaches to NAT are called *DNAT* and *SNAT*:

Key Topic

- **DNAT:** In the preceding example, the inside local addresses were automatically assigned an inside global address from a pool of available addresses. This approach to NAT is referred to as dynamic NAT (DNAT).

- **SNAT:** Sometimes, you might want to statically configure the inside global address assigned to a specific device inside your network. For example, you might have an e-mail server inside your company, and you want other e-mail servers on the Internet to send e-mail messages to your server. Those e-mail servers on the Internet need to point to a specific IP address, not one that was randomly picked from a pool of available IP addresses. In such a case, you can statically configure the mapping of an inside local address (the IP address of your internal e-mail server) to an inside global address (the IP address to which e-mail servers on the Internet will send e-mail for your company). This approach to NAT is referred to as static NAT (SNAT).

PAT

A challenge with basic NAT, however, is that there is a one-to-one mapping of inside local addresses to inside global addresses, meaning that a company would need as many publicly routable IP addresses as it had internal devices needing IP addresses. This does not scale well because, often, a service provider will provide a customer with only a single IP address or a small block of IP addresses.

Fortunately, many routers support *Port Address Translation* (PAT), which allows multiple inside local addresses to share a single inside global address (a single publicly routable IP address). In Chapter 2, "Dissecting the OSI Model," you learned about how IP communications relies on port numbers. As a review, when a client sends an IP packet, not only does that packet have a source and destination IP address, it has a source and destination port number. PAT leverages these port numbers to track separate communication flows.

As an example, consider Figure 6-14. Unlike the example shown in Figure 6-13, in which each inside local address was translated to its own inside global address, the example shown in Figure 6-14 only has one inside global address. This single inside global address is shared among all the devices inside a network. The different communication flows are kept separate in router R1's NAT translation table by considering port numbers.

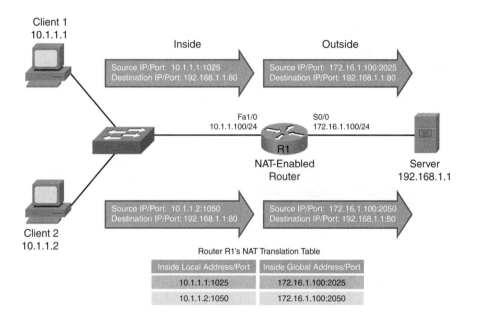

Figure 6-14 PAT Topology

When client 1 sends a packet to the web server (with an IP address of 192.168.1.1), the client's ephemeral port number (its source port selected, which is greater than 1023) is 1025. Router R1 notes that port number and translates the inside local address of 10.1.1.1 with a port number of 1025 to an inside global address of 172.16.1.100 with a port number of 2025. When client 1 sends a packet to the same web server, its inside local address of 10.1.1.2 with a port number of 1050 is translated into an outside local address of 172.16.1.100 with a port number of 2050.

Notice that both client 1 and client 2 had their inside local addresses translated into the same inside global address of 172.16.1.100. Therefore, when the web server sends packets back to client 1 and client 2, those packets are destined for the same IP address (172.16.1.100). However, when router R1 receives those packets, it knows to which client each packet should be forwarded based on the destination port number. For example, if a packet from the web server (192.168.1.1) arrived at router R1 with a destination IP address of 172.16.1.100 and a destination port number of 2050, router R1 would translate the destination IP address to 10.1.1.2 with a port number of 1050, which would be forwarded to client 2.

Multicast Routing

Chapter 5 introduced the concept of multicast transmission, where a multicast sender could send traffic destined for a Class D IP address, known as a *multicast group*, and devices on a network wanting to receive that transmission could join that multicast group. Let us now consider how a client joins a multicast group and how routers route multicast traffic. Keep in mind that one of the main goals with multicast traffic is to send that traffic only to devices in a network wanting to receive that traffic. Two primary protocols used for multicast are *Internet Group Management Protocol* (IGMP) and *Protocol Independent Multicast* (PIM).

> **NOTE**   A surprising amount of networking literature incorrectly states that IGMP stands for Internet Group Multicast Protocol.

IGMP

The protocol used between clients (for example, PCs) and routers to let routers know which of their interfaces have multicast receivers attached is IGMP. Although three versions of IGMP exist (as described in the list that follows), only two versions (version 1 and version 2) are in wide-scale deployment:

- **IGMP version 1 (IGMPv1):** When a PC wants to join a multicast group, it sends an IGMP report message to its router, letting the router know it wants to receive traffic for a specific group. Every 60 seconds, by default, the router sends an IGMP query message to determine if the PC still wants to belong to the group. There can be up to a 3-minute delay before a router realizes the receiver left the group. The destination address of this router query is 224.0.0.1, which addresses all IP multicast hosts.

- **IGMP version 2 (IGMPv2):** Similar to IGMPv1, except IGMP version 2 can send queries to a specific group and a *leave* message is supported. Specifically, a receiver can proactively send a leave message when it no longer wants to participate in a multicast group, allowing the router to prune its interface earlier than it would have with IGMPv1.

- **IGMP version 3 (IGMPv3):** Adds a feature called *Source-Specific Multicast* (SSM), which allows a client to request traffic not only destined for a particular multicast group but also sourced from a specific server. For example, you could have multiple video servers streaming different video streams, all destined for the same multicast group. However, when a client joined that group, with SSM (as supported by IGMPv3), that client could request that it only receive traffic sourced from a specific server. This would provide support for multiple multicast sessions while consuming only one Class D IP address.

Consider Figure 6-15, which shows a basic multicast topology. Of the three PCs on the network, only PC2 wants to receive the multicast traffic. How do the switch and router know to only forward traffic out ports leading to PC2 (the multicast receiver)?

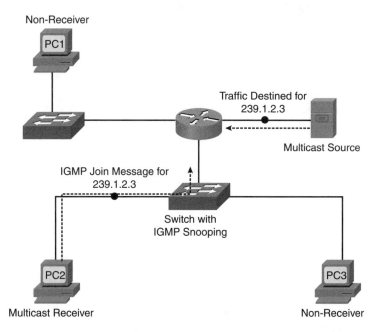

Figure 6-15 Multicast Receiver Joining a Multicast Group

PC2 indicates it wants to belong to the multicast group of 239.1.2.3 by sending an IGMP join message to its default gateway. The switch through which the IGMP join message passes is enabled with the *IGMP snooping* feature, which allows the switch to eavesdrop on the IGMP join message and determine the multicast group that PC2 wants to join. Then, in the future, when the switch receives traffic from the router destined for 239.1.2.3, the switch will only forward those packets out the port connected to PC2.

When the router receives the IGMP join message from PC2, it knows that it should only forward traffic destined for 239.1.2.3 out the interface on which a IGMP join message was received. As a result, when the multicast source sends a stream of traffic, that traffic is only forwarded out the router port and the switch port leading to PC2, as shown in Figure 6-16.

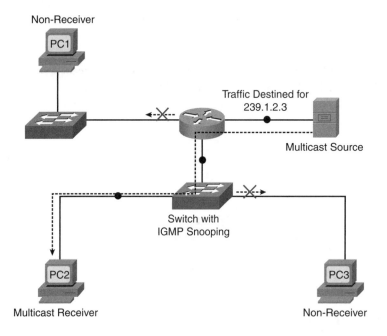

Figure 6-16 Multicast Traffic Only Being Forwarded to the Multicast Receiver

PIM

Although IGMP allows a multicast receiver to join a multicast group, we still have a need for a multicast routing protocol, which routes multicast traffic between multicast-enabled routers. The most popular multicast routing protocol is PIM. PIM's main purpose is to form a *multicast distribution tree*, which is the path (or paths) over which multicast traffic flows. PIM has two modes of operation: PIM dense mode (PIM-DM) and PIM sparse mode (PIM-SM).

PIM-DM

PIM-DM uses a *source distribution tree*, meaning that an optimal path is formed between the source router in a multicast network (that is, the router closest to the multicast sender) and each last-hop router (the router closest to each multicast receiver). However, before this optimal source distribution tree is formed, traffic from the multicast source is initially flooded throughout the entire network, as shown in Figure 6-17.

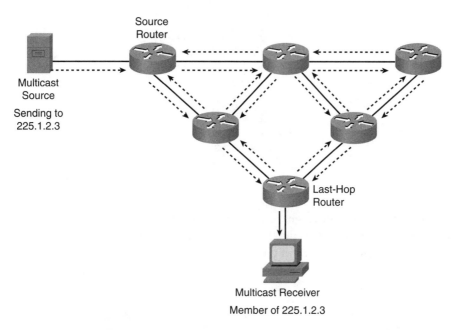

Figure 6-17   PIM-DM Flooding

Obviously, this initial flooding of multicast traffic causes traffic to be sent to routers not needing the multicast traffic, and it can unnecessarily consume bandwidth on the links between routers. After this initial flooding occurs, if a router interface receives the multicast traffic, and that traffic is not needed by the router (or if the traffic is needed by the router, but on a different interface), the router interface sends a *prune* message to its neighboring router, asking that it be pruned off of the source distribution tree, as shown in Figure 6-18.

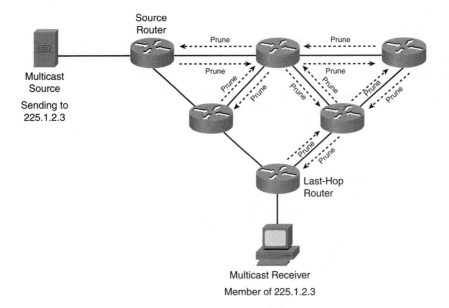

Figure 6-18 PIM-DM Pruning

After sending these prune messages, the resulting source distribution tree (the path over which the multicast packets flow) is an optimal path between the source router and the last-hop router, as shown in Figure 6-19.

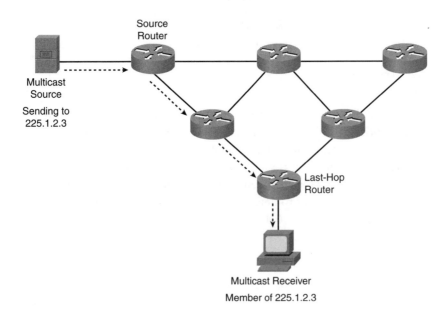

Figure 6-19 PIM-DM Source Distribution Tree After Pruning

A benefit of PIM-DM is that an optimal path is formed between the source router and each last-hop router. However, the drawback of PIM-DM is that a network must undergo the *flood and prune behavior*, as previously described, to form the optimal distribution tree. Also, even after the optimal distribution tree is formed, the flooding and pruning repeats every 3 minutes. Such a periodic flooding of traffic might cause a significant performance impact on a network.

PIM-SM

PIM-SM uses a *shared distribution tree*. A shared distribution tree does not initially form an optimal path between a source router and each last-hop router. Instead, a multicast source sends traffic directly to another router, called a *rendezvous point* (RP). When another router in the multicast network wants to join the multicast distribution tree (because it received an IGMP join message from a client), that last-hop router sends a join message to the RP to join the shared distribution tree, as shown in Figure 6-20. The tree is called a shared distribution tree, because all last-hop routers (routers with downstream multicast receivers) send join messages to the same RP.

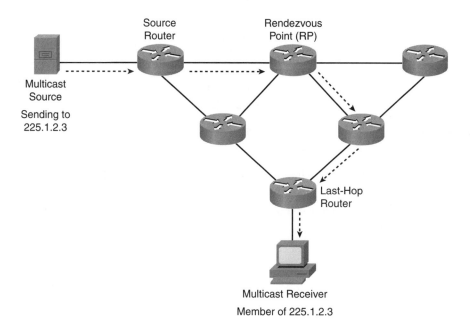

Figure 6-20 PIM-SM Shared Distribution Tree

The benefit of PIM-SM is that the flood and prune behavior of PIM-DM is avoided. However, by inspecting Figure 6-20, you might conclude that a drawback of PIM-SM is a suboptimal distribution tree might be formed. Although that is initially true, after a last-hop router receives the first multicast packet from the multicast source, it can see the IP address of the multicast source. Then, based on its unicast routing table, a last-hop router can form an optimal distribution tree and then prune off the branch of the tree connecting it to the RP. This behavior is called *shortest path tree* (SPT) *switchover*. The resulting distribution tree is shown in Figure 6-21.

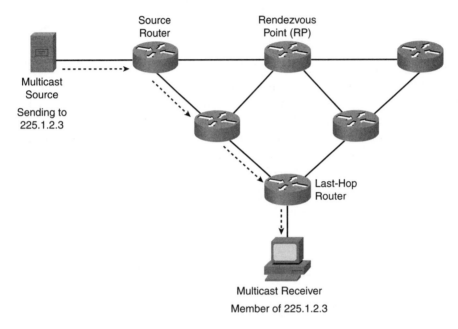

Figure 6-21   PIM-SM Distribution Tree After SPT Switchover

With the addition of the SPT switchover feature, PIM-SM is the preferred approach to forming a multicast distribution tree, because it gives you an optimal path from the source router to each last-hop router, and it avoids the flood and prune behavior of PIM-DM.

Summary

The main topics covered in this chapter are the following:

- How routers forward traffic through a network based on source and destination IP addresses.

- The sources of route information used to populate a router's routing table. These sources include directly connected routes, statically configured routes, and dynamically learned routes.

- A distinction was made between routed protocols (for example, IP) and routing protocols (such as OSPF or EIGRP).

- Some routing sources are more trustworthy than other routing sources, based on their administrative distances (AD).

- Different routing protocols use different metrics to select the best route in the presence of multiple routes.

- This chapter distinguished between IGPs (which run within an autonomous system) and EGPs (which run between autonomous systems).

- The behavior of distance-vector and link-state routing protocols were contrasted, and you saw how spilt horizon and poison reverse could prevent a routing loop in a distance-vector routing protocol environment.

- Today's most popular routing protocols (including RIP, OSPF, IS-IS, EIGRP, and BGP) were presented, along with their characteristics.

- NAT can be used to translate private IP addresses inside a network to publicly routable IP addresses. Additionally, this chapter contrasted variations of NAT: PAT, SNAT, and DNAT.

- This chapter discussed the IGMP and PIM protocols used in multicast networks. These protocols work together to allow a network to only forward multicast traffic over links needing that traffic.

Exam Preparation Tasks

Review All the Key Topics

Review the most important topics from inside the chapter, noted with the Key Topic icon in the outer margin of the page. Table 6-4 lists these key topics and the page numbers where each is found.

Table 6-4   Key Topics for Chapter 6

Key Topic Element	Description	Page Number
Step list	Basic routing processes	190
Table 6-1	Administrative distance	198
Figure 6-9	IGPs versus EGPs	199
List	Approaches for preventing routing loops	202
List	Routing protocol examples	203
Figure 6-13	Basic NAT topology	204
Table 6-2	Names of NAT IP addresses	205
List	NAT variations	206
Figure 6-14	PAT topology	207
Figure 6-15	Multicast receiver joining a multicast group	209

Complete Tables and Lists from Memory

Print a copy of Appendix C, "Memory Tables" (found on the CD), or at least the section for this chapter, and complete the tables and lists from memory. Appendix D, "Memory Table Answer Key," also on the CD, includes the completed tables and lists so you can check your work.

Define Key Terms

Define the following key terms from this chapter, and check your answers in the Glossary:

ARP, TTL, default static route, next-hop, routed protocol, routing protocol, administrative distance, metric, IGP, EGP, distance-vector, link-state, hold-down timer, split horizon, poison reverse, LSA, RIP, OSPF, IS-IS, EIGRP, BGP, route redistribution, NAT, DNAT, SNAT, PAT, IGMP, PIM

Review Questions

The answers to these review questions are in Appendix A, "Answers to Review Questions."

1. If a PC on an Ethernet network attempts to communicate with a host on a different subnet, what destination IP address and destination MAC address will be placed in the packet/frame header sent by the PC?

    a. **Dest. IP:** IP address of default gateway. **Dest. MAC:** MAC address of default gateway.

    b. **Dest. IP:** IP address of remote host. **Dest. MAC:** MAC address of default gateway.

    c. **Dest. IP:** IP address of remote host. **Dest. MAC:** MAC address of remote host.

    d. **Dest. IP:** IP address of remote host. **Dest. MAC:** MAC address of local PC.

2. What protocol is used to request a MAC address that corresponds to a known IP address?

    a. IGMP

    b. TTL

    c. ICMP

    d. ARP

3. What is the network address and subnet mask of a default route?

    a. 255.255.255.255/32

    b. 0.0.0.0/32

    c. 255.255.255.255/0

    d. 0.0.0.0/0

4. What routing protocol characteristic indicates the believability of the routing protocol (as opposed to other routing protocols)?

    a. Weight

    b. Metric

    c. Administrative distance

    d. SPF algorithm

5. Which of the following are distance-vector routing protocol features that can prevent routing loops? (Choose two.)

   a. Reverse path forwarding (RPF) check

   b. Split horizon

   c. Poison reverse

   d. Rendezvous point

6. Which of the following is a distance-vector routing protocol with a maximum hop count of 15?

   a. BGP

   b. IS-IS

   c. RIP

   d. OSPF

7. Which of the following routing protocols is an EGP?

   a. BGP

   b. IS-IS

   c. RIP

   d. OSPF

8. What NAT IP address is a public IP address that references an inside device?

   a. Inside local

   b. Inside global

   c. Outside local

   d. Outside global

9. What NAT variation automatically assigns an inside global address from a pool of available addresses?

   a. SNAT

   b. DNAT

   c. PAT

   d. GNAT

10. What multicast protocol is used between clients and routers to let routers know which of their interfaces are connected to a multicast receiver?

   a. IGMP

   b. PIM-DM

   c. PIM-SM

   d. SPT switchover

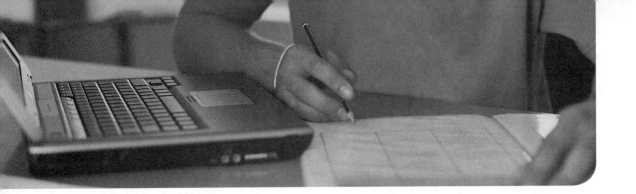

After completion of this chapter, you will be able to
answer the following questions:

- What are three categories of wide-area network (WAN) connections?

- How are data rates measured on various WAN technologies?

- Which types of media (or wireless technologies) might be used in WAN connections?

- What are the characteristics of the following WAN technologies: dedicated leased line, digital subscriber line (DSL), cable modem, Synchronous Optical Network (SONET), satellite, Plain Old Telephone Service (POTS), Integrated Services Digital Network (ISDN), Frame Relay, Asynchronous Transfer Mode (ATM), and Multiprotocol Label Switching (MPLS)?

CHAPTER 7

Introducing Wide-Area Networks

In the early 1990s, computer-networking design guides invoked the *Pareto Principle* and stated that 80 percent of your network traffic stays local, while only 20 percent of your network traffic leaves the local network. This was an information technology (IT) extrapolation of Vilfredo Pareto's *80-20 rule*. With the advent of Internet browsers, cloud storage, and streaming audio and video, today's network traffic patterns are more closely approximated with a 20-80 rule, meaning that the vast majority of network traffic leaves the local network, over a wide-area network (WAN) connection.

As defined in Chapter 1, "Introducing Computer Networks," a WAN is a network that spans large geographical distances. This chapter discusses the properties of WAN connections, followed by a survey of common WAN technologies.

Foundation Topics

WAN Properties

To select an appropriate WAN technology for a network you are designing, or to better understand a WAN technology in a currently installed network, you need the ability to compare one WAN technology to another. This section identifies a collection of WAN connection properties that can be used to contrast various WAN technologies.

WAN Connection Types

Some WAN connections are considered to be *always on*, in that the connection is always available without having to first set up the connection. Conversely, some WAN technologies are *on demand*, meaning that the connection is not established until needed. Then, when the connection is needed, it is brought up.

Another distinguishing characteristic of WAN connections is whether multiple users share bandwidth. For example, some WAN connections provide dedicated bandwidth to a service provider's customer, while other WAN connections allow multiple customers of a service provider to share a common pool of available bandwidth.

A WAN connection can generally be classified into one of three categories: a *dedicated leased line*, a *circuit-switched connection*, or a *packet-switched connection*:

- **Dedicated leased line:** A connection interconnecting two sites. This logical connection might physically connect through a service provider's facility or a telephone company's central office (CO). The expense of a dedicated leased line is typically higher than other WAN technologies offering similar data rates, because with a dedicated leased line, a customer does not have to share bandwidth with other customers.

  As discussed in the section, "WAN Technologies," a T1 circuit, as shown in Figure 7-1, is an example of a dedicated leased line technology commonly found in North America. A common Layer 2 protocol that could run over a dedicated leased line is *Point-to-Point Protocol* (PPP), which is discussed later in this chapter.

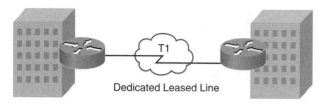

Figure 7-1   Dedicated Leased Line Sample Topology

- **Circuit-switched connection:** A connection that is brought up on an as-needed basis. In fact, a circuit-switched connection is analogous to a phone call, where you pick up your phone, dial a number, and a connection is established based on the number you dial. As discussed later in this chapter, *Integrated Services Digital Network* (ISDN) can operate as a circuit-switched connection, bringing up a *virtual circuit* (VC) on demand. This approach to on-demand bandwidth can be a cost savings for some customers who only need periodic connectivity to a remote site. Figure 7-2 illustrates a circuit-switched connection.

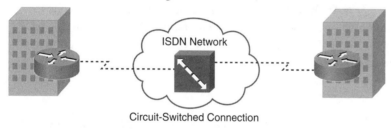

Figure 7-2   Circuit-Switched Connection Sample Topology

- **Packet-switched connection:** Similar to a dedicated leased line, because most packet-switched networks are always on. However, unlike a dedicated leased line, packet-switched connections allow multiple customers to share a service provider's bandwidth.

Even though bandwidth is being shared among customers, customers can purchase a *service-level agreement* (SLA), which specifies performance metrics (for example, available bandwidth and maximum delay) guaranteed for a certain percentage of time. For example, an SLA might guarantee a customer that he has a minimum of 256 kbps of bandwidth available 80 percent of the time.

Frame Relay, which is discussed in the section, "WAN Technologies," is an example of a packet-switched connection. As shown in Figure 7-3, a Frame Relay network allows multiple customers to connect to a service provider's network, and virtual circuits (VC, as indicated with the dashed lines) logically interconnect customer sites.

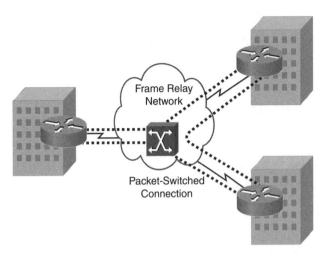

Figure 7-3   Packet-Switched Connection Sample Topology

Asynchronous Transfer Mode (ATM) is often categorized as a packet-switched connection. However, to be technically accurate, ATM is a *cell-switched* connection, because ATM uses fixed-length (that is, 53 byte) cells, as opposed to variable-length frames.

NOTE   These connection types are meant to be general categories, and not all WAN technologies will strictly meet the previous definitions. For example, *digital subscriber line* (DSL) is a technology that could be configured for on-demand access (like a circuit-switched connection) or it could be configured for always-on access. Also, DSL typically provides a customer with an amount of bandwidth that the customer does not have to share with other customers (like a dedicated leased line). However, DSL uses ATM technologies to connect back to the service provider's equipment (like a cell-switched connection). So, use these three categories of WAN connection types as general guidelines, not strict definitions.

WAN Data Rates

WAN links are typically faster than LAN links; however, some WAN technologies (for example, *Synchronous Optical Network* [SONET]) boast a bandwidth capacity in the tens of Gbps. One could argue that some of these higher-speed WAN technologies are actually *metropolitan-area network* (MAN) technologies. However, this chapter considers a WAN to be an interconnection of geographically dispersed networks, which also encompasses MAN technologies.

Aside from measuring bandwidth in kbps, Mbps, or Gbps, high-speed optical networks often use *optical carrier* (OC) levels to indicate bandwidth. As a base reference point, the speed of an OC-1 link is 51.84 Mbps. Other OC levels are simply multiples of an OC-1. For example, an OC-3 link has three times the bandwidth of an OC-1 link (that is, 3 * 51.84 Mbps = 155.52 Mbps).

Although a variety of speeds are available from different service providers, Table 7-1 offers typical bandwidths of several common WAN technologies.

Table 7-1   Typical WAN Data Rates

WAN Technology	Typical Available Bandwidth
Frame Relay	56 kbps–1.544 Mbps
T1	1.544 Mbps
T3	44.736 Mbps
E1	2.048 Mbps
E3	34.4 Mbps
ATM	155 Mbps–622 Mbps
SONET	51.84 Mbps (OC-1)–159.25 Gbps (OC-3072)

WAN Media Types

WAN links might be physical hard-wired links (for example, copper or fiber-optic cable running from your site back to your service provider's site and then to the remote site with which your site communicates). Alternately, some WAN links are wireless. These wireless solutions might be appropriate for locations where more conventional WAN technologies are unavailable or for accommodating the needs of mobile users.

Physical Media

The physical media used for WAN connections is similar to the physical media found in LAN connections:

- **Unshielded twisted pair (UTP):** Both analog and digital circuits coming into your location from a local telephone central office commonly use UTP cabling. This cabling might be Category 3 (Cat 3) cabling, as opposed to higher categories used in LANs. Examples of WAN technologies using UTP cabling include T1 circuits, DSL connections, dial-up analog modems, or ISDN circuits.

- **Coaxial cable:** A common residential WAN solution (primarily for connecting out to the Internet) is a cable modem. As the name suggests, a cable modem uses a coaxial cable (for example, an RG-6 coaxial cable) for transmission. In fact, the same coaxial cable providing a variety of television programming for your home might also be used to carry data (upstream and downstream) using specific frequency ranges.

- **Fiber-optic cable:** WAN connections needing a high bandwidth capacity or needing to span a large distance might use fiber-optic cabling. Another benefit of fiber-optic cabling is its immunity from electromagnetic interference (EMI).

- **Electric power lines:** With such an expansive existing infrastructure, electric power lines can be attractive candidates to provide broadband Internet access to residential locations. This is made possible with *broadband over power lines* (BPL) technology. Although implementations vary widely, bandwidth offered to an end user typically maxes out at approximately 2.7 Mbps.

Although the physical media on a WAN closely resembles LAN media, keep in mind that the Layer 2 protocols running over the media is usually different for WAN links, as opposed to LAN links.

Wireless Media

Wireless media adds flexibility to WAN connections and often reduces cost. Some examples of wireless media include the following:

- **Cellular phone:** Some cellular-phone technologies (for example, *Long-Term Evolution* (LTE), which supports a 100-Mbps data rate to mobile devices and a 1-Gbps data rate for stationary devices) can be used to connect a mobile device (such as a smart phone) to the Internet. The term *tethering* is commonly used with today's smart phones. Tethering allows a smart phone's data connection to be used by another device, such as a laptop. Also, *mobile hot spots* are growing in popularity, because these devices connect to a cell phone company's data network and make that data network available to nearby devices (typically, a maximum of five devices) via wireless networking technologies. This, for example, allows multiple passengers in a car to share a mobile hot spot and have Internet connectivity from their laptops when riding down the road.

> **NOTE**   The term *Internet connection sharing* (ICS) is sometimes used interchangeably with the term *tethering*. However, be aware the ICS is a Microsoft Windows solution, allowing a Microsoft Windows-based computer with an Internet connection (possibly via an internal cellular data card) to share its connection with other devices.

- **Satellite:** Some locations do not have WAN connectivity options, such as DSL connections or cable modems, commonly available in urban areas. However, these locations might be able to connect to the Internet, or to a remote office, using satellite communications, where a transmission is bounced off of a satellite, received by a satellite ground station, and then sent to its destination using either another satellite hop or a wired WAN connection.

- **WiMAX:** *Worldwide Interoperability for Microwave Access* (WiMAX) provides wireless broadband access to fixed locations (as an alternative to technologies such as DSL) and mobile devices. Depending on the WiMAX service provider, WiMAX coverage areas could encompass entire cities or small countries.

- **HSPA+:** Like WiMAX, *Evolved High-Speed Packet Access* (HSPA+) is a technology offering wireless broadband service. The maximum data rate for HSPA+ is 84 Mbps.

- **Radio:** The range of frequencies (measured in *Hertz* [Hz], which represents the number of cycles of a waveform per second) typically considered to be in the radio frequency spectrum includes frequencies of 3 kHz through 300 GHz. Different countries have their own standards bodies that dictate which frequency ranges can be used for what purposes. For example, in the United States, the *Federal Communications Commission* (FCC) regulates the use of frequencies in the radio frequency spectrum. Therefore, while multiple radio-based WAN solutions exist, their implementation might vary by country.

A couple of potential downsides of wireless WAN media include experiencing increased delay and higher packet error rates, as compared with physical links.

WAN Technologies

The previous section presented a collection of WAN connection properties. Understanding these properties can now help you better understand the collection of WAN technologies presented in this section.

Dedicated Leased Line

A dedicated leased line is typically a *point-to-point* connection interconnecting two sites. All the bandwidth on that dedicated leased line is available to those sites. This means that, unlike a packet-switched connection, the bandwidth of a dedicated leased line connection does not need to be shared among multiple service provider customers.

WAN technologies commonly used with dedicated leased lines include digital circuits, such as T1, E1, T3, and E3 circuits. These circuits can use multiplexing technology to simultaneously carry multiple conversations in different 64-kbps channels. A single 64-kbps channel is called a *Digital Signal 0* (DS0).

When one of these circuits comes into your location, it terminates on a device called a channel service unit/data service unit (CSU/DSU). Also, be aware that a common Layer 2 protocol used on dedicated leased lines is *Point-to-Point Protocol* (PPP).

NOTE   A less common protocol used on dedicated leased lines (as compared to PPP) is *High-Level Data Link Control* (HDLC). HDLC lacks many of the features of PPP, and in its standards-based implementation, it can only support a single Layer 3 protocol on a circuit. However, Cisco has its own HDCL implementation in which the HDLC header has a protocol field, thus allowing the simultaneous transmission of multiple Layer 3 protocols.

T1

T1 circuits were originally used in telephony networks, with the intent of one voice conversation being carried in a single channel (that is, a single DS0). A T1 circuit is comprised of 24 DS0s, which is called a *Digital Signal 1* (DS1). The bandwidth of a T1 circuit is 1.544 Mbps:

- The size of a T1 frame = 193 bits (that is, 24 channels * 8 bits per channel + 1 framing bit = 193 bits).

- The *Nyquist Theorem* requires 8,000 samples to be sent per second for a voice conversation (that is, a rate at least twice the highest frequency of 4000 Hz).

- Total bandwidth = 193 bit frames * 8,000 samples per second = 1.544 Mbps.

In a T1 environment, more than one frame is sent at once. Two popular approaches to grouping these frames together are the following:

- **Super Frame (SF):** Combines 12 standard 193-bblit frames into a *super frame*.

- **Extended Super Frame (ESF):** Combines 24 standard 193-bit frames into an *extended super frame.*

T1 circuits are popular in North America and Japan.

E1

An E1 circuit contains 32 channels, in contrast to the 24 channels on a T1 circuit. Only 30 of those 32 channels, however, can transmit data (or voice or video). Specifically, the first of those 32 channels is reserved for framing and synchronization, and the seventeenth channel is reserved for signaling (that is, setting up, maintaining, and tearing down a call).

Because an E1 circuit has more DS0s than a T1, it has a higher bandwidth capacity. Specifically, an E1 has a bandwidth capacity of 2.048 Mbps (8,000 samples per second as required by the Nyquist Theorem * 8 bits per sample * 32 channels = 2,048,000 bits per second).

Unlike a T1 circuit, an E1 circuit does not group frames together in a SF or an ESF. Rather, an E1 circuit groups 16 frames together in a *multiframe.*

E1 circuits are popular outside of North America and Japan.

T3

In the same T-carrier family of standards as a T1, a T3 circuit offers an increased bandwidth capacity. Although a T1 circuit combines 24 DS0s into a single physical connection to offer 1.544 Mbps of bandwidth, a T3 circuit combines 672 DS0s into a single physical connection, which is called a *Digital Signal 3* (DS3). A T3 circuit has a bandwidth capacity of 44.7 Mbps.

E3

Just as a T3 circuit provided more bandwidth than a T1 circuit, an E3 circuit's available bandwidth of 34.4 Mbps is significantly more than the 2.048 Mbps of bandwidth offered by an E1 circuit. A common misconception is that the bandwidth of an E3 is greater than the bandwidth of a T3, because an E1's bandwidth was greater than a T1's bandwidth. However, that is not the case, with a T3 having a greater bandwidth (that is, 44.7 Mbps) than an E3 (that is, 34.4 Mbps).

CSU/DSU

Although far less popular than they once were, analog modems allowed a phone line to come into a home or business and terminate on analog modems, which provided data connections for devices such as PCs. These analog modems supported a single data conversation per modem.

However, digital circuits (for example, T1, E1, T3, or T3 circuits) usually have multiple data conversations multiplexed together on a single physical connection. Therefore, a digital modem is needed, as opposed to an analog modem. This digital modem needs to be able to distinguish between data arriving on various DS0s. Such a digital modem is called a *channel service unit/data service unit* (CSU/DSU).

As shown in Figure 7-4, a CSU/DSU circuit can terminate an incoming digital circuit from a service provider and send properly formatted bits to a router. A CSU/DSU uses clocking (often provided by the service provider) to determine when one bit stops and another bit starts. Therefore, the circuit coming from a service provider and terminating on a CSU/DSU is a *synchronous circuit* (where the synchronization is made possible by clocking).

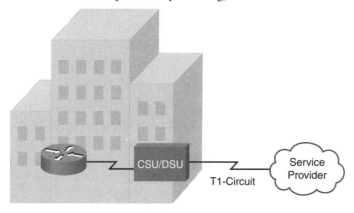

Figure 7-4   CSU/DSU Terminating a Synchronous Circuit

NOTE   Because a CSU/DSU works with bits, it is classified as a Layer 1 device.

Point-to-Point Protocol

A common Layer 2 protocol used on dedicated leased lines is *Point-to-Point Protocol* (PPP). PPP has the capability to simultaneously transmit multiple Layer 3 protocols (for example, IP and IPX) through the use of *control protocols* (CP). IP, as an example, uses the *IP control protocol* (IPCP).

Each Layer 3 CP runs an instance of PPP's *Link Control Protocol* (LCP). Four primary features offered by LCP include the following:

- **Multilink interface:** PPP's multilink interface feature allows multiple physical connections to be bonded together into a logical interface. This logical interface allows load balancing across multiple physical interfaces.

- **Looped link detection:** A Layer 2 loop (of PPP links) can be detected and prevented.

- **Error detection:** Frames containing errors can be detected and discarded by PPP.

- **Authentication:** A device at one end of a PPP link can authenticate the device at the other end of the link. Three approaches to perform PPP authentication are as follows:

  - **Password Authentication Protocol (PAP):** PAP performs one-way authentication (a client authenticates with a server), as shown in Figure 7-5. A significant drawback to PPP, other than its unidirectional authentication, is the security vulnerability of its clear text transmission of credentials, which could permit an eavesdropper to learn the authentication credentials being used.

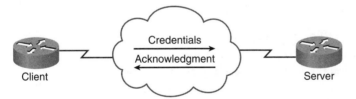

Figure 7-5   PAP Authentication

  - **Challenge-Handshake Authentication Protocol (CHAP):** Like PAP, CHAP performs a one-way authentication. However, authentication is performed through a three-way handshake (challenge, response, and acceptance messages) between a server and a client, as shown in Figure 7-6. The three-way handshake allows a client to be authenticated without sending credential information across a network.

Figure 7-6   CHAP Authentication

- **Microsoft Challenge-Handshake Authentication Protocol (MS-CHAP):** MS-CHAP is a Microsoft-enhanced version of CHAP, offering a collection of additional features, including two-way authentication.

> **NOTE**   These PPP features are optional and are not necessarily going to be found in a given PPP connection.

Point-to-Point Protocol over Ethernet

A popular WAN technology (specifically, an Internet access technology) in residences and as businesses is *digital subscriber line* (DSL). DSL is described later in this section. However, as part of the PPP discussion, note that DSL connections use a variant of PPP called *PPP over Ethernet* (PPPoE).

As Figure 7-7 illustrates, PPPoE is commonly used between a DSL modem in a home (or business) and a service provider. Specifically, PPPoE encapsulates PPP frames within Ethernet frames. PPP is used to leverage its features, such as authentication. For example, when you set up a DSL modem in your home, you typically have to provide authentication credentials. Although Ethernet does not handle authentication, PPP does. By combining Ethernet with PPP, Ethernet-based devices (for example, PCs) can take advantage of PPP features, such as authentication.

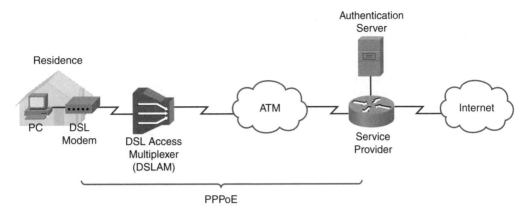

Figure 7-7   PPPoE Sample Topology

Microsoft RRAS

PPP is often the protocol used by *Microsoft Routing and Remote Access Server* (RRAS), which is a Microsoft Windows Server feature that allows Microsoft Windows clients to remotely access a Microsoft Windows network. Figure 7-8 shows the RRAS configuration window being used to configure a static route.

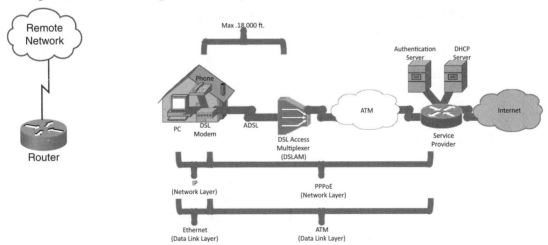

Figure 7-8   Microsoft RRAS

Using PPP along with Microsoft RRAS allows support for PPP features, such as the multilink interface feature. The multilink interface feature could, for example, allow multiple dial-up modem connections to be bonded together into a single logi-cal connection, giving increased bandwidth to a remote Microsoft Windows client.

PPP is not required for Microsoft RRAS, which could alternately use *Serial Line Internet Protocol* (SLIP). However, PPP is preferred over SLIP, because of PPP's fea-tures (for example, multilink interface and error detection).

> **NOTE**   Microsoft RRAS was previously known as *Microsoft RAS* (Remote Access Server).

> **NOTE**   An alternative to RRAS, where remote clients can become members of a Mi-crosoft Windows network, is *remote desktop control*. With remote desktop control, a remote computer does not directly become a member of an internal network (for ex-ample, a network inside a corporation). Rather, it controls a computer that is already part of an internal network (which could be Microsoft Windows based, or based on some other *operating system* (OS), such as Linux or Mac OS X). With remote desktop control, a remote user can see the screen of the internal computer and control the computer with a keyboard and mouse. One example of a protocol that supports re-mote desktop control is *Independent Computer Architecture* (ICA), which is a product of Citrix.
>
> Yet another technology that supports the remote control of a computer's desktop is *virtual network computing* (VNC).

Digital Subscriber Line

Commonplace in many residential and small business locations (also known as *small office / home office* or SOHO locations), *digital subscriber line* (DSL) is a group of tech-nologies that provide high-speed data transmission over existing telephone wiring. DSL has several variants, which differ in data rates and distance limitations.

Three popular DSL variants include *asymmetric DSL* (ADSL), *symmetric DSL* (SDSL), and very high bit-rate DSL (VDSL):

- **Asymmetric DSL (ADSL):** A popular Internet-access solution for residential locations. Figure 7-9 shows a sample ADSL topology. Note that ADSL allows an existing analog telephone to share the same line used for data for simulta-neous transmission of voice and data.

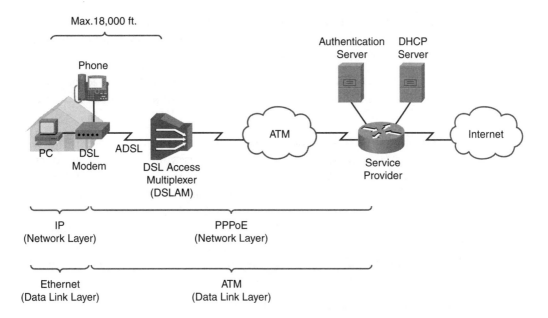

Figure 7-9   ADSL Sample Topology

Also notice in Figure 7-9 that the maximum distance from a DSL modem to a *DSL access multiplexer* (DSLAM) is 18,000 ft. This limitation stems from a procedure telephone companies have used for decades to change the impedance of telephone lines.

Here is a brief history: If wires in a telephone cable run side-by-side for several thousand feet, capacitance builds up in the line (which can cause echo). To counteract this capacitance, after 18,000 ft. of cable, telephone companies insert a *load coil*, which adds inductance to the line. Electrically speaking, inductance is the opposite of capacitance. So, by adding a load coil, much of the built-up capacitance in a telephone cable is reduced. However, ADSL signals cannot cross a load coil, thus the 18,000 ft. distance limitation for ADSL.

Figure 7-9 also shows how a telephone line leaving a residence terminates on a DSLAM. A DSLAM acts as an aggregation point for multiple connections, and it connects via an ATM network back to a service provider's router. The service provider authenticates user credentials, provided via PPPoE, using an authentication server. Also, the service provider has a DHCP server to hand out IP address information to end-user devices (for example, a PC or a wireless router connected to a DSL modem).

The term *asymmetric* in asymmetric DSL implies the upstream and downstream speeds can be different. Typically, downstream speeds are greater than upstream speeds in an ADSL connection.

The theoretical maximum downstream speed for an ADSL connection is 8 Mbps, and the maximum upstream speed is 1.544 Mbps (the speed of a T1 circuit).

■ **Symmetric DSL (SDSL):** While ADSL has asymmetric (unequal) upstream and downstream speeds, by definition, SDSL has symmetric (equal) upstream and downstream speeds. Another distinction between ADSL and SDSL is that SDSL does not allow simultaneous voice and data on the same phone line. Therefore, SDSL is less popular in residential installations, because an additional phone line is required for data. Although service providers vary, a typical maximum upstream/downstream data rate for an SDSL connection is 1.168 Mbps. Also, SDSL connections are usually limited to a maximum distance of 12,000 ft. between a DSL modem and its DSLAM.

■ **Very High Bit-Rate DSL (VDSL):** VDSL boasts a much higher bandwidth capacity than ADSL or SDSL, with a common downstream limit of 52 Mbps, and a limit of 12 Mbps for upstream traffic.

VDSL's distance limitation is 4,000 ft. of telephone cable between a cable modem and a DSLAM. This constraint might seem too stringent for many potential VDSL subscribers, based on their proximity to their closest telephone central office (CO). However, service providers and telephone companies offering VDSL service often extend their fiber-optic network into their surrounding communities. This allows VDSL gateways to be located in multiple communities. The 4,000 ft. limitation then becomes a distance limitation between a DSL modem and the nearest VDSL gateway, thus increasing the number of potential VDSL subscribers.

Cable Modem

Cable television companies have a well-established and wide-reaching infrastructure for television programming. This infrastructure might contain both coaxial and fiber-optic cabling. Such an infrastructure is called a *hybrid fiber-coax* (HFC) distribution network. These networks can designate specific frequency ranges for upstream and downstream data transmission. The device located in a residence (or a business) that can receive and transmit in those data frequency ranges is known as a *cable modem*, as illustrated in Figure 7-10.

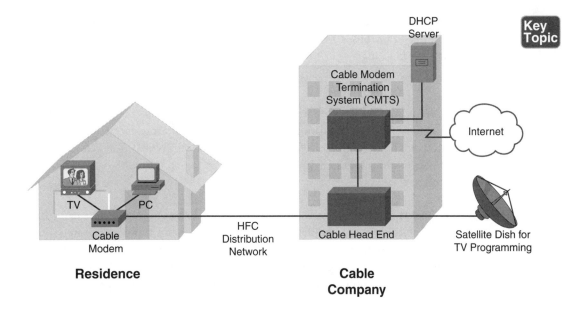

Figure 7-10   Cable Modem Sample Topology

The frequency ranges typically allocated for upstream and downstream data are as follows:

■ **Upstream data frequencies:** 5 MHz–42 MHz

■ **Downstream data frequencies:** 50 MHz–860 MHz

Although the theoretical maximum upstream/downstream bandwidth limits are greater (and is dependent on the HFC distribution network in use), most upstream speeds are limited to 2 Mbps, with downstream speeds limited to 10 Mbps. As HFC distribution networks continue to evolve, greater bandwidth capacities will be available.

The frequencies dedicated to data transmission are specified by a *Data-Over-Cable Service Interface Specification* (DOCSIS) version. Although DOCSIS is an international standard, European countries use their own set of frequency ranges, their own standard known as *Euro-DOCSIS*.

Synchronous Optical Network

Synchronous Optical Network (SONET) is a Layer 1 technology that uses fiber-optic cabling as its media. Because SONET is a Layer 1 technology, it can be used to transport various Layer 2 encapsulation types, such as Asynchronous Transfer Mode

(ATM). Also, because SONET uses fiber-optic cabling, it offers high data rates, typically in the 155 Mbps–10 Gbps range, and long-distance limitations, typically in the 20 km–250 km range.

> **NOTE** The term SONET is often used synonymously with the term *Synchronous Digital Hierarchy* (SDH), which is another fiber-optic multiplexing standard. Although these standards are similar, SONET is usually seen in North America, while SDH has greater worldwide popularity.

A SONET network can vary in its physical topology. For example, devices can connect as many as 16 devices in a linear fashion (similar to a bus topology) or in a ring topology. A metropolitan-area network (MAN), as depicted in Figure 7-11, often uses a ring topology. The ring might circumnavigate a large metropolitan area. Sites within that metropolitan area could then connect to the nearest point on the SONET ring.

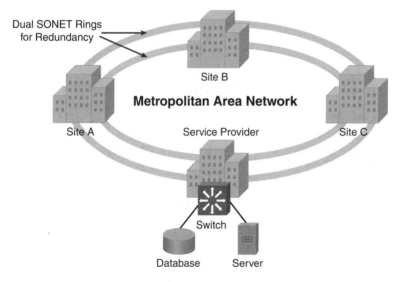

Figure 7-11 SONET Sample Topology

NOTE A SONET network uses a single wavelength of light, along with time-division multiplexing (TDM) to support multiple data flows on a single fiber. This approach differs from *dense wavelength division multiplexing* (DWDM), which is another high-speed optical network commonly used in MANs. DWDM uses as many as 32 light wavelengths on a single fiber, where each wavelength can support as many as 160 simultaneous transmissions.

NOTE Another optical WAN technology to be aware of is *passive optical network* (PON), which allows a single fiber cable to service as many as 128 subscribers. This is made possible via unpowered (that is, passive) optical splitters.

Satellite

Many rural locations lack the option of connecting to an IP WAN or to the Internet via physical media (for example, a DSL modem or a cable modem connection). For such locations, a satellite WAN connection, as shown in Figure 7-12, might be an option.

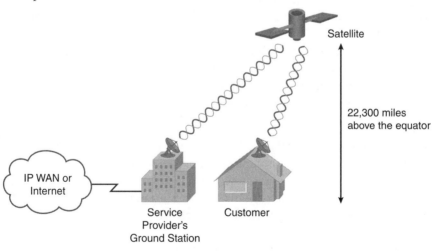

Figure 7-12 Satellite WAN Sample Topology

Most satellites used for WAN connectivity are in orbit above the earth's equator, about 22,300 miles high. Therefore, if a customer in North America, for example, had a clear view of the southern sky, she would be able to install a satellite dish and establish a line-of-sight communication path with the orbiting satellite.

The satellite would then relay transmissions back and forth between the customer's site and the service provider's ground station. The ground station could then provide connectivity, via physical media, to an IP WAN or to the Internet.

Two significant design considerations include the following:

- **Delay:** Radio waves travel at the speed of light, which is 186,000 miles per second, or $3 * 10^8$ meters per second. This speed is specifically the speed of light (and radio waves) in a vacuum; however, for the purposes of this discussion, assume these commonly known values, even though, technically, the speed of light (and radio waves) is a bit slower when traveling through air, as opposed to traveling through a vacuum. Although these are fast speeds, consider the distance between a customer and the satellite. If a customer were located 2,000 miles north of the equator, the approximate distance between the customer site and the satellite could be calculated using the Pythagorean Theorem: $d^2 = 2000^2 + 22,300^2$. Solving the equation for d, which is the distance between the customer and the satellite, yields a result of approximately 22,390 miles.

  A transmission from a customer to a destination on the Internet (or IP WAN) would have to travel from the customer to the satellite, from the satellite to the ground station, and then out to the Internet (or IP WAN). The propagation delay alone introduced by bouncing a signal off of the satellite is approximately 241 ms (that is, (22,390 * 2) / 186,000 = .241 seconds = 241 ms). And to that, you have to add other delay components, such as processing delay (by the satellite and other networking devices), making the one-way delay greater than $1/4^{th}$ of a second, and therefore the round-trip delay greater than 1/2 of a second. Such delays are not conducive to latency-sensitive applications, such as Voice over IP (VoIP).

- **Sensitivity to weather conditions:** Because communication between a customer's satellite dish and an orbiting satellite must travel through the earth's atmosphere, weather conditions can impede communications. For example, if a thunderstorm is in the vicinity of the customer location, that customer might temporarily lose connectivity with her satellite.

Based on these design considerations, even though satellite WAN technology offers tremendous flexibility in terms of geographical location, more terrestrial-based solutions are usually preferred.

Plain Old Telephone Service

The *Public Switched Telephone Network* (PSTN) is comprised of multiple telephone carriers from around the world. An end-user location (for example, a home or business) gets to the PSTN by connecting to its local telephone company, known as a *local exchange carrier* (LEC). Analog connections (both voice and data connections) using the PSTN are referred to as *Plain Old Telephone Service* (POTS) connections.

With the PSTN as we know it today, you can place a telephone call to just about anywhere in the world from just about anywhere in the world. Although the bandwidth available on the PSTN is limited, the PSTN is such an expansive network, it is more likely to be available in a given location that other wired WAN solutions. So, the benefit of availability has the tradeoff of performance.

A POTS connection can be used to access the Internet (or an IP WAN) by connecting a computer to a modem with a serial cable (or using a computer with an internal modem), connecting the modem to a POTS phone line, and dialing into a service provider. The service provider then connects out to the Internet (or an IP WAN), as shown in Figure 7-13.

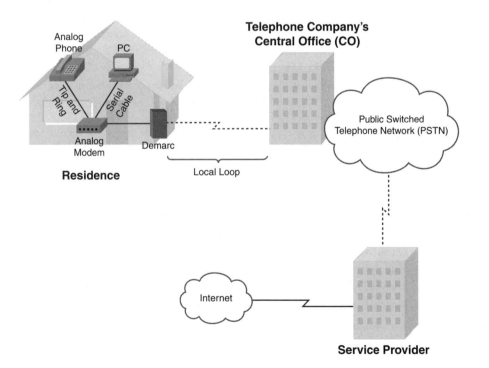

Figure 7-13 Dial-Up Modem Sample Topology

As previously stated, the performance of a POTS connection (using a dial-up modem) is limited. Although modems are rated as 56-kbps modems, in the United States and Canada, a modem's upstream data rate is limited to 48.0 kbps, and its downstream data rate is limited to 53.3 kbps. These limits are imposed not based on a technical limitation, but based on regulations from these countries' communications commissions.

Table 7-2 offers a collection of common terms used when working with POTS connections, for both voice and data.

Table 7-2   Common POTS Terms

Term	Definition
Telco	A *telco* is a telephone company. Some countries have government-maintained telcos, while other countries have multiple competitive telcos.
Local loop	A *local loop* is a connection between a customer premise and their local telephone central office (CO).
Central office (CO)	A building containing a telephone company's telephone switching equipment is referred to a *central office* (CO). COs are categorized into five hierarchical classes. A Class 1 CO is a long-distance office serving a regional area. A Class 2 CO is a second-level long-distance office (it's subordinate to a Class 1 office). A Class 3 CO is a third-level long-distance office. A Class 4 CO is a fourth-level long-distance office that provides telephone subscribers access to a live operator. A Class 5 CO is at the bottom of the five-layer hierarchy and physically connects to customer devices in the local area.
Tip and ring	The *tip and ring* wires are the red and green wires found in an RJ-11 wall jack, which carry voice, ringing voltage, and signaling information between an analog device (for example, a phone or a modem) and a telephone's wall jack.
Demarc	A *demarc* (also known as a *demarcation point* or a *demarc extension*) is the point in a telephone network where the maintenance responsibility passes from a telephone company to the subscriber (unless the subscriber has purchased inside wiring maintenance). This demarc is typically located in a box mounted to the outside of a customer's building (for example, a residential home). This box is called a *network interface device* (NID).
Smart jack	A *smart jack* is a type of network interface device (see the definition for demarc) that adds circuitry. This circuitry adds such features as converting between framing formats on digital circuit (for example, a T1), supporting remote diagnostics, and regenerating a digital signal.

Integrated Services Digital Network

Integrated Services Digital Network (ISDN) is a digital telephony technology that supports multiple 64-kbps channels (known as *bearer channels [B channels]*) on a single connection. ISDN was popular back in the 1980s and was used to connect *private branch exchanges* (PBX), which are telephone switches owned by and operated by a company, to a CO. ISDN has the capability to carry voice, video, or data over its B channels. ISDN also offers a robust set of signaling protocols: Q.921 for Layer 2 signaling and Q.931 for Layer 3 signaling. These signaling protocols run on a separate channel in an ISDN circuit (known as the *delta channel*, *data channel*, or *D channel*).

ISDN circuits are classified as either a *basic rate interface* (BRI) circuit or a *primary rate interface* (PRI) circuit:

- **BRI:** A BRI circuit contains two 64-kbps B channels and one 16-kbps D channel. Although such a circuit can carry two simultaneous voice conversations, the B channels can be logically bonded into a single VC (using the multilink interface feature of PPP as discussed earlier in this chapter) to offer a 128-kbps data path.

- **PRI:** A PRI circuit is an ISDN circuit built on a T1 or E1 circuit. Recall that a T1 circuit has 24 channels. Therefore, if a PRI circuit is built on a T1 circuit, the ISDN PRI circuit has 23 B channels and a one 64-kbps D channel. The 24th channel in the T1 circuit is used as the ISDN D channel (the channel used to carry the Q.921 and Q.931 signaling protocols, which are used to set up, maintain, and tear down connections).

  Also, recall that an E1 circuit has 32 channels, with the first channel being reserved for framing and synchronization and the seventeenth channel being served for signaling. Therefore, an ISDN PRI circuit built on an E1 circuit has 30 B channels and one D channel, which is the seventeenth channel.

Figure 7-14 depicts the constituent elements of an ISDN network.

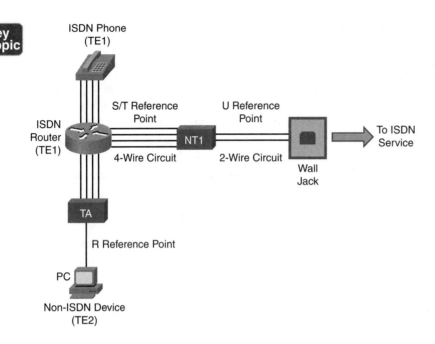

Figure 7-14   ISDN Sample Topology

Some ISDN circuits are four-wire circuits, while some are two-wire. Also, some devices in an ISDN network might not natively be ISDN devices, or they might need to connect to a four-wire ISDN circuit or a two-wire ISDN circuit. As a result of all these variables, an ISDN network, as pictured in Figure 7-14, categorizes various reference points in the network and various elements in the network. Definitions of these reference points and elements are presented in Table 7-3.

Table 7-3   ISDN Network Reference Points and Elements

Term	Definition
R reference point	The *R reference point* resides between a non-ISDN device and a terminal adapter (TA).
S/T reference point	The *S/T reference point* resides between a network termination 1 (NT1) and a terminal endpoint 1 (TE1).
U reference point	The *U reference point* resides between a network termination 1 (NT1) and the wall jack connecting back to an ISDN service provider.
Terminal adapter (TA)	A *TA* performs protocol conversion between a non-ISDN device and a terminal endpoint 1 (TE1) device.

Term	Definition
Terminal endpoint 1 (TE1)	A *TE1* is a device (such as an ISDN phone) that natively supports ISDN.
Terminal endpoint 2 (TE2)	A *TE2* is a device (such as a PC) that does not natively support ISDN.
Network termination 1 (NT1)	An *NT1* is a device that interconnects a four-wire ISDN circuit and a two-wire ISDN circuit.

Frame Relay

Although it is starting to wane in popularity because of the proliferation of technologies such as cable modems and DSL connections, for many years, Frame Relay was *the* WAN technology of choice for many companies. Frame Relay offers widespread availability and relatively low cost compared to leased lines.

Figure 7-15 shows a sample Frame Relay topology. Frame Relay sites are interconnected using *virtual circuits* (VC). So, a single router interface can have multiple VCs. For example, in Figure 7-15, notice that the New York router has two VCs (as indicated by the dashed lines) emanating from a single interface. One VC is destined for the Austin router, and the other VC is destined for the Orlando router. These VCs could be either point-to-point circuits, where the VC between New York and Austin belongs to the same IP subnet, and the VC between New York and Orlando belongs to a separate subnet. Alternately, the connection from New York to Austin and Orlando could be a *point-to-multipoint* connection, where all routers belong to the same subnet.

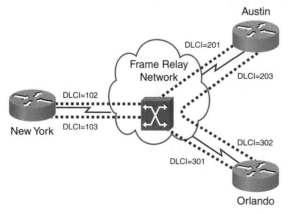

Figure 7-15   Frame Relay Sample Topology

Frame Relay is a Layer 2 technology, and a router uses locally significant identifiers for each VC. These identifiers are called *data-link connection identifiers* (DLCI). Because DLCIs are locally significant, DLCIs at the different ends of a VC do not need to match (although they could). For example, note the VC that interconnects New York with Orlando. From the perspective of the New York router, the VC is denoted with a DLCI of 103. However, from the perspective of the Orlando router, the same VC is referenced with a DLCI of 301.

If a VC is always connected, it is considered to be a *permanent virtual circuit* (PVC). However, some VCs can be brought up on an as-needed basis, and they are referred to as *switched virtual circuits* (SVC).

Unlike a dedicated leased line, Frame Relay shares a service provider's bandwidth with other customers of its service provider. Therefore, subscribers might purchase an SLA (previously described) to guarantee a minimum level of service. In SLA terms, a minimum bandwidth guarantee is called a *committed information rate* (CIR).

During times of congestion, a service provider might need a sender to reduce his transmission rate below its CIR. A service provider can ask a sender to reduce his rate by setting the *backwards explicit congestion notification* (BECN) bit in the Frame Relay header of a frame destined for the sender that needs to slow down. If the sender is configured to respond to BECN bits, it can reduce its transmission rate by as much as 25 percent per timing interval (which is 125 ms by default). CIR and BECN configurations are both considered elements of *Frame Relay Traffic Shaping* (FRTS).

Another bit to be aware of in a Frame Relay header is the discard eligible (DE) bit. Recall that a CIR is a minimum bandwidth guarantee for a service provider's customer. However, if the service is not congested, a customer might be able to temporarily transmit at a higher rate. However, frames sent in excess of the CIR have the DE bit in their header set. Then, if the Frame Relay service provider experiences congestion, it might first drop those frames marked with a DE bit.

Asynchronous Transfer Mode

Like Frame Relay, Asynchronous Transfer Mode (ATM) is a Layer 2 WAN technology that operates using the concept of PVCs and SVCs. However, ATM uses fixed-length *cells* as its protocol data unit (PDU), as opposed to the variable frames used by Frame Relay.

As shown in Figure 7-16, an ATM cell contains a 48-byte payload and a 5-byte header. Table 7-4 describes the fields of an ATM header.

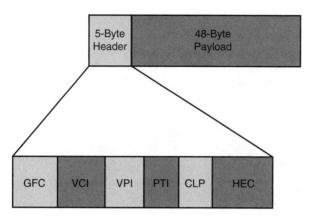

Figure 7-16   ATM Cell Structure

Table 7-4   ATM Header Fields

Field	Description
GFC (4 bits)	The *Generic Flow Control* (GFC) field uses 4 bits to locally indicate a congestion condition.
VCI (16 bits)	The *Virtual Circuit Identifier* (VCI) field usually uses 16 bits to indicate a VC. However, to fully identify a VC, the virtual path within which that VC resides must also be defined.
VPI (8 bits)	The *Virtual Path Identifier* (VPI) field uses 8 bits to identify an ATM virtual path, which could contain multiple virtual circuits.
PTI (3 bits)	The *Payload Type Indicator* (PTI) field uses 3 bits to indicate the type of payload being carried in a cell (for example, user data versus ATM management data).
HEC (8 bits)	The *Header Error Control* (HEC) field uses 8 bits to detect and correct errors in an ATM cell header.

An ATM cell's 48-byte payload size resulted from a compromise between the wishes of different countries as an international standard for ATM was being developed. Some countries, such as France and Japan, wanted a 32-byte payload size, because smaller payload sizes worked well for voice transmission. However, other countries, including the United States, wanted a 64-byte payload size, because they felt such a size would better support the transmission of both voice and data. In the end, the compromise was to use the average of 32 bytes and 64 bytes (that is, 48 bytes).

Although ATM uses VCs to send voice, data, and video, those VCs are not identified with DLCIs. Rather, ATM uses a pair of numbers to identify a VC. One of the numbers represents the identifier of an ATM virtual path. A single virtual path can contain multiple virtual circuits, as shown in Figure 7-17.

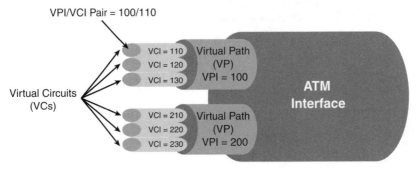

Figure 7-17   ATM Virtual Circuits

Also note in Figure 7-17 that a virtual path is labeled with a *virtual path identifier* (VPI), and a virtual circuit is labeled with a *virtual circuit identifier* (VCI). Therefore, an ATM VC can be identified with a *VPI/VCI pair* of numbers. For example, 100/110 can be used to represent a VC with a VPI of 100 and a VCI of 110.

Figure 7-18 provides an example of an ATM network topology. Notice that interconnections between ATM switches and ATM endpoints are called *user-network interfaces* (UNI), while interconnections between ATM switches are called *network-node interfaces* (NNI).

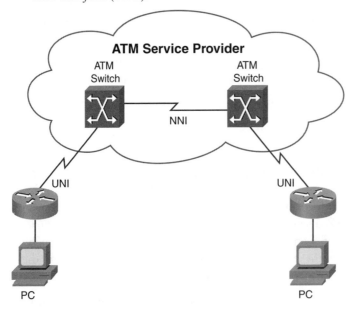

Figure 7-18   ATM Sample Topology

Multiprotocol Label Switching

Multiprotocol Label Switching (MPLS) is growing in popularity as a WAN technology used by service providers. This growth in popularity is due in part to MPLS' capability to support multiple protocols on the same network—for example, an MPLS network can accommodate users connecting via Frame Relay or ATM on the same MPLS backbone—and MPLS's capability to perform traffic engineering (which allows traffic to be dynamically routed within an MPLS cloud based on current load conditions of specific links and availability of alternate paths).

MPLS inserts a 32-bit header between Layer 2 and Layer 3 headers. Because this header is shimmed between the Layer 2 and Layer 3 headers, it is sometimes referred to as a *shim header*. Also, because the MPLS header resides between the Layer 2 and Layer 3 headers, MPLS is considered to be a Layer 2 1/2 technology.

The 32-bit header contains a 20-bit label. This label is used to make forwarding decisions within an MPLS cloud. Therefore, the process of routing MPLS frames through an MPLS cloud is commonly referred to as *label switching*.

Figure 7-19 shows a sample MPLS network. Table 7-5 defines the various MPLS network elements shown in the figure.

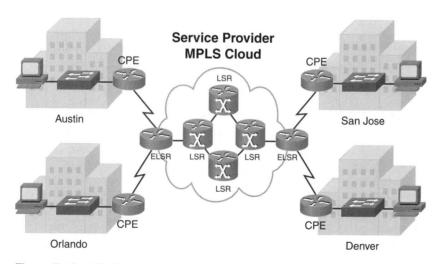

Figure 7-19 MPLS Sample Topology

Table 7-5 MPLS Network Elements

Element	Description
CPE	A *customer premise equipment* (CPE) device resides at a customer site. A router, as an example, could be a CPE that connects a customer with an MPLS service provider.
ELSR	An *edge label switch router* (ELSR) resides at the edge of an MPLS service provider's cloud and interconnects a service provider to one or more customers.
LSR	A *label switch router* (LSR) resides inside a service provider's MPLS cloud and makes frame-forwarding decisions based on labels applied to frames.

An MPLS frame does not maintain the same label throughout the MPLS cloud. Rather, an LSR receives a frame, examines the label on the frame, makes a forwarding decision based on the label, relabels the frame, and forwards the frame to the next LSR. This process of label switching is more efficient than routing based on Layer 3 IP addresses.

Summary

The main topics covered in this chapter are the following:

- This chapter identified the three categories of WAN connections: dedicated leased lines, circuit-switched connections, and packet-switched connections.

- Data rates of various WAN technologies were contrasted.

- Various types of WAN media were identified. These types could be categorized as either *physical media* (including unshielded twisted pair (UTP), coaxial cable, fiber-optic cable, and electric power lines) or *wireless technologies* (including cellular phone, satellite, WiMAX, HSPA+, and radio technologies).

- The basic theory and operation of various WAN technologies were discussed, including dedicated leased line, digital subscriber line (DSL), cable modem, Synchronous Optical Network (SONET), satellite, Plain Old Telephone Service (POTS), Integrated Services Digital Network (ISDN), Frame Relay, Asynchronous Transfer Mode (ATM), and Multiprotocol Label Switching (MPLS).

Exam Preparation Tasks

Review All the Key Topics

Review the most important topics from inside the chapter, noted with the Key Topic icon in the outer margin of the page. Table 7-6 lists these key topics and the page numbers where each is found.

Table 7-6 Key Topics for Chapter 7

Key Topic Element	Description	Page Number
List	WAN connection types	222
Table 7-1	Typical WAN data rates	225
List	Types of physical WAN media	226
List	Types of wireless WAN technologies	226
List	PPP features	231
List	Types of DSL connections	234
Figure 7-10	Cable modem sample topology	237
Figure 7-12	Satellite sample topology	239
Figure 7-13	Dial-up modem sample topology	241
Table 7-2	Common POTS terms	242
List	Types of ISDN circuits	243
Figure 7-14	ISDN sample topology	244
Figure 7-15	Frame Relay sample topology	245
Figure 7-16	ATM cell structure	247
Figure 7-19	MPLS sample topology	249

Complete Tables and Lists from Memory

Print a copy of Appendix C, "Memory Tables" (found on the CD), or at least the section for this chapter, and complete the tables and lists from memory. Appendix D, "Memory Table Answer Key," also on the CD, includes the completed tables and lists so you can check your work.

Define Key Terms

Define the following key terms from this chapter, and check your answers in the Glossary:

dedicated leased line, circuit-switched connection, packet-switched connection, optical carrier, T1, E1, T3, E3, channel service unit/data service unit (CSU/DSU), Point-to-Point Protocol (PPP), Password Authentication Protocol (PAP), Challenge-Handshake Authentication Protocol (CHAP), Microsoft Challenge-Handshake Authentication Protocol (MS-CHAP), Point-to-Point Protocol over Ethernet (PPPoE), Microsoft Routing and Remote Access Server (RRAS), digital subscriber line (DSL), cable modem, Synchronous Optical Network (SONET), satellite (WAN technology), Public Switched Telephone Network (PSTN), Plain Old Telephone Service (POTS), telco, local loop, central office (CO), tip and ring, demarc, Integrated Services Digital Network (ISDN), basic rate interface (BRI), primary rate interface (PRI), Frame Relay, Asynchronous Transfer Mode (ATM), Multiprotocol Label Switching (MPLS), customer premise equipment (CPE), edge label switch router (ELSR), label switch router (LSR)

Review Questions

The answers to these review questions are in Appendix A, "Answers to Review Questions."

1. ISDN is considered to be what type of WAN connection?

   a. Dedicated leased line

   b. Circuit-switched connection

   c. Packet-switched connection

   d. Cell-switched connection

2. What is the data rate of an OC-3 connection?

   a. 51.84 Mbps

   b. 622 Mbps

   c. 155.52 Mbps

   d. 159.25 Gbps

3. Which of the following WAN technologies commonly use unshielded twisted pair (UTP)? (Choose three.)

   a. Cable modem

   b. ISDN

   c. DSL modem

   d. POTS dial-up modem

4. How many channels on an E1 circuit are available for voice, video, or data?

   a. 23

   b. 24

   c. 30

   d. 32

5. Which PPP authentication method provides one-way authentication and sends credentials in clear text?

   a. WEP

   b. MS-CHAP

   c. PAP

   d. CHAP

6. What DSL variant has a distance limitation of 18,000 ft. between a DSL modem and its DSLAM?

   a. HDSL

   b. ADSL

   c. SDSL

   d. VDSL

7. What kind of network is used by many cable companies to service their cable modems, and contains both fiber-optic and coaxial cabling?

   a. Head-end

   b. DOCSIS

   c. Composite

   d. HFC

8. What locally significant identifier is used by a Frame Relay network to reference a virtual circuit?

   a. VPI/VCI

   b. DLCI

   c. TEI

   d. MAC

9. How big is the payload portion of an ATM cell?

   a. 5 bytes

   b. 48 bytes

   c. 53 bytes

   d. 64 bytes

10. What is the size of an MPLS header?

   a. 4 bits

   b. 8 bits

   c. 16 bits

   d. 32 bits

After completion of this chapter, you will be able to
answer the following questions:

- How do various *wireless LAN* (WLAN) technologies function, and what wireless standards are in common use?

- What are some of the most important WLAN design considerations?

- What WLAN security risks exist, and how can those risks be mitigated?

CHAPTER 8

Connecting Wirelessly

The popularity of *wireless LANs* (WLAN) has exploded over the past decade, allowing users to roam within a WLAN coverage area, allowing users to take their laptops with them and maintain network connectivity as they move throughout a building or campus environment. Many other devices, however, can take advantage of wireless networks, such as gaming consoles, smart phones, and printers.

This chapter introduces WLAN technology, along with various wireless concepts, components, and standards. WLAN design considerations are then presented, followed by a discussion of WLAN security.

Foundation Topics

Introducing Wireless LANs

This section introduces the basic building blocks of WLANs and discusses how WLANs connect into a wired local-area network (LAN). Various design options, including antenna design, frequencies, and communications channels are discussed, along with a comparison of today's major wireless standards, which are all some variant of IEEE 802.11.

WLAN Concepts and Components

Wireless devices, such as laptops and smart phones, often have a built-in wireless card that allows those devices to communicate on a WLAN. But, what is the device to which they communicate? It could be, as one example, another laptop with a wireless card. This would be an example of an *ad-hoc* WLAN. However, enterprise-class WLANs, and even most WLANs in homes, are configured in such a way that a wireless client connects to some sort of a wireless base station, such as a *wireless access point* (AP) or a *wireless router*.

This communication might be done using a variety of antenna types, frequencies, and communication channels. The following sections consider some of these elements in more detail.

Wireless Routers

Consider the basic WLAN topology shown in Figure 8-1. Such a WLAN might be found in a residence whose Internet access is provided by digital subscriber line (DSL) modem. In this topology, a wireless router and switch are shown as separate components. However, in many residential networks, a wireless router integrates switch ports and wireless routing functionality into a single device.

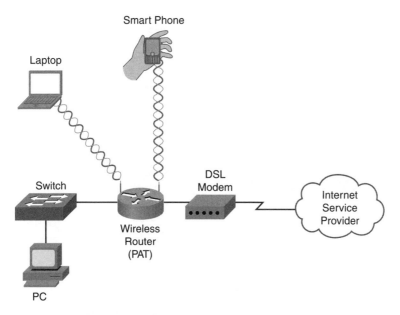

Figure 8-1   Basic WLAN Topology with a Wireless Router

In Figure 8-1, the wireless router obtains an IP address via DHCP from the *Internet service provider* (ISP). Then, the router uses Port Address Translation (PAT), as described in Chapter 6, "Routing Traffic," to provide IP addresses to devices attaching to it wirelessly or through a wired connection. The process through which a wireless client (for example, a laptop or a smart phone) attaches with a wireless router (or wireless AP) is called *association*. All wireless devices associating with a single AP share a collision domain. Therefore, for scalability and performance reasons, WLANs might include multiple APs.

Wireless Access Point

Although a *wireless access point* (AP) interconnects a wired LAN with a WLAN, it does not interconnect two networks (for example, the service provider's network with an internal network). Figure 8-2 shows a typical deployment of an AP.

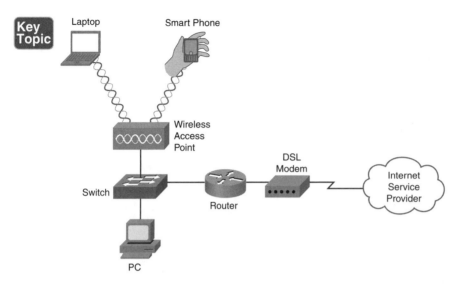

Figure 8-2 Basic WLAN Topology with a Wireless AP

The AP connects to the wired LAN, and the wireless devices that connect to the wired LAN via the AP are on the same subnet as the AP (no Network Address Translation [NAT] or PAT is being performed).

Antennas

The coverage area of a WLAN is largely determined by the type of antenna used on a wireless AP or a wireless router. Although some lower-end, consumer-grade wireless APs have fixed antennas, higher-end, enterprise-class wireless APs often support various antenna types.

Design goals to keep in mind when selecting an antenna include the following:

- Required distance between an AP and a wireless client

- Pattern of coverage area (for example, the coverage area might radiate out in all directions, forming a spherical coverage area around an antenna, or an antenna might provide increased coverage in only one or two directions)

- Indoor or outdoor environment

- Avoiding interference with other APs

The strength of the electromagnetic waves being radiated from an antenna is referred to as *gain*, which involves a measurement of both direction and efficiency of a transmission. For example, the gain measurement for a wireless AP's antenna transmitting a signal is a measurement of how efficiently the power being applied to the antenna is converted into electromagnetic waves being broadcast in a specific direction. Conversely, the gain measurement for a wireless AP's antenna receiving a signal is a measurement of how efficiently the received electromagnetic waves arriving from a specific direction are converted back into electricity leaving the antenna.

Gain is commonly measured using the *dBi* unit of measure. In this unit of measure, the *dB* stands for *decibels* and the *i* stands for *isotropic*. A decibel, in this context, is a ratio of radiated power to a reference value. In the case of dBi, the reference value is the signal strength (power) radiated from an *isotropic antenna*, which represents a theoretical antenna that radiates an equal amount of power in all directions (in a spherical pattern). An isotropic antenna is considered to have gain of 0 dBi.

The most common formula used for antenna gain is the following:

$$GdBi = 10 * \log^{10} (G)$$

Based on this formula, an antenna with a peak power gain of 4 (*G*) would have a gain of 6.02 dBi. Antenna theory can become mathematical (heavily relying on the use of *Maxwell's equations*). However, to put this discussion in perspective, generally speaking, if one antenna has 3 dB more gain than another antenna, it has approximately twice the effective power.

Antennas are classified not just by their gain but also by their coverage area. Two broad categories of antennas, which are based on coverage area, are as follows:

- **Omnidirectional:** An omnidirectional antenna radiates power at relatively equal power levels in all directions (somewhat similar to the theoretical isotropic antenna). Omnidirectional antennas, an example of which is depicted in Figure 8-3, are popular in residential WLANs and small office/home office (SOHO) locations.

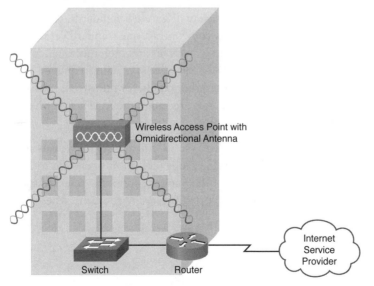

Wireless Access Point with
Omnidirectional Antenna

Switch   Router

Internet
Service
Provider

Figure 8-3 Omnidirectional Antenna Coverage

■ **Unidirectional:** Unidirectional antennas can focus their power in a specific direction, thus avoiding potential interference with other wireless devices and perhaps reaching greater distances than those possible with omnidirectional antennas. One application for unidirectional antennas is interconnecting two nearby buildings, as shown in Figure 8-4.

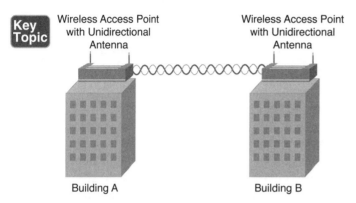

Figure 8-4   Unidirectional Antenna Coverage

Another consideration for antenna installation is the horizontal or vertical orientation of the antenna. For best performance, if two wireless APs communicate with one another, they should have matching antenna orientations, which is referred to as the *polarity* of the antenna.

Frequencies and Channels

Later in this chapter, you are introduced to a variety of wireless standards, which are all variants of the *IEEE 802.11* standard. As you contrast one standard versus another, a characteristic to watch out for is the frequencies at which these standards operate. Although there are some country-specific variations, certain frequency ranges (or *frequency bands*) have been reserved internationally for industrial, scientific, and medical purposes. These frequency bands are called the *ISM bands*, where ISM derives from *i*ndustrial, *s*cientific, and *m*edical.

Two of these bands are commonly used for WLANs. Specifically, WLANs can use the range of frequencies in the 2.4 GHz–2.5 GHz range (commonly referred to as the *2.4-GHz band*) or in the 5.725 GHz–5.875 GHz range (commonly referred to as the *5-GHz band*). In fact, some WLANs support a mixed environment, where 2.4 GHz devices run alongside 5-GHz devices.

Within each band are specific frequencies (or *channels*) at which wireless devices operate. To avoid interference, nearby wireless APs should use frequencies that do not overlap one another. Merely selecting different channels is not sufficient, however, because transmissions on one channel spill over into nearby channels.

As an example, consider the 2.4-GHz band. Here, channel frequencies are separated by 5 MHz (with the exception of channel 14, which has 12 MHz of separation from channel 13). However, a single channel's transmission can spread over a frequency range of 22 MHz. As a result, channels must have five channels of separation (5 * 5 MHz = 25 MHz, which is greater than 22 MHz). You can see from Figure 8-5 that, in the United States, you could select nonoverlapping channels of 1, 6, and 11.

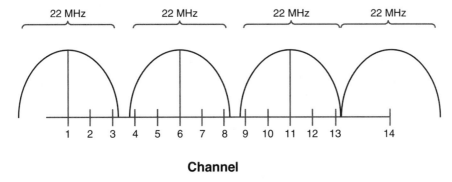

Figure 8-5 Nonoverlapping Channels in the 2.4 GHz Band

NOTE Even though some countries use channel 14 as a nonoverlapping channel, it is not supported in the United States.

As a reference, Table 8-1 shows the specific frequencies for each of the channels in the 2.4-GHz band.

Table 8-1   Channel Frequencies in the 2.4-GHz Band

Channel	Frequency (GHz)	Recommended as a Nonoverlapping Channel
1	2.412	Yes
2	2.417	No
3	2.422	No
4	2.427	No
5	2.432	No
6	2.437	Yes
7	2.442	No
8	2.447	No
9	2.452	No
10	2.457	No
11	2.462	Yes
12	2.467	No
13	2.472	No
14	2.484	Yes (not supported in the United States)

The 5-GHz band has a higher number of channels, as compared to the 2.4-GHz band. Table 8-2 lists the recommended nonoverlapping channels for the 5-GHz band in the United States. Note that additional channels are supported in some countries.

Table 8-2   Nonoverlapping Channels in the 5-GHz Band Recommended for Use in the United States

Channel	Frequency (GHz)
36	5.180
40	5.200
44	5.220
48	5.240
52	5.260*
56	5.280*
60	5.300*
64	5.320*

100	5.500**
104	5.520**
108	5.540**
112	5.560**
116	5.580**
136	5.680**
140	5.700**
149	5.745
153	5.765
157	5.785
161	5.805
165	5.825

*Must support dynamic frequency selection to prevent interference with RADAR

**Must be professionally installed

CSMA/CA

In Chapter 4, "Understanding Ethernet," you learned about Ethernet's *carrier sense multiple access collision detection* (CSMA/CD) technology. WLANs use a similar technology called *carrier sense multiple access collision avoidance* (CSMA/CA). Just as CSMA/CD is needed for half-duplex Ethernet connections, CSMA/CA is needed for WLAN connections, because of their half-duplex operation. Similar to how an Ethernet device listens to an Ethernet segment to determine if a frame exists on the segment, a WLAN device listens for a transmission on a wireless channel to determine if it is safe to transmit. Additionally, the collision avoidance part of the CSMA/CA algorithm causes wireless devices to wait for a random backoff time before transmitting.

Transmission Methods

In the previous discussion, you saw the frequencies used for various wireless channels. However, be aware that those frequencies are considered to be the *center frequencies* of a channel. In actual operation, a channel uses more than one frequency, which is a transmission method called *spread spectrum*. These frequencies are, however, very close to one another, which results in a *narrowband transmission*.

The three variations of spread-spectrum technology to be aware of for your study of WLANs include the following:

- **Direct-sequence spread spectrum (DSSS):** Modulates data over an entire range of frequencies using a series symbols called *chips*. A chip is shorter in duration than a bit, meaning that chips are transmitted at a higher rate than the actual data. These chips not only encode the data to be transmitted, but also what appears to be random data. Although both parties involved in a DSSS communication know which chips represent actual data and which chips do not, if a third party intercepted a DSSS transmission, it would be difficult for him to eavesdrop in on the data, because he would not easily know which chips represented valid bits. DSSS is more subject to environmental factors, as opposed to FHSS and OFDM, because of its use of an entire frequency spectrum.

- **Frequency-hopping spread spectrum (FHSS):** Allows the participants in a communication to hop between predetermined frequencies. Security is enhanced, because the participants can predict the next frequency to be used while a third party cannot easily predict the next frequency. FHSS can also provision extra bandwidth by simultaneously using more than one frequency.

- **Orthogonal frequency division multiplexing (OFDM):** While DSSS used a high modulation rate for the symbols it sends, OFDM uses a relatively slow modulation rate for symbols. This slower modulation rate, combined with the simultaneous transmission of data over 52 data streams, helps OFDM support high data rates while resisting interference between the various data streams.

Of these three wireless modulation techniques, only DSSS and OFDM are commonly used in today's WLANs.

WLAN Standards

Most modern WLAN standards are variations of the original IEEE 802.11 standard, which was developed in 1997. This original standard supported a DSSS and a FHSS implementation, both of which operated in the 2.4-GHz band. However, with supported speeds of 1 Mbps or 2 Mbps, the original 802.11 standard lacks sufficient bandwidth to meet the needs of today's WLANs. The most popular variants of the 802.11 standard in use today are 802.11a, 802.11b, 802.11g, and 802.11n, as described in detail in the following sections.

802.11a

The 802.11a WLAN standard, which was ratified in 1999, supports speeds as high as 54 Mbps. Other supported data rates (which can be used if conditions are not suitable for the 54 Mbps rate) include 6, 9, 12, 18, 24, 36, and 48 Mbps. The 802.11a standard uses the 5-GHz band and uses the OFDM transmission method.

Interestingly, 802.11a never gained widespread adoption, because it was not backwards compatible with 802.11b, while 802.11g was backwards compatible.

802.11b

The 802.11b WLAN standard, which was ratified in 1999, supports speeds as high as 11 Mbps. However, 5.5 Mbps is another supported data rate. The 802.11b standard uses the 2.4-GHz band and uses the DSSS transmission method.

802.11g

The 802.11g WLAN standard, which was ratified in 2003, supports speeds as high as 54 Mbps. Like 802.11a, other supported data rates include 6, 9, 12, 18, 24, 36, and 48 Mbps. However, like 802.11b, 802.11g operates in the 2.4-GHz band, which allows it to offer backwards compatibility to 802.11b devices. 802.11g can use either the OFDM or the DSSS transmission method.

802.11n

The 802.11n WLAN standard, which was ratified in 2009, supports a wide variety of speeds, depending on its implementation. Although the speed of an 802.11n network could exceed 300 Mbps (through the use of *channel bonding*, as discussed later), many 802.11n devices on the market have speed ratings in the 130–150 Mbps range. Interestingly, an 802.11n WLAN could operate in the 2.4 GHz band, the 5-GHz band, or both simultaneously. 802.11n uses the OFDM transmission method.

One way 802.11n achieves superior throughput is through the use of a technology called *multiple input, multiple output* (MIMO). MIMO uses multiple antennas for transmission and reception. These antennas do not interfere with one another, thanks to MIMO's use of *spatial multiplexing*, which encodes data based on the antenna from which the data will be transmitted. Both reliability and throughput can be increased with MIMO's simultaneous use of multiple antennas.

Yet another technology implemented by 802.11n is *channel bonding*. With channel bonding, two wireless bands can be logically bonded together, forming a band with twice the bandwidth of an individual band. Some literature refers to channel bonding as *40-MHz mode*, which refers to the bonding of two adjacent 20-MHz bands into a 40-MHz band.

Table 8-3 acts as a reference to help you contrast the characteristics of the 802.11 standards.

Table 8-3 Characteristics of 802.11 Standards

Standard	Band	Max. Bandwidth	Transmission Method	Max. Range
802.11	2.4 GHz	1 Mbps or 2 Mbps	DSSS or FHSS	20 m indoors/100 m outdoors
802.11a	5 GHz	54 Mbps	OFDM	35 m indoors/120 m outdoors
802.11b	2.4 GHz	11 Mbps	DSSS	32 m indoors/140 m outdoors
802.11g	2.4 GHz	54 Mbps	OFDM or DSSS	32 m indoors/140 m outdoors
802.11n	2.4 GHz or 5 GHz (or both)	> 300 Mbps (with channel bonding)	OFDM	70 m indoors/250 m outdoors

Deploying Wireless LANs

When designing and deploying WLANs, you have a variety of installation options and design considerations. This section delves into your available options and provides you with some best practice recommendations.

Types of WLANs

WLANs can be categorized based on their use of wireless APs. The three main categories are *independent basic service set* (IBSS), *basic service set* (BSS), and *extended service set* (ESS). An IBSS WLAN operates in an *ad-hoc* fashion, while BSS and ESS WLANs operate in *infrastructure mode*. The following sections describe the three types of WLANs in detail.

IBSS

As shown in Figure 8-6, a WLAN can be created without the use of an AP. Such a configuration, called an IBSS, is said to work in an ad-hoc fashion. An ad-hoc WLAN is useful for temporary connections between wireless devices. For example, you might temporarily interconnect two laptop computers to transfer a few files.

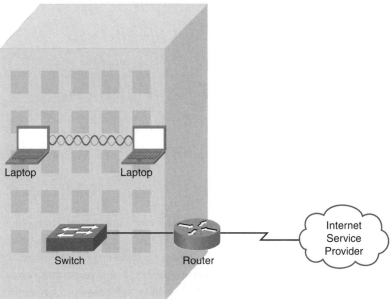

Figure 8-6   Independent Basic Service Set (IBSS) WLAN

BSS

Figure 8-7 depicts a WLAN using a single AP. WLANs that have just one AP are called BSS WLANs. BSS WLANs are said to run in infrastructure mode, because wireless clients connect to an AP, which is typically connected to a wired network infrastructure. A BSS network is often used in residential and SOHO locations, where the signal strength provided by a single AP is sufficient to service all the WLAN's wireless clients.

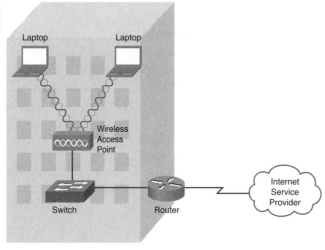

Figure 8-7   Basic Service Set (BSS) WLAN

ESS

Figure 8-8 illustrates a WLAN using two APs. WLANs containing more than one AP are called ESS WLANs. Like BSS WLANs, ESS WLANs operate in infrastructure mode. When you have more than one AP, take care to prevent one AP from interfering with another. Specifically, the previously discussed nonoverlapping channels (channels 1, 6, and 11 for the 2.4-GHz band) should be selected for adjacent wireless coverage areas.

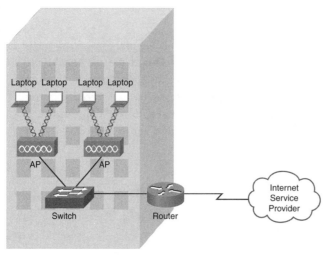

Figure 8-8   Extended Service Set (ESS) WLAN

Sources of Interference

A major issue for WLANs is *radio frequency interference* (RFI) caused by other devices using similar frequencies to the WLAN devices. Also, physical obstacles can impede or reflect WLAN transmissions. The following are some of the most common sources of interference:

- **Other WLAN devices:** Earlier in this chapter, you read about nonoverlapping channels for both the 2.4-GHz and 5-GHz bands. However, if two or more WLAN devices are in close proximity and use overlapping channels, those devices could interfere with one another.

- **Cordless phones:** Several models of cordless phones operate in the 2.4-GHz band and can interfere with WLAN devices. However, if you need cordless phones to coexist in an environment with WLAN devices using the 2.4-GHz band, consider the use of *digital enhanced cordless telecommunications* (DECT) cordless phones. Although the exact frequencies used by DECT cordless phones vary based on country, DECT cordless phones do not use the 2.4-GHz band. For example, in the United States, DECT cordless phones use frequencies in the range 1.92 GHz–1.93 GHz.

- **Microwave ovens:** Older microwave ovens, which might not have sufficient shielding, can emit relatively high-powered signals in the 2.4-GHz band, resulting in significant interference with WLAN devices operating in the 2.4-GHz band.

- **Wireless security system devices:** Most wireless security cameras operate in 2.4-GHz frequency range, which can cause potential issues with WLAN devices.

- **Physical obstacles:** In electromagnetic theory, radio waves cannot propagate through a perfect conductor. So, although metal filing cabinets and large appliances are not perfect conductors, they are sufficient to cause degradation of a WLAN signal. For example, a WLAN signal might hit a large air conditioning unit, causing the radio waves to be reflected and scattered in multiple directions. Not only does this limit the range of the WLAN signal, but radio waves carrying data might travel over different paths. This *multipath* issue can cause data corruption.

- **Signal strength:** The range of a WLAN device is a function of the device's signal strength. Lower-cost consumer-grade APs do not typically allow an administrative adjustment of signal strength. However, enterprise-class APs often allow signal strength to be adjusted to assure sufficient coverage of a specific area, while avoiding interference with other APs using the same channel.

As you can see from this list, most RFI occurs in the 2.4-GHz band as opposed to the 5-GHz band. Therefore, depending on the wireless clients you need to support, you might consider using the 5-GHz band, which is an option for 802.11a and 802.11n WLANs.

Wireless AP Placement

WLANs using more than one AP (an ESS WLAN) require careful planning to prevent the APs from interfering with one another, while still servicing a desired coverage area. Specifically, an overlap of coverage between APs should exist to allow uninterrupted roaming from one WLAN *cell* (which is the coverage area provided by an AP) to another. However, those overlapping coverage areas should not use overlapping frequencies.

Figure 8-9 shows how nonoverlapping channels in the 2.4-GHz band can overlap their coverage areas to provide seamless roaming between AP coverage areas. A common WLAN design recommendation is to have a 10–15 percent overlap of coverage between adjoining cells.

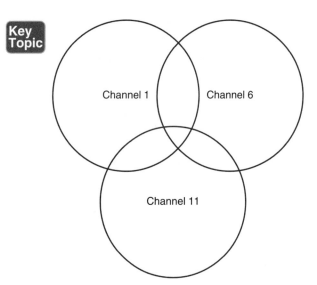

Figure 8-9   10–15 Percent Coverage Overlap in Coverage Areas for Nonoverlapping Channels

If a WLAN has more than three APs, the APs can be deployed in a honeycomb fashion to allow an overlap of AP coverage areas while avoiding an overlap of identical channels. The example shown in Figure 8-10 shows an approach to channel selection for adjoining cells in the 2.4-GHz band. Notice that cells using the same nonoverlapping channels (channels 1, 6, and 11) are separated by another cell. For example, notice that none of the cells using channel 11 overlap another cell using channel 11.

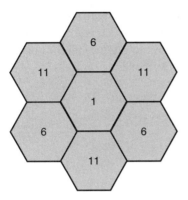

Figure 8-10   Nonoverlapping Coverage Cells for the 2.4-GHz Band

NOTE   Although a honeycomb channel assignment scheme can be used for the 5-GHz band, identical channels should be separated by at least two cells, rather than the single cell shown for the 2.4 GHz band.

Securing Wireless LANs

WLANs introduce some unique concerns to your network. For example, improperly installed wireless APs are roughly equivalent to putting an Ethernet port in a building's parking lot, where someone can drive up and access to your network. Fortunately, a variety of features are available to harden the security of your WLAN, as discussed in this section.

Security Issues

In the days when dial-up modems were popular, malicious users could run a program on their computer to call all phone numbers in a certain number range. Phone numbers that answered with modem tone became targets for later attacks. This type of reconnaissance was known as *war dialing*. A modern-day variant of war dialing is *war driving*, where potentially malicious users drive around looking for unsecured WLANs. These users might be identifying unsecured WLANs for nefarious purposes or simply looking for free Internet access.

Other WLAN security threats include the following:

- **Warchalking:** Once an open WLAN (or a WLAN whose SSID and authentication credentials are known) is found in a public place, a user might write a symbol on a wall (or some other nearby structure), to let others know the characteristics of the discovered network. This practice, which is a variant of the decades-old practice of hobos leaving symbols as messages to fellow hobos, is called *warchalking*. Figure 8-11 shows common warchalking symbols.

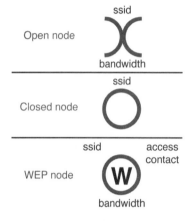

Figure 8-11 Warchalking Symbols

- **WEP and WPA security cracking:** As discussed later in this chapter, various security standards are available for encrypting and authenticating a WLAN client with an AP. Two of the less secure standards include *Wired Equivalent Privacy* (WEP) and *Wi-Fi Protected Access* (WPA). Although WPA is considered more secure than WEP, utilities are available on the Internet for cracking each of these approaches to wireless security. By collecting enough packets transmitted by a secure AP, these cracking utilities can use mathematical algorithms to determine the *preshared key* (PSK) configured on a wireless AP, with which an associating wireless client must also be configured.

- **Rogue access point:** A malicious user could set up his own AP to which legitimate users would connect. Such an AP is called a *rogue access point*. That malicious user could then use a *packet sniffer* (which displays information about unencrypted traffic, including the traffic's data and header information) to eavesdrop on communications flowing through their AP. To cause unsuspecting users to connect to the rogue AP, the malicious user could configure the rogue AP with the same *service set identifier* (SSID) as used by a legitimate AP. When a rogue AP is configured with the SSID of legitimate AP, the rogue AP is commonly referred to as an *evil twin*.

> **NOTE**   An SSID is a string of characters identifying a WLAN. APs participating in the same WLAN (in an ESS) can be configured with identical SSIDs. An SSID shared among multiple APs is called an *extended service set identifier* (ESSID).

Approaches to WLAN Security

A WLAN that does not require any authentication or provide any encryption for wireless devices (for example, a publicly available WLAN found in many airports) is said to be using *open authentication*. To protect WLAN traffic from eavesdroppers, a variety of security standards and practices have been developed, including the following:

- **MAC address filtering:** An AP can be configured with a listing of MAC addresses that are permitted to associate with the AP. If a malicious user attempts to connect via his laptop (whose MAC address is not on the list of trusted MAC addresses), that user is denied access. One drawback to MAC address filtering is the administrative overhead required to keep an approved list of MAC addresses up-to-date. Another issue with MAC address filtering is that a knowledgeable user could falsify the MAC address of his wireless network card, making his device appear to be approved.

- **Disabling SSID broadcast:** An SSID can be broadcast by an AP to let users know the name of the WLAN. For security purposes, an AP might be configured not to broadcast its SSID. However, knowledgeable users could still determine the SSID of an AP by examining captured packets.

- **Preshared key:** To encrypt transmission between a wireless client and an AP (in addition to authenticating a wireless client with an AP), both the wireless client and the AP could be preconfigured with a matching string of characters (a *preshared key* [PSK], as previously described). The PSK could be used as part of a mathematical algorithm to encrypt traffic, such that if an eavesdropper intercepted in the encrypted traffic, he would not be able to decrypt the traffic without knowing the PSK. Although using a PSK can be effective in providing security for a small network (for example, a SOHO network), it lacks scalability. For example, in a large corporate environment, a PSK being compromised would necessitate the reconfiguration of all devices configured with that PSK.

> **NOTE**   WLAN security based on a PSK technology is called *personal mode*.

■ **IEEE 802.1X:** Rather than having all devices in a WLAN be configured with the same PSK, a more scalable approach is to require all wireless users to authenticate using their own credentials (for example, a username and password). Allowing each user to have his own set of credentials prevents the compromising of one password from impacting the configuration of all wireless devices. *IEEE 802.1x* is a technology that allows wireless clients to authenticate with an authentication server (typically, a *Remote Authentication Dial-In User Service* [RADIUS] server).

NOTE   WLAN security based on IEEE 802.1x is called *enterprise mode*.

Chapter 4 discussed IEEE 802.1x in detail and described the role of a *supplicant*, an *authenticator*, and an *authentication server*; however, Chapter 4 showed how IEEE 802.1x was used in a wired network. Figure 8-12 shows a wireless implementation of IEEE 8021x.

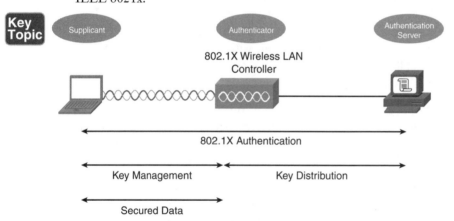

Figure 8-12   IEEE 802.1x Security for a WLAN

NOTE   IEEE 802.1x works in conjunction with an *Extensible Authentication Protocol* (EAP) to perform its job of authentication. A variety of EAP types exist, including *Lightweight Extensible Authentication Protocol* (LEAP), *EAP-Flexible Authentication via Secure Tunneling* (EAP-FAST), *EAP-Transport Layer Security* (EAP-TLS), *Protected EAP–Generic Token Card* (PEAP-GTC), and *Protected EAP–Microsoft Challenge Hand- shake Authentication Protocol version 2* (PEAP-MSCHAPv2). Although these EAP types differ in their procedures, the overriding goal for each EAP type is to securely authenticate a supplicant and provide the supplicant and the authenticator a *session key* that can be used during a single session in the calculation of security algorithms (for example, encryption algorithms).

Security Standards

When configuring a wireless client for security, the most common security standards from which you can select are as follows:

- Wired Equivalent Privacy (WEP)

- Wi-Fi Protected Access (WPA)

- Wi-Fi Protected Access version 2 (WPA2)

The following sections describe these standards in detail.

WEP

The original 802.11 standard did address security; however, the security was a WEP key. With WEP, an AP is configured with a static WEP key. Wireless clients needing to associate with an AP are configured with an identical key (making this a PSK approach to security). The 802.11 standard specifies a 40-bit WEP key, which is considered to be a relatively weak security measure.

Because a WEP key is a static string of characters, it could be compromised with a brute-force attack, where an attacker attempts all possible character combinations until a match for the WEP key is found. Another concern, however, is that WEP uses *RC4* as its encryption algorithm.

NOTE   RC4 (which stands for *Ron's Code* or *Rivest Cipher*, because it was developed by Ron Rivest of RSA Security) is sometimes pronounced *arc 4*.

RC4 uses a 24-bit *initialization vector* (IV), which is a string of characters added to the transmitted data, such that the same plain text data frame will never appear as the same WEP-encrypted data frame. However, the IV is transmitted in clear text. So, if a malicious user, using packet-capture software, captures enough packets having the same WEP key, and because the malicious user can see the IV in clear text, he can use a mathematical algorithm (which can be performed with WEP-cracking software found on the Internet) to determine the static WEP key.

Some WEP implementations support the use of a longer WEP key (for example, 128 bits instead of 40 bits), making a WEP key more difficult to crack; however, both the wireless clients and their AP must support the longer WEP key.

WPA

The Wi-Fi Alliance (a nonprofit organization formed to certify interoperability of wireless devices) developed its own security standard, WPA, to address the weaknesses of WEP. Some of the security enhancements offered by WPA include the following:

- WPA operating in enterprise mode can require a user to be authenticated before keys are exchanged.

- In enterprise mode, the keys used between a wireless client and an access point are temporary session keys.

- WPA uses *Temporal Key Integrity Protocol* (TKIP) for enhanced encryption. Although TKIP does rely on an initialization vector, the IV is expanded from WEP's 24-bit IV to a 48-bit IV. Also, broadcast key rotation can be used, which causes a key to change so quickly, an eavesdropper would not have time to exploit a derived key.

- TKIP leverages *Message Integrity Check* (MIC), which is sometimes referred to as *Message Integrity Code* (MIC). MIC can confirm that data was not modified in transit.

Although not typically written as WPA1, when you see the term *WPA*, consider it to be WPA version 1 (WPA1). WPA version 2, however, is written as *WPA2*.

WPA2

In 2004, the *IEEE 802.11i* standard was approved, and required stronger algorithms for encryption and integrity checking than those seen in previous WLAN security protocols such as WEP and WPA. The requirements set forth in the IEEE 802.11i standard are implemented in the Wi-Fi Alliance's *WPA version 2* (WPA2) security standard. WPA2 uses *Counter Mode with Cipher Block Chaining Message Authentication Code Protocol* (CCMP) for integrity checking and *Advanced Encryption Standard* (AES) for encryption.

Summary

The main topics covered in this chapter are the following:

- Various components, technologies, and terms used in WLANs were identified.

- WLAN design considerations were presented, such as the selection of WLAN standards, bands, and nonoverlapping channels. Potential sources of interference were also identified.

- Some of the security risks posed by a WLAN were described and the technologies available for mitigating those risks were presented.

Exam Preparation Tasks

Review All the Key Topics

Review the most important topics from inside the chapter, noted with the Key Topic icon in the outer margin of the page. Table 8-4 lists these key topics and the page numbers where each is found.

Table 8-4   Key Topics for Chapter 8

Key Topic Element	Description	Page Number
Figure 8-1	Basic WLAN topology with a wireless router	259
Figure 8-2	Basic WLAN topology with a wireless access point	260
Figure 8-3	Omnidirectional antenna coverage	261
Figure 8-4	Unidirectional antenna coverage	262
Figure 8-5	Nonoverlapping channels in the 2.4-GHz band	263
List	Spread spectrum transmission methods	266
Table 8-3	Characteristics of 802.11 standards	268
Figure 8-6	Independent basic service set (IBSS) WLAN	269
Figure 8-7	Basic service set (IBSS) WLAN	270
Figure 8-8	Extended service set (ESS) WLAN	270
List	Sources of interference	271
Figure 8-9	10–15 percent coverage overlap in coverage areas for nonoverlapping channels	272
Figure 8-10	Nonoverlapping coverage cells for the 2.4-GHz band	273
List	Wireless security threats	274
List	Security standards and best practices	275
Figure 8-12	IEEE 802.1x security for a WLAN	276

Complete Tables and Lists from Memory

Print a copy of Appendix C, "Memory Tables" (found on the CD), or at least the section for this chapter, and complete the tables and lists from memory. Appendix D, "Memory Table Answer Key," also on the CD, includes the completed tables and lists so you can check your work.

Define Key Terms

Define the following key terms from this chapter, and check your answers in the Glossary:

wireless access point (AP), wireless router, decibel (dB), omnidirectional antenna, unidirectional antenna, carrier sense multiple access collision avoidance (CSMA/CA), direct-sequence spread spectrum (DSSS), frequency-hopping spread spectrum (FHSS), Orthogonal Frequency Division Multiplexing (OFDM), 802.11a, 802.11b, 802.11g, 802.11n, multiple input, multiple output (MIMO), channel bonding, independent basic service set (IBSS), basic service set (BSS), extended service set (ESS), warchalking, service set identifier (SSID), Wired Equivalent Privacy (WEP), Wi-Fi Protected Access (WPA), Wi-Fi Protected Access version 2 (WPA2)

Review Questions

The answers to these review questions are in Appendix A, "Answers to Review Questions."

1. What type of antenna, commonly used in wireless APs and wireless routers in SOHO locations, radiates relatively equal power in all directions?

   a. Unidirectional

   b. Yagi

   c. Parabolic

   d. Omnidirectional

2. When using the 2.4-GHz band for multiple access points in a WLAN located in the United States, which nonoverlapping channels should you select? (Choose three.)

   a. 0

   b. 1

   c. 5

   d. 6

e. 10

f. 11

g. 14

3. What technology do WLANs use to determine when they gain access to the wireless media?

   a. SPF

   b. CSMA/CA

   c. RSTP

   d. DUAL

4. What IEEE 802.11 variant supports a maximum speed of 54 Mbps and uses the 2.4-GHz band?

   a. 802.11a

   b. 802.11b

   c. 802.11g

   d. 802.11n

5. Which of the following is used by IEEE 802.11n to achieve high throughput through the use of multiple antennas for transmission and reception?

   a. MIMO

   b. DSSS

   c. FHSS

   d. LACP

6. A WLAN formed directly between wireless clients (without the use of a wireless AP) is referred to as what type of WLAN?

   a. Enterprise mode

   b. IBSS

   c. Personal mode

   d. BSS

7. When extended the range for a 2.4-GHz WLAN, you can use nonoverlapping channels for adjacent coverage cells. However, there should be some overlap in coverage between those cells (using nonoverlapping channels) to prevent a connection from dropping as a user roams from one coverage cell to another. What percentage of coverage overlap is recommended for these adjacent cells?

   a. 5–10 percent

   b. 10–15 percent

   c. 15–20 percent

   d. 20–25 percent

8. If a WLAN does not require a user to provide any credentials to associate with a wireless AP and access the WLAN, what type of authentication is said to be in use?

   a. WEP

   b. SSID

   c. Open

   d. IV

9. WEP's RC4 approach to encryption uses a 24-bit string of characters added to transmitted data, such that the same plain text data frame will never appear as the same WEP-encrypted data frame. What is this string of characters called?

   a. Initialization vector

   b. Chips

   c. Orthogonal descriptor

   d. Session key

10. What standard developed by the Wi-Fi Alliance implements the requirements of IEEE 802.11i?

   a. TKIP

   b. MIC

   c. WEP

   d. WPA2

Upon completion of this chapter, you will be able to
answer the following questions:

- Why is high availability a requirement in today's network designs, and
  what mechanisms can help provide that high availability?

- What various technologies optimize network performance?

- What QoS mechanisms can help optimize network performance?

- Using what you have learned in this and previous chapters, how do you
  design a SOHO network based on a set of requirements?

CHAPTER 9

Optimizing Network Performance

If you saw the movie *The Field of Dreams*, you've heard this statement: "If you build it, they will come." That statement has proven itself to be true in today's networks. These networks, which were once relegated to the domain of data, can now carry voice and video. These additional media types, in addition to mission-critical data applications, need a network to be up and available for its users.

For example, think about how often your telephone service has been unavailable versus how often your data network has been unavailable. Unfortunately, data networks have traditionally been less reliable than voice networks; however, today's data networks often *are* voice networks, contributing to this increased demand for uptime.

Beyond basic availability, today's networks need optimization tools to make the most of their available bandwidth. This book already addressed several network optimization tools, which are reviewed in this chapter.

Quality of service (QoS) is an entire category of network-optimization tools. QoS, as one example, can give priority treatment to *latency-sensitive* (delay-sensitive) traffic, such as Voice over IP (VoIP). This chapter devotes a section to exploring these tools.

Finally, based on what you learn in this chapter and what you have learned in previous chapters, you are presented with a design challenge. Specifically, a case study presents various design requirements for a small office/home office (SOHO) network. After you create your own network design, you can compare your solution with a suggested solution, keeping in mind that multiple solutions are valid.

Foundation Topics

High Availability

If a network switch or router stops operating correctly (meaning that a *network fault* occurs), communication through the network could be disrupted, resulting in a network becoming unavailable to its users. Therefore, network availability, called *uptime*, is a major design consideration. This consideration might, for example, lead you to add fault-tolerant devices and fault-tolerant links between those devices. This section discusses the measurement of high availability along with a collection of high-availability design considerations.

High-Availability Measurement

The availability of a network is measured by its uptime during a year. For example, if a network has *five nines* of availability, it is up 99.999 percent of the time, which translates to a maximum of 5 minutes of downtime per year. If a network has *six nines* of availability (it's up 99.9999 percent of the time), it is down less than 30 seconds per year.

As a designer, one of your goals is to select components, topologies, and features that maximize network availability within certain parameters (for example, a budget). Be careful not to confuse *availability* with *reliability*. A *reliable* network, as an example, does not drop many packets. However, an *available* network is up and operational.

NOTE   The availability of a network increases as the *mean time to repair* (MTTR) of the network devices decreases and as the *mean time between failures* (MTBF) increases. Therefore, selecting reliable networking devices that are quick to repair is crucial to a high-availability design.

Fault-Tolerant Network Design

Two approaches to designing a fault-tolerant network include the following:

- **Single points of failure:** If the failure of a single network device or link (for example, a switch, router, or WAN connection) would result in a network becoming unavailable, that single device or link is a potential *single point of failure*. To eliminate single points of failure from your design, you might include redundant links and redundant hardware. For example, some high-end Ethernet switches support two power supplies, and if one power supply fails, the switch continues to operate by using the backup power supply. Port redundancy and link redundancy, as shown in Figure 9-1, can be achieved by interconnecting network infrastructure components using more than one physical link. So, even if a switch or router completely failed, the network would go down, a network with these single points of failure can still offer redundancy.

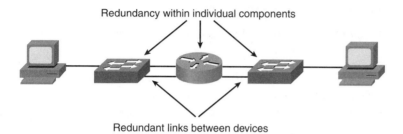

Figure 9-1   Redundant Network with Single Points of Failure

■ **No single points of failure:** A network without any single point of failure contains redundant network-infrastructure components (for example, switches and routers). Additionally, these redundant devices are interconnected with redundant links. Although a network host could have two network interface cards (NIC), each of which connects to a different switch, such a design is rarely implemented because of the increased costs. Instead, as shown in Figure 9-2, a network with no single points of failure in the backbone allows any single switch or router in the backbone to fail or any single link in the backbone to fail, while maintaining end-to-end network connectivity.

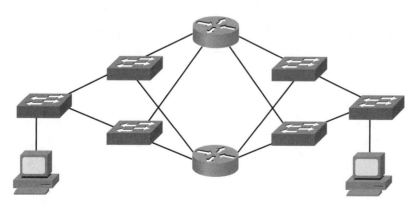

Figure 9-2   Redundant Network with No Single Point of Failure

These two approaches to fault-tolerant network design can be used together to increase a network's availability even further.

Hardware Redundancy

Having redundant route processors in a switch or router chassis improves the chassis' reliability. If, for example, a multilayer switch has two route processors, one of the route processors could be active, with the other route processor standing by to take over in the event the active processor became unavailable.

An end system can have redundant NICs. The two modes of NIC redundancy are as follows:

- **Active-active:** Both NICs are active at the same time, and they each have their own MAC address. This makes troubleshooting more complex, while giving you slightly better performance than the Active-Standby approach.

- **Active-standby:** Only one NIC is active at a time. This approach allows the client to appear to have a single MAC address and IP address, even in the event of a NIC failure.

NIC redundancy is most often found in strategic network hosts, rather than in end-user client computers, because of the expense and administrative overhead incurred with a redundant NIC configuration.

Layer 3 Redundancy

End systems, not running a routing protocol, point to a default gateway. The default gateway is traditionally the IP address of a router on the local subnet. However, if the default gateway router fails, the end systems are unable to leave their subnet. Chapter 4, "Understanding Ethernet," introduced two first-hop redundancy technologies (which offer Layer 3 redundancy):

- **Hot Standby Router Protocol (HSRP):** A Cisco proprietary approach to first-hop redundancy. Figure 9-3 shows a sample HSRP topology.

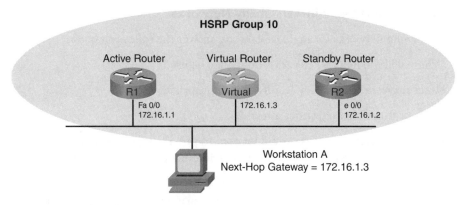

Figure 9-3 HSRP Sample Topology

In Figure 9-3, workstation A is configured with a default gateway (that is, a next-hop gateway) of 172.16.1.3. To prevent the default gateway from becoming a single point of failure, HSRP enables routers R1 and R2 to each act as the default gateway, although only one of the routers will act as the default gateway at any one time. Under normal conditions, router R1 (that is, the *active router*) forwards packets sent to 172.16.1.3. However, if router R1 is unavailable, router R2 (that is, the *standby router*) can take over and start forwarding traffic sent to 172.16.1.3. Notice that neither router R1 nor R2 have a physical interface with an IP address of 172.16.1.3. Instead, a logical router (called a *virtual router*), which is serviced by either router R1 or R2, maintains the 172.16.1.3 IP address.

- **Common Address Redundancy Protocol (CARP):** CARP is an open-standard variant of HSRP.

With each of these technologies, the MAC address and the IP address of a default gateway can be serviced by more than one router (or multilayer switch). Therefore, if a default gateway becomes unavailable, the other router (or multilayer switch) can take over, still servicing the same MAC and IP addresses.

Another type of Layer 3 redundancy is achieved by having multiple links between devices and selecting a routing protocol that load balances over the links. Link Aggregation Control Protocol (LACP), discussed in Chapter 4, enables you to assign multiple physical links to a logical interface, which appears as a single link to a route processor. Figure 9-4 illustrates a network topology using LACP.

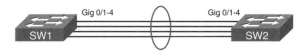

Figure 9-4 LACP Sample Topology

Design Considerations for High-Availability Networks

When designing networks for high availability, answer the following questions:

- Where will module and chassis redundancy be used?

- What software redundancy features are appropriate?

- What protocol characteristics affect design requirements?

- What redundancy features should be used to provide power to an infrastructure device (for example, using an uninterruptable power supply [UPS] or a generator)?

- What redundancy features should be used to maintain environmental conditions (for example, dual air-conditioning units)?

> **NOTE**   Module redundancy provides redundancy within a chassis by allowing one module to take over in the event that a primary module fails. Chassis redundancy provides redundancy by having more than one chassis, thus providing a path from the source to destination, even in the event of a chassis or link failure.

High-Availability Best Practices

The following steps are five best practices for designing high-availability networks:

1. Examine technical goals.

2. Identify the budget to fund high-availability features.

3. Categorize business applications into profiles, each of which require a certain level of availability.

4. Establish performance standards for high-availability solutions.

5. Define how to manage and measure the high-availability solution.

Although existing networks can be retrofitted to make them highly available networks, network designers can often reduce such expenses by integrating high-availability best practices and technologies into the initial design of a network.

Content Caching

Chapter 3, "Identifying Network Components," introduced the concept of a *content engine* (also known as a *caching engine*). A content engine is a network appliance that can receive a copy of content stored elsewhere (for example, a video presentation located on a server at a corporate headquarters) and serve that content to local clients, thus reducing the bandwidth burden on an IP WAN. Figure 9-5 shows a sample topology using a content engine as a network optimization technology.

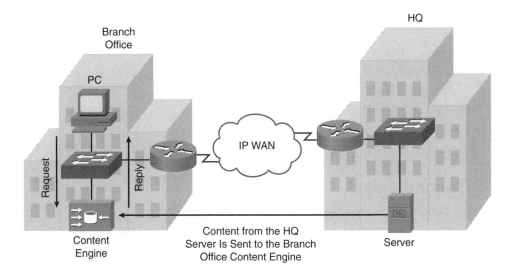

Figure 9-5   Content Engine Sample Topology

Load Balancing

Another network optimization technology introduced in Chapter 3 was *content switching*, which allows a request coming into a server farm to be distributed across multiple servers containing identical content. This approach to load balancing lightens the load on individual servers in a server farm and allows servers to be taken out of the farm for maintenance without disrupting access to the server farm's data. Figure 9-6 illustrates a sample content switching topology, which performs load balancing across five servers (containing identical content) in a server farm.

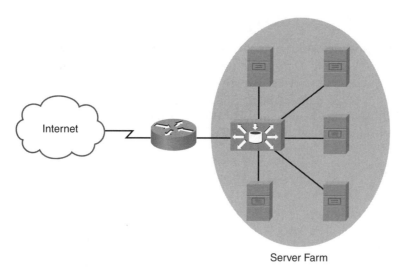

Figure 9-6   Content Switching Sample Topology

QoS Technologies

Quality of service (QoS) is a suite of technologies that allows you to strategically optimize network performance for select traffic types. For example, in today's converged networks (that is, networks simultaneously transporting voice, video, and data), some applications (for example, voice) might be more intolerant of delay (that is, *latency*) than other applications (for example, an FTP file transfer is less latency sensitive than a Voice over IP [VoIP] call). Fortunately, through the use of QoS technologies, you can identify which traffic types need to be sent first, how much bandwidth to allocate to various traffic types, which traffic types should be dropped first in the event of congestion, and how to make the most efficient use of the relatively limited bandwidth of an IP WAN. This section introduces QoS and a collection QoS of mechanisms.

Introduction to QoS

A lack of bandwidth is the overshadowing issue for most quality problems. Specifically, when there is a lack of bandwidth, packets might suffer from one or more of the symptoms shown in Table 9-1.

Table 9-1   Three Categories of Quality Issues

Issue	Description
Delay	Delay is the time required for a packet to travel from its source to its destination. You might have witnessed delay on the evening news, when the news anchor is talking via satellite to a foreign news correspondent. Because of the satellite delay, the conversation begins to feel unnatural.
Jitter	Jitter is the uneven arrival of packets. For example, imagine a VoIP conversation where packet 1 arrives at a destination router. Then, 20 ms later, packet 2 arrives. After another 70 ms, packet 3 arrives, and then packet 4 arrives 20 ms behind packet 3. This variation in arrival times (that is, variable delay) is not dropping packets, but this jitter might be interpreted by the listener as dropped packets.
Drops	Packet drops occur when a link is congested and a router's interface queue overflows. Some types of traffic, such as UDP traffic carrying voice packets, are not retransmitted if packets are dropped.

Fortunately, QoS features available on many routers and switches can recognize important traffic and then treat that traffic in a special way. For example, you might want to allocate 128 kbps of bandwidth for your VoIP traffic and give that traffic priority treatment.

Consider water flowing through a series of pipes with varying diameters. The water's flow rate through those pipes is limited to the water's flow rate through the pipe with the smallest diameter. Similarly, as a packet travels from its source to its destination, its effective bandwidth is the bandwidth of the slowest link along that path. For example, consider Figure 9-7. Notice that the slowest link speed is 256 kbps. This weakest link becomes the effective bandwidth between client and server.

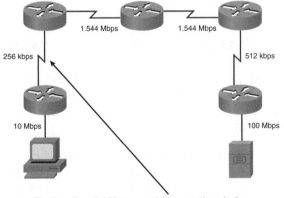

The "weakest link" between the two stations is the "effective bandwidth" between those stations.

Figure 9-7   Effective Bandwidth of 256 kbps

Because the primary challenge QoS is a lack of bandwidth, the logical question is, "How do we increase available bandwidth?" A knee-jerk response to that question is often, "Add more bandwidth." Although there is no substitute for more bandwidth, it often comes at a relatively high cost.

Compare your network to a highway system in a large city. During rush hour, the lanes of the highway are congested, but the lanes might be underutilized during other periods of the day. Instead of just building more lanes to accommodate peak traffic rates, the highway engineers might add a carpool lane. Cars with two or more riders can use the reserved carpool lane. These cars have a higher priority on the highway. Similarly, you can use QoS features to give your mission-critical applications higher-priority treatment in times of network congestion.

QoS Configuration Steps

The mission statement of QoS could read something like, "To categorize traffic and apply a policy to those traffic categories, in accordance with a QoS policy." Understanding this underlying purpose of QoS can help you better understand the three basic steps to QoS configuration:

1. Determine network performance requirements for various traffic types. For example, consider these design recommendations for voice, video, and data traffic:

   - **Voice:** No more than 150 ms of one-way delay; no more than 30 ms of jitter; and no more than 1 percent packet loss.

   - **Video:** No more than 150 ms of one-way delay for interactive voice applications (for example, video conferencing); no more than 30 ms of jitter; no more than 1 percent packet loss.

   - **Data:** Applications have varying delay and loss requirements. Therefore, data applications should be categorized into predefined *classes* of traffic, where each class is configured with specific delay and loss characteristics.

2. Categorize traffic into specific categories. For example, you might have a category named *Low Delay*, and you decide to place voice and video packets in that category. You might also have a *Low Priority* class, where you place traffic such as music downloads from the Internet.

3. Document your QoS policy and make it available to your users. Then, for example, if a user complains that his network-gaming applications are running slowly, you can point him to your corporate QoS policy, which describes how applications such as network gaming have *best-effort* treatment while VoIP traffic receives *priority* treatment.

The actual implementation of these steps varies based on the specific device you are configuring. In some cases, you might be using the command-line interface (CLI) of a router or switch. In other cases, you might have some sort of graphical-user interface (GUI) through which you configure QoS on your routers and switches.

QoS Components

QoS features are categorized into one of the three categories shown in Table 9-2.

Table 9-2 Three Categories of QoS Mechanisms

Issue	Description
Best-effort	Best-effort treatment of traffic does not truly provide QoS to that traffic, because there is no reordering of packets. Best-effort uses a *first-in, first-out* (FIFO) queuing strategy, where packets are emptied from a queue in the same order that they entered the queue.
Integrated Services (IntServ)	IntServ is often referred to as *hard QoS*, because it can make strict bandwidth reservations. IntServ uses signaling among network devices to provide bandwidth reservations. *Resource Reservation Protocol* (RSVP) is an example of an IntServ approach to QoS. Because IntServ must be configured on every router along a packet's path, the main drawback of IntServ is its lack of scalability.
Differentiated services	DiffServ, as its name suggests, differentiates between multiple traffic flows. Specifically, packets are *marked*, and routers and switches can then make decisions (for example, dropping or forwarding decisions) based on those markings. Because DiffServ does not make an explicit reservation, it is often called *soft QoS*. Most modern QoS configurations are based on the DiffServ approach.

Figure 9-8 summarizes these three QoS categories.

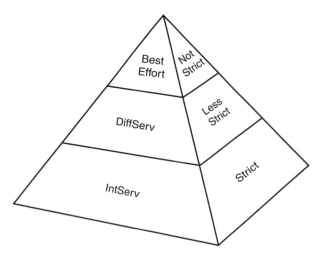

Figure 9-8 QoS Categories

QoS Mechanisms

As previously mentioned, a DiffServ approach to QoS marks traffic. However, for markings to impact the behavior of traffic, a QoS tool must reference those markings and alter the packets' treatment based on them. The following is a collection of commonly used QoS mechanisms:

- Classification
- Marking
- Congestion management
- Congestion avoidance
- Policing and shaping
- Link efficiency

The following sections describe each QoS mechanism in detail.

Classification

Classification is the process of placing traffic into different categories. Multiple characteristics can be used for classification. For example, POP3, IMAP, SMTP, and Exchange traffic could all be placed in an *E-MAIL* class. Classification does not, however, alter any bits in the frame or packet.

Marking

Marking alters bits within a frame, cell, or packet to indicate how the network should treat that traffic. Marking alone does not change how the network treats a packet. Other tools (such as queuing tools) can, however, reference those markings and make decisions based on the markings.

Various packet markings exist. For example, inside an IPv4 header, there is a byte called the *type of service* (ToS) byte. You can mark packets, using bits within the ToS byte, using either *IP Precedence* or *Differentiated Service Code Point* (DSCP) markings, as shown in Figure 9-9.

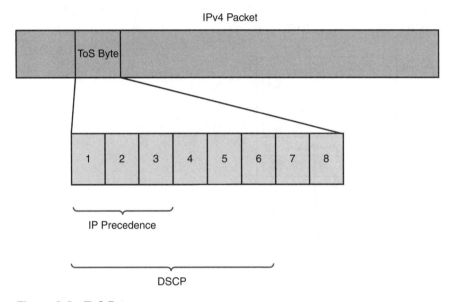

Figure 9-9 ToS Byte

IP Precedence uses the three left-most bits in the ToS byte. With 3 bits at its disposal, IP Precedence markings can range from 0–7. However, 6 and 7 should not be used, because those values are reserved for network use.

For more granularity, you might choose DSCP, which uses the six left-most bits in the ToS byte. Six bits yield 64 possible values (0–63).

Congestion Management

When a device, such as a switch or a router, receives traffic faster than it can be transmitted, the device attempts to buffer (or store) the extra traffic until bandwidth becomes available. This buffering process is called *queuing* or *congestion management*. However, queuing algorithms (for example, weighted fair queuing [WFQ], low latency queuing [LLQ], or weighted round robin [WRR]) can be configured on routers and switches. These algorithms divide an interface's buffer into multiple logical queues, as shown in Figure 9-10. The queuing algorithm then empties packets from those logical queues in a sequence and amount determined by the algorithm's configuration. For example, traffic could first be sent from a priority queue (which might contain VoIP packets) up to a certain bandwidth limit, after which packets could be sent from a different queue.

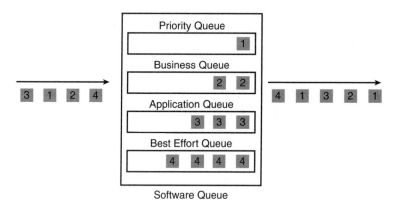

Figure 9-10   Queuing Example

Congestion Avoidance

If an interface's output queue fills to capacity, newly arriving packets are discarded (or *tail dropped*). To prevent this behavior, a congestion-avoidance technique called *random early detection* (RED) can be used, as illustrated in Figure 9-11. After a queue depth reaches a configurable level (*minimum threshold*), RED introduces the possibility of a packet discard. As the queue depth continues to increase, the possibility of a discard increases until a configurable *maximum threshold* is reached. After the queue depth exceeds the maximum threshold for traffic with a specific priority, there is a 100 percent chance of discard for those traffic types. If those discarded packets are TCP-based (connection-oriented), the sender knows which packets are discarded and can retransmit those dropped packets. However, if those dropped packets are

UDP-based (that is, connectionless), the sender does not receive any indication that the packets were dropped.

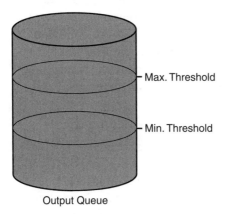

Max. Threshold

Min. Threshold

Output Queue

Figure 9-11   Random Early Detection (RED)

Policing and Shaping

Instead of making a minimum amount of bandwidth available for specific traffic types, you might want to limit available bandwidth. Both *policing* and *traffic-shaping* tools can accomplish this objective. Collectively, these tools are called *traffic conditioners*.

Policing can be used in either the inbound or outbound direction, and it typically discards packets that exceed the configured rate limit, which you can think of as a *speed limit* for specific traffic types. Because policing drops packets, resulting in retransmissions, it is recommended for higher-speed interfaces.

Shaping buffers (and therefore delays) traffic exceeding a configured rate. Therefore, shaping is recommended for slower-speed interfaces.

NOTE   Special emphasis is placed on traffic shaping, because of its relevance to the Network+ exam.

Because traffic shaping (and policing) can limit the speed of packets exiting a router, a question arises: "How do we send traffic out of an interface at a rate that is less than the physical clock rate of the interface?" For this to be possible, shaping and policing tools do not transmit all the time. Specifically, they send a certain number of bits or bytes at line rate, and then they stop sending, until a specific timing interval (for example, 1/8th of a second) is reached. After the timing interval is reached, the interface again sends a specific amount of traffic at line rate. It stops and waits for the next timing interval to occur. This process continually repeats, allowing an interface to send an average bandwidth that might be below the physical speed of the interface. This average bandwidth is called the *committed information rate* (CIR). The number of bits (the unit of measure used with shaping tools) or bytes (the unit of measure used with policing tools) that are sent during a timing interval is called the *Committed Burst* (Bc). The timing interval is written as *Tc*.

For example, imagine that you have a physical line rate of 128 kbps, but the CIR is only 64 kbps. Also, assume there are eight timing intervals in a second (that is, Tc = 1/8th of a second = 125 ms), and during each of those timing intervals, 8,000 bits (the committed burst parameter) are sent at line rate. Therefore, over the period of a second, 8,000 bits were sent (at line rate) eight times, for a grand total of 64,000 bits per second, which is the CIR. Figure 9-12 illustrates this shaping of traffic to 64 kbps on a line with a rate of 128 kbps.

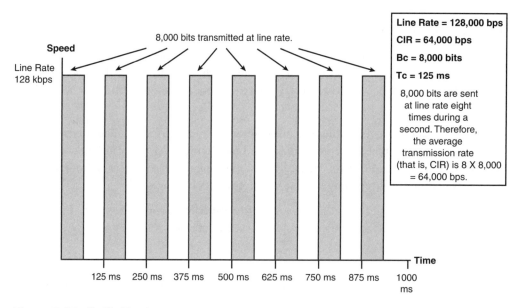

Figure 9-12   Traffic Shaping

If all the Bc bits (or bytes) were not sent during a timing interval, there is an option to *bank* those bits and use them during a future timing interval. The parameter that allows this storing of unused potential bandwidth is called the *Excess Burst* (Be) parameter. The Be parameter in a shaping configuration specifies the maximum number of bits or bytes that can be sent in excess of the Bc during a timing interval, if those bits are indeed available. For those bits or bytes to be available, they must have gone unused during previous timing intervals. Policing tools, however, use the Be parameter to specify the maximum number of bytes that can be sent during a timing interval. Therefore, in a policing configuration, if the Bc equals the Be, no excess bursting occurs. If excess bursting occurs, policing tools consider this excess traffic as *exceeding traffic*. Traffic that conforms to (does not exceed) a specified CIR is considered by a policing tool to be *conforming traffic*.

The relationship between the Tc, Bc, and CIR is given with this formula: $CIR = Bc / Tc$. Alternately, the formula can be written as $Tc = Bc / CIR$. Therefore, if you want a smaller timing interval, configure a smaller Bc.

Link Efficiency

To make the most of the limited bandwidth available on slower-speed links, you might choose to implement *compression* or *link fragmentation and interleaving* (LFI). Although you could compress a packet's payload or header to conserve bandwidth, as one example, consider header compression. With VoIP packets, the Layer 3 and Layer 4 headers total 40 bytes in size. However, depending on how you encode voice, the voice payload might be only 20 bytes in size. As a result, VoIP benefits most from header compression, as opposed to payload compression.

VoIP sends packets using *Real-Time Transport Protocol* (RTP), which is a Layer 4 protocol. RTP is then encapsulated inside UDP (another Layer 4 protocol), which is then encapsulated inside of IP (at Layer 3). *RTP header compression* (cRTP) can take the Layer 3 and Layer 4 headers and compress them to only 2 or 4 bytes in size (2 bytes if UDP checksums are not used and 4 bytes if UDP checksums are used), as shown in Figure 9-13.

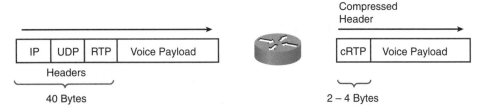

Figure 9-13   RTP Header Compression (cRTP)

LFI addresses the issue of *serialization delay*, which is the amount of time required for a packet to exit an interface. A large data packet, for example, on a slower-speed link might create excessive delay for a voice packet, because of the time required for the data packet to exit the interface. LFI fragments the large packets and interleaves the smaller packets in among the fragments, reducing the serialization delay experienced by the smaller packets. Figure 9-14 shows the operation of LFI, where the packets labeled *D* are data packets, and the packets labeled *V* are voice packets.

Link Fragmentation and Interleaving (LFI)

Figure 9-14   Link Fragmentation and Interleaving (LFI)

Case Study: SOHO Network Design

Based on what you learned from previous chapters and this chapter, this section challenges you to create a network design to meet a collection of criteria. Because network design is part science and part art, multiple designs can meet the specified requirements. However, as a reference, this section presents one solution, against which you can contrast your solution.

Case Study Scenario

While working through your design, consider the following:

- Meeting all requirements
- Media distance limitations
- Network device selection
- Environmental factors
- Compatibility with existing and future equipment

The following are your design scenario and design criteria for this case study:

- Company ABC leases two buildings (building A and building B) in a large office park, as shown in Figure 9-15. The office park has a conduit system that allows physical media to run between buildings. The distance (via the conduit system) between building A and building B is 1 km.

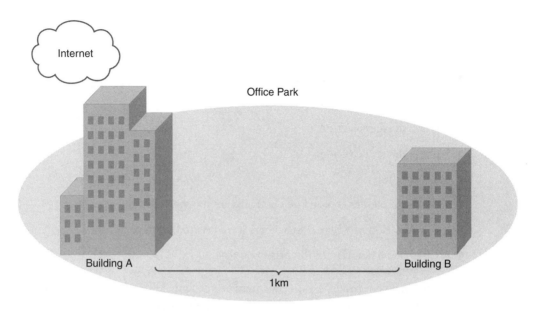

Figure 9-15 Case Study Topology

- Company ABC will use the Class B address of 172.16.0.0/16 for its sites. You should subnet this classful network to support not only the two buildings (one subnet per building), but to allow as many as five total sites in the future, as Company ABC continues to grow.

- Company ABC needs to connect to the Internet, supporting a speed of at least 30 Mbps, and this connection should come into building A.

- Cost is a primary design consideration, while performance is a secondary design consideration.

- Each building contains various Wi-Fi client devices (for example, smart phones, tablets, and laptops).

- Table 9-3 identifies the number of hosts contained in each building and the number of floors contained in each building.

Table 9-3 Case Study Information for Buildings A and B

Building	Number of Hosts	Floors (and Wireless Coverage)
A	200	Three floors, each of which can be services with a single wireless access point
B	100	One floor, which can be serviced by a single wireless access point

Your design should include the following information:

- Network address and subnet mask for building A

- Network address and subnet mask for building B

- Layer 1 media selection

- Layer 2 device selection

- Layer 3 device selection

- Wireless design

- Any design elements based on environmental considerations

- An explanation of where cost savings were created from performance tradeoffs

- A topological diagram of the proposed design

On separate sheets of paper, create your network design. After your design is complete, perform a sanity check by contrasting the listed criteria against your design. Finally, while keeping in mind that multiple designs could meet the design criteria, you can review the following suggested solution. In the real world, reviewing the logic behind other designs can often give you a fresh perspective for future designs.

Suggested Solution

This suggested solution begins by IP address allocation. Then, consideration is given to the Layer 1 media, followed by Layer 2 and Layer 3 devices. Wireless design decisions are presented. Design elements based on environmental factors are discussed. The suggested solution also addresses how cost savings were achieved through performance tradeoffs. Finally, a topological diagram of the suggested solution is presented.

IP Addressing

Questions you might need to ask when designing the IP addressing of a network include the following:

- How many hosts do you need to support (now and in the future)?

- How many subnets do you need to support (now and in the future)?

From the scenario, you know that each subnet must accommodate at least 200 hosts. Also, you know that you must accommodate at least five subnets. In this solution, the subnet mask is based on the number of required subnets. Eight subnets are supported with three borrowed bits, while two borrowed only support four subnets, based on this formula:

Number of subnets = 2^s,

where s is the number of borrowed bits

With three borrowed bits, we have 13 bits left for host IP addressing, which is far more than needed to accommodate 200 host IP addresses. These three borrowed bits yield a subnet mask of 255.255.224.0. Because the third octet is the last octet to contain a binary 1 in the subnet mask, the third octet is the *interesting octet*.

The block size can be calculated by subtracting the subnet decimal value in the interesting octet from 256: 256 - 224 = 32. Because the block size is 32, and the interesting octet is the third octet, the following subnets are created with the 255.255.224.0 (that is, /19) subnet mask:

- 172.16.0.0 /19
- 172.16.32.0 /19
- 172.16.64.0 /19
- 172.16.96.0 /19
- 172.16.128.0 /19
- 172.16.160.0 /19
- 172.16.192.0 /19
- 172.16.224.0 /19

The first two subnets are selected for the building A and building B subnet, as shown in Table 9-4.

Table 9-4   Case Study Suggested Solution: Network Addresses

Building	Subnet
A	172.16.0.0 /19
B	172.16.32.0 /19

Layer 1 Media

Questions you might need to ask when selecting the Layer 1 media types of a network include the following:

- What speeds need to be supported (now and in the future)?

- What distances between devices need to be supported (now and in the future)?

Within each building, Category 6a (Cat 6a) unshielded-twisted pair (UTP) cabling is selected to interconnect network components. The installation is based on Gigabit Ethernet. However, if 10-Gigabit Ethernet devices are installed in the future, Cat 6a is rated for 10GBASE-T for distances as long as 100 m.

The 1-km distance between building A and building B is too far for UTP cabling. Therefore, multimode fiber (MMF) is selected. The speed of the fiber link will be 1 Gbps. Table 9-5 summarizes these media selections.

Table 9-5 Case Study Suggested Solution: Layer 1 Media

Connection Type	Media Type
LAN links within buildings	Cat 6a UTP
Link between building A and building B	MMF

Layer 2 Devices

Questions you might need to ask when selecting Layer 2 devices in a network include the following:

- Where will the switches be located?

- What port densities are required on the switches (now and in the future)?

- What switch features need to be supported (for example, STP or LACP)?

- What media types are used to connect to the switches?

A collection of Ethernet switches interconnect network devices within each building. Assuming the 200 hosts in building A are distributed relatively evenly across the three floors (each floor contains approximately 67 hosts). Therefore, each floor will have a wiring closet containing two Ethernet switches: one 48-port density switch and one 24-port density switch. Each switch is connected to a multilayer switch located in building A using four connections logically bundled together using *Link Aggregation Control Protocol* (LACP).

Within building B, two Ethernet switches, each with 48 ports, and one Ethernet switch, with 24 ports, are installed in a wiring closet. These switches are interconnected in a stacked configuration, using four connections logically bundled together using LACP. One of the switches has a MMF port, which allows it to connect via fiber to building A's multilayer switch.

Table 9-6 summarizes the switch selections.

Table 9-6 Case Study Suggested Solution: Layer 2 Devices

Building	Quantity of 48-Port Switches	Quantity of 24-Port Switches
A	3	3
B	2	1

Layer 3 Devices

Questions you might need to ask when selecting Layer 3 devices for a network include the following:

- How many interfaces are needed (now and in the future)?
- What types of interfaces need to be supported (now and in the future)?
- What routing protocol(s) need to be supported?
- What router features (for example, HSRP or security features) need to be supported?

Layer 3 devices consist of a multilayer switch located in building A. All switches within building A home back to the multilayer switch using four LACP-bundled links. The multilayer switch is equipped with at least one MMF port, which allows a connection with one of the Ethernet switches in building B.

The multilayer switch connects to a router via a FastEthernet connection. This router contains a serial interface, which connects to the Internet via a T3 connection.

Wireless Design

Questions you might need to ask when designing the wireless portion of a network include the following:

- What wireless speeds need to be supported (now and in the future)?
- What distances need to be supported between wireless devices and wireless access points (now and in the future)?
- What IEEE wireless standard(s) needs to be supported?
- What channel(s) should be used?
- Where should wireless access points be located?

Because the network needs to support various Wi-Fi clients, the 2.4 GHz band is chosen, because it is the most commonly used band. Within building A, a wireless access point (AP) is placed on each floor of the building. To avoid interference, the nonoverlapping channels of 1, 6, and 11 are chosen. The 2.4 GHz band also allows compatibility with IEEE 802.11 b/g/n.

Within building B, a single wireless AP accommodates Wi-Fi clients. Table 9-7 summarizes the wireless AP selection.

Table 9-7   Case Study Suggested Solution: Wireless AP Selection

AP Identifier	Building	Band	Channel
1	A (1st floor)	2.4 GHz	1
2	A (2nd floor)	2.4 GHz	6
3	A (3rd floor)	2.4 GHz	11
4	B	2.4 GHz	1

Environmental Factors

Questions you might need to ask when considering environmental factors of a network design include the following:

- What temperature or humidity controls exist in the rooms containing network equipment?

- What power redundancy system(s) is needed to provide power to network equipment in the event of a power outage?

Because the multilayer switch in building A could be a single point of failure for the entire network, the multilayer switch is placed in a well-ventilated room, which can help dissipate heat in the event of an air conditioning failure. To further enhance the availability of the multilayer switch, the switch is connected to a UPS, which can help the multilayer switch continue to run, for a brief time, in the event of a power outage. Protection against an extended power outage could be achieved with the addition of a generator. However, no generator is included in this design because of budgetary reasons.

Cost Savings Versus Performance

When assimilating all the previously gathered design elements, you need to weigh budgetary constraints against network performance metrics. In this example, Gigabit Ethernet was chosen over 10 Gigabit Ethernet. Additionally, the link between building A and building B could become a bottleneck, because it runs at a speed of

1 Gbps, although it transports an aggregation of multiple 1 Gbps. However, cost savings are achieved through using 1 Gbps switch interfaces as opposed to 10 Gbps interfaces or a bundle of multiple 1 Gbps fiber links.

Topology

Figure 9-16 shows the topology of the proposed design based on the collection of previously listed design decisions.

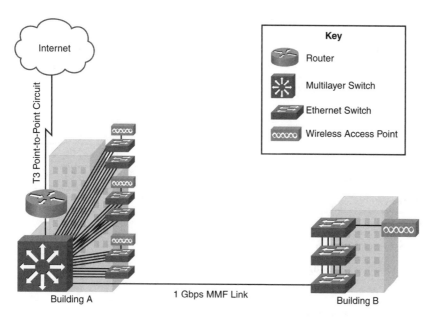

Figure 9-16   Case Study Proposed Topology

Summary

The main topics covered in this chapter are the following:

- Network availability was discussed, including how availability is measured and can be achieved through redundant designs.

- Performance optimization strategies were discussed, including the use of content caching, link aggregation, and load balancing.

- A variety of QoS technologies were reviewed, with an emphasis on traffic shaping, which can limit the rate of data transmission on a WAN link to the CIR.

- You were given a case study, where you were challenged to design a network to meet a collection of criteria.

Exam Preparation Tasks

Review All the Key Topics

Review the most important topics from inside the chapter, noted with the Key Topic icon in the outer margin of the page. Table 9-8 lists these key topics and the page numbers where each is found.

Table 9-8   Key Topics for Chapter 9

Key Topic Element	Description	Page Number
List	Fault-tolerant network design approaches	286
List	First-hop redundant technologies	288
List	Design considerations for high-availability networks	290
Step list	High-availability best practices	290
Table 9-1	Three categories of quality issues	293
Table 9-2	Three categories of Quality of Service mechanisms	295
Section	QoS mechanism: Classification	296
Section	QoS mechanism: Marking	297
Section	QoS mechanism: Congestion management	298
Section	QoS mechanism: Congestion avoidance	298
Section	QoS mechanism: Policing and shaping	299
Section	QoS mechanism: Link efficiency	301

Complete Tables and Lists from Memory

Print a copy of Appendix C, "Memory Tables" (found on the CD), or at least the section for this chapter, and complete the tables and lists from memory. Appendix D, "Memory Table Answer Key," also on the CD, includes the completed tables and lists so you can check your work.

Define Key Terms

Define the following key terms from this chapter, and check your answers in the Glossary:

availability, reliability, Common Address Redundancy Protocol (CARP), uninterruptable power supply (UPS), latency, jitter, integrated services (IntServ), differentiated services, classification, marking, congestion management, congestion avoidance, policing, traffic shaping, committed information rate (CIR), link efficiency

Review Questions

The answers to these review questions are in Appendix A, "Answers to Review Questions."

1. If a network has the five nines of availability, how much downtime does it experience per year?

   a. 30 seconds

   b. 5 minutes

   c. 12 minutes

   d. 26 minutes

2. What mode of NIC redundancy uses has only one NIC active at a time?

   a. Publisher-subscriber

   b. Client-server

   c. Active-standby

   d. Active-subscriber

3. What performance optimization technology uses a network appliance, which can receive a copy of content stored elsewhere (for example, a video presentation located on a server at a corporate headquarters), and serve that content to local clients, thus reducing the bandwidth burden on an IP WAN?

   a. Content engine

   b. Load balancer

   c. LACP

   d. CARP

4. A lack of bandwidth can lead to which QoS issues? (Choose three.)

   a. Delay

   b. Jitter

   c. Prioritization

   d. Packet drops

5. What is the maximum recommended one-way delay for voice traffic?

   a. 25 ms

   b. 75 ms

   c. 125 ms

   d. 150 ms

6. Which of the following QoS mechanisms is considered an IntServ mechanism?

   a. LLQ

   b. RSVP

   c. RED

   d. cRTP

7. Identify the congestion avoidance mechanism from the following list of QoS tools.

   a. LLQ

   b. RSVP

   c. RED

   d. cRTP

8. Which traffic-shaping parameter is a measure of the average number of bits transmitted during a timing interval?

   a. CIR

   b. Tc

   c. Bc

   d. Be

9. RTP header compression can compress the combined Layer 3 and Layer 4 headers from 40 bytes down to how many bytes?

   a. 1–3 bytes

   b. 2–4 bytes

   c. 3–5 bytes

   d. 4–6 bytes

10. What type of delay is the amount of time required for a packet to exit a router's serial interface?

    a. Serialization delay

    b. Packetization delay

    c. Propagation delay

    d. Queuing delay

After completion of this chapter, you will be able to
answer the following questions:

- What are some of the more useful Microsoft Windows® commands for
  configuring and troubleshooting network clients and servers?

- What are some of the more useful UNIX commands for configuring and
  troubleshooting network clients and servers?

CHAPTER 10

Using Command-Line Utilities

Your configuration and troubleshooting of networks will undoubtedly involve issuing commands at an operating system (OS) prompt of an end-user computer (a client) or a server. This chapter provides you with a collection of commands that you can use at those OS prompts. The two OSs for which commands are provided include Microsoft Windows and UNIX.

Some commands, you will notice, exist on both Microsoft Windows and UNIX platforms. For example, the **ping** command can be used by both platforms to check network reachability; however, other commands are OS-specific. For example, the IP address settings on a Microsoft Windows PC can be viewed by entering the **ipconfig** command. However, a slightly different command, the **ifconfig** command, is used to gather similar information on UNIX hosts.

Many of the commands presented in this chapter have multiple command-line arguments; however, this chapter focuses on the more popular options for these commands. As a result, this chapter is not an exhaustive reference, listing all available options, for the commands presented.

Foundation Topics

Windows Commands

The Microsoft Windows OS (generically referred to as *Windows* in this chapter) allows you to access a command prompt by opening the *Command Prompt* application or by typing **cmd** in the **Start > Run** dialog box (on some Windows platforms, such as Windows XP) or in the **Start > Search Programs and Files** dialog box (on other Windows platforms, such as Windows 7). Although slight variations exist in these Windows commands based on your version of Windows, this chapter describes these Windows commands as they exist in Windows 7. Also, note that all the commands listed in this section are commands on the Network+ exam (N10-005) blueprint.

arp

The **arp** command can be used to see what a Layer 2 MAC address corresponds to a known Layer 3 IP address. Additionally, the **arp** command can be used to statically add a MAC address to IP address mapping to a PC's ARP table (sometimes called the *ARP cache*).

The syntax of the **arp** command is as follows:

```
arp -s inet_addr eth_addr [if_addr]
arp -d inet_addr [if_addr]
arp -a [inet_addr] [-N if_addr] [-v]
```

Table 10-1 describes the previously listed *switches* (for example, *-s*, *-d*, or *-a*) and *arguments* (for example, *inet_addr* or *if_addr*).

Table 10-1 Parameters for the Windows **arp** Command

Parameter	Purpose
-a or **-g**	These options display current entries in a PC's ARP table.
-v	This option, where the *v* stands for *verbose*, includes any invalid and loopback interface entries in an ARP table.
inet_addr	This option is a specific IP address.
-N *if_addr*	This option shows ARP entries learned for a specified network.
-d	An ARP entry for a host can be deleted with this option, in combination with the *inet_addr* parameter. A wildcard character of * can delete all host entries.
-s	This option, used in conjunction with the *inet_addr* and *eth_addr* parameters, statically adds a host entry in the ARP table.

Parameter	Purpose
eth_addr	This parameter is a 48-bit MAC address.
if_addr	If a host has multiple interfaces, an ARP entry might be associated with a specific interface. This option can be used for statically adding or deleting an ARP entry to or from a specified interface.

Example 10-1 shows the **arp -a** command being issued on a PC. The output shows what MAC addresses have been learned for the listed IP addresses. The dynamically learned addresses have *dynamic* listed in the *Type* column, while statically configured addresses (which are addresses configured by a user or the OS) are listed with *static* in the *Type* column. From the output, as one example, you can determine that the network device with an IP address of 172.16.202.1 has a MAC address of 00-50-56-c0-00-08, which could alternately be written as 0050.56c0.0008. Also, you can determine from the output that this information was dynamically learned, as opposed to being statically configured.

Example 10-1 Sample Output from the Windows **arp -a** Command

```
C:\>arp -a
Interface: 172.16.202.128 --- 0xb
  Internet Address        Physical Address      Type
  172.16.202.1            00-50-56-c0-00-08     dynamic
  172.16.202.2            00-50-56-fd-65-2c     dynamic
  172.16.202.254          00-50-56-e8-84-fc     dynamic
  172.16.202.255          ff-ff-ff-ff-ff-ff     static
  224.0.0.22              01-00-5e-00-00-16     static
  224.0.0.252             01-00-5e-00-00-fc     static
  255.255.255.255         ff-ff-ff-ff-ff-ff     static

Interface: 172.16.202.129 --- 0x14
  Internet Address        Physical Address      Type
  172.16.202.1            00-50-56-c0-00-08     dynamic
  172.16.202.2            00-50-56-fd-65-2c     dynamic
  172.16.202.254          00-50-56-e8-84-fc     dynamic
  172.16.202.255          ff-ff-ff-ff-ff-ff     static
  224.0.0.22              01-00-5e-00-00-16     static
  224.0.0.252             01-00-5e-00-00-fc     static
  224.0.1.60              01-00-5e-00-01-3c     static
  255.255.255.255         ff-ff-ff-ff-ff-ff     static
```

From a troubleshooting perspective, keep in mind that static ARP entries tend to be more problematic than dynamic entries. For example, a static entry might be added to a laptop computer, and the computer later connects to a different network. If a PC then attempted to reach the IP address specified in the static ARP entry, the Layer 2 frame would have the incorrect destination MAC address (which should then be the MAC address of the PC's default gateway) in its header.

ipconfig

The **ipconfig** command can be used to display IP address configuration parameters on a Windows PC. Additionally, if the PC uses Dynamic Host Configuration Protocol (DHCP), the **ipconfig** command can be used to release and renew a DHCP lease, which is often useful when troubleshooting.

The syntax of the **ipconfig** command, along with some of its more commonly used parameters, is as follows:

```
ipconfig [/all | /renew | /release | /renew6 | /release6]
```

Table 10-2 describes the previously listed parameters for the **ipconfig** command.

Table 10-2 Parameters for the Windows `ipconfig` Command

Parameter	Purpose
/all	The **ipconfig** command entered by itself displays summary information about a PC's IP address configuration. This parameter gives more verbose information, including such information as DNS and WINS server IP addresses.
/release or **/release6**	These options release a DHCP lease for an IPv4 and IPv6 address, respectively.
/renew or **renew6**	These options renew a DHCP lease for an IPv4 and IPv6 address, respectively.

Example 10-2 shows the **ipconfig** command, without any extra parameters, being issued on a PC. The PC contains an Ethernet and a wireless network interface card (NIC). From the output, you can conclude that one of the NICs has an IP address of 172.16.202.129, while the other NIC has an IP address of 172.16.202.128. Also, you can see that these two NICs share a common default gateway of 172.16.202.2.

Example 10-2   Sample Output from the Windows `ipconfig` Command

```
C:\>ipconfig
Windows IP Configuration
Ethernet adapter Local Area Connection 3:
   Connection-specific DNS Suffix  . : localdomain
   Link-local IPv6 Address . . . . . : fe80::5101:b420:4354:d496%20
   IPv4 Address. . . . . . . . . . . : 172.16.202.129
   Subnet Mask . . . . . . . . . . . : 255.255.255.0
   Default Gateway . . . . . . . . . : 172.16.202.2
Ethernet adapter Local Area Connection:
   Connection-specific DNS Suffix  . : localdomain
   Link-local IPv6 Address . . . . . : fe80::a10f:cff4:15e4:aa6%11
   IPv4 Address. . . . . . . . . . . : 172.16.202.128
   Subnet Mask . . . . . . . . . . . : 255.255.255.0
   Default Gateway . . . . . . . . . : 172.16.202.2
   OUTPUT OMITTED...
```

Example 10-3 shows the **ipconfig /all** command being issued on a PC. Notice the additional output from this command, not shown in the output of the **ipconfig** command. As a couple of examples, you can see the MAC address (labeled as the *physical address*) for each NIC and the DNS server's IP address of 172.16.202.2.

Example 10-3   Sample Output from the Windows `ipconfig /all` Command

```
C:\>ipconfig /all
Windows IP Configuration
   Host Name . . . . . . . . . . . . : WIN-OD1IG7JF47P
   Primary Dns Suffix  . . . . . . . :
   Node Type . . . . . . . . . . . . : Hybrid
   IP Routing Enabled. . . . . . . . : No
   WINS Proxy Enabled. . . . . . . . : No
   DNS Suffix Search List. . . . . . : localdomain
Ethernet adapter Local Area Connection 3:
   Connection-specific DNS Suffix  . : localdomain
   Description . . . . . . . . . . . : Intel(R) PRO/1000 MT Network
      Connection #2
   Physical Address. . . . . . . . . : 00-0C-29-3A-21-67
   DHCP Enabled. . . . . . . . . . . : Yes
   Autoconfiguration Enabled . . . . : Yes
   Link-local IPv6 Address . . . . . : fe80::5101:b420:4354:d496%20
      (Preferred)
```

```
    IPv4 Address. . . . . . . . . . . : 172.16.202.129(Preferred)
    Subnet Mask . . . . . . . . . . . : 255.255.255.0
    Lease Obtained. . . . . . . . . . : Saturday, May 28, 2011 6:28:08
       PM
    Lease Expires . . . . . . . . . . : Saturday, May 28, 2011 9:28:08
       PM
    Default Gateway . . . . . . . . . : 172.16.202.2
    DHCP Server . . . . . . . . . . . : 172.16.202.254
    DHCPv6 IAID . . . . . . . . . . . : 419433513
    DHCPv6 Client DUID. . . . . . . . : 00-01-00-01-14-A6-11-77-00-0C-
       29-3A-21-5D
    DNS Servers . . . . . . . . . . . : 172.16.202.2
    Primary WINS Server . . . . . . . : 172.16.202.2
    NetBIOS over Tcpip. . . . . . . . : Enabled
Ethernet adapter Local Area Connection:
    Connection-specific DNS Suffix  . : localdomain
    Description . . . . . . . . . . . : Intel(R) PRO/1000 MT Network
       Connection
    Physical Address. . . . . . . . . : 00-0C-29-3A-21-5D
    DHCP Enabled. . . . . . . . . . . : Yes
    Autoconfiguration Enabled . . . . : Yes
    Link-local IPv6 Address . . . . . : fe80::a10f:cff4:15e4:aa6%11
       (Preferred)
    IPv4 Address. . . . . . . . . . . : 172.16.202.128(Preferred)
    Subnet Mask . . . . . . . . . . . : 255.255.255.0
    Lease Obtained. . . . . . . . . . : Saturday, May 28, 2011 6:27:56
       PM
    Lease Expires . . . . . . . . . . : Saturday, May 28, 2011 9:28:08
       PM
    Default Gateway . . . . . . . . . : 172.16.202.2
    DHCP Server . . . . . . . . . . . : 172.16.202.254
    DHCPv6 IAID . . . . . . . . . . . : 234884137
    DHCPv6 Client DUID. . . . . . . . : 00-01-00-01-14-A6-11-77-00-0C-
       29-3A-21-5D
    DNS Servers . . . . . . . . . . . : 172.16.202.2
    Primary WINS Server . . . . . . . : 172.16.202.2
    NetBIOS over Tcpip. . . . . . . . : Enabled
    OUTPUT OMITTED...
```

If you are troubleshooting a PC and suspect that IP addressing might be an issue, you can release the PC's current DHCP lease with the **ipconfig /release** command, as shown in Example 10-4. Then, you can renew the DHCP lease with the **ipconfig /renew** command, as shown in Example 10-5.

Example 10-4   Sample Output from the Windows **ipconfig /release** Command

```
C:\>ipconfig /release
Windows IP Configuration
Ethernet adapter Local Area Connection 3:
   Connection-specific DNS Suffix  . :
   Link-local IPv6 Address . . . . . : fe80::5101:b420:4354:d496%20
   Default Gateway . . . . . . . . . :
Ethernet adapter Local Area Connection:
   Connection-specific DNS Suffix  . :
   Link-local IPv6 Address . . . . . : fe80::a10f:cff4:15e4:aa6%11
   Default Gateway . . . . . . . . . :
   OUTPUT OMITTED...
```

Example 10-5   Sample Output from the Windows **ipconfig /renew** Command

```
C:\>ipconfig /renew
Windows IP Configuration
Ethernet adapter Local Area Connection 3:
   Connection-specific DNS Suffix  . : localdomain
   Link-local IPv6 Address . . . . . : fe80::5101:b420:4354:d496%20
   IPv4 Address. . . . . . . . . . . : 172.16.202.129
   Subnet Mask . . . . . . . . . . . : 255.255.255.0
   Default Gateway . . . . . . . . . : 172.16.202.2
Ethernet adapter Local Area Connection:
   Connection-specific DNS Suffix  . : localdomain
   Link-local IPv6 Address . . . . . : fe80::a10f:cff4:15e4:aa6%11
   IPv4 Address. . . . . . . . . . . : 172.16.202.128
   Subnet Mask . . . . . . . . . . . : 255.255.255.0
   Default Gateway . . . . . . . . . : 172.16.202.2
   OUTPUT OMITTED...
```

nbtstat

The **nbtstat** command displays NetBIOS information for IP-based networks. The *nbt* prefix of the **nbtstat** command refers to *NetBIOS over TCP/IP*, which is called *NBT* or *NetBT*. This command can, for example, display a listing of NetBIOS device names learned by a Windows PC.

The syntax of the **nbtstat** command is as follows:

```
nbtstat [ [-a remote_name] [-A ip_address] [-c] [-n] [-r] [-R] [-S] ]
```

Table 10-3 describes the previously listed parameters for the **nbtstat** command.

Table 10-3   Parameters for the Windows **nbtstat** Command

Parameter	Purpose
-a *remote_name*	This option allows you to see the NetBIOS table of a remote PC with a NetBIOS name as specified by the remote_name argument.
-A *ip_address*	This option allows you to see the NetBIOS table of a remote PC with an IP address as specified by the *ip_address* argument.
-c	This option displays the contents of a PC's NetBIOS name cache along with the IP addresses corresponding to those NetBIOS names.
-n	This option displays NetBIOS names that have been registered by an application, such as a server application.
-r	This option shows statistical NetBIOS information, such as the number of NetBIOS names resolved by broadcasting and the number of NetBIOS names resolved by a WINS server.
-R	This option purges a PC's NetBIOS cache and reloads entries from a PC's *LMHOSTS* file (which is a text file containing NetBIOS to IP address mappings) that have *#PRE* following the entry. The #PRE option in an LMHOSTS file causes those entries to be preloaded into a PC's NetBIOS cache.
-S	This option provides a listing of the NetBIOS session table, along with the IP addresses of the listed NetBIOS names.

When troubleshooting, it often helps to know the IP address of a known NetBIOS name. You can view a PC's NetBIOS name cache, which lists this information, with the **nbtstat -c** command, as shown in Example 10-6.

Example 10-6   Sample Output from the Windows **nbtstat -c** Command

```
C:\>nbtstat -c
Local Area Connection:
Node IpAddress: [192.168.1.50] Scope Id: []

                    NetBIOS Remote Cache Name Table

        Name                 Type        Host Address     Life [sec]
     ---------------------------------------------------------------
     192.168.1.150   <20>   UNIQUE          192.168.1.150        440
```

```
192.168.1.241   <20>   UNIQUE          192.168.1.241       395
192.168.1.50    <20>   UNIQUE          192.168.1.50        392
AZSCO-CISCO-S2 <00>    UNIQUE          192.168.1.150       555
AZSCO-CISCO-S2 <20>    UNIQUE          192.168.1.150       555
THE-WALLACES-TI<20>    UNIQUE          192.168.1.1         202
THE-WALLACES-TI<00>    UNIQUE          192.168.1.1         202
IMAC-3026FE     <00>   UNIQUE          192.168.1.240       552
IMAC-3026FE     <20>   UNIQUE          192.168.1.240       550
LIVE-DELIVERY   <20>   UNIQUE          192.168.1.50        222
```

If you want to verify that a PC is successfully resolving NetBIOS names, either by using a broadcast or from a WINS server, the **nbtstat -r** command, as demonstrated in Example 10-7, can help.

Example 10-7   Sample Output from the Windows **nbtstat -r** Command

```
C:\>nbtstat -r
    NetBIOS Names Resolution and Registration Statistics
    ----------------------------------------------------
    Resolved By Broadcast     = 6
    Resolved By Name Server   = 0

    Registered By Broadcast   = 4
    Registered By Name Server = 0

    NetBIOS Names Resolved By Broadcast
---------------------------------------------
        AZSCO-CISCO-S2 <00>
        AZSCO-CISCO-S2
        IMAC-3026FE      <00>
        IMAC-3026FE
        THE-WALLACES-TI<00>
        THE-WALLACES-TI
```

The **nbtstat** command even allows you to view the NetBIOS table of a remote PC with the **nbtstat -a** command, as shown in Example 10-8. Note, however, that the *Node IpAddress* parameter shows the IP address of the PC issuing the **nbtstat** command. However, the *MAC Address* parameter shows the MAC address of the remote PC.

Example 10-8   Sample Output from the Windows **nbtstat -a** Command

```
C:\>nbtstat -a AZSCO-CISCO-S2
Local Area Connection:
Node IpAddress: [192.168.1.50] Scope Id: []
            NetBIOS Remote Machine Name Table
        Name                    Type         Status
    ---------------------------------------------------
    AZSCO-CISCO-S2 <00>    UNIQUE       Registered
    KITCHEN        <00>    GROUP        Registered
    AZSCO-CISCO-S2 <20>    UNIQUE       Registered
    KITCHEN        <1E>    GROUP        Registered
    KITCHEN        <1D>    UNIQUE       Registered
    .._MSBROWSE__.<01>     GROUP        Registered
        MAC Address = 00-13-72-79-4C-9D
```

netstat

The **netstat** command can be used to display various information about IP-based connections on a PC. For example, you can view information about current sessions, including source and destination IP addresses and port numbers. You can also display protocol statistics. This might be useful for troubleshooting purposes. As an example, you might issue the **netstat** command and see that your PC has sessions open to an unknown host on the Internet. These sessions might warrant further investigation to determine why the sessions are open and if they might be resulting in performance issues on your PC or possibly posing a security risk.

The following is the syntax for the **netstat** command, with some of its commonly used options:

netstat [-a] [-b] [-e] [-f] [-p *proto*] **[-r] [-s]**

Table 10-4 explains the usage of the previously listed command options.

Table 10-4 Parameters for the Windows **netstat** Command

Parameter	Purpose
-a	This option displays all of a PC's active IP-based sessions, along with the TCP and UDP ports of each session.
-b	This option shows you the names of the program that opened up a session.
-e	This option shows statistical information for an interface's IP-based traffic, such as the number of bytes sent and received.
-f	This option displays *fully qualified domain names* (FQDN) of destination addresses appearing in a listing of active sessions.
-p *proto*	This option displays connections for a specific protocol, which might be **icmp**, **icmpv6**, **ip**, **ipv6**, **tcp**, **tcpv6**, **udp**, or **udpv6**.
-r	This option displays a PC's IP routing table. Note: This command generates the same output as the **route print** command.
-s	This option displays statistical information for the following protocols: icmpv4, icmpv6, ipv4, ipv6, tcpv4, tcpv6, udpv4, and udpv6.

The **netstat** command issued without any options lists source and destination IP addresses and port numbers for all IP-based sessions. Example 10-9 shows sample output from this command.

Example 10-9 Sample Output from the Windows **netstat** Command

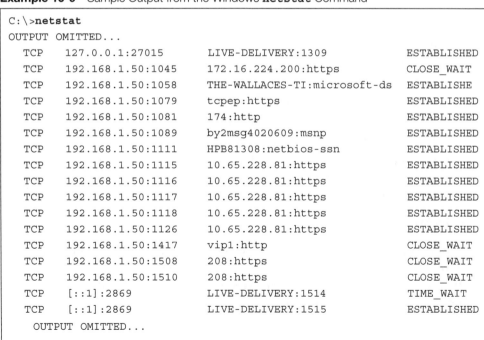

```
C:\>netstat
OUTPUT OMITTED...
  TCP    127.0.0.1:27015        LIVE-DELIVERY:1309            ESTABLISHED
  TCP    192.168.1.50:1045      172.16.224.200:https         CLOSE_WAIT
  TCP    192.168.1.50:1058      THE-WALLACES-TI:microsoft-ds ESTABLISHE
  TCP    192.168.1.50:1079      tcpep:https                  ESTABLISHED
  TCP    192.168.1.50:1081      174:http                     ESTABLISHED
  TCP    192.168.1.50:1089      by2msg4020609:msnp           ESTABLISHED
  TCP    192.168.1.50:1111      HPB81308:netbios-ssn         ESTABLISHED
  TCP    192.168.1.50:1115      10.65.228.81:https           ESTABLISHED
  TCP    192.168.1.50:1116      10.65.228.81:https           ESTABLISHED
  TCP    192.168.1.50:1117      10.65.228.81:https           ESTABLISHED
  TCP    192.168.1.50:1118      10.65.228.81:https           ESTABLISHED
  TCP    192.168.1.50:1126      10.65.228.81:https           ESTABLISHED
  TCP    192.168.1.50:1417      vip1:http                    CLOSE_WAIT
  TCP    192.168.1.50:1508      208:https                    CLOSE_WAIT
  TCP    192.168.1.50:1510      208:https                    CLOSE_WAIT
  TCP    [::1]:2869             LIVE-DELIVERY:1514           TIME_WAIT
  TCP    [::1]:2869             LIVE-DELIVERY:1515           ESTABLISHED
   OUTPUT OMITTED...
```

You might notice an open connection using a specific port, and you are not sure what application opened that connection. As seen in Example 10-10, the **netstat -b** command shows which application opened a specific connection. In this example, *Dropbox.exe, iTunex.exe, firefox.exe,* and *OUTLOOK.exe* are applications that have currently open connections.

Example 10-10 Sample Output from the Windows `netstat -b` Command

```
C:\>netstat -b
Active Connections
OUTPUT OMITTED...
  Proto  Local Address           Foreign Address         State
  TCP    127.0.0.1:1068          LIVE-DELIVERY:19872     ESTABLISHED
[Dropbox.exe]
  TCP    127.0.0.1:1309          LIVE-DELIVERY:27015     ESTABLISHED
[iTunes.exe]
  TCP    127.0.0.1:1960          LIVE-DELIVERY:1961      ESTABLISHED
[firefox.exe]
  TCP    192.168.1.50:1115       10.1.228.81:https       ESTABLISHED
[OUTLOOK.EXE]
  TCP    192.168.1.50:1116       10.1.228.81:https       ESTABLISHED
[OUTLOOK.EXE]
   OUTPUT OMITTED...
```

nslookup

Although the **nslookup** command offers various command options, this section focuses on the most common use for the command. Specifically, the **nslookup** command can be used to resolve an FQDN to an IP address. This can, as a couple of examples, help you determine if a DNS record is correct, and verify that your DNS server is operating.

The **nslookup** command can be issued along with an FQDN, or it can be used in an interactive mode, where you are prompted to enter command parameters. Therefore, the syntax can be summarized as follows:

`nslookup [fqdn]`

In non-interactive mode, you issue the **nslookup** command followed by a FQDN to display the IP address corresponding to the FQDN. To illustrate, consider Example 10-11, where the **nslookup** command is issued to resolve the IP address of the author's website *1ExamAMonth.com*, which appears to be *172.31.194.74*. (Note: A private IP address is used for illustrative purposes; in a real-world example, a public IP address would display.)

Example 10-11   Sample Output from the Windows **nslookup** Non-Interactive Command

```
C:\>nslookup 1ExamAMonth.com
Server:   UnKnown
Address:   192.168.1.1


Non-authoritative answer:
Name:     1ExamAMonth.com
Address:   172.31.194.74
```

In interactive mode, the **nslookup** command is entered, after which you enter command parameters from the **>** prompt. In Example 10-12, 1ExamAMonth.com is entered at the prompt to see the IP address corresponding to that FQDN. Also, notice that entering a question mark (**?**) displays a help screen that shows command options. Entering **quit** exits you from interactive mode.

Example 10-12   Sample Output from the Windows **nslookup** Interactive Command

```
C:\>nslookup
Default Server:   UnKnown
Address:   192.168.1.1

> 1ExamAMonth.com
Server:   UnKnown
Address:   192.168.1.1


Non-authoritative answer:
Name:     1ExamAMonth.com
Address:   172.31.194.74


> ?
Commands:   (identifiers are shown in uppercase, [] means optional)
NAME              - print info about the host/domain NAME using default
   server
NAME1 NAME2       - as above, but use NAME2 as server
help or ?         - print info on common commands
```

```
set OPTION        - set an option
    all                      - print options, current server and host
    [no]debug                - print debugging information
    [no]d2                   - print exhaustive debugging information
    [no]defname              - append domain name to each query
    [no]recurse              - ask for recursive answer to query
    [no]search               - use domain search list
    [no]vc                   - always use a virtual circuit
    domain=NAME              - set default domain name to NAME
    srchlist=N1[/N2/.../N6] - set domain to N1 and search list to
        N1,N2, etc.
    root=NAME                - set root server to NAME
OUTPUT OMITTED...
>quit
    C:\>
```

ping

The **ping** command is one of the most commonly used command-line commands. It can be used to check IP connectivity between two network devices. Multiple platforms (for example, routers, switches, and hosts) support the **ping** command.

The **ping** command uses *Internet Control Message Protocol* (ICMP), which is a Layer 4 protocol. If you issue a **ping** command from your PC, your PC sends an *ICMP echo* message to the specified destination host. Assuming the destination host is reachable, the host responds with an *ICMP echo reply* message. Other ICMP messages can be returned to your PC, from your PC's default gateway, to indicate that a destination host is unreachable, that an ICMP echo timed out, or that a *Time to Live* (TTL) value (which is decremented by 1 at each router hop) has expired (decremented to a value of 0).

The syntax of the **ping** command, along with some of its commonly used options, is as follows:

ping [**-t**] [**-n** *count*] [**-l** *size*] [**-f**] [**-i** *TTL*] [**-S** *srcaddr*] *target_ name*

Table 10-5 explains the usage of the previously listed command options.

Table 10-5 Parameters for the Windows `ping` Command

Parameter	Purpose
-t	This option repeatedly sends pings (ICMP echo messages) until you stop it by pressing <CTRL>-C.
-n *count*	This option specifies the number of pings to send.
-f	This option sets the Do Not Fragment bit in a packet's header. If the packet tries to cross a router that attempts to fragment the packet, the packet is dropped and an ICMP error message is returned.
-i *TTL*	This option sets the TTL value in a packet's header. The TTL is decremented for each router hop. A packet is discarded when its TTL value reaches 0.
-S *srcaddr*	If the PC from which you are issuing the **ping** command has more than one IP address, this option allows you to specify the source IP address from which the ICMP echo messages should be sent.
target_name	This option specifies the name or the IP address of the device to which you are sending ICMP echo messages.

A Windows **ping** command specifying only the *target_name* parameter sends four ICMP echo messages to the specified target, as shown in Example 10-13. In the output, notice that none of the packets were dropped.

Example 10-13 Sample Output from the Windows `ping` Command

```
C:\>ping 192.168.1.2
Pinging 192.168.1.2 with 32 bytes of data:
Reply from 192.168.1.2: bytes=32 time=2ms TTL=64
Reply from 192.168.1.2: bytes=32 time=1ms TTL=64
Reply from 192.168.1.2: bytes=32 time=1ms TTL=64
Reply from 192.168.1.2: bytes=32 time=1ms TTL=64

Ping statistics for 192.168.1.2:
    Packets: Sent = 4, Received = 4, Lost = 0 (0% loss),
Approximate round trip times in milli-seconds:
        Minimum = 1ms, Maximum = 2ms, Average = 1ms
```

If the specified target address is unreachable, output from the **ping** command indicates that the target cannot be reached, as shown in Example 10-14.

Example 10-14   Windows `ping` Command Indicating an Unreachable Destination

```
C:\>ping 192.168.1.200

Pinging 192.168.1.200 with 32 bytes of data:
Reply from 192.168.1.50: Destination host unreachable.
Reply from 192.168.1.50: Destination host unreachable.
Reply from 192.168.1.50: Destination host unreachable.
Reply from 192.168.1.50: Destination host unreachable.

Ping statistics for 192.168.1.200:
        Packets: Sent = 4, Received = 4, Lost = 0 (0% loss),
```

route

The **route** command can display a PC's current IP routing table. Additionally, the **route** command can be used to add or delete entries to or from that routing table. Syntax of the **route** command, with a collection of commonly used options, is as follows:

```
C:\>route [-f] [-p] command [destination] [mask netmask] [gateway]
[metric metric] [if interface]
```

Table 10-6 explains the usage of the previously listed command options.

Table 10-6   Parameters for the Windows `route` Command

Parameter	Purpose
-f	This option clears gateway entries from the routing table. If this option is used with another option, the clearing of gateways from the routing table occurs before any other specified action.
-p	This option can be used with the **add** command to make a statically configured route persistent, meaning that the route will remain in a PC's routing table even after a reboot.
command	Supported commands include print, add, delete, and change. The print option lists entries in a PC's routing table. The add option adds a route entry. The delete option removes a route from the routing table, while the change option can modify an existing route.
destination	This option specifies the destination host or subnet to add to a PC's routing table.

Parameter	Purpose
mask *netmask*	This option, used in conjunction with the destination option, specifies the subnet mask of the destination. If the destination is the IP address of a host, the netmask parameter is *255.255.255.255*.
gateway	This option specifies the IP address of the next-hop router used to reach the specified destination.
metric *metric*	This option specifies the cost to reach a specified destination. If a routing table contains more than one route to reach the destination, the route with the lowest cost is selected.
if *interface*	If you want to forward traffic to a specified destination out of a specific interface, use this option.

Example 10-15 illustrates the use of the **route print** command, which displays the contents of a PC's routing table. Notice that the output identifies a listing of the PC's interfaces, along with IPv4 routes and IPv6 routes. From the output, you see that the 10.0.0.0 255.0.0.0 network is reachable via two gateways (192.168.1.77 and 192.168.1.11). Also, notice that there is a persistent route (a route entry that survives a reboot) to act as a default gateway for the PC, which is 192.168.1.1.

Example 10-15 Sample Output from the Windows **route print** Command

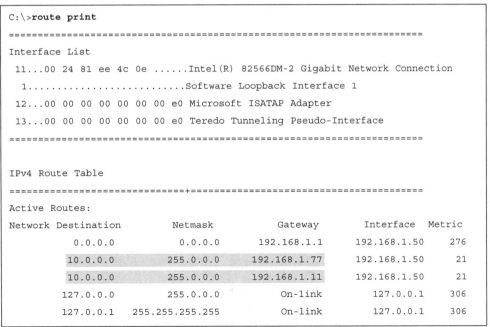

```
C:\>route print
===========================================================================
Interface List
 11...00 24 81 ee 4c 0e ......Intel(R) 82566DM-2 Gigabit Network Connection
  1...........................Software Loopback Interface 1
 12...00 00 00 00 00 00 00 e0 Microsoft ISATAP Adapter
 13...00 00 00 00 00 00 00 e0 Teredo Tunneling Pseudo-Interface
===========================================================================

IPv4 Route Table
===========================================================================
Active Routes:
Network Destination        Netmask          Gateway       Interface  Metric
          0.0.0.0          0.0.0.0      192.168.1.1    192.168.1.50     276
         10.0.0.0        255.0.0.0     192.168.1.77    192.168.1.50      21
         10.0.0.0        255.0.0.0     192.168.1.11    192.168.1.50      21
        127.0.0.0        255.0.0.0          On-link       127.0.0.1     306
        127.0.0.1  255.255.255.255          On-link       127.0.0.1     306
```

```
        127.255.255.255   255.255.255.255          On-link          127.0.0.1   306
              172.16.0.0       255.255.0.0     192.168.1.11      192.168.1.50    21
             192.168.0.0     255.255.255.0     192.168.1.11      192.168.1.50    21
             192.168.1.0     255.255.255.0          On-link      192.168.1.50   276
            192.168.1.50   255.255.255.255          On-link      192.168.1.50   276
           192.168.1.255   255.255.255.255          On-link      192.168.1.50   276
               224.0.0.0         240.0.0.0          On-link         127.0.0.1   306
               224.0.0.0         240.0.0.0          On-link      192.168.1.50   276
         255.255.255.255   255.255.255.255          On-link         127.0.0.1   306
         255.255.255.255   255.255.255.255          On-link      192.168.1.50   276
===========================================================================
Persistent Routes:
  Network Address            Netmask   Gateway Address   Metric
         0.0.0.0             0.0.0.0       192.168.1.1   Default
===========================================================================


IPv6 Route Table
===========================================================================
Active Routes:
 If Metric Network Destination      Gateway
 13     58 ::/0                     On-link
  1    306 ::1/128                  On-link
 13     58 2001::/32                On-link
 13    306 2001:0:4137:9e76:10e2:614f:b34e:ea84/128
                                    On-link
 11    276 fe80::/64                On-link
 13    306 fe80::/64                On-link
 13    306 fe80::10e2:614f:b34e:ea84/128
                                    On-link
 11    276 fe80::f46d:4a34:a9c4:51a0/128
                                    On-link
  1    306 ff00::/8                 On-link
 13    306 ff00::/8                 On-link
 11    276 ff00::/8                 On-link
===========================================================================
Persistent Routes:
     None
```

Imagine that you want to remove one of the route entries for the 10.0.0.0 255.0.0.0 network. Example 10-16 shows how one of the two entries (specifically, the entry pointing to 192.168.1.11) can be removed from the routing table. Notice from the output that after the **route delete 10.0.0.0 mask 255.0.0.0 192.168.1.11** command is issued, the route no longer appears in the routing table.

Example 10-16   Sample Output from the Windows **route delete** Command

```
C:\>route delete 10.0.0.0 mask 255.0.0.0 192.168.1.11
 OK!
C:\>route print
OUTPUT OMITTED...
IPv4 Route Table
===========================================================================
Active Routes:
Network Destination        Netmask          Gateway       Interface  Metric
          0.0.0.0          0.0.0.0      192.168.1.1      192.168.1.50     276
         10.0.0.0        255.0.0.0     192.168.1.77      192.168.1.50      21
        127.0.0.0        255.0.0.0         On-link        127.0.0.1       306
        127.0.0.1  255.255.255.255         On-link        127.0.0.1       306
  127.255.255.255  255.255.255.255         On-link        127.0.0.1       306
       172.16.0.0      255.255.0.0     192.168.1.11      192.168.1.50      21
      192.168.0.0    255.255.255.0     192.168.1.11      192.168.1.50      21
      192.168.1.0    255.255.255.0         On-link      192.168.1.50     276
     192.168.1.50  255.255.255.255         On-link      192.168.1.50     276
    192.168.1.255  255.255.255.255         On-link      192.168.1.50     276
        224.0.0.0        240.0.0.0         On-link        127.0.0.1       306
        224.0.0.0        240.0.0.0         On-link      192.168.1.50     276
  255.255.255.255  255.255.255.255         On-link        127.0.0.1       306
  255.255.255.255  255.255.255.255         On-link      192.168.1.50     276
===========================================================================
    OUTPUT OMITTED...
```

A route can be added by using the **route add** command. Example 10-17 shows and confirms the addition of a route pointing to the 10.2.1.0 255.255.255.0 network, with a next-hop route (gateway) of 192.168.1.1.

Example 10-17   *Sample Output from the Windows* **route add** *Command*

```
C:\>route add 10.2.1.0 mask 255.255.255.0 192.168.1.1
 OK!

C:\>route print
OUTPUT OMITTED...
IPv4 Route Table
===========================================================================
Active Routes:
Network Destination        Netmask          Gateway       Interface  Metric
          0.0.0.0          0.0.0.0      192.168.1.1    192.168.1.50     276
         10.0.0.0        255.0.0.0     192.168.1.77    192.168.1.50      21
         10.2.1.0    255.255.255.0      192.168.1.1    192.168.1.50      21
        127.0.0.0        255.0.0.0          On-link       127.0.0.1     306
        127.0.0.1  255.255.255.255          On-link       127.0.0.1     306
  127.255.255.255  255.255.255.255          On-link       127.0.0.1     306
       172.16.0.0      255.255.0.0     192.168.1.11    192.168.1.50      21
      192.168.0.0    255.255.255.0     192.168.1.11    192.168.1.50      21
      192.168.1.0    255.255.255.0          On-link    192.168.1.50     276
     192.168.1.50  255.255.255.255          On-link    192.168.1.50     276
    192.168.1.255  255.255.255.255          On-link    192.168.1.50     276
        224.0.0.0        240.0.0.0          On-link       127.0.0.1     306
        224.0.0.0        240.0.0.0          On-link    192.168.1.50     276
  255.255.255.255  255.255.255.255          On-link       127.0.0.1     306
  255.255.255.255  255.255.255.255          On-link    192.168.1.50     276
===========================================================================
    OUTPUT OMITTED...
```

tracert

In an earlier section, you were introduced to the **ping** command, which can verify Layer 3 connectivity to a remote host. If the ping were unsuccessful, or if the round-trip response times seem too long, the **tracert** command might help isolate the issue. Specifically, the **tracert** command pings every router hop from the source to the destination and reports the round-trip time for each router hop.

If a router is not reachable, you might want to investigate the router hop just before or just after the hop that timed out. However, in many cases, a router does not respond to a tracert, because it has been configured not to respond to ICMP messages (which is what the **tracert** command uses) for security reasons. So, a failed response does not always indicate a router-configuration issue or a bad link between two routers. However, even if the **tracert** output shows every route hop from the source to the destination, the round-trip delay time can help identify congested links.

Although the **tracert** command has a few optional parameters, usually, the command simply specifies a target IP address or FQDN, as follows:

```
C:\>tracert destination
```

Example 10-18 shows a successful trace from a PC to a destination FQDN of *pearsonitcertification.com*. Even though the trace was successful, the output still helps identify any slow links interconnecting routers along the path from the source to the destination.

Example 10-18   Sample Output from a Successful Windows **tracert** Command

```
C:\>tracert pearsonitcertification.com
Tracing route to pearsonitcertification.com [64.28.85.25]
over a maximum of 30 hops:
  1    <1 ms    <1 ms    <1 ms   THE-WALLACES-TI [192.168.1.1]
  2    12 ms    18 ms     9 ms   CPE-76-177-16-1.natcky.res.rr.com
       [76.177.16.1]
  3     8 ms    13 ms    11 ms   gig2-0-0.rcmdky-mx41.natcky.rr.com
       [65.28.199.205]
  4    32 ms    35 ms    34 ms   tge0-2-0.chcgileq-rtr1.kc.rr.com
       [65.28.199.97]
  5    30 ms    28 ms    35 ms   ae-4-0.cr0.chi10.tbone.rr.com
       [66.109.6.100]
  6    28 ms    36 ms    51 ms   ae-0-0.pr0.chi10.tbone.rr.com
       [66.109.6.153]
  7    32 ms    37 ms    32 ms   if-4-0-0.core1.CT8-Chicago.as6453.net
       [66.110.14.21]
  8    32 ms    31 ms    33 ms   if-1-0-0-1878.core2.CT8-Chicago.
       as6453.net [66.110.27.78]
  9    58 ms    60 ms    56 ms   63.243.186.25
 10    95 ms    64 ms    73 ms   cr2-pos-0-8-0-3.nyr.savvis.net
       [208.173.129.29]
 11    66 ms    61 ms    72 ms   hr1-tengig-13-0-0.waltham2bo2.savvis.
       net [204.70.198.182]
 12    62 ms    67 ms    62 ms   das3-v3038.bo2.savvis.net
       [209.202.187.182]
 13    62 ms    63 ms    66 ms   blhosting.bridgelinesw.com
       [64.14.81.46]
 14    63 ms    62 ms    76 ms   www1.webdialogs.com [64.28.85.25]
    Trace complete.
```

Example 10-19 shows an unsuccessful trace. The first-hop router (192.168.1.1) responded; however, the router beyond that did not respond. So, in a troubleshooting situation, you might focus your attention to the interconnection between those two routers.

Example 10-19   Sample Output from an Unsuccessful Windows `tracert` Command

```
C:\>tracert 172.16.1.1
Tracing route to 172.16.1.1 over a maximum of 30 hops
  1     <1 ms     <1 ms     <1 ms    THE-WALLACES-TI [192.168.1.1]
  2      *         *         *       Request timed out.
  3      *         *         *       Request timed out.
  4      *         *         *       Request timed out.
  5      *         *         *       Request timed out.
  6      *         *         *       Request timed out.
  7      *         *         *       Request timed out.
  8      *         *         *       Request timed out.
  9      *         *         *       Request timed out.
   OUTPUT OMITTED...
```

UNIX Commands

This discussion of UNIX OS commands is more generic than Windows, in that there are many variations of UNIX implementations: some open-standard implementations and some vendor-specific implementations. This chapter describes UNIX commands as they exist in Apple's OS X (10.6 Snow Leopard) OS, which runs a variant of UNIX at its core.

Although some of the following UNIX command can be used for the same purposes as some of the Windows commands, the syntax might vary slightly. Again, this chapter is not an exhaustive syntax reference, but a quick reference for common use cases and common options for the selected commands.

One of the benefits of UNIX is its extensive syntax reference in the form of *manual pages* (*man pages*). These man pages can be invoked with the following syntax:

HOST# **man** *command*

For example, if you want detailed information about the **arp** command, you can enter **man arp** to produce the output shown in Example 10-20.

Example 10-20   Sample Output from a Sample UNIX **man** Command

```
HOST# man arp


ARP(8)                          BSD System Manager's Manual
ARP(8)


NAME
     arp -- address resolution display and control

SYNOPSIS
     arp [-n] [-i interface] hostname
     arp [-n] [-i interface] -a
     arp -d hostname [pub] [ifscope interface]
     arp -d [-i interface] -a
     arp -s hostname ether_addr [temp] [reject] [blackhole] [pub [only]]
         [ifscope interface]
     arp -S hostname ether_addr [temp] [reject] [blackhole] [pub [only]]
         [ifscope interface]
     arp -f filename

DESCRIPTION
     The arp utility displays and modifies the Internet-to-Ethernet address
     translation tables used by the address resolution protocol (arp(4)).
     With no flags, the program displays the current ARP entry for hostname.
     The host may be specified by name or by number, using Internet dot
notation.


   :
     OUTPUT OMITTED...
```

Other than the **man** command, all the UNIX commands listed in this section are commands listed in the Network+ exam (N10-005) blueprint.

arp

Similar to the Windows **arp** command, the UNIX **arp** command can be used to display MAC-address-to-IP-address mappings. The syntax of the **arp** command is as follows:

```
arp [-a]
arp [-n] [-i interface] -a
```

```
arp -s hostname ether_addr [temp] [reject] [blackhole] [ifscope
interface]
arp -d hostname [ifscope interface]
arp -d [-i interface] -a
    arp -f filename
```

Table 10-7 explains the usage of the previously listed command options.

Table 10-7   Parameters for the UNIX **arp** Command

Parameter	Purpose
-a	This option displays current ARP entries in a UNIX hosts' ARP table.
-n	This option displays network addresses as numbers instead of symbols.
-i *interface*	This option specifies that the **arp** command should be limited to a specified interface.
-d	An ARP entry for a host can be deleted with this option, in combination with the inet_addr parameter. A wildcard character of * can delete all host entries.
-s	This option, used in conjunction with the hostname and eth_addr parameters, statically adds a host entry in the ARP table.
ifscope *interface*	This option indicates that the **arp** command should be limited to a specified interface.
hostname	This option is the IP address of the host to be associated with a specified MAC address.
eth_addr	This parameter specifies a 48-bit MAC address.
temp	Used in conjunction with the **-s** option, the **temp** option says that the static ARP entry is only temporary, as opposed to the default of being permanent.
reject	Used in conjunction with the **-s** option, this option says that traffic to the destination specified in the static ARP entry will be rejected, and the sender will be notified that the host is unreachable.
blackhole	Similar to the **reject** option, the **blackhole** option says that traffic to the destination specified in the static ARP entry will be rejected. However, the sender is not notified.
-f *filename*	This option allows an external file to be used to import a collection of ARP entries. The entries in the external file should be in the following format: **hostname** *ether_addr* [**temp**] [**ifscope** *interface*]

To illustrate a few uses of the **arp** command, first imagine that you want to add an entry in your UNIX host's ARP cache for an IP address of *192.168.1.32*. You know the MAC address of that device is *11:22:33:44:55:66*, and you know that the device is available off of interface *en0*. You can enter the **arp** command with the **-s** option, as demonstrated in Example 10-21, to add a static ARP entry. The example then confirms the entry has been made by issuing the **arp -a** command.

Example 10-21   Adding and Confirming a Static ARP Entry with the UNIX `arp` Command

```
HOST# arp -s 192.168.1.32 11:22:33:44:55:66 ifscope en0
HOST# arp -a
? (172.16.53.255) at (incomplete) on vmnet1 ifscope [ethernet]
? (172.16.202.255) at (incomplete) on vmnet8 ifscope [ethernet]
? (192.168.1.1) at 0:1f:f3:c9:39:fe on en0 ifscope [ethernet]
? (192.168.1.2) at 0:18:f8:50:ad:35 on en0 ifscope [ethernet]
? (192.168.1.32) at 11:22:33:44:55:66 on en0 ifscope [ethernet]
? (192.168.1.50) at 0:24:81:ee:4c:e on en0 ifscope [ethernet]
? (192.168.1.235) at 0:21:5a:b8:13:9 on en0 ifscope [ethernet]
? (192.168.1.240) at 0:23:12:18:a1:bd on en0 ifscope [ethernet]
? (192.168.1.248) at 0:21:47:3:6:94 on en0 ifscope [ethernet]
    ? (192.168.1.255) at (incomplete) on en0 ifscope [ethernet]
```

Next, imagine that you want to delete the entry you just added. Example 10-22 shows how the **-d** option of the **arp** command can remove an entry from a host's ARP cache. The output then confirms that the entry was removed.

Example 10-22   Deleting and Confirming the Deletion of a Static ARP Entry with the UNIX `arp` Command

```
HOST# arp -d 192.168.1.32 ifscope en0
192.168.1.32 (192.168.1.32) deleted
HOST# arp -a
? (172.16.53.255) at (incomplete) on vmnet1 ifscope [ethernet]
? (172.16.202.255) at (incomplete) on vmnet8 ifscope [ethernet]
? (192.168.1.1) at 0:1f:f3:c9:39:fe on en0 ifscope [ethernet]
? (192.168.1.2) at 0:18:f8:50:ad:35 on en0 ifscope [ethernet]
? (192.168.1.50) at 0:24:81:ee:4c:e on en0 ifscope [ethernet]
? (192.168.1.235) at 0:21:5a:b8:13:9 on en0 ifscope [ethernet]
? (192.168.1.240) at 0:23:12:18:a1:bd on en0 ifscope [ethernet]
? (192.168.1.248) at 0:21:47:3:6:94 on en0 ifscope [ethernet]
? (192.168.1.255) at (incomplete) on en0 ifscope [ethernet]
```

dig and nslookup

The Windows **nslookup** command was used to resolve a given FQDN to its IP address. UNIX has a similar **nslookup** command, which can also be used for FQDN-to-IP-address resolution.

The **dig** command can similarly be used to resolve FQDNs to IP addresses. Unlike the **nslookup** command, however, the **dig** command is entirely a command-line command (**dig** lacks the interactive mode of the **nslookup** command).

Example 10-23 compares the output of the **nslookup** and **dig** commands. Notice that the **dig** command offers more information than the **nslookup** command. For example, the *A* in the *QUESTION SECTION* output of the **dig** command identifies the DNS record type (an *A record*, which is an *alias record*). If you peruse the output, you can find a few other pieces of information present in the **dig** command output, not found in the **nslookup** command output; however, the **dig** command is rarely used to glean these more subtle pieces of information. Rather, the **dig** command is used by many UNIX administrators as simply an alternate way of resolving FQDNs to IP addresses. Notice that both commands indicate that the IP address corresponding to the FQDN of *www.pearsonitcertification* is *64.28.85.25*.

Example 10-23   Comparing Output from the UNIX `dig` and `nslookup` Commands

```
HOST# nslookup www.pearsonitcertification.com
Server:     192.168.1.1
Address:    192.168.1.1#53


Non-authoritative answer:
Name:    www.pearsonitcertification.com
Address: 64.28.85.25


HOST# dig www.pearsonitcertification.com

; <<>> DiG 9.6.0-APPLE-P2 <<>> www.pearsonitcertification.com
;; global options: +cmd
;; Got answer:
;; ->>HEADER<<- opcode: QUERY, status: NOERROR, id: 10821
;; flags: qr rd ra; QUERY: 1, ANSWER: 1, AUTHORITY: 0, ADDITIONAL: 0

;; QUESTION SECTION:
;www.pearsonitcertification.com.      IN        A


;; ANSWER SECTION:
www.pearsonitcertification.com.      10791 IN A    64.28.85.25
```

```
;; Query time: 5 msec
;; SERVER: 192.168.1.1#53(192.168.1.1)
;; WHEN: Mon May 30 13:36:11 2011
  ;; MSG SIZE  rcvd: 64
```

host

Yet another approach to resolving FQDNs to IP addresses is to use the **host** command. The **host** command offers a variety of options, and you can read more about them by issuing the **man host** command from a UNIX prompt. However, this discussion focuses on the most frequent use of the **host** command, which is FQDN-to-IP-address resolution.

Example 10-24 shows output from **host www.pearsonitcertification.com**. Notice that the resolved IP address of *64.28.85.25* matches the IP address resolved by both the **dig** and **nslookup** commands.

Example 10-24 Sample Output from the UNIX **host** Command

```
HOST# host www.pearsonitcertification.com
   www.pearsonitcertification.com has address 64.28.85.25
```

ifconfig

The UNIX **ifconfig** command is most similar to the Windows **ipconfig** command, although the output is noticeably different. Issued by itself, the **ifconfig** command displays a UNIX host's interfaces along with configuration information about those interfaces, including MAC address, maximum transmission unit (MTU), IPv4 address, and IPv6 address information.

Beyond just displaying interface information, the **ifconfig** command can also configure interface parameters. For example, an interface's IP address can be configured with the **ifconfig** command.

Although many options are available (see the UNIX man pages for more details), the following syntax shows how to use the previously described **ifconfig** command functions:

```
ifconfig [interface [inet ip_addr netmask netmask]]
```

For example, if want to configure interface *en0* with an IP address of *192.168.1.26* with a subnet mask of *255.255.255.0*, you could issue the command **ifconfig en0 inet 192.168.1.26 netmask 255.255.255.0**. Example 10-25 shows this command being issued, followed by the display generated from the **ifconfig** command to confirm that the change took effect.

Example 10-25 Configuring and Verifying the Configuration of an Interface's IP Address with the UNIX **ifconfig** Command

```
HOST# ifconfig en0 inet 192.168.1.26 netmask 255.255.255.0
HOST# ifconfig
lo0: flags=8049<UP,LOOPBACK,RUNNING,MULTICAST> mtu 16384
        inet 127.0.0.1 netmask 0xff000000
        inet6 ::1 prefixlen 128
        inet6 fe80::1%lo0 prefixlen 64 scopeid 0x1
        inet6 fdb9:537c:6f1c:705f:5a55:caff:fefa:1551 prefixlen 128
gif0: flags=8010<POINTOPOINT,MULTICAST> mtu 1280
stf0: flags=0<> mtu 1280
en0: flags=8863<UP,BROADCAST,SMART,RUNNING,SIMPLEX,MULTICAST> mtu 1500
        ether 58:55:ca:fa:15:51
        inet6 fe80::5a55:caff:fefa:1551%en0 prefixlen 64 scopeid 0x4
        inet 192.168.1.26 netmask 0xffffff00 broadcast 192.168.1.255
        media: autoselect
        status: active
    OUTPUT OMITTED...
```

traceroute

The **traceroute** UNIX command can be used for the same purpose as the **tracert** Windows command. Specifically, you can help isolate which router hop along the path from a source device to a destination device is having issues. Also, based on the round-trip response time information reported for each hop, you can better determine which network segment might be causing excessive delay because of congestion. Example 10-26 offers sample output from the **traceroute** command, which is identifying the 13 router hops a UNIX host must transit to reach *pearsonitcertifica-tion.com*.

Example 10-26   Sample Output from the UNIX `traceroute` Command

```
HOST# traceroute pearsonitcertification.com
traceroute to pearsonitcertification.com (64.28.85.25), 64 hops max,
52 byte packets
 1   192.168.1.1 (192.168.1.1)   3.480 ms   2.548 ms   2.404 ms
 2   cpe-76-177-16-1.natcky.res.rr.com (76.177.16.1)   22.150 ms   11.300
     ms   9.719 ms
 3   gig2-0-0.rcmdky-mx41.natcky.rr.com (65.28.199.205)   9.242 ms
     19.940 ms   11.735 ms
 4   tge0-2-0.chcgileq-rtr1.kc.rr.com (65.28.199.97)   38.459 ms   38.821
     ms   36.157 ms
 5   ae-4-0.cr0.chi10.tbone.rr.com (66.109.6.100)   41.903 ms   37.388 ms
     31.966 ms
 6   ae-0-0.pr0.chi10.tbone.rr.com (66.109.6.153)   75.757 ms   46.287 ms
     35.031 ms
 7   if-4-0-0.core1.ct8-chicago.as6453.net (66.110.14.21)   48.020 ms
     37.248 ms   45.446 ms
 8   if-1-0-0-1878.core2.ct8-chicago.as6453.net (66.110.27.78)   108.466
     ms   55.465 ms   87.590 ms
 9   63.243.186.25 (63.243.186.25)   64.045 ms   63.582 ms   69.200 ms
10   cr2-pos-0-8-0-3.nyr.savvis.net (208.173.129.29)   64.933 ms   65.113
     ms   61.759 ms
11   hr1-tenqiq-13-0-0.waltham?bo2.savvis.net (204.70.198.182)   71.964
     ms   65.430 ms   74.397 ms
12   das3-v3038.bo2.savvis.net (209.202.187.182)   65.777 ms   64.483 ms
     82.383 ms
13   blhosting.bridgelinesw.com (64.14.81.46)   63.448 ms !X *   68.879
     ms !X
```

netstat

The UNIX **netstat** command serves the same basic purpose of the Windows **netstat** command, which is to display various information about current connections. This information includes source and destination IP addresses and port numbers. You can also display protocol statistics with the **netstat** command.

The following is the syntax for the **netstat** command, with some of its commonly used options:

netstat [**-a**] [**-b**] [**-r**] [**-s**]

Table 10-8 explains the usage of the previously listed command options.

Table 10-8   Parameters for the Windows `netstat` Command

Parameter	Purpose
-a	This option displays all of a UNIX host's active IP-based sessions, along with the TCP and UDP ports of each session.
-b	This option shows you the names of the program that opened up a session.
-r	This option displays a UNIX host's IP routing table.
-s	This option displays statistical information for protocols such as udp, ip, icmp, igmp, ipsec, ip6, icmp6, ipsec6, rip6, and pfkey (**Note:** These protocols vary depending on your UNIX platform.)

As with Windows, the UNIX **netstat** command issued by itself produces output that details each current session, as shown in Example 10-27.

Example 10-27   Sample Output from the UNIX `netstat` Command

```
HOST# netstat
Active Internet connections
Proto Recv-Q Send-Q  Local Address            Foreign Address         (state)
tcp4     37      0   192.168.1.245.49499      172.20.202.51-st.https  CLOSE_WAIT
tcp4     37      0   192.168.1.245.49495      192.168.202.51-st.https CLOSE_WAIT
tcp4      0      0   192.168.1.26.49472       192.168.1.50.17500      ESTABLISHED
tcp4      0      0   192.168.1.26.49471       192.168.1.240.17501     ESTABLISHED
tcp4      0      0   192.168.1.245.49436      172.16.30.42-sta.http   ESTABLISHED
tcp4      0      0   192.168.1.245.17500      192.168.1.50.2583       ESTABLISHED
tcp4      0      0   192.168.1.245.17500      192.168.1.240.60687     ESTABLISHED
tcp4      0      0   192.168.1.245.49423      10.243.202.51-st.https  CLOSE_WAIT
tcp4      0      0   192.168.1.245.49321      172.16.62.121.https     ESTABLISHED
tcp4      0      0   localhost.26164          localhost.49184         ESTABLISHED
tcp4      0      0   192.168.1.26.49505       192.168.1.240.netbios-  TIME_WAIT
OUTPUT OMITTED...
```

The **netstat** command with the **-r** option can also be used to view the IP routing table of a UNIX host, as shown in Example 10-28.

Example 10-28   Sample Output from the UNIX `netstat -r` Command

```
HOST# netstat -r
Routing tables

Internet:
Destination         Gateway            Flags       Refs       Use    Netif Expire
default             192.168.1.1        UGSc          45        40       en0
127                 localhost          UCS            0         0       lo0
localhost           localhost          UH             2        14       lo0
169.254             link#4             UCS            0         0       en0
172.16.53/24        link#6             UC             3         0     vmnet1
172.16.53.1         0:50:56:c0:0:1     UHLWI          0       107       lo0
172.16.53.255       link#6             UHLWbI         2       184     vmnet1
172.16.202/24       link#5             UC             2         0     vmnet8
172.16.202.255      link#5             UHLWbI         2       184     vmnet8
192.168.1           link#4             UC            10         0       en0
192.168.1.1         0:1f:f3:c9:39:fe   UHLWI         67       257       en0
1183
192.168.1.2         0:18:f8:50:ad:35   UHLWI          0         0       en0
1032
192.168.1.50        0:24:81:ee:4c:e    UHLWI          2       481       en0
```

ping

The UNIX **ping** command is most typically used to test network reachability to a specified destination, such as the Windows version **ping** command. However, unlike the Windows **ping** command, the UNIX **ping** command sends continuous pings, as opposed to the Windows default of only four pings.

Syntax for the UNIX **ping** command, along with some of its commonly used parameters, is as follows:

`ping [-c count] [-D] [-S srcaddr] target_name`

Table 10-9 explains the usage of the previously listed command options.

Table 10-9   Parameters for the UNIX `ping` Command

Parameter	Purpose
-c *count*	This option specifies the number of pings to send.
-D	This option sets the Do Not Fragment bit in a packet's header. If the packet tries to cross a router that attempts to fragment the packet, the packet is dropped and an ICMP error message is returned.
-S *srcaddr*	If the UNIX host from which you are issuing the **ping** command has more than one interface, this option allows you to specify the source IP address from which the ICMP echo messages should be sent.
target_name	This option specifies the name or the IP address of the device to which you are sending ICMP echo messages.

Example 10-29 shows output from a **ping** command limited to sending only five ICMP echo packets.

Example 10-29   *Sample Output from the UNIX ping -c Command*

```
HOST# ping -c 5 192.168.1.1
PING 192.168.1.1 (192.168.1.1): 56 data bytes
64 bytes from 192.168.1.1: icmp_seq=0 ttl=255 time=7.386 ms
64 bytes from 192.168.1.1: icmp_seq=1 ttl=255 time=7.490 ms
64 bytes from 192.168.1.1: icmp_seq=2 ttl=255 time=7.485 ms
64 bytes from 192.168.1.1: icmp_seq=3 ttl=255 time=2.575 ms
64 bytes from 192.168.1.1: icmp_seq=4 ttl=255 time=7.584 ms


--- 192.168.1.1 ping statistics ---
5 packets transmitted, 5 packets received, 0.0% packet loss
round-trip min/avg/max/stddev = 2.575/6.504/7.584/1.965 ms
            route
```

Although the UNIX **route** command is not used to display a host's IP routing table, which is a use of the Windows **route** command, it can be used to modify a UNIX host's IP routing table. The **route** command has multiple options; however, this discussion focuses on using the **route** command to add or delete a route from a UNIX host's routing table.

A partial syntax description for the UNIX **route** command, which focuses on adding and deleting routes from a UNIX host's routing table, is as follows:

```
route [-qv] [[add | delete] net network/mask gateway]
```

Table 10-10 explains the usage of the previously listed command options.

Table 10-10 Parameters for the UNIX `route` Command Used to Add and Delete Routes

Parameter	Purpose
-q	This option, where the q stands for *quiet*, suppresses any output from appearing onscreen after entering the **route** command.
-v	This option, where the v stands for *verbose*, causes additional details about the **route** command's execution to be shown onscreen.
add	This option adds a route to a UNIX host's routing table.
delete	This option deletes a route from a UNIX host's routing table.
net	This option specifies that the next parameter is a network address.
network	This option specifies the network to add or remove from a UNIX host's routing table.
mask	This option is the number of bits in a specified network's subnet mask.
gateway	This option is the IP address of the gateway, which is the next hop toward the specified network.

Example 10-30 illustrates an example of using the UNIX **route** command to add a static route to a UNIX host's routing table. Specifically, a route to *10.1.2.0/24* with a next-hop gateway of *192.168.1.1* is being added. Also, notice that the **netstat -r** command issued after the **route** command to confirm the insertion of the 10.1.2.0/24 route into the UNIX host's routing table.

Example 10-30   Adding a Static Route with the UNIX **route** Command

```
HOST# route add 10.1.2.0/24 192.168.1.1
add net 10.1.2.0: gateway 192.168.1.1
HOST# netstat -r
Routing tables

Internet:
Destination      Gateway          Flags     Refs      Use   Netif Expire
default          192.168.1.1      UGSc        15        0   en0
10.1.2/24        192.168.1.1      UGSc         0        0   en0
127              localhost        UCS          0        0   lo0
localhost        localhost        UH           2        8   lo0
169.254          link#4           UCS          0        0   en0
     OUTPUT OMITTED...
```

Summary

The main topics covered in this chapter are the following:

- A collection of Windows CLI commands can be useful to monitor and troubleshoot a network. These commands include **arp**, **ipconfig**, **nbtstat**, **netstat**, **nslookup**, **ping**, **route**, and **tracert**.

- A series of UNIX CLI commands include **man**, **arp**, **dig**, **nslookup**, **host**, **ifconfig**, **traceroute**, **netstat**, **ping**, and **route**.

Exam Preparation Tasks

Review All the Key Topics

Review the most important topics from inside the chapter, noted with the Key Topic icon in the outer margin of the page. Table 10-11 lists these key topics and the page numbers where each is found.

Table 10-11   Key Topics for Chapter 10

Key Topic Element	Description	Page Number
Example 10-1	Sample output from the Windows **arp -a** command	317
Example 10-2	Sample output from the Windows **ipconfig /all** command	319
Example 10-6	Sample output from the Windows **nbtstat -c** command	322
Example 10-9	Sample output from the Windows **netstat** command	325
Example 10-11	Sample output from the Windows **nslookup** non-interactive command	327
Example 10-13	Sample output from the Windows **ping** command	329
Example 10-15	Sample output from the Windows **route print** command	331
Example 10-16	Sample output from a successful Windows **tracert** command	333
Example 10-21	Adding and confirming a static ARP entry with the UNIX **arp** command	339
Example 10-23	Comparing output from the UNIX **dig** and **nslookup** commands	340
Example 10-24	Sample output from the UNIX **host** command	341
Example 10-25	Configuring and verifying the configuration of an interface's IP address with the UNIX **ifconfig** command	342
Example 10-26	Sample output from the UNIX **traceroute** command	343
Example 10-27	Sample output from the UNIX **netstat** command	344
Example 10-29	Sample output from the UNIX **ping -c** command	346
Example 10-30	Adding a static route with the UNIX **route** command	348

Complete Tables and Lists from Memory

Print a copy of Appendix C, "Memory Tables" (found on the CD), or at least the section for this chapter, and complete the tables and lists from memory. Appendix D, "Memory Table Answer Key," also on the CD, includes the completed tables and lists so you can check your work.

Define Key Terms

Define the following key terms from this chapter, and check your answers in the Glossary:

arp command, **ipconfig** command, **nbtstat** command, **netstat** command, **nslookup** command, **ping** command, **route** command, **tracert** command, **dig** command, **host** command, **traceroute** command

Review Questions

The answers to these review questions are in Appendix A, "Answers to Review Questions."

1. Consider the following output:

    ```
    C:\>arp -a

    Interface: 172.16.202.128 --- 0xb
       Internet Address      Physical Address      Type
       172.16.202.2          00-50-56-fd-65-2c     dynamic
       172.16.202.255        ff-ff-ff-ff-ff-ff     static
       224.0.0.22            01-00-5e-00-00-16     static
       224.0.0.252           01-00-5e-00-00-fc     static
       255.255.255.255       ff-ff-ff-ff-ff-ff     static
    ```

    What is the IP MAC address corresponding to the IP address of 172.16.202.2?

    a. ff-ff-ff-ff-ff-ff

    b. 00-50-56-fd-65-2c

    c. 01-00-5e-00-00-16

    d. 01-00-5e-00-00-fc

2. What option would you specify after the **ipconfig** command to display a Windows PC's DNS server's IP address?

   a. No option is needed, because the **ipconfig** displays DNS server information by default.

   b. /full

   c. /fqdn

   d. /all

3. Which Windows commands could have produced the following output? (Choose two.)

```
===============================================================================
Interface List
 20...00 0c 29 3a 21 67 ......Intel(R) PRO/1000 MT Network Connection #2
 11...00 0c 29 3a 21 5d ......Intel(R) PRO/1000 MT Network Connection
  1.......................... Software Loopback Interface 1
 12...00 00 00 00 00 00 00 e0 Microsoft ISATAP Adapter
 13...00 00 00 00 00 00 00 e0 Teredo Tunneling Pseudo-Interface
===============================================================================


IPv4 Route Table
===============================================================================
Active Routes:
Network Destination        Netmask          Gateway        Interface  Metric
          0.0.0.0          0.0.0.0      172.16.202.2   172.16.202.128      10
          0.0.0.0          0.0.0.0      172.16.202.2   172.16.202.129      10
        127.0.0.0        255.0.0.0         On-link         127.0.0.1     306
        127.0.0.1  255.255.255.255         On-link         127.0.0.1     306
  127.255.255.255  255.255.255.255         On-link         127.0.0.1     306
     172.16.202.0    255.255.255.0         On-link    172.16.202.128     266
     172.16.202.0    255.255.255.0         On-link    172.16.202.129     266
   172.16.202.128  255.255.255.255         On-link    172.16.202.128     266
   172.16.202.129  255.255.255.255         On-link    172.16.202.129     266
   172.16.202.255  255.255.255.255         On-link    172.16.202.128     266
   172.16.202.255  255.255.255.255         On-link    172.16.202.129     266
        224.0.0.0        240.0.0.0         On-link         127.0.0.1     306
        224.0.0.0        240.0.0.0         On-link    172.16.202.129     266
        224.0.0.0        240.0.0.0         On-link    172.16.202.128     266
  255.255.255.255  255.255.255.255         On-link         127.0.0.1     306
  255.255.255.255  255.255.255.255         On-link    172.16.202.129     266
  255.255.255.255  255.255.255.255         On-link    172.16.202.128     266
```

    a. netstat -a

    b. route print

    c. netstat -r

    d. nbtstat -r

4. Which of the following Windows commands is used to display NetBIOS over TCP/IP information?

    a. route

    b. nbtstat

    c. dig

    d. netstat

5. What Layer 4 protocol is used by the **ping** command?

    a. IGMP

    b. PIM

    c. ICMP

    d. RTP

6. Which of the following commands is used on a UNIX host to generate information about each along the path from a source to a destination?

    a. ping -t

    b. tracert

    c. ping -r

    d. traceroute

7. Which of the following UNIX commands can be used to check FQDN-to-IP-address resolution? (Choose three.)

    a. nslookup

    b. netstat

    c. dig

    d. host

8. Which of the following commands would you issue on a UNIX host to send five ICMP echo messages to a device with an IP address of 10.1.1.1?

   a. **ping 10.1.1.1** (No options are required, because five is the default number of pings.)

   b. **ping -c 5 10.1.1.1**

   c. **ping -t 5 10.1.1.1**

   d. **ping 10.1.1.1 -t 5**

9. What command produced the following snippet of output?
   ```
   OUTPUT OMITTED...
   ;; global options: +cmd
   ;; Got answer:
   ;; ->>HEADER<<- opcode: QUERY, status: NOERROR, id: 62169
   ;; flags: qr rd ra; QUERY: 1, ANSWER: 1, AUTHORITY: 0,
   ADDITIONAL: 0

   ;; QUESTION SECTION:
   ;pearsonitcertification.com. IN          A

   ;; ANSWER SECTION:
   pearsonitcertification.com. 10800 IN        A
   64.28.85.25

   ;; Query time: 202 msec
   ;; SERVER: 192.168.1.1#53(192.168.1.1)
   ;; WHEN: Wed Jun  1 20:41:57 2011
   ;; MSG SIZE   rcvd: 60
   OUTPUT OMITTED...
   ```

   a. **traceroute -d pearsonitcertification.com**

   b. **dig pearsonitcertification.com**

   c. **netstat -a pearsonitcertification.com**

   d. **nbtstat pearsonitcertification.com**

10. What command produced the following snippet of output?

```
OUTPUT OMITTED...
lo0: flags=8049<UP,LOOPBACK,RUNNING,MULTICAST> mtu 16384
     inet 127.0.0.1 netmask 0xff000000
     inet6 ::1 prefixlen 128
     inet6 fe80::1%lo0 prefixlen 64 scopeid 0x1
     inet6 fd4e:f9d5:c34e:acd1:5a55:caff:fefa:1551 prefixlen 128
gif0: flags=8010<POINTOPOINT,MULTICAST> mtu 1280
stf0: flags=0<> mtu 1280
en0: flags=8863<UP,BROADCAST,SMART,RUNNING,SIMPLEX,MULTICAST>
  mtu 1500
     ether 58:55:ca:fa:15:51
     inet6 fe80::5a55:caff:fefa:1551%en0 prefixlen 64 scopeid 0x4
     inet 192.168.1.245 netmask 0xffffff00 broadcast
       192.168.1.255
     media: autoselect
     status: active
OUTPUT OMITTED...
```

a ifconfig

b ipconfig

c ipconfig /all

d ifconfig /all

After completion of this chapter, you will be able to
answer the following questions:

- What are some of the more common tools used to physically maintain a network?

- What components are involved in configuration management?

- What sorts of network monitoring tools are available to network administrators, and what types of information are included in various logs?

CHAPTER 11

Managing a Network

Even with a network's increasing dependence on wireless technologies, physical cabling still comprises the critical backbone of a network. Therefore, network management, monitoring, and troubleshooting require a familiarity with a variety of cable maintenance tools. These tools might, for example, be used to physically terminate cabling and troubleshoot cabling issues. This chapter addresses these and other maintenance tools, providing an overview of each.

Another key network-management element is documentation, which encompasses, as one example, managing device-configuration information. Such configuration repositories are continually evolving entities requiring ongoing attention. This chapter discusses several of the most important configuration element components.

Finally, this chapter addresses network monitoring resources and reports whose information can be gleaned from monitoring resources. For example, the primary network management protocol used by network management systems (NMS) is *Simple Network Management Protocol* (SNMP), and this chapter discusses the various versions of SNMP. Additionally, syslog servers and a variety of reports are considered.

Foundation Topics

Maintenance Tools

The number of troubleshooting issues occurring in a network can be reduced by proper installation and configuration. For example, improper wiring might function immediately following an installation; however, over time, the wiring might start to experience intermittent issues that cause network disruptions. In such a situation, you, as a network administrator, need to be familiar with a collection of maintenance tools to help diagnose, isolate, and resolve the wiring issue.

Therefore, this chapter presents you with a collection of popular network tools. Having this understanding can help you better perform initial installations and resolve issues with existing installations.

Bit-Error Rate Tester

Interference on a transmission medium, or faulty cabling, can cause errors in the transmission of binary data (or bits). A common measurement for bit errors is called *bit error rate* (BER), which is calculated as follows:

BER = Bit errors / Bits transmitted

For example, imagine that a network device transmitted the binary pattern of 10101010; however, the pattern received by the destination device was 10101111. Comparing these two bit patterns reveals that the sixth and eighth bits were incorrectly received. Therefore, the BER could be calculated by dividing the number of bit errors (two) by the number of transmitted bits (eight), resulting in a BER of 25 percent (BER = 2 / 8 = .25).

When troubleshooting a link where you suspect a high BER, you can use a piece of test equipment called a *bit-error rate tester* (BERT), as shown in Figure 11-1. A BERT contains both a *pattern generator* (which can generate a variety of bit patterns) and an *error detector* (which is synchronized with the pattern generator and can determine the number of bit errors), and it can calculate a BER for the tested transmission link.

Figure 11-1 Bit-Error Rate Tester (BERT) (Photo Courtesy of BBN International [www.bbnint.co.uk])

Butt Set

A *butt set* is a piece of test equipment typically used by telephone technicians. The clips on the butt set can connect a punch-down block (for example, a 66 block or a 110 block) connecting to a telephone. This allows the technician to check a line (for example, to determine if a dial tone is present on the line or to determine if a call can be placed from the line).

The name of *butt set* (which is sometimes called a *butt in*) comes from the device's capability to butt into (or interrupt) a conversation in progress. For example, a telephone technician might be at the top of a telephone pole and connect to the wires of a phone currently in a call. The technician would then butt into the call, identifying himself and stating that he was testing the line.

Although a butt set is an extremely common piece of test equipment for telephone technicians, it has less usefulness to you as a network administrator. One exception, however, is if you are working on a digital subscriber line (DSL) line. You could use a butt set while working on DSL wiring to confirm dial tone is present on the line.

Cable Certifier

Chapter 3, "Identifying Network Components," introduced you to a variety of unshielded twisted pair (UTP) wiring categories (for example, Cat 3, Cat 5, and Cat 5e). Different UTP categories support different data rates over specific distances. If you are working with existing cable and want to determine its category, or if you simply want to test the supported frequency range (and therefore data throughput) of a cable, you can use a *cable certifier*.

Cable Tester

A *cable tester* can test the conductors in an Ethernet cable. Notice the two parts that comprise the cable tester. By connecting these parts of the cable tester to each end of a cable under test, you can check the wires in the cable for continuity (that is, check to make sure there are no opens, or breaks, in a conductor). Additionally, you can verify an RJ-45 connector's pinouts (wires are connected to appropriate pins on an RJ-45 connector).

Connectivity Software

When you are physically separate from the network you are maintaining or trouble-shooting, you might be able to access the network through *remote connectivity software*. *RealVNC* and *GoToMyPC* are two examples of software that allow you to take control of a PC that's located on a remote network. Additionally, Microsoft has its own proprietary protocol called *Remote Desktop Protocol* (RDP), which supports remotely connecting to a Microsoft Windows computer. Figure 11-2 shows Microsoft's *Remote Desktop Connection* application (which comes with Microsoft Windows 7). In the figure, you see a dialog box prompting a user for an IP address of the remote computer with which they want to connect.

Figure 11-2 Microsoft's Remote Desktop Connection

Crimper

A *crimper*, as pictured in Figure 11-3, can be used to attach a connector (for example, an RJ-45 connector) to the end of a UTP cable. To accompany a crimper, you might want to purchase a spool of cable (for example, Category 6 UTP cable) and a box of RJ-45 connectors. You will then be equipped to make your own Ethernet patch cables, which might be less expensive than buying preterminated UTP cables, and convenient when you need a patch cable of a nonstandard length or when you need a nonstandard pinout on the RJ-45 connectors (for example, when you need a T1 crossover cable).

Figure 11-3   Crimper

Electrostatic Discharge Wrist Strap

Do you remember a time when you touched a metallic object and received a shock, due to the static electricity you built up (for example, by walking on a carpeted floor)? That static discharge was probably a few thousand volts. Although the shock might have caused you to recoil your hand, you survived this event, because the amperage of the shock was low (probably just a few milliamps). Although no damage was done to your hand or the object you touched, if the static discharge occurred when you touched a component on a circuit board, you could destroy that component.

Viewed under a microscope, the damage done to electrical components subjected to static shock is very evident, with visible craters in the components. Therefore, care must be taken when handling circuit boards (for example, *blades* used in modular switches or routers), to avoid destroying potentially expensive equipment.

As a precaution, you can wear an *electrostatic discharge* (ESD) *wrist strap*. The strap is equipped with a clip that you attach to something with a ground potential (for example, a large metal desk). While wearing the wrist strap, if you have any static buildup in your body, the static flows to the object with a ground potential, to which your strap is clipped, thus avoiding damage to any electrical components you might touch.

NOTE   Some ESD wrist straps contain a resistor to prevent you from being harmed if you come in contact with a voltage source capable of producing a significant current. Specifically, the formula for voltage is $V = R * I$, where V is voltage, R is resistance, and I is current. By rewriting the formula as $I = V / R$, you can see that if electricity has to flow through a greater resistance, the resulting current will be lower and, therefore, safer.

Environmental Monitor

Components (for example, routers, switches, and servers) making up a computer network are designed to operate within certain environmental limits. If the temperature rises too high in a server farm, for example, possibly because of an air-conditioner outage, components could begin to fail. To prevent such an occurrence, *environmental monitors* can be used to send an alert if the temperature in a room rises above or drops below administratively configured thresholds. By alerting appropriate personnel about a suspicious temperature variation before it becomes an issue, action can hopefully be taken to, for example, repair an air-conditioning unit or provide extra ventilation, thus preventing a system failure. In addition to monitoring a room's temperature, some environmental monitors also monitor a room's humidity.

Environmental monitors can alert appropriate personnel in a variety of ways. For example, some environmental monitors can send an alert to a *Simple Network Management Protocol* (SNMP) server. This alert is known as an *SNMP trap*. Another common notification option allows an environmental monitor to send an e-mail to alert appropriate personnel about the suspect environmental condition.

Loopback Plug

When troubleshooting a network device, you might want to confirm that a network interface is functional (for example, that it can transmit and receive traffic). One way to perform such a test is to attach a *loopback plug* to a network interface and run diagnostic software designed to use the loopback plug. A loopback plug takes the transmit pins on an Ethernet connector and connects them to the receive pins, such that everything that is transmitted is received back on the interface. Similarly, a fiber-optic loopback plug, as shown in Figure 11-4, interconnects a fiber-connector's transmit fiber with a connector's receive fiber. The diagnostic software can then transmit traffic out of a network interface and confirm its successful reception on that same interface.

Figure 11-4   Fiber-Optic Loopback Plug (Photo Courtesy of Digi-Key Corporation [www.digikey.com])

Multimeter

When working with copper cabling (as opposed to fiber-optic cabling), a *multimeter* can check a variety of a cable's electrical characteristics. These characteristics include *resistance* (in Ohms), *current* (in Amps), and *voltage* (in Volts). Figure 11-5 shows an example of a multimeter.

Figure 11-5   Multimeter

As one example, you could use the *ohmmeter* function of a multimeter (the resistance feature) to check continuity of an Ethernet cable. If you connect the two leads of a multimeter to two pins of a cable, the resulting resistance is approximately 0 Ohms if those two pins are connected, and the resulting resistance approaches an infinite number of Ohms if the pins do not connect with one another.

Another common use of a multimeter is to use the *voltmeter* function (the voltage feature). As an example, you could check leads of an Ethernet cable to see if DC voltage is being applied to a device needing to receive *Power over Ethernet* (PoE).

Protocol Analyzer

If you understand the characteristics of the protocols running on your network (for example, understanding the fields in a protocol's header), a *protocol analyzer* (also known as a *network sniffer*) can be a tremendous troubleshooting asset. A protocol analyzer can be a standalone device or software running on a laptop computer. You can use a protocol analyzer to capture traffic flowing through a network switch, using the port mirroring feature of a switch, as described in Chapter 4, "Understanding Ethernet." By examining the captured packets, you can discern the details of communication flows (sessions) as they are being set up, maintained, and torn down. The examination of these captured packets is referred to as *traffic analysis*, which provides an administrator with valuable insights about the nature of traffic flowing through the veins of the network.

Although protocol analyzers come in a wide range of features and costs, *Wireshark* is a free software program, which can make your laptop act as a protocol analyzer. You can download your free copy of Wireshark from www.wireshark.org. Figure 11-6 shows the Wireshark application.

Figure 11-6   Wireshark Protocol Analyzer Software

Punch-Down Tool

When terminating wires on a punch-down block (for example, a 110 block), an insulated wire is inserted between two *contact blades*. These blades cut through the insulation and make electrical contact with the inner wire. As a result, you do not have to strip off the insulation.

However, if you attempt to insert the wire between the two contact blades using a screwdriver, for example, the blades might be damaged to the point where they will not make a good connection. Therefore, you should use a *punch-down tool*, which is designed to properly insert an insulated wire between the two contact blades without damaging the blades.

Throughput Tester

Networks often perform differently when they are under a heavy load, as opposed to little or no load, which might be the case if you are mocking up a design in a testbed environment (which is a test network isolated from any production network). Also, you might simply want to verify a network's maximum throughput. Either scenario could benefit from a *throughput tester*.

A throughput tester is a network appliance, which typically has multiple network interfaces and can generate high volumes of pseudo-random data. You could, for example, connect a throughput tester to a proposed network that has been mocked up in a test bed, to observe how the network performs under a heavy load. Also, you can attach a throughput tester to a production network to determine the actual throughput of that existing network. Figure 11-7 shows an example of a throughput tester appliance.

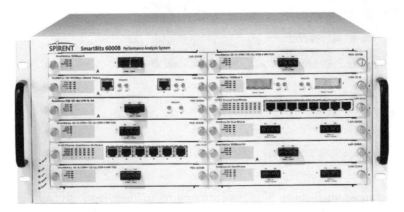

Figure 11-7   Throughput Tester (Photo Courtesy of NSS Labs [www.nsslabs.com])

Time Domain Reflectometer/Optical Time Domain Reflectometer

Imagine that you have been troubleshooting a network cable (either copper or fiber optic), and you determine that there is a break in (or physical damage to) the cable. However, identifying exactly where the break exists in a long length of cable can be problematic. Fortunately, you can use a *time domain reflectometer* (TDR) for copper cabling or an *optical time domain reflectometer* (OTDR) for fiber-optic cabling to locate the cable fault.

Both light and electricity travel at speeds approaching $3 * 10^8$ meters per second (approximately 186,000 miles per second), although the speeds are a bit slower and vary depending on the medium. A TDR can send an electric signal down a copper cable (or an OTDR sends light down a fiber-optic cable), and when the electric signal (or light) encounters a cable fault, a portion of the electric signal (or light) reflects back to the source. Based on the speed of electricity, or light, in the medium and on the amount of time required for the reflected electric signal or light to be returned to the source, a TDR or an OTDR can mathematically determine where the cable fault lies. Figure 11-8 shows an example of an OTDR.

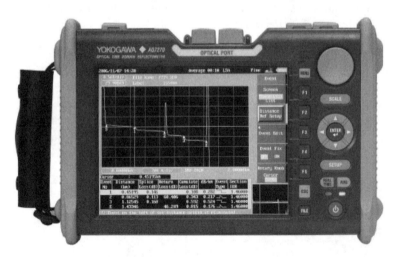

Figure 11-8   Optical Time Domain Reflectometer (Photo Courtesy of Coral-i Solutions [www.coral-i.com])

Toner Probe

If you are working on a punch-down block and attempting to identify which pair of wires connect back to an end-user's location (for example, someone's office), you can use a *toner probe*. A toner probe allows you to place a *tone generator* at one end of a connection (for example, someone's office), and use a *probe* on a punch-down block to audibly detect to which pair of wires the tone generator is connected.

A toner probe, therefore, comes in two pieces: the tone generator and the probe. Another common name for a toner probe is a *fox and hound*, where the tone generator is the *fox*, and the probe (which searches for the tone) is the *hound*.

Configuration Management

Configuration management (CM) focuses on maintaining up-to-date documentation of a network's configuration. As a result, CM helps ensure consistent configuration practices across network devices. CM encompasses a variety of procedures, including the following:

- **Asset management:** *Asset management*, as related to networks, is a formalized system of tracking network components and managing the lifecycle of those components. As an example, Cisco defines the *Cisco Lifecycle Services* maintenance model, which defines distinct phases in the lifecycle of a network asset using the acronym PPDIOO, which stands for the following:

  - Prepare

  - Plan

  - Design

  - Implement

  - Operate

  - Optimize

- **Baselining:** When troubleshooting a network issue, one of the first things you should do, after clearly defining the problem, is to gather information. This information might come from diagnostic commands you issue on network routers or switches, as a couple of examples. Information contained in the output of those diagnostic commands might include a link's bandwidth utilization, a router's CPU utilization, or a switch's memory utilization. For those numbers to be meaningful, however, you need to have previously collected similar data when the network was operating properly. The collection of such data under normal operating conditions is known as *baselining*. With comprehensive baseline data in your possession (which might include data collected at different times of the day and different days of the week), you can better notice any deviations from the norm when analyzing the data you collect when a problem exists on a network.

- **Cable management:** Designing and troubleshooting large networks requires documentation about a network's existing cable (that is, copper and fiber-optic cable) infrastructure. This documentation might include a diagram of a network's conduit system (if nearby buildings are interconnected), locations of punch-down blocks, and a listing of the sources and destinations of a network's cable runs that includes a consistent numbering system to clearly identify different cable pairs.

- **Change management:** When you make a change in a network, such as upgrading the operating system on a router requiring a network outage of fifteen minutes, realize that your actions could impact a business' operation. Therefore, many large companies institute a *change management* system, which is commonly in the form of software used by network administrators to alert other network administrators about an upcoming network change (for example, an Internet access outage required to swap out a router). Then, when other network administrators receive that notification, if they know of a conflict, where the planned network outage would impact a critical network function at a critical time (for example, a planned Internet outage might be scheduled for a time when a company is conducting a webcast for its customers), they can give feedback to the originator of the change notification. The two network administrators might then choose a different time to implement the planned change.

- **Network documentation:** Although having an up-to-date collection of network documentation is vital for effective network troubleshooting, be aware that having outdated network documentation can be worse than having no documentation at all. For example, if you attempt to troubleshoot an issue by relying on outdated (and therefore inaccurate) network documentation, you could make incorrect assumptions about which switch ports were connected to which end-user stations. As a result, you could draw erroneous conclusions.

Therefore, take care to ensure the ongoing upkeep of a complete set of network documentation. Although the elements comprising this set of documentation can vary from network to network, the following are some of more common elements:

- **Contact information:** In larger networks, where different devices fall under different administrative authorities, you need to be able to quickly reach a responsible party to respond to an event. Additionally, you should have ready access to contact information for a network's service provider, which might also include the circuit ID of a service provider's incoming WAN link.

- **Policies:** When debate arises concerning activity on a network and the way the network is configured to handle various traffic types, a network administrator can benefit from having a set of network policies in place. These policies, such as an *acceptable use policy*, a *security policy*, or a *quality of service policy*, should have received approval by an authority within an organization (for example, the *chief information officer* [CIO]), rather than coming directly from the enforcing party (such as a network administrator).

- **Network maps:** A collection of network maps should include both a map of a network's physical topology and a map of a network's logical topology. For example, a physical topology map shows such information circuit IDs, port numbers, fiber pairs, and locations of network devices. Conversely, a logical topology map might show a network's VLANs.

- **Wiring schemes:** Network documentation should include information about the wiring within and between buildings. For example, what conduit systems exist, and how many copper pairs are in the riser cable interconnecting the first and second floors? How are pairs of fiber-optic cables numbered? Wiring scheme documentation should, therefore, complement a network's physical topology map.

Although this section addressed some of the more common elements of configuration management, realize that configuration management entails any network activity (from documentation to using best practices) that helps ensure consistent configuration practices, helps document a network's configuration, or helps preserve device configurations in the event of a device failure.

Monitoring Resources and Reports

Network administrators routinely monitor network resources and review reports to be proactive in their administration. For example, a potential network issue might be averted by spotting a trend (for example, increasing router CPU utilization or an increasing bandwidth demand on a WAN link). Monitoring resources and reports come from various sources, such as a *syslog server*, a *Simple Network Management Protocol* (SNMP) server, *Event Viewer* logs found on a Microsoft Windows server, or packet captures from a network sniffer. This section introduces you to these resources for monitoring network information.

SNMP

The first *Request for Comments* (RFC) for SNMP came out in 1988. Since then, SNMP has become the de facto standard of network-management protocols. The original intent for SNMP was for SNMP to manage network nodes, such as network servers, routers, switches, and hubs. SNMP version 1 (SNMPv1) and SNMP version 2c (SNMPv2c) specify three major components of an SNMP solution, as detailed in Table 11-1.

Table 11-1 Components of an SNMPv1 and SNMPv2c Network-Management Solution

Component	Description
SNMP manager	An SNMP manager runs a network management application. This SNMP manager is sometimes referred to as a *Network Management Server* (NMS).
SNMP agent	An SNMP agent is a piece of software that runs on a managed device (for example, a server, router, or switch).
Management Information Base (MIB)	Information about a managed device's resources and activity is defined by a series of objects. The structure of these management objects is defined by a managed device's *Management Information Base* (MIB).

As depicted in Figure 11-9, an SNMP manager (an NMS) can send information to, receive request information from, or receive unsolicited information from a managed device (a managed router, in this example). The managed device runs an SNMP agent and contains the MIB.

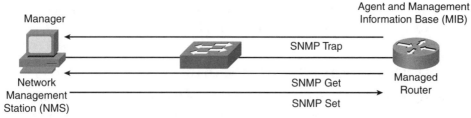

Figure 11-9 SNMPv1 and SNMPv2c Network-Management Components and Messages

Even though multiple SNMP messages might be sent between an SNMP manager and a managed device, consider the three broad categories of SNMP message types:

- **GET:** An SNMP GET message retrieves information from a managed device.

- **SET:** An SNMP SET message sets a variable in a managed device or to trigger an action on a managed device.

- **Trap:** An SNMP trap message is an unsolicited message sent from a managed device to an SNMP manager, which can notify the SNMP manager about a significant event that occurred on the managed device.

SNMP offers security against malicious users attempting to collect information from a managed device, change the configuration of a managed device, or intercepting information being sent to an NMS. However, the security integrated with SNMPv1 and SNMPv2c is considered weak. Specifically, SNMPv1 and SNMPv2c use *community strings* to gain read-only access or read-write access to a managed device. You can think of a community string like a password. Also, be aware that multiple SNMP-compliant devices on the market today have a default read-only community string of *public* and a default read-write community string of *private*. As a result, such devices, left at their default SNMP settings, could be compromised.

NOTE   Notice that this section refers to SNMPv2c as opposed to SNMPv2. SNMPv2 contained security enhancements, in addition to other performance enhancements. However, few network administrators adopted SNMPv2 because of the complexity of the newly proposed security system. Instead, *Community-Based Simple Network Management Protocol* (SNMPv2c) gained widespread acceptance, because SNMPv2c included the performance enhancements of SNMPv2 without using SNMPv2's complex security solution. Instead, SNMPv2c kept the SNMPv1 concept of community strings.

Fortunately, the security weaknesses of SNMPv1 and SNMPv2c are addressed in SNMPv3. To better understand these security enhancements, consider the concept of a security model and a security level:

- **Security model:** Defines an approach for user and group authentications (for example, SNMPv1, SNMPv2c, and SNMPv3).

- **Security level:** Defines the type of security algorithm performed on SNMP packets. The three security levels discussed here are the following:

  - **noAuthNoPriv:** The *noAuthNoPriv* (no authorization, no privacy) security level uses community strings for authorization and does not use encryption to provide privacy.

  - **authNoPriv:** The *authNoPriv* (authorization, no privacy) security level provides authorization using *hashed message authentication code* (HMAC) with *message digest 5* (MD5) or *Secure Hash Algorithm* (SHA). However, no encryption is used.

  - **authPriv:** The *authPriv* (authorization, privacy) security level offers HMAC MD5 or SHA authentication and provides privacy through encryption. Specifically, the encryption uses the Cipher Block Chaining (CBC) Data Encryption Standard (DES) (DES-56) algorithm.

As summarized in Table 11-2, SNMPv3 supports all three security levels. Notice that SNMPv1 and SNMPv2 only support the noAuthNoPriv security level.

Table 11-2   Security Models and Security Levels Supported by Cisco IOS

Security Model	Security Level	Authentication Strategy	Encryption Type
SNMPv1	noAuthNoPriv	Community string	None
SNMPv2c	noAuthNoPriv	Community string	None
SNMPv3	noAuthNoPriv	Username	None
SNMPv3	authNoPriv	MD5 or SHA	None
SNMPv3	authPriv	MD5 or SHA	CBC-DES (DES-56)

Through the use of security algorithms, as shown in Table 11-2, SNMPv3 dramatically increases the security of network-management traffic, as compared to SNMPv1 and SNMPv2c. Specifically, SNMPv3 offers three primary security enhancements:

- **Integrity:** Using hashing algorithms, SNMPv3 ensures that an SNMP message was not modified in transit.

- **Authentication:** Hashing allows SNMPv3 to validate the source of an SNMP message.

- **Encryption:** Using the CBC-DES (DES-56) encryption algorithm, SNMPv3 provides privacy for SNMP messages, making them unreadable by an attacker who might capture an SNMP packet.

NOTE   Many of the security concepts mentioned in this discussion are covered in more detail in Chapter 12, "Securing a Network."

In addition to its security enhancements, SNMPv3 also differs architecturally from SNMPv1 and SNMPv2c. SNMPv3 defines SNMP entities, which are groupings of individual SNMP components. As shown in Figure 11-10, SNMP applications and an SNMP manager combine into an NMS SNMP entity, while an SNMP agent and a MIB combine into a managed node SNMP entity.

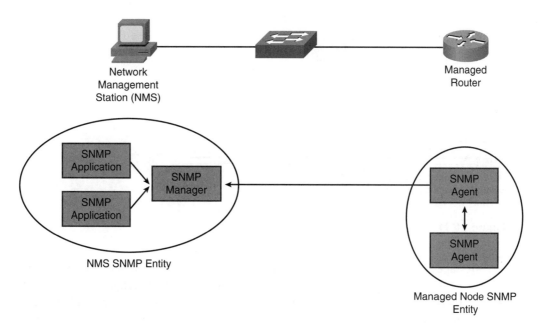

Figure 11-10 SNMPv3 Entities

Syslog

A variety of network components (for example, routers, switches, and servers) can send their log information to a common *syslog* server. By having log information for multiple devices in a common log, network administrators can better correlate events occurring on one network devices with events occurring on a different network device, by examining time stamps. A syslog-logging solution consists of two primary components:

- **Syslog servers:** A syslog server receives and stores log messages sent from syslog clients.

- **Syslog clients:** As shown in Figure 11-11, various types of network devices can act as syslog clients and send logging information to a syslog server.

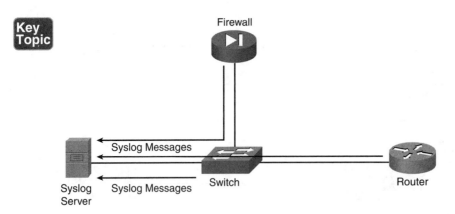

Figure 11-11   Sample Syslog Clients

Messages sent from a syslog client to a syslog server vary in their severity levels. Table 11-3 lists the eight severity levels of syslog messages. The higher the syslog level, the more detailed the logs. Keep in mind that more detailed logs require additional storage space on a syslog server.

Table 11-3   Syslog Severity Levels

Level	Name	Description
0	Emergencies	The most severe error conditions, which render the system unusable
1	Alerts	Conditions requiring immediate attention
2	Critical	A less severe condition, as compared to alerts, which should be addressed to prevent an interruption of service
3	Errors	Notifications about error conditions within the system, which do not render the system unusable
4	Warnings	Notifications that specific operations failed to complete successfully
5	Notifications	Non-error notifications that alert an administrator about state changes within a system
6	Informational	Detailed information about the normal operation of a system
7	Debugging	Highly detailed information (for example, information about individual packets), which is typically used for troubleshooting purposes

Consider the format of a syslog message, as illustrated in Figure 11-12. The syslog log entries contain timestamps, which are helpful in understanding how one log message relates to another. The log entries also include severity level information, in addition to the text of the syslog messages.

Names of Log Message
and Severity Levels

Time Stamps   Text of Syslog Messages

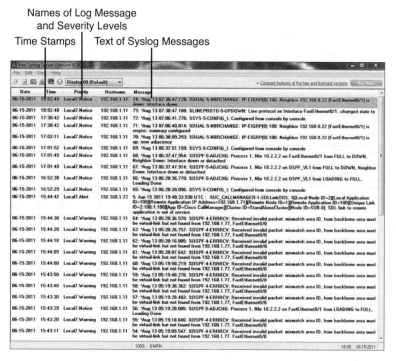

Figure 11-12   Structure of a Syslog Message

NOTE   A variety of systems can act as syslog servers. In the previous example, the *Free Kiwi Syslog Server* was used. This free utility can be downloaded from http:// solarwinds.com/downloads.

Logs

In addition to logs generated by routers, switches, and other infrastructure gear, the operating systems powering network clients and servers generally have the capability to produce log output. Rather than containing *general log* information (meaning log information about all a system's tracked components), Microsoft Windows incorporates an *Event Viewer* application that allows you to view various log types, including *application*, *security*, and *system* logs. These logs can be archived for later review. These *history logs* can be used to spot network trends and serve as data for creating baselines.

Application Logs

Microsoft Windows application logs contain information about software applications running on the underlying operating system. Notice, in Figure 11-13, the three levels of severity associated with the events in the log: Information, Warning, and Error. The events provide a collection of information about the event, such as the source (for example, the application) that caused the event, the severity level of the event, and a date/time stamp of the event.

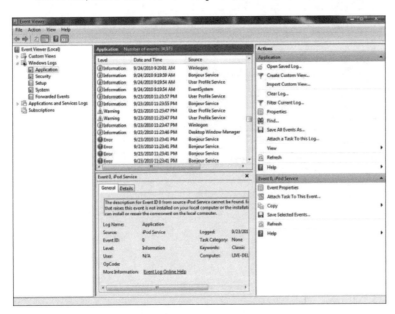

Figure 11-13 Application Log

Security Logs

Figure 11-14 shows an example of a Microsoft Windows security log. In this example, successful and failed login attempts are shown.

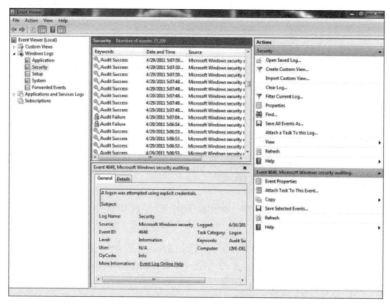

Figure 11-14 Security Log

System Logs

A Microsoft Windows system log, an example of which is shown in Figure 11-15, lists events generated by the underlying operating system.

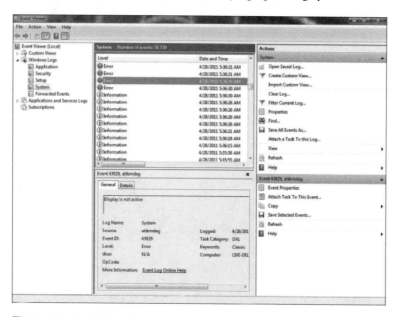

Figure 11-15 System Log

Summary

The main topics covered in this chapter are as follows:

- The purpose of various tools that could be used to physically maintain a network were identified. Examples include BERT, butt set, cable certifier, cable tester, connectivity software, crimper, ESD wrist strap, environmental monitor, loop back plug, multimeter, protocol analyzer, punch-down tool, throughput tester, TDR, OTDR, and toner probe.

- The operation of SNMP was discussed, along with an explanation of the security enhancements available in SNMPv3.

- The operation of syslog was reviewed, along with an explanation of the syslog message severity levels.

- Examples of logs collected by the Microsoft Windows Event Viewer application were given. Specifically, examples of Microsoft Windows application, security, and system logs were presented.

Exam Preparation Tasks

Review All the Key Topics

Review the most important topics from inside the chapter, noted with the Key Topic icon in the outer margin of the page. Table 11-4 lists these key topics and the page numbers where each is found.

Table 11-4   Key Topics for Chapter 11

Key Topic Element	Description	Page Number
Figure 11-3	Crimper	361
Figure 11-5	Multimeter	363
Figure 11-6	Wireshark Protocol Analyzer Software	364
List	Configuration management procedures	367
Table 11-1	Components of an SNMPv1 and SNMPv2 network management solution	370
Figure 11-9	SNMPv1 and SNMPv2c network management components and messages	370
List	Syslog logging components	373
Figure 11-11	Sample syslog clients	374
Table 11-3	Syslog severity levels	374

Complete Tables and Lists from Memory

Print a copy of Appendix C, "Memory Tables" (found on the CD), or at least the section for this chapter, and complete the tables and lists from memory. Appendix D, "Memory Table Answer Key," also on the CD, includes the completed tables and lists so you can check your work.

Define Key Terms

Define the following key terms from this chapter, and check your answers in the Glossary:

bit-error rate tester (BERT), butt set, cable certifier, cable tester, crimper, electrostatic discharge (ESD) wrist strap, punch-down tool, time domain reflectometer (TDR), optical time domain reflectometer (OTDR), toner probe, asset management, baseline, Simple Network Management Protocol (SNMP), syslog

Review Questions

The answers to these review questions are in Appendix A, "Answers to Review Questions."

1. One error occurred during the transmission of 8 bits. What is the BER?

   a. .0125

   b. .025

   c. .125

   d. .25

2. What device, traditionally used by telephone technicians, allows you to tap into a phone line to, for example, check a line for dial tone?

   a. Tester

   b. Butt set

   c. TDR

   d. Fox and hound

3. Which piece of test equipment can be used to test the throughput of a Cat 5 cable?

   a. OTDR

   b. Multimeter

   c. BERT

   d. Cable certifier

4. What is a best practice to prevent you from damaging a circuit board with static from your body?

   a. Wear an ESD wrist strap.

   b. Apply antistatic spray to the circuit board.

   c. Ground the circuit board.

   d. Stand on a carpeted floor (or a rug) when working on a circuit board to provide insulation between your body and an electric ground potential.

5. A toner probe is also known as what?

   a. TDR

   b. Fox and hound

   c. Tip and ring

   d. OTDR

6. What piece of test equipment can be used to locate a break in a fiber-optic cable?

   a. TDR

   b. Cable certifier

   c. Crimper

   d. OTDR

7. SNMP uses a series of objects to collect information about a managed device. The structure, similar to a database, containing these objects is referred to as what?

   a. RIB

   b. MIB

   c. DUAL

   d. LSA

8. A notification that a specific operation failed to complete successfully is classified as what syslog severity level?

   a. Informational (1)

   b. Critical (2)

   c. Errors (5)

   d. Warnings (4)

9. Identify the broad categories of SNMP message types? (Choose three.)

   a. GET

   b. PUT

   c. SET

   d. Trap

10. What Microsoft Windows application allows you to view a variety of log types, including application, security, and system logs?

   a. Event Viewer

   b. Performance Monitor

   c. Microsoft Management Console

   d. Control Panel

Upon completion of this chapter, you will be able to answer the following questions:

- What are the goals of network security, and what sorts of attacks do you need to defend against?

- What best practices can be implemented to defend against security threats?

- What are the characteristics of various remote-access security technologies?

- How can firewalls be used to protect an organization's internal network, while allowing connectivity to an untrusted network, such as the Internet?

- How can *virtual private networks* (VPN) be used to secure traffic as that traffic flows over an untrusted network?

- What is the difference between *intrusion prevention* and *intrusion detection* systems, and how do they protect an organization from common security threats?

CHAPTER 12

Securing a Network

Today's networks are increasingly dependent on connectivity with other networks. However, connecting an organization's trusted network to untrusted networks, such as the Internet, introduces security risks. Security risks even exist within an organization.

To protect your organization's data from malicious users, you need to understand the types of threats against which you might have to defend. Then, you need to know the options you have for defending your network. A key security concept to understand is that you need multiple layers of security for your network, not just a single solution, such as a firewall. Rather, you might combine user training, security policies, remote-access security protocols, firewalls, virtual private networks, and intrusion prevention systems. Combined, these solutions offer overlapping layers of network protection.

This chapter begins by introducing you to the fundamentals of security, which includes a discussion of common network attacks. Then, you focus on how to defend against those attacks. Remote-access security options are reviewed, along with the functions and deployment considerations of dedicated security solutions, including firewalls, virtual private networks, and intrusion detection/prevention systems.

Foundation Topics

Security Fundamentals

Security is a vast topic, and to begin our discussion, this section introduces the goals that security can help you meet. Then, to better understand what you are defending against, this section identifies several categories of network attacks.

Network Security Goals

For most of today's corporate networks, the demands of e-commerce and customer contact require connectivity between internal corporate networks and the outside world. Two basic assumptions, from a security standpoint, about modern corporate networks are the following:

- Today's corporate networks are large, interconnect with other networks, and run both standards-based and proprietary protocols.

- The devices and applications connecting to and using corporate networks are continually increasing in complexity.

Because almost all (if not all) corporate networks require network security, consider the three primary goals of network security:

- Confidentiality

- Integrity

- Availability

The following sections explain these goals in more detail.

Confidentiality

Data confidentiality implies keeping data private. This privacy could entail physically or logically restricting access to sensitive data or encrypting traffic traversing a network. A network that provides confidentiality would, as a few examples:

- Use network-security mechanisms (for example, firewalls and access control lists [ACL]) to prevent unauthorized access to network resources.

- Require appropriate credentials (such as usernames and passwords) to access specific network resources.

- Encrypt traffic such that any traffic captured off of the network by an attacker cannot be deciphered by the attacker.

Confidentiality can be provided by *encryption*. Encryption allows a packet to be encoded in such a way that it can be decoded by an intended party. However, if a malicious user intercepted an encrypted packet in transit, he would not be able to decrypt the packet. The way most modern encryption algorithms prevent decryption by a third party is through the use of a *key*. Because the encryption or decryption algorithm uses a key in its mathematical calculation, a third party, who does not possess the key, cannot interpret any encrypted data that he intercepts.

Encryption has two basic forms: *symmetric encryption* and *asymmetric encryption*.

Symmetric Encryption

Symmetric encryption is fast, in comparison to asymmetric encryption. The word *symmetric* in symmetric encryption implies that the same key is used by both the sender and receiver to encrypt or decrypt a packet. Examples of symmetric encryption algorithms include the following:

- **DES:** *Data Encryption Standard* (DES) is an older encryption algorithm (developed in the mid 1970s) using a 56-bit key and is considered *weak* by today's standards.

- **3DES:** *Triple DES* (3DES), developed in the late 1990s, uses three 56-bit DES keys (for a total of 168 bits) and is usually considered a strong encryption algorithm. However, the security of 3DES varies based on the way it is implemented. Specifically, 3DES has three *keying options*, where all three keys are different (keying option 1); two of the three keys are the same (keying option 2); or all three keys are the same (keying option 3) to maintain backwards compatibility with DES.

- **AES:** *Advanced Encryption Standard* (AES), released in 2001, is typically considered the preferred symmetric encryption algorithm. AES is available in 128-bit key, 192-bit key, and 256-bit key versions.

Figure 12-1 illustrates an example of symmetric encryption, where both parties have a shared key to be used during a session (called a *session key*).

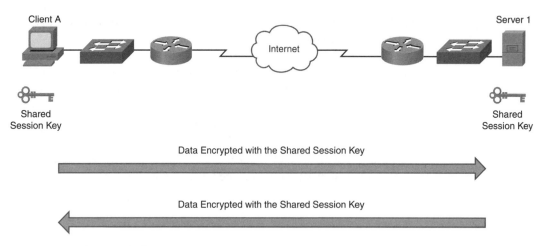

Figure 12-1 Symmetric Encryption Example

Asymmetric Encryption

Asymmetric encryption is slow, in comparison to symmetric encryption, but balances this with higher security. As its name suggests, asymmetric encryption uses asymmetric (different) keys for the sender and the receiver of a packet. Because of its speed, asymmetric encryption algorithms are not typically used to encrypt large quantities of real-time data. Rather, asymmetric encryption might be used to encrypt a small chunk of data used to, for example, authenticate the other party in a conversation or to exchange a shared key to be used during a session (after which, the parties in the conversation could start using symmetric encryption). One of the most popular asymmetric encryption algorithms in use today is RSA; its name comes from the last initials of its inventors: Ronald L. Rivest, Adi Shamir, and Leonard M. Adleman.

> **NOTE** Another widely deployed asymmetric encryption algorithm is *pretty good privacy* (PGP), which is often used to encrypt e-mail traffic. A free variant of PGP is *GNU Privacy Guard* (GPC).

RSA is commonly used as part of a *public key infrastructure* (PKI) system. Specifically, PKI uses *digital certificates* and a *certificate authority* (CA) to allow secure communication across a public network.

For example, when client A wants to communicate securely with server 1, as illustrated in Figure 12-2, the following steps occur (which are outlined in the following list).

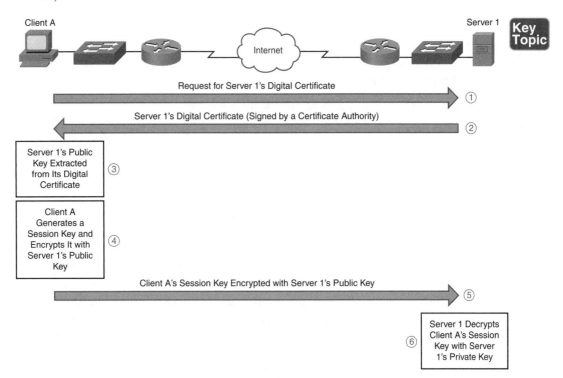

Figure 12-2 Asymmetric Encryption Example

1. Client A requests server 1's digital certificate.

2. Server 1 sends its digital certificate, and client A knows the received certificate is really from server 1, because the certificate has been authenticated (*signed*) by a trusted third party, called a *certificate authority*.

3. Client A extracts server 1's public key from server 1's digital certificate. Data encrypted using server 1's public key can only be decrypted with server 1's private key, which only server 1 has.

4. Client A generates a random string of data called a *session key*.

5. The session key is then encrypted using server 1's public key and sent to server 1.

6. Server 1 decrypts the session key using its private key.

At this point, both client A and server 1 know the session key, which can be used to symmetrically encrypt traffic during the session.

Integrity

Data integrity ensures that data has not been modified in transit. Also, a data integrity solution might perform origin authentication to verify that traffic is originating from the source that should send the traffic.

Examples of integrity violations include the following:

- Modifying the appearance of a corporate website

- Intercepting and altering an e-commerce transaction

- Modifying financial records that are stored electronically

Hashing is one approach to providing integrity to data transmissions crossing a network. Specifically, hashing takes a string of data (such as a password) and runs it through an algorithm. The result of the algorithm is called a *hash* or a *hash digest*. If the sender of that data runs a hashing algorithm on the data and sends the hash digest along with the data, when the recipient receives the data, she can also run the data through the same hashing algorithm. If the recipient calculates the same hash digest, she might conclude that the data has not been modified in transit (that is, she has confirmed the integrity of the data). Note that a hashing algorithm produces hash digests of the same length regardless of the size of the data being hashed.

Two of the most common hashing algorithms are the following:

- **Message Digest 5 (MD5):** Creates 128-bit hash digests

- **Secure Hash Algorithm 1 (SHA-1):** Creates 160-bit hash digests

Hashing by itself, however, does not guarantee data integrity, because an attacker could intercept a string of data, manipulate it, and recalculate the hash value based on the manipulated data. The victim would then determine that the hash was valid based on the data.

To overcome this limitation of pure hashing, *hash-based message authentication code* (HMAC) uses an additional secret key in the calculation of a hash value. So, an attacker would not be able to create a valid hash value, because he would not know the secret key.

NOTE   *Challenge-Response Authentication Mechanism Message Digest 5* (CRAM-MD5) is a common variant of HMAC frequently used in e-mail systems.

Availability

The availability of data is a measure of the data's accessibility. For example, if a server was down only 5 minutes per year, the server would have an availability of 99.999 percent (that is, the *five nines of availability*).

A couple of examples of how an attacker could attempt to compromise the availability of a network include the following:

- Send improperly formatted data to a networked device, resulting in an unhandled exception error.

- Flood a network system with an excessive amount of traffic or requests, which would consume a system's processing resources and prevent the system from responding to many legitimate requests. This type of attack is referred to as a denial of service (DoS) attack.

The topic of availability was elaborated on in Chapter 9, "Optimizing Network Performance."

Categories of Network Attacks

The previous discussion identified confidentiality, integrity, and availability as the three primary goals of network security. Therefore, we need to better understand the types of attacks that attempt to compromise these areas.

Confidentiality Attacks

A *confidentiality attack* attempts to make confidential data (for example, personnel records, usernames, passwords, credit-card numbers, or e-mails) viewable by an attacker. Because an attacker often makes a copy of the data, rather than trying to manipulate the data or crash a system, confidentiality attacks often go undetected. Even if auditing software to track file access were in place, if no one suspected an issue, the audit logs might never be examined.

Figure 12-3 illustrates an example confidentiality attack.

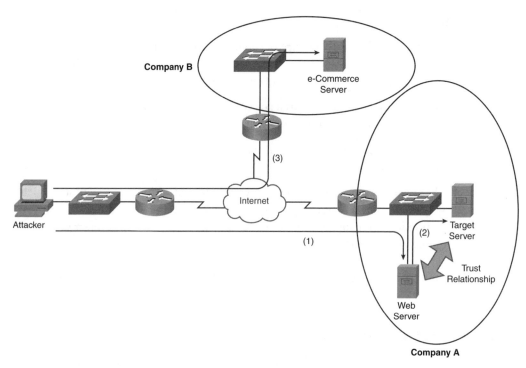

Figure 12-3   Confidentiality Attack Example

In Figure 12-3, a web server and a database server have a mutual trust relationship. The database server houses confidential customer information, such as customer credit-card information. As a result, company A decided to protect the database server (for example, patching known software vulnerabilities) better than the web server. However, the attacker leverages the trust relationship between the two servers to obtain customer credit-card information and then make a purchase from company B using the stolen credit-card information. The procedure is as follows:

1. The attacker exploits a vulnerability in company A's web server and gains control of that server.

2. The attacker uses the trust relationship between the web server and the database server to obtain customer credit-card information from the database server.

3. The attacker uses the stolen credit-card information to make a purchase from company B.

Table 12-1 identifies several methods that attackers might use in a confidentiality attack.

Table 12-1 Confidentiality Attack Tactics

Tactic	Description
Packet capture	A packet-capture (also known as *packet sniffing*) utility (such as *Wireshark* [wireshark.org]) can capture packets visible by a PC's network interface card (NIC), by placing the NIC in *promiscuous mode*. Some protocols (for example, Telnet and HTTP) are sent in plain text. Therefore, these types of captured packets can be read by an attacker, perhaps allowing the attacker to see confidential information.
Ping sweep and port scan	A confidentiality attack might begin with a scan of network resources to identify attack targets on a network. A *ping sweep* could be used to ping a series of IP addresses. Ping replies might indicate to an attacker that network resources were reachable at those IP addresses. After a collection of IP addresses is identified, the attacker might scan a range of UDP and/or TCP ports to see what services are available on the hosts at the specified IP addresses. Also, port scans often help attackers identify the operating system running on a target system.
Dumpster diving	Because many companies throw away confidential information, without proper shredding, some attackers rummage through company dumpsters in hopes of discovering information that could be used to compromise network resources.
Electromagnetic interference (EMI) interception	Because data is often transmitted over wire (for example, unshielded twisted pair), attackers can sometimes copy information traveling over the wire, by intercepting the *electromagnetic interference* (EMI) being emitted by the transmission medium. These EMI emissions are sometimes called *emanations*.
Wiretapping	If an attacker gains physical access to a wiring closet, he might physically tap into telephone cabling to eavesdrop on telephone conversations, or he might insert a shared media hub in-line with a network cable, allowing an attacker to connect to the hub and receive copies of packets flowing through the network cable.
Social engineering	Attackers sometimes use social techniques (which often leverage people's desire to be helpful) to obtain confidential information. For example, an attacker might pose as a member of an organization's IT department and ask a company employee for his login credentials in order for the "IT staff to test the connection."

Table 12-1   Confidentiality Attack Tactics

Tactic	Description
Sending information over overt channels	An attacker might send or receive confidential information over a network using an *overt channel*. An example of using an overt channel is tunneling one protocol inside another (for example, sending instant-messaging traffic via HTTP). *Steganography* is another example of sending information over an overt channel. An example of steganography is sending a digital image, made up of millions of pixels, with "secret" information encoded in specific pixels, where only the sender and the receiver know which pixels represent the encoded information.
Sending information over covert channels	An attacker might send or receive confidential information over a network using a *covert channel*, which can communicate information as a series of codes and/or events. For example, binary data could be represented by sending a series of pings to a destination. A single ping within a certain period of time could represent a binary 0, while two pings within that same time period represented a binary 1.
FTP bounce	FTP supports a variety of commands for setting up a session and managing file transfers. One of these commands is the **PORT** command, and it can, in some cases, be used by an attacker to access a system that would otherwise deny the attacker. Specifically, an attacker connects to an FTP server using the standard port of 21. However, FTP uses a secondary connection to send data. The client issues a **PORT** command to specify the destination port and destination IP address for the data transmission. Normally, the client would send its own IP address and an ephemeral port number. The FTP server would then use a source port of 20 and a destination port specified by the client when sending data to the client. However, an attacker might issue a **PORT** command specifying the IP address of a device they want to access, along with an open port number on that device. As a result, the targeted device might allow an incoming connection from the FTP server's IP address, while a connection coming in from the attacker's IP address would be rejected. Fortunately, most modern FTP servers do not accept the **PORT** command coming from a device that specifies a different IP address than the client's IP address.

Integrity Attacks

Integrity attacks attempt to alter data (compromise the integrity of the data). As an example of an integrity attack, consider Figure 12-4.

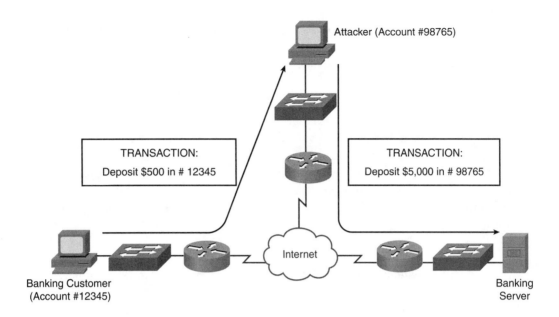

Traffic diverted to attacker due to a man-in-the-middle attack

Figure 12-4   Integrity Attack

In Figure 12-4, a *man-in-the-middle attack* has been launched by an attacker. This attack causes data flowing between the banking customer and the banking server to be sent via the attacker's computer. The attacker can then not only intercept but also manipulate the data. In the figure, notice that the banking customer attempts to deposit $500 into her account. However, the attacker intercepts and changes the details of the transaction, such that the instruction to the banking server is to deposit $5,000 in the attacker's account.

The following list identifies multiple methods attackers might leverage in order conduct an integrity attack:

- **Salami attack:** A salami attack is a collection of small attacks that result in a larger attack when combined. For example, if an attacker had a collection of stolen credit-card numbers, the attacker could withdraw small amounts of money from each credit card (possibly unnoticed by the credit-card holders). Although each individual withdrawal was small, the combination of the multiple withdrawals results in a significant sum for the attacker.

- **Data diddling:** The process of *data diddling* changes data before it is stored in a computing system. Malicious code in an input application or a virus could perform data diddling. For example, a *virus, Trojan horse,* or *worm* could be written to intercept keyboard input, and while displaying the appropriate characters onscreen (so the user does not see an issue), manipulated characters could be entered into a database application or sent over a network.

> **NOTE** For the Network+ exam, you need to understand the difference between a *virus*, a *worm*, and a *Trojan horse*. A virus is a piece of code (for example, a program or a script) that an end user executes. A worm, however, can infect a system or propagate to other systems without any intervention from the end user. Finally, a Trojan horse is a program that appears to be for one purpose (for example, a game), but secretly performs another task (such as collecting a list of contacts from an end user's e-mail program).

- **Trust relationship exploitation:** Different devices in a network might have a trust relationship between themselves. For example, a certain host might be trusted to communicate through a firewall using specific ports, while other hosts are denied passage through the firewall using those same ports. If an attacker were able to compromise the host that had a trust relationship with the firewall, then the attacker could use the compromised host to pass normally denied data through a firewall. Another example of a trust relationship is a web server and a database server mutually trusting one another. In that case, if an attacker gained control of the web server, he might be able to leverage that trust relationship to compromise the database server.

- **Password attack:** A password attack, as its name suggests, attempts to determine the password of a user. Once the attacker gains the username and password credentials, he can attempt to log into a system as that user and inherit that user's set of permissions. Various approaches are available to determine passwords. For example:

  - **Trojan horse:** A *Trojan horse* is a program that appears to be a useful application, but might capture a user's password and then make it available to the attacker.

  - **Packet capture:** A packet-capture utility can capture packets seen on a PC's NIC. Therefore, if the PC can see a copy of a plain-text password being sent over a link, the packet-capture utility can be used to glean the password.

  - **Keylogger:** A program that runs in a computer's background, and it logs keystrokes that a user makes. Therefore, after a user enters a password, the password is stored in the log created by the keylogger. An attacker can then retrieve the log of keystrokes to determine the user's password.

- **Brute force:** This attack tries all possible password combinations until a match is made. For example, the brute-force attack might start with the letter *a* and go through the letter *z*. Then, the letters *aa* through *zz* are attempted, until the password is determined. Therefore, using a mixture of upper- and lowercase, in addition to special characters and numbers, can help mitigate a brute-force attack.

- **Dictionary attack:** Similar to a brute-force attack, in that multiple password guesses are attempted. However, the dictionary attack is based on a dictionary of commonly used words, rather than the brute-force method of trying all possible combinations. Picking a password that is not a common word helps mitigate a dictionary attack.

- **Botnet:** A software *robot* is typically thought of as an application on a machine that can be controlled remotely (for example, a Trojan horse or a backdoor in a system). If a collection of computers are infected with such software robots, called *bots*, this collection of computers (each of which are known as a *zombie*) is called a *botnet*. Because of the potentially large size of a botnet, it might compromise the integrity of a large amount of data.

- **Hijacking a session:** An attacker could hijack a TCP session, for example, by completing the third step in the three-way TCP handshake process between an authorized client and a protected server. If an attacker successfully hijacked a session of an authorized device, he might be able to maliciously manipulate data on the protected server.

Availability Attacks

Availability attacks attempt to limit the accessibility and usability of a system. For example, if an attacker were able to consume the processor or memory resources on a target system, that system might be unavailable to legitimate users.

Availability attacks vary widely, from consuming the resources of a target system to doing physical damage to that system. The following sections describe various availability attacks that might be employed by attackers.

Denial of Service (DoS)

An attacker can launch a denial of service (DoS) attack on a system by either sending the target system a flood of data or requests that consume the target system's resources. Alternately, some operating systems (OS) and applications might crash when they receive specific strings of improperly formatted data, and the attacker could leverage such OS and/or application vulnerabilities to render a system or application inoperable. The attacker often uses IP spoofing to conceal his identity when launching a DoS attack, as illustrated in Figure 12-5.

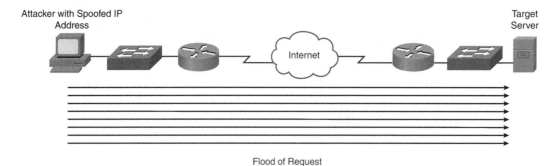

Figure 12-5   DoS Attack

Distributed Denial of Service (DDoS)

Distributed denial of service (DDoS) attacks can increase the amount of traffic flooded to a target system. Specifically, an attacker compromises multiple systems, and those compromised systems, called *zombies*, can be instructed by the attacker to simultaneously launch a DDoS attack against a target system.

TCP SYN Flood

One variant of a DoS attack is for an attacker to initiate multiple TCP sessions by sending SYN segments, but then never complete the three-way TCP handshake. As illustrated in Figure 12-6, the attack can send multiple SYN segments to a target system with false source IP addresses in the header of the SYN segments. Because many servers limit the number of TCP sessions they can have open simultaneously, a SYN flood can render a target system incapable of opening a TCP session with a legitimate user.

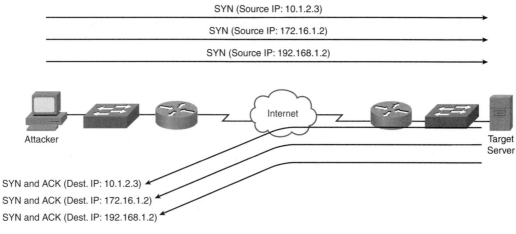

Figure 12-6   TCP SYN Flood Attack Example

Buffer Overflow

Consider a computer program that has been given a dedicated area of memory to which it can write. This area of memory is called a *buffer*. However, if the program attempts to write more information than the buffer can accommodate, a *buffer overflow* can occur. If permitted to do so, the program can fill up its buffer and then have its output spill over into the memory area being used for a different program. This could potentially cause the other program to crash. Some programs are known to have this vulnerability (that is, the characteristic of overrunning their memory buffers) and can be exploited by attackers.

ICMP Attacks

Many networks permit the use of ICMP traffic (for example, ping traffic), because pings can be useful for network troubleshooting. However, attackers can use ICMP for DoS attacks. One ICMP DoS attack variant is called the *ping of death*, which uses ICMP packets that are too big. Another variant sends ICMP traffic as a series of fragments, in an attempt to overflow the fragment reassembly buffers on the target device. Also, a *Smurf attack* can use ICMP traffic, directed to a subnet, to flood a target system with ping replies, as illustrated in Figure 12-7. Notice in the figure that the attacker sends a ping to the subnet broadcast address of 172.16.0.0/16. This collection of pings instruct devices on that subnet to send their ping replies to the target system at IP address 10.2.2.2, thus flooding the target system's bandwidth and processing resources.

NOTE   For illustrative purposes, Figure 12-7 only shows three systems in the subnet being used for the Smurf attack. However, realize that thousands of systems could potentially be involved and send ping replies to the target system.

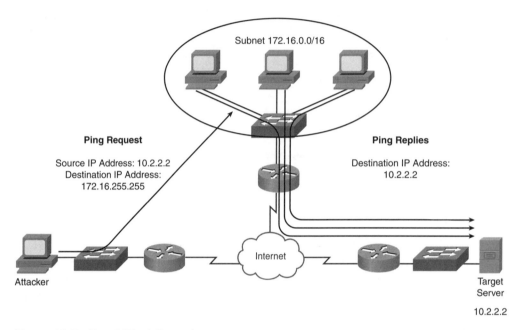

Figure 12-7   Smurf Attack Example

Electrical Disturbances

At a physical level, an attacker could launch an availability attack by interrupting or interfering with the electrical service available to a system. For example, if an attacker gained physical access to a data center's electrical system, he might be able to cause a variety of electrical disturbances, such as the following:

- **Power spikes:** Excess power for a brief period of time

- **Electrical surges:** Excess power for an extended period of time

- **Power fault:** A brief electrical outage

- **Blackout:** An extended electrical outage

- **Power sag:** A brief reduction in power

- **Brownout:** An extended reduction in power

To combat such electrical threats, you might want to install *uninterruptable power supplies* (UPS) and generator backups for strategic devices in your network. Also, you need to routinely test the UPS and generator backups.

NOTE   A *standby power supply* (SPS) is a lower-end version of a UPS. Although it's less expensive than a traditional UPS, an SPS' battery is not in-line with the electricity coming from a wall outlet. Instead, an SPS' battery operates in parallel with the wall power, standing by in the event that the wall power is lost. Because of this configuration, there is a brief period of time between a power outage and the SPS taking over, which could result in the attached equipment shutting down.

Attacks on a System's Physical Environment

Attackers could also intentionally damage computing equipment by influencing the equipment's physical environment. For example, attackers could attempt to manipulate such environmental factors as the following:

- **Temperature:** Because computing equipment generates heat (for example, in data centers or server farms), if an attacker interferes with the operation of an air-conditioning system, the computing equipment could overheat.

- **Humidity:** Because computing equipment is intolerant of moisture, an attacker could, over time, cause physical damage to computing equipment by creating a high level of humidity in a computing environment.

- **Gas:** Because gas can often be flammable, if an attacker injects gas into a computing environment, small sparks in that environment could cause a fire.

Consider the following recommendations to mitigate such environmental threats:

- Computing facilities should be locked (and not accessible via a drop ceiling, a raised floor, or any other way other than a monitored point of access).

- Access should require access credentials (for example, via a card swipe or a biometric scan).

- Access points should be visually monitored (for example, via local security personnel or remotely via a camera system).

- Climate control systems should maintain temperature and humidity, and send alerts if specified temperature or humidity thresholds are exceeded.

- The fire detection and suppression systems should be designed not to damage electronic equipment.

With this understanding of the three primary targets of an attack (that is, confidentiality, integrity, and availability) and examples of common attacks, the next section presents you with strategies for defending against such attacks.

Defending Against Attacks

Upcoming sections in this chapter address how to defend against security threats using network devices (that is, switches, routers, firewalls, VPN concentrators, and IDS/IPS sensors). However, this section presents a collection of best practices for defending a network against attacks.

User Training

Many attacks require user intervention in order to be carried out. For example, a user needs to execute an application containing a virus before the virus takes any action. Similarly, social engineering requires a user to give sensitive information (such as username and password credentials) to an attacker in order for the attacker to access the user's account. As a result, several potential attacks can be thwarted through effective user training. As a few examples, users could be trained on using policies such as the following:

- Never give out your password to anyone, even if they claim to be from IT.

- Do not open e-mail attachments from unknown sources.

- Select strong passwords, consisting of at least eight characters and containing a mixture of alphabetical (upper- and lowercase), numeric, and special characters.

- Change your passwords monthly.

This list is only an example, and you should develop a collection of best practices for your users based on your network's specific circumstances.

Patching

Some attacks are directed at vulnerabilities known to exist in various OSs and applications. As these vulnerabilities are discovered, the vendors of the OSs or applications often respond by releasing a *patch*. A patch is designed to correct a known bug or fix a known vulnerability in a piece of software. Therefore, network administrators should have a plan for implementing patches as they become available.

NOTE   A *patch* is different from an *update*, which, in addition to fixing known bug or vulnerability, adds one or more features to the software being updated.

Security Policies

One of the main reasons security breaches occur within an organization is the lack of a *security policy* or, if a security policy is in place, the lack of effectively communicating/enforcing that security policy to all concerned. A security policy is a continually changing document that dictates a set of guidelines for network use. These guidelines complement organizational objectives by specifying rules for how a network is used.

The main purpose of a security policy is to protect the assets of an organization. An organization's assets include more than just tangible items. Assets also entail things such as intellectual property, processes and procedures, sensitive customer data, and specific server functions (for example, e-mail or web functions).

Aside from protecting an organization's assets, a security policy serves other purposes, such as the following:

- Making employees aware of their obligations in regard to security practices

- Identifying specific security solutions required to meet the goals of a security policy

- Acting as a baseline for ongoing security monitoring

One of the more well-known components of a security policy is an *acceptable use policy* (AUP), also known as an *appropriate use policy*. An AUP identifies what users of a network are and are not allowed to do on a network. For example, retrieving sports scores during working hours via an organization's Internet connection might be deemed inappropriate by an AUP.

Because an organization's security policy applies to various categories of employees (such as management, technical staff, and end users), a single document might not be sufficient. For example, managerial personnel might not be concerned with the technical intricacies of a security policy. However, the technical personnel might be less concerned with why a policy is in place, while end users might be more likely to comply with the policy if they did understand the reasoning behind the rules. Therefore, a security policy might be a collection of congruent, yet separate, documents. Figure 12-8 offers a high-level overview of these complementary documents.

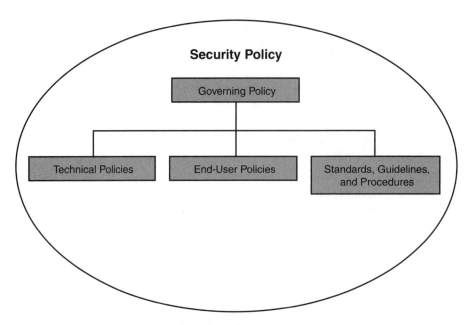

Figure 12-8   Components of a Security Policy

Governing Policy

At a very high level, a governing policy addresses security concepts deemed important to an organization. The governing policy is primarily targeted toward managerial and technical employees. The following are typical elements of a governing policy:

- Identification of the issue addressed by the policy
- Discussion of the organization's view of the issue
- Examination of the relevance of the policy to the work environment
- Explanation of how employees are to comply with the policy
- Enumeration of appropriate activities, actions, and processes
- Explanation of the consequences of noncompliance

You might want to consult with your company's legal counsel when formulating a governing policy.

Technical Policies

Technical policies provide a more detailed treatment of an organization's security policy, as opposed to the governing policy. Typical components of technical policies include specific duties of the security and IT staff in areas such as the following:

- E-mail

- Wireless networks

- Remote access

Security and IT personnel are the intended target of these technical policies, and these personnel use these policies in performing their day-to-day tasks.

End User Policies

End user policies address security issues and procedures relevant to end users. For example, an end user might be asked to sign an AUP for Internet access. That AUP might state that Internet access is only for business purposes. Then, if an end user is found using the Internet for personal reasons, she could face the consequences outlined in the governing policy.

More Detailed Documents

Because the governing policy, technical policies, and end user policies each target a relatively large population of personnel, these policies tend to be general in nature. However, a comprehensive security policy requires a highly granular treatment of an organization's procedures. Therefore, more detailed documents, such as the following, are often contained in a security policy:

- **Standards:** Standards support consistency within a network. For example, a standard might specify a limited number of OSs to be supported in the organization, because it would be impractical for the IT staff to support any OS that a user happened to select. Also, standards could apply to configuring devices, such as routers (for example, having a standardized routing protocol).

- **Guidelines:** While standards tend to be mandatory practices, guidelines tend to be suggestions. For example, a series of best practices might constitute a security policy's guidelines.

- **Procedures:** To support consistency in a network, and as dictated by the previously mentioned standards, a security policy might include a collection of procedures. These procedures are detailed documents that provide step-by-step instructions for completing specific tasks (for example, steps for configuring port security on an Ethernet switch).

Keep in mind that this list is not comprehensive, and you need to create a set of documents to match the security needs of your company.

Incident Response

How an organization reacts to a security violation is called its *incident response*. Many *deterrent controls* might display warnings such as, "Violators will be prosecuted to the fullest extent of the law." However, to successfully prosecute an attacker, litigators typically require the following elements to present an effective argument:

- **Motive:** A motive describes why the attacker committed the act. For example, was the attacker a disgruntled employee? Also, potential motives can be valuable to define during an investigation. Specifically, an investigation might begin with those that had a motive to carry out the attack.

- **Means:** With all the security controls in place to protect data or computer systems, you need to determine if the accused had the means (for example, the technical skills) to carry out the attack.

- **Opportunity:** The question of whether the accused had the opportunity to commit an attack asks if the accused was available to commit the attack. For example, if the accused claims to have been at a ball game at the time of the attack, and if there are witnesses to verify her assertion, then it is less likely that the accused indeed committed the attack.

Another challenge with prosecuting computer-based crime stems from the fragility of data. A timestamp can easily be changed on a file without detection. To prevent such evidence tampering, strict policies and procedures for data handling must be followed. For example, before any investigative work is done on a computer system, a policy might require that multiple copies of a hard drive be made. One or more master copies could be locked up, and copies could be given to the defense and prosecution for their investigation.

Also, to verify the integrity of data since a security incident occurred, you need to be able to show a *chain of custody*. A chain of custody documents who has been in possession of the data (evidence) since a security breach occurred.

Vulnerability Scanners

After you deploy your network-security solution, components of that solution might not behave as expected. Additionally, you might not be aware of some of the vulnerabilities in your network devices. Therefore, you should periodically test your network for weaknesses. Such a test can be performed using applications designed to check for a variety of know weaknesses. These applications are known as *vulnerability scanners*. Examples of these vulnerability scanners include Nessus and Nmap (network mapper).

Nessus

Tenable Network Security has a vulnerability scanning product called Nessus, which is available from www.tenable.com/products/nessus. A few of the product features include the following:

- Performing audits on systems without requiring an agent to be installed on the systems

- Checking system configurations for compliance with an organization's policy

- Auditing systems for specific content (for example, credit-card information or adult content)

- Performing continuous scanning, thus reducing the time required to identify a network vulnerability

- Scheduling scans to run once, daily, weekly, or monthly

Tenable Network Security offers a version of Nessus for home use and another version for business use. Figure 12-9 shows an example of a Nessus scan result.

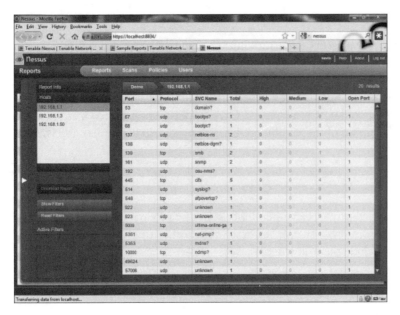

Figure 12-9   Nessus

Nmap

As another example of a vulnerability scanner, consider the Nmap utility. Nmap is a publicly available scanner that can be downloaded from www.insecure.org/ nmap. Nmap offers features such as the following:

- Scanning and sweeping features, which identify services running on systems in a specified range of IP addresses

- Using a stealth approach to scanning and sweeping, making the scanning and sweeping less detectible by hosts and IPS technology

- Using OS fingerprinting technology to identify an OS running on a target system (including a percentage of confidence that the OS was correctly detected)

Figure 12-10 illustrates a GUI version of Nmap, where a collection of host IP addresses are scanned for open ports, in addition to a variety of other fingerprinting operations.

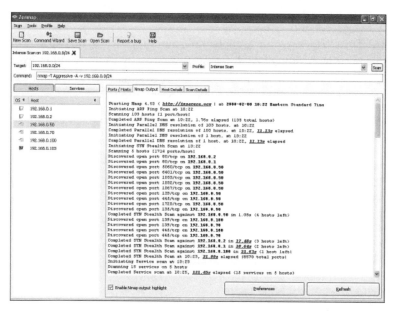

Figure 12-10   Nmap

Honey Pots and Honey Nets

A *honey pot* acts as a distracter. Specifically, a system designated as a honey pot appears to be an attractive attack target. One school of thought on the use of a honey pot is to place one or more honey pot systems in a network to entice attackers into thinking a system is real. The attackers then use their resources attacking the honey pot, the end result of which is that the attackers leave the real servers alone.

Another use of a honey pot is to use it as a system that is extensively monitored to learn what an attacker is attempting to do on the system. A honey pot could, as an example, be a UNIX system configured with a weak password. After an attacker logs in, surveillance software could log what the attacker does on the system. This knowledge could then be used to protect real servers in the network.

NOTE   For larger networks, a network administrator might deploy multiple honey pots, which forms a *honey net*.

Access Control Lists

Access control lists (ACL) are rules, typically applied to router interfaces, that specify permitted and denied traffic. Although ACL features can vary by router vendor, examples of filtering criteria include IP addresses (source or destination), port number (source or destination), and MAC addresses (source or destination).

As an example, consider Figure 12-11, which shows an ACL being applied to an interface on a Cisco IOS router.

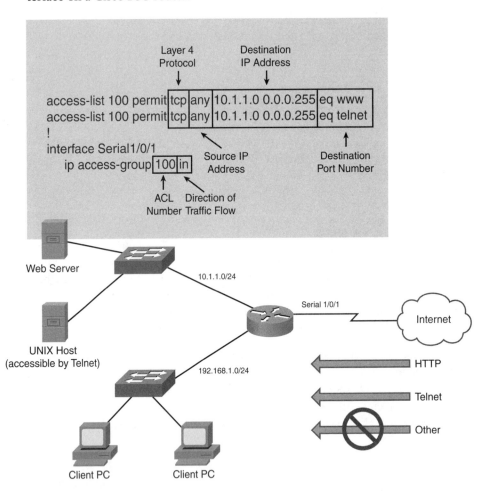

Figure 12-11   ACL Example

This syntax tells the router interface of Serial 1/0/1 to permit incoming Telnet and HTTP traffic from any source and destined for a network of 10.1.1.0/24. However, you might be curious about all the other traffic that attempts to enter interface

Serial 1/0/1. Because there is no *deny* instruction seen in the syntax, is that traffic permitted? Actually, in the case of Cisco IOS routers, ACLs have an implicit (and invisible) *deny all* instruction. Therefore, any traffic not explicitly permitted is rejected.

Remote Access Security

Although ACLs can be used to permit or deny specific connections flowing *through* a router (or switch), you also need to control connections *to* network devices (for example, routers, switches, or servers). Many of these remote-access security methods have been introduced in preceding chapters. However, as a review, Table 12-2 provides a summary of these protocols and procedures.

Table 12-2   Remote Access Security Methods

Method	Description
RAS	Microsoft *Remote Access Server* (RAS) is the predecessor to Microsoft *Routing and Remote Access Server* (RRAS). RRAS is a Microsoft Windows Server feature that allows Microsoft Windows® clients to remotely access to a Microsoft Windows® network.
RDP	*Remote Desktop Protocol* (RDP) is a Microsoft protocol that allows a user to view and control the desktop of a remote computer.
PPPoE	*Point-to-Point Protocol over Ethernet* (PPPoE) is a commonly used protocol between a DSL modem in a home (or business) and a service provider. Specifically, PPPoE encapsulates PPP frames within Ethernet frames. This approach allows an Ethernet connection to leverage the features of PPP, such as authentication.
PPP	*Point-to-Point Protocol* (PPP) is a common Layer 2 protocol that offers features such as multilink interface, looped link detection, error detection, and authentication.
ICA	*Independent Computing Architecture* (ICA) is a Citrix Systems proprietary protocol that allows an application running on one platform (for example, Microsoft Windows®) to be seen and controlled from a remote client, independent of the client platform (for example, UNIX).
SSH	*Secure Shell* is a protocol used to securely connect to a remote host (typically via a terminal emulator).
Kerberos	Kerberos is a client-server authentication protocol, which supports mutual authentication between a client and a server. Kerberos uses the concept of a *trusted third party* (a *key distribution center*) that hands out *tickets* that are used instead of a username and password combination.

Table 12-2   Remote Access Security Methods

Method	Description
AAA	*Authentication, authorization, and accounting* (AAA) allows a network to have a single repository of user credentials. A network administrator can then, for example, supply the same credentials to log onto various network devices (for example, routers and switches). RADIUS and TACACS+ are protocols commonly used to communicate with a AAA server.
RADIUS	*Remote Authentication Dial-In User Service* (RADIUS) is a UDP-based protocol used to communicate with a AAA server. Unlike TACACS+, RADIUS does not encrypt an entire authentication packet, but only the password. However, RADIUS does offer more robust accounting features than TACACS+. Also, RADIUS is a standards-based protocol, while TACACS+ is a Cisco proprietary protocol.
TACACS+	*Terminal Access Controller Access-Control System Plus* (TACACS+) is a TCP-based protocol used to communicate with a AAA server. Unlike RADIUS, TACACS+ encrypts an entire authentication packet, rather than just the password. TACACS+ does offer accounting features, but they are not as robust as the accounting features found in RADIUS. Also, unlike RADIUS, TACACS+ is a Cisco proprietary protocol.
NAC	*Network Admission Control* (NAC) can permit or deny access to a network based on characteristics of the device seeking admission, rather than just checking user credentials. For example, a client's OS and version of antivirus software could be checked against a set of requirements before allowing the client to access a network. This process of checking a client's characteristics is called *posture assessment*.
IEEE 802.1X	*IEEE 802.1X* is a type of NAC that can permit or deny a wireless or wired LAN client access to a network. If IEEE 802.1X is used to permit access to a LAN via a switch port, then IEEE 802.1X is being used for *port security*. The device seeking admission to the network is called the *supplicant*. The device to which the supplication connects (either wirelessly or through a wired connection) is called the *authenticator*. The device that checks the supplicant's credentials and permits or denies the supplicant to access the network is called an *authentication server*. Usually, an authentication server is a RADIUS server.
CHAP	*Challenge-Handshake Authentication Protocol* (CHAP) performs a one-way authentication for a remote-access connection. However, authentication is performed through a three-way handshake (challenge, response, and acceptance messages) between a server and a client. The three-way handshake allows a client to be authenticated without sending credential information across a network.

Table 12-2 Remote Access Security Methods

Method	Description
MS-CHAP	*Microsoft Challenge-Handshake Authentication Protocol* (MS-CHAP) is a Microsoft-enhanced version of CHAP, offering a collection of additional features not present with CHAP, including two-way authentication.
EAP	An *Extensible Authentication Protocol* (EAP) specifies how authentication is performed by an IEEE 802.1X. A variety of EAP types exist: *Extensible Authentication Protocol-Flexible Authentication via Secure Tunneling* (EAP-FAST), *Extensible Authentication Protocol-Message Digest 5* (EAP-MD5), and *Extensible Authentication Protocol-Transport Layer Security* (EAP-TLS).
Two-factor authentication	*Two-factor authentication* (TFA) requires two types of authentication from a user seeking admission to a network. For example, a user might have to *know* something (for example, a password) and *have* something (such as a specific fingerprint, which can be checked with a biometric authentication device).
Multifactor authentication	Similar to two-factor authentication, *multifactor authentication* requires two or more types of successful authentication before granting access to a network.
Single sign-on	Single sign-on (SSO) allows a user to authenticate only once to gain access to multiple systems, without requiring the user to independently authenticate with each system.

Firewalls

At this point, this chapter has introduced you to various security threats, along with best practices to protect your network from those threats. Additionally, you reviewed a collection of remote-access security methods. In the remainder of this chapter, you are introduced to three additional layers of security that can be applied to a network, often in the form of a dedicated security appliance. These additional layers consist of *firewalls*, *virtual private networks*, and *intrusion detection and prevention systems*. This section focuses on firewalls.

Firewall Types

A firewall defines a set of rules to dictate which types of traffic are permitted or denied as that traffic enters or exits a firewall interface. The actual firewall devices can be either a software firewall or a hardware firewall:

- **Software firewall:** A computer running firewall software, which can protect the computer itself (for example, preventing incoming connections to the computer). Alternately, a software firewall could be a computer with more than one NIC running firewall software. This type of software firewall could filter traffic attempting to pass through the computer (that is, coming in one of the NICs and leaving via a different NIC).

- **Hardware firewall:** A network appliance that acts as a firewall. This appliance can have multiple interfaces for connecting to areas of a network that require varying levels of security.

As traffic flows into or out of a firewall, the firewall checks the traffic against a set of *firewall rules*, which might permit or deny the traffic. Additionally, many firewalls also perform *Network Address Translation* (NAT) or *Port Address Translation* (PAT), which are described in Chapter 6, "Routing Traffic."

Firewall Inspection Types

Some firewalls inspect traffic based solely on a packet's header. This type of firewall is called a *packet-filtering* firewall. Other firewalls, however, can recognize that a packet is part of a session that might have originated inside the local network or outside the local network. This type of firewall is called a *stateful firewall*.

Packet-Filtering Firewall

Earlier, this chapter described the function of ACLs. An ACL can decide if a packet should be permitted or denied based on the contents of its header (for example, based on source and destination IP address information or source and destination port number information).

A device that filters traffic based on ACL-like rules is a packet filtering firewall. However, a packet-filtering firewall lacks flexibility. For example, in Figure 12-12, a router is acting as a firewall. The ACL applied to interface Serial 1/0/1 permits all traffic from the inside network to go out to the Internet. However, all traffic coming from the Internet is blocked as it attempts to enter the router. Although this might seem like a reasonable ACL, it can prevent a session from being set up between a client on the inside network with a host on the Internet, even if the session originated from the inside client.

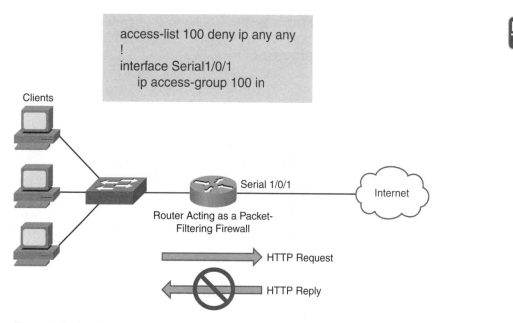

Figure 12-12   Packet-Filtering Firewall

For example, imagine that an inside client running a web browser attempts to contact a web server on the Internet. Although the outgoing HTTP request is permitted, the returning HTTP reply is blocked by the incoming ACL applied to interface Serial 1/0/1. As a result, the HTTP session cannot be established.

Stateful Firewall

Unlike a packet-filtering firewall, a *stateful firewall* inspects traffic leaving the inside network as it goes out to the Internet. Then, when returning traffic from the same session (as identified by source and destination IP addresses and port numbers) attempts to enter the inside network, the stateful firewall permits that traffic. The process of inspecting traffic to identify unique sessions is called *stateful inspection*.

As an example, consider Figure 12-13, where a stateful firewall allows return traffic from the Internet for a Telnet session initiated from the inside network (session A). However, Telnet traffic coming from the Internet is blocked, if the Telnet session is initiated from a device on the Internet (session B).

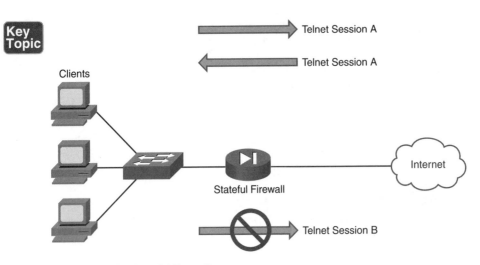

Figure 12-13 Stateful Firewall

Firewall Zones

A firewall's interfaces can be defined as belonging to different *firewall zones*. After you define which interfaces belong to which zones, you can set up rules saying what types of traffic are permitted to flow between zones. As an example, consider Figure 12-14. The firewall interface connecting to the inside network (trusted network) is configured as belonging to the INSIDE zone. The firewall interface connecting to the Internet (an untrusted network) is configured as belonging to the OUTSIDE zone. In this example, a rule has been applied to the firewall stating that the traffic source from the INSIDE zone is allowed to go to the OUTSIDE zone. Return traffic from sessions originating in the INSIDE zone is also permitted to come back into the INSIDE zone from the OUTSIDE zone, thanks to stateful inspection. However, traffic from sessions originating in the OUTSIDE zone are not permitted to come into the INSIDE zone.

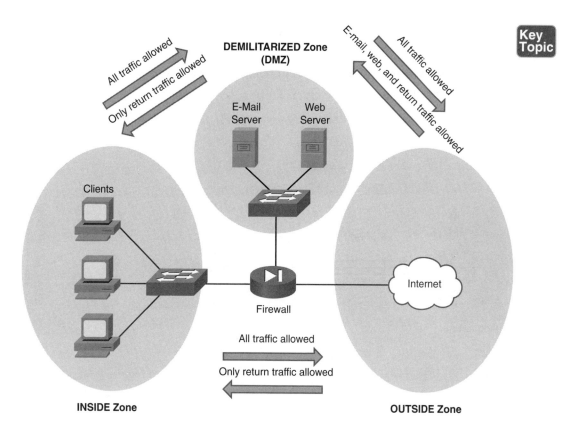

Figure 12-14   Firewall Zone Example

Notice the *DEMILITARIZED zone (DMZ)*. A DMZ often contains servers that should be accessible from the public Internet. This approach would, in this example, allow users on the Internet to initiate an e-mail or a web session coming into an organization's e-mail or web server. However, other protocols would be blocked.

Virtual Private Networks

Much of today's workforce (approximately 40 percent, according to Cisco Systems) is located outside of a corporate headquarters location. Some employees work in remote offices, while others telecommute. These remote employees can connect to their main corporate network by using a variety of WAN technologies (such as leased lines and PVCs, found in Frame Relay and/or ATM networks). However, these WAN technologies typically cost more than widely available broadband technologies, such as DSL and cable, which might also offer faster speeds. Fortunately, *virtual private networks* (VPN) support secure communication between two sites over an untrusted network (for example, the Internet). The two primary categories of VPNs are *site-to-site* and *client-to-site*:

- **Site-to-site:** A site-to-site VPN interconnects two sites, as an alternative to a leased line, at a reduced cost. Figure 12-15 shows a sample site-to-site VPN.

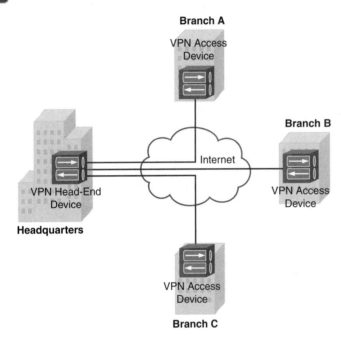

Figure 12-15 Sample Site-to-Site VPN

- **Client-to-site:** A client-to-site VPN (also known as a remote-access VPN) interconnects a remote user with a site, as an alternative to dial-up or ISDN connectivity, at a reduced cost. Figure 12-16 shows a sample client-to-site VPN.

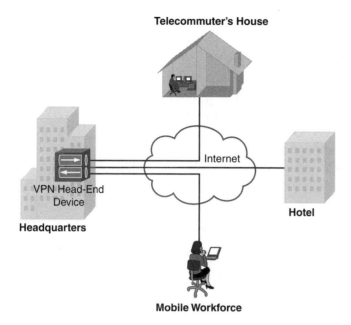

Figure 12-16   Sample Client-to-Site VPN

Although a VPN tunnel might physically pass through multiple service provider routers, the tunnel appears to be a single router hop from the perspective of the routers at each end of the tunnel.

Although a client-to-site VPN allows a user, with software on their client computer, to connect to a centralized VPN termination device, a site-to-site VPN interconnects two sites without requiring the computers at those sites to have any specialized VPN software installed.

Overview of IPsec

Broadband technologies, such as cable and DSL, in addition to other VPN transport mechanisms, often traverse an untrusted network, such as the Internet. Therefore, a primary concern with using a broadband technology as a VPN transport is security.

Although different VPN technologies (for example, IPsec, GRE, L2TP, and L2F) offer a variety of features, IPsec VPNs offer strong security features. Specifically, *IP security* (IPsec) offers the following protections for VPN traffic:

- **Confidentiality:** Data confidentiality is provided by encrypting data. If a third-party intercepts the encrypted data, he would not be able to interpret the data.

- **Integrity:** Data integrity ensures that data is not modified in transit. For example, routers at each end of a tunnel can calculate a checksum value or a hash value for the data, and if both routers calculate the same value, the data has most likely not been modified in transit.

- **Authentication:** Data authentication allows parties involved in a conversation to verify that the other party is the party they claim to be.

IPsec also scales to a wide range of networks. IPsec operates at Layer 3 of the OSI model (the network layer). As a result, IPsec is transparent to applications, which means that applications do not require any sort of integrated IPsec support.

IKE Modes and Phases

IPsec uses a collection of protocols to provide its features. One of the primary protocols that IPsec uses is the *Internet Key Exchange* (IKE) protocol. Specifically, IPsec can provide encryption between authenticated peers using encryption keys, which are periodically changed. IKE, however, allows an administrator to manually configure keys.

IKE can use the three modes of operation to set up a secure communicate path between IPsec peers. These modes are explained in Table 12-3.

Table 12-3   IKE Modes

Mode	Description
Main mode	Main mode involves three exchanges of information between the IPsec peers. One peer, called the *initiator*, sends one or more proposals to the other peer, called the *responder*. The proposal(s) include supported encryption and authentication protocols and key lifetimes. Additionally, the proposal(s) indicate whether or not *perfect forward secrecy* (PFS) should be used. PFS makes sure that a session key remains secure, even if one of the private keys used to derive the session key becomes compromised. The three main mode exchanges are summarized as follows: Exchange #1: The responder selects a proposal it received from the initiator. Exchange #2: *Diffie-Hellman* (DH) securely establishes a shared secret key over the unsecured medium. Exchange #3: An *Internet Security Association and Key Management Protocol* (ISAKMP) session is established. This secure session is then used to negotiate an IPsec session.

Table 12-3   IKE Modes

Mode	Description
Aggressive mode	Aggressive mode more quickly achieves the same results of main mode, using only three packets. The initiator sends the first packet, which contains all the information necessary to establish a *security association* (SA) (an agreement between the two IPsec peers about the cryptographic parameters to be used in the ISAKMP session). The responder sends the second packet, which contains the security parameters selected by the responder (the proposal, keying material, and its ID). This second packet is also used by the responder to authenticate the session. The third and final packet, which is sent by the initiator, finalizes the authentication of the ISAKMP session.
Quick mode	Quick mode negotiates the parameters (the SA) for the IPsec session, and this negotiation occurs within the protection of an ISAKMP session.

The IKE modes reflect the two primary phases of establishing an IPsec tunnel. For example, during IKE Phase 1, a secure ISAKMP session is established using either main mode or aggressive mode. During IKE Phase 1, the IPsec endpoints establish *transform sets* (which are a collection of encryption and authentication protocols), hash methods, and other parameters needed to establish a secure ISAKMP session (sometimes called an *ISAKMP tunnel* or an *IKE Phase 1 tunnel*). As a reminder, this collection of parameters is called a *security association* (SA). With IKE Phase 1, the SA is bidirectional, which means that the same key exchange is used for data flowing across the tunnel in either direction.

IKE Phase 2 occurs within the protection of an IKE Phase 1 tunnel, using the previously described *quick mode* of parameter negotiation. A session formed during IKE Phase 2 is sometimes called an *IKE Phase 2 tunnel* or simply an *IPsec tunnel*. However, unlike IKE Phase 1, IKE Phase 2 performs unidirectional SA negotiations, which means that each data flow uses a separate key exchange.

Although an IPsec tunnel can be established using just IKE Phase 1 and IKE Phase 2, an optional IKE Phase 1.5 can be used. IKE Phase 1.5 uses the Extended Authentication (XAUTH) protocol to perform user authentication of IPsec tunnels. Like IKE Phase 2, IKE Phase 1.5 is performed within the protection of an IKE Phase 1 tunnel. The user authentication provided by this phase adds an additional layer of authentication for VPN clients. Also, parameters such as IP, WINS, and DNS server information can be provided to a VPN client during this optional phase.

Authentication Header and Encapsulating Security Payload

In addition to IKE, which establishes the IPsec tunnel, IPsec also relies on either the *Authentication Header* (AH) protocol (IP protocol number 51) or the *Encapsulating Security Payload* (ESP) protocol (IP protocol number 50). Both AH and ESP offer origin authentication and integrity services, which ensure that IPsec peers are who they claim to be and that the data was not modified in transit.

However, the main distinction between AH and ESP is encryption support. ESP encrypts the original packet, while AH does not offer any encryption. As a result, ESP is far more popular on today's networks.

Both AH and ESP can operate in one of two modes: *transport mode* or *tunnel mode*. Figure 12-17 illustrates the structure of an ESP transport mode packet versus an ESP tunnel mode packet.

Transport Mode

ESP Auth	ESP Trailer	Payload	ESP Header	Original IP Header

Tunnel Mode

ESP Auth	ESP Trailer	Payload	Original IP Header	ESP Header	New IP Header

Figure 12-17   Transparent Mode Versus Tunnel Mode

Following is a detailed description of these two modes:

- **Transport mode:** Uses a packet's original IP header, as opposed to adding an additional tunnel header. This approach works well in networks where increasing a packet's size might cause an issue. Also, transport mode is frequently used for client-to-site VPNs, where a PC running VPN client software connects back to a VPN termination device at a headquarters location.

- **Tunnel mode:** Unlike transport mode, tunnel mode encapsulates an entire packet. As a result, the encapsulated packet has a new header (an IPsec header). This new header has source and destination IP address information that reflects the two VPN termination devices at different sites. Therefore, tunnel mode is frequently used in an IPsec site-to-site VPN.

NOTE   You might be concerned that transport mode allows the IP address of the IPsec peers to remain visible during transit, because the original packet's IP header is used to route a packet. However, IPsec is often used in conjunction with the *generic routing encapsulation* (GRE) tunneling protocol. In such a scenario, the original IP packet is encapsulated inside of a GRE tunnel packet, which adds a new GRE tunnel header. The GRE packet is then sent over an IPsec tunnel. Even if the IPsec tunnel were running in transport mode, the original packet's IP header would still not be visible. Instead, the GRE packet's header would be visible.

One reason a GRE tunnel might be used with an IPsec tunnel is a limitation on the part of IPsec. Specifically, an IPsec tunnel can only transmit unicast IP packets. The challenge is that large enterprise networks might have a significant amount of broadcast or multicast traffic (for example, routing protocol traffic). GRE can take any traffic type and encapsulate the traffic in a GRE tunnel packet, which is a unicast IP packet that can then be sent over an IPsec tunnel. Take, for example, a multicast packet used by a routing protocol. Although IPsec cannot directly transport the multicast packet, if the packet is first encapsulated by GRE, the GRE packet can then be sent over an IPsec tunnel, thereby securing the transmission of the multicast packet.

The Five Steps in Setting Up and Tearing Down an IPsec Site-to-Site VPN

The process of establishing, maintaining, and tearing down an IPsec site-to-site VPN consists of five primary steps. These steps are illustrated in Figure 12-18 and described in detail in the following list.

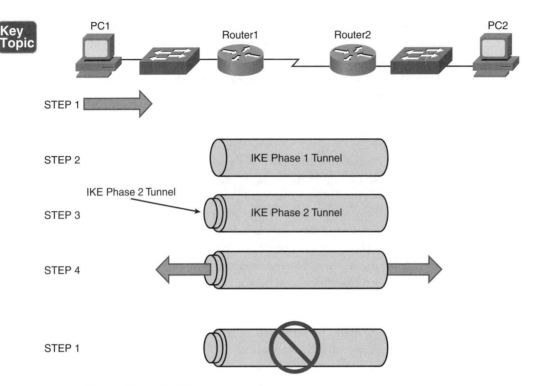

Figure 12-18   IPsec VPN Steps

1. PC1 sends traffic destined for PC2. Router1 classifies the traffic as "interesting" traffic, which initiates the creation of an IPsec tunnel.

2. Router1 and Router2 negotiate a security association (SA) used to form an IKE Phase 1 tunnel, which is also known as an ISAKMP tunnel.

3. Within the protection of the IKE Phase 1 tunnel, an IKE Phase 2 tunnel is negotiated and set up. An IKE Phase 2 tunnel is also known as an IPsec tunnel.

4. After the IPsec tunnel is established, interesting traffic (for example, traffic classified by an ACL) flows through the protected IPsec tunnel. Note that traffic not deemed interesting can still be sent between PC1 and PC2. However, the noninteresting traffic is transmitted outside of the protection of the IPsec tunnel.

5. After no interesting traffic is seen for a specified amount of time, or if the IPsec SA is deleted, the IPsec tunnel is torn down.

Although the previous example described an IPsec site-to-site VPN, the procedure is similar for a client-to-site VPN.

Other VPN Technologies

Although IPsec VPNs are popular for securely interconnecting sites, or connecting a remote client to a site, you need to be aware of other VPN protocols, examples of which are provided in Table 12-4.

Table 12-4 Examples of VPN Protocols

Protocol	Description
SSL	*Secure Sockets Layer* (SSL) provides cryptography and reliability for upper layers (Layers 5–7) of the OSI model. SSL, which was introduced in 1995, has largely been replaced by *Transport Layer Security* (TLS). However, recent versions of SSL (for example, SSL 3.3) have been enhanced to be more comparable with TLS. Both SSL and TLS provide secure web browsing via *Hypertext Transfer Protocol Secure* (HTTPS).
L2TP	*Layer 2 Tunneling Protocol* (L2TP) is a VPN protocol that lacks security features, such as encryption. However, L2TP can still be used for a secure VPN connection if it is combined with another protocol that does provide encryption.
L2F	*Layer 2 Forwarding* (L2F) is a VPN protocol designed (by Cisco Systems) with the intent of providing a tunneling protocol for PPP. Like L2TP, L2F lacks native security features.
PPTP	*Point-to-Point Tunneling Protocol* (PPTP) is an older VPN protocol (which supported the dial-up networking feature in older versions of Microsoft Windows®). Like L2TP and L2F, PPTP lacks native security features. However, Microsoft's versions of PPTP bundled with various versions of Microsoft Windows® were enhanced to offer security features.
TLS	*Transport Layer Security* (TLS) has largely replaced SSL as the VPN protocol of choice for providing cryptography and reliability to upper layers of the OSI model. For example, when you securely connect to a website using HTTPS, you are probably using TLS.

Intrusion Detection and Prevention

When an attacker launches an attack against a network, *intrusion detection system* (IDS) and *intrusion prevention system* (IPS) technologies are often able to recognize the attack and respond appropriately. Attacks might be recognizable by comparing incoming data streams against a database of well-known attack signatures. Other mechanisms for detecting attacks include policy-based and anomaly-based approaches. In addition to dedicated *network-based intrusion prevention system* (NIPS) sensors, IPS software can be installed on a host to provide a *host-based intrusion prevention system* (HIPS) solution.

IDS Versus IPS

Although both IDS and IPS devices can recognize network attacks, they primarily differ in their network placement. Specifically, while an IDS device receives a copy of traffic to be analyzed, an IPS device resides in-line with the traffic, as illustrated in Figure 12-19.

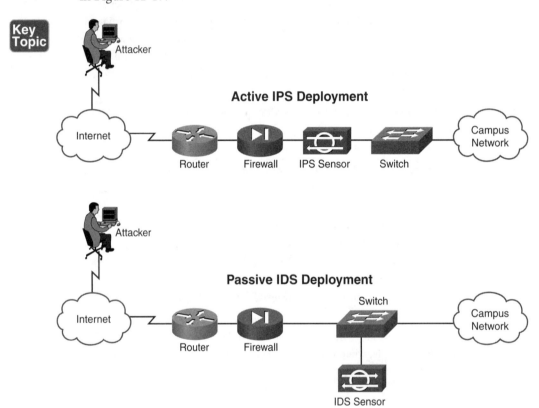

Figure 12-19 IDS and IPS Network Placement

Because the analyzed traffic does not flow through the IDS device, the IDS device is considered to be *passive*, while the IPS device is considered to be *active*. Both the IDS and IPS devices can send alerts to, for example, a management station. Although an IDS device can also communicate with a security appliance or a router to prevent subsequent attack packets, the initially offending traffic reaches its destination. Conversely, an IPS device can drop the traffic in-line, thus preventing even the first malicious packet from reaching its intended target.

The previous discussion of IDS versus IPS devices might seem to suggest that IPS devices should always be used instead of IDS devices. However, in some network environments, these two solutions complement one another. For example, an IDS device can add value to a network that already employs an IPS device by verifying that the IPS device is still operational. The IDS device might also identify suspicious traffic and send alerts about that traffic without having the IPS device drop the traffic.

IDS and IPS Device Categories

IDS and IPS devices can be categorized based on how they detect malicious traffic. Alternately, IPS devices can be categorized based on whether they run on a network device or on a host.

Detection Methods

Consider the following approaches for detecting malicious traffic:

- Signature-based detection

- Policy-based detection

- Anomaly-based detection

The following is a detailed discussion of each method.

Signature-Based Detection

The primary method used to detect and prevent attacks using IDS or IPS technologies is *signature-based*. A signature could be a string of bytes, in a certain context, that triggers detection.

For example, attacks against a web server typically take the form of URLs. Therefore, URLs could be searched for a certain string that would identify an attack against a web server.

As another example, the IDS or IPS device could search for a pattern in the MIME header of an e-mail message. However, because signature-based IDS/IPS is, as its name suggests, based on signatures, the administrator needs to routinely update those signature files.

Policy-Based Detection

Another approach to IDS/IPS detection is *policy based*. With a policy-based approach, the IDS/IPS device needs a specific declaration of the security policy. For example, you could write a network access policy that identified which networks could communicate with other networks. The IDS/IPS device could then recognize *out-of-profile* traffic that does not conform to the policy, and then report that activity.

Anomaly-Based Detection

A third approach to detecting or preventing malicious traffic is *anomaly based*. This approach is prone to false positives, because a *normal* condition is difficult to measurably define. However, there are a couple of options for detecting anomalies:

- **Statistical anomaly detection:** This approach watches network-traffic patterns over a period of time and dynamically builds a baseline. Then, if traffic patterns significantly vary from the baseline, an alarm can be triggered.

- **Nonstatistical anomaly detection:** This approach allows an administrator to define what traffic patterns are supposed to look like. However, imagine that Microsoft released a large service pack for its Windows 7 OS, and your company has hundreds of computers that are configured to automatically download that service pack. If multiple employees turn on their computers at approximately the same time tomorrow morning, and multiple copies of the service pack simultaneously start to download from www.microsoft.com, the IDS/IPS device might consider that traffic pattern to be significantly outside of the baseline. As a result, the nonstatistical anomaly detection approach could lead to a false positive (an alarm being triggered in the absence of malicious traffic).

NOTE   Anomaly-based detection is also known as *behavior-based detection*.

Deploying Network-Based and Host-Based Solutions

NIPS and HIPS solutions can work in tandem. For example, although a NIPS solution can inspect traffic flowing through the network, what if a host had a SSL connection to a server, and the malicious traffic traveled over the SSL connection? In that instance, the NIPS hardware would be unable to analyze the malicious traffic, because it would be encrypted inside of the SSL connection. However, a HIPS software solution could analyze the malicious traffic after the traffic was decrypted on the host. Similarly, a NIPS device might be able to prevent a DoS attack or recognize network reconnaissance patterns, while a HIPS solution could focus on the protection of applications and host resources.

Figure 12-20 illustrates the deployment of *network-based IDS* (NIDS), NIPS, and HIPS technologies in the same network. Notice the sensors are strategically deployed at network boundaries (that is, coming into the network from the Internet and going into the DMZ). As previously discussed, both NIDS and NIPS devices complement the functions of one another. Additionally, HIPS software is deployed on strategic hosts, which are the HTTP, DNS, and e-mail hosts in this example. The NIDS, NIPS, and HIPS devices can all send any alarms triggered on their respective devices to a management console. Using input from these diverse sources, the management console software might be able to perform *event correlation* to recognize broader network attack patterns, rather than just examining a single attack against a single device.

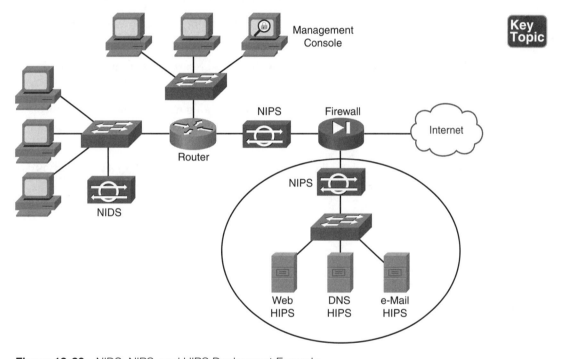

Figure 12-20   NIDS, NIPS, and HIPS Deployment Example

Summary

The main topics covered in this chapter are the following:

- Security fundamentals were discussed. Specifically, you were introduced to the security goals of confidentiality, integrity, and availability. Then, you were presented with several examples of common network threats.

- You reviewed best practice recommendations for defending against threats to network security. These recommendations included such things as user training, patching, having a security policy, having an incident response policy, testing your own network with vulnerability scanners, distracting attackers with honey pots, and blocking unwanted traffic with access control lists.

- A collection of remote-access security technologies were presented (for example, SSH, AAA, and NAC).

- Firewalls were discussed, along with firewall types, inspection types, and firewall zones.

- Virtual private networks were introduced, along with various VPN protocols. However, the primary focus was on IPsec, and you saw a detailed explanation of how an IPsec tunnel is established.

- You saw how to defend your network against well-known attacks using IDS and IPS sensors.

Exam Preparation Tasks

Review All the Key Topics

Review the most important topics from inside the chapter, noted with the Key Topic icon in the outer margin of the page. Table 12-5 lists these key topics and the page numbers where each is found.

Table 12-5   Key Topics for Chapter 12

Key Topic Element	Description	Page Number
List	Network security goals	386
List	Symmetric encryption algorithms	387
Figure 12-2	Asymmetric encryption example	389
List	Types of integrity attacks	390
Table 12-1	Confidentiality attack tactics	393
Figure 12-11	ACL example	410
Table 12-2	Remote-access security methods	411
List	Firewall types	414
Figure 12-12	Packet-filtering firewall	415
Figure 12-13	Stateful firewall	416
Figure 12-14	Firewall zone example	417
List	VPN categories	418
Figure 12-17	Transparent mode versus tunnel mode	422
Figure 12-18	IPsec VPN steps	424
Table 12-4	Examples of VPN protocols	425
Figure 12-19	IDS and IPS network placement	426
List	IDS/IPS detection methods	427
Figure 12-20	NIDS, NIPS, and HIPS deployment example	429

Complete Tables and Lists from Memory

Print a copy of Appendix C, "Memory Tables" (found on the CD), or at least the section for this chapter, and complete the tables and lists from memory. Appendix D, "Memory Table Answer Key," also on the CD, includes the completed tables and lists so you can check your work.

Define Key Terms

Define the following key terms from this chapter, and check your answers in the Glossary:

symmetric encryption, asymmetric encryption, Advanced Encryption Standard (AES), RSA, pretty good privacy (PGP), GNU Privacy Guard (GPC), public key infrastructure (PKI), Challenge-Response Authentication Mechanism Message Digest 5 (CRAM-MD5), denial of service (DoS), social engineering, FTP bounce, distributed denial of service (DDoS), buffer overflow, security policy, acceptable use policy (AUP), Nessus®, Nmap, honey pot, honey net, access control list (ACL), Kerberos, Remote Authentication Dial-In User Service (RADIUS), Terminal Access Controller Access-Control System Plus (TACACS+), two-factor authentication, multifactor authentication, single sign-on (SSO), software firewall, hardware firewall, stateful firewall, demilitarized zone (DMZ), virtual private network (VPN), site-to-site VPN, client-to-site, remote access VPN, IP security (IPsec), Internet Key Exchange (IKE), Internet Security Association and Key Management Protocol (ISAKMP), security association (SA), Authentication Header (AH), Encapsulating Security Payload (ESP), Secure Sockets Layer (SSL), Layer 2 Tunneling Protocol (L2TP), Layer 2 Forwarding (L2F), Point-to-Point Tunneling Protocol (PPTP), intrusion detection system (IDS), intrusion prevention system (IDS), network-based IDS (NIDS), network-based IPS (NIPS), host-based IPS (HIPS)

Review Questions

The answers to these review questions are in Appendix A, "Answers to Review Questions."

1. Which of the following is a symmetric encryption algorithm, available in 128-bit, 192-bit, and 256-bit key versions?

   a. RSA

   b. 3DES

   c. AES

   d. TKIP

2. In what type of attack does the attacker compromise multiple systems and then instruct those compromised systems, called *zombies*, to simultaneously flood a target system with traffic?

   a. DoS

   b. TCP SYN flood

   c. Buffer overflow

   d. DDoS

3. Which of the following is a continually changing document that dictates a set of guidelines for network use?

   a. Security policy

   b. Post-mortem report

   c. Syslog report

   d. QoS policy

4. What type of software application should network administrators routinely use to verify the security of their network and check for any weaknesses?

   a. Honey pot

   b. Posture monitor

   c. Profile scanner

   d. Vulnerability scanner

5. Which of the following are characteristics of RADIUS? (Choose two.)

   a. TCP-based

   b. UDP-based

   c. Encrypts an entire authentication packet

   d. Only encrypts the password in an authentication packet

6. What feature allows a firewall to permit traffic to flow from a trusted network (for example, a corporate intranet) to an untrusted network (for example, the Internet), and then allow return traffic for that session, while blocking sessions initiated on the untrusted network?

   a. Packet filtering

   b. Stateful inspection

   c. Demilitarized zone

   d. Implicit deny all instruction

7. Which of the following is an IPsec protocol that provides authentication and integrity services, but does not support encryption?

   a. IKE Phase I

   b. IKE Phase II

   c. AH

   d. ESP

8. Which of the following protocols are most commonly used to provide security for an HTTPS connection? (Choose two.)

   a. L2TP

   b. SSL

   c. PPTP

   d. TLS

9. Which of the following security solutions consists of software running on a host to protect that host against a collection of well-known attacks?

   a. HIPS

   b. NIDS

   c. L2F

   d. NIPS

10. From the following list, identify the detection methods commonly used by IPS sensors. (Choose three.)

    a. Signature-based

    b. Distribution-based

    c. Policy-based

    d. Behavior-based

After completion of this chapter, you will be able to
answer the following questions:

- What are the elements in a structured troubleshooting model?

- What common physical layer troubleshooting issues might you encounter?

- What potential Layer 2 issues are you most likely to face when troubleshooting a network containing Ethernet switches?

- Aside from routing protocol troubleshooting, what Layer 3 troubleshooting issues are common in a routed network?

- How do characteristics unique to wireless networks impact your troubleshooting of a network containing wireless access points?

CHAPTER 13

Troubleshooting Network Issues

As you perform your day-to-day tasks of administering a network, a significant percentage of your time will be dedicated to resolving network issues. Whether the issues that you are troubleshooting were reported by an end user or were issues you discovered, you need an effective plan to respond to those issues. Specifically, you need a systematic approach to clearly articulate the issue, gather information about the issue, hypothesize the underlying cause of the issue, validate your hypothesis, create an action plan, implement that action plan, observe results, and document your resolution. Without a plan, your efforts might be inefficient, as you try one thing after another, possibly causing other issues in the process.

Although your troubleshooting efforts can most definitely benefit from a structured approach, realize that troubleshooting is part art and part science. Specifically, your intuition and instincts play a huge role in isolating an issue. Of course, those skills are developed over time and come with experience and exposure to more and more scenarios.

To help you start developing, or continue honing, your troubleshooting skills, this chapter begins by presenting you with a formalized troubleshooting methodology, which can act as a guide for addressing most any network issue. Then, the remainder of this chapter presents you with a collection of common network issues to consider in your real-world troubleshooting efforts (and issues to consider on the Network+ exam).

These common network issues are broken down into the following categories: physical layer issues, data link layer issues, network layer issues, and wireless network issues.

Troubleshooting Basics

Troubleshooting network issues is implicit in the responsibilities of a network administrator. Such issues could arise as a result of human error (for example, a misconfiguration), from equipment failure, software bugs, or traffic patterns (for example, high utilization or a network being under attack by malicious traffic).

Many network issues can be successfully resolved using a variety of approaches. This section begins by introducing you to troubleshooting fundamentals. Then, you are presented with a structured troubleshooting methodology you should know for the Network+ exam.

Troubleshooting Fundamentals

The process of troubleshooting, at its essence, is the process of responding to a problem report (sometimes in the form of a *trouble ticket*), diagnosing the underlying cause of the problem, and resolving the problem. While you normally think of the troubleshooting process beginning when a user reports an issue, realize that through effective network monitoring, you might detect a situation that might become a troubleshooting issue and resolve that situation before it impacts users.

After an issue is reported, the first step toward resolution is clearly defining the issue. After you have a clearly defined troubleshooting target, you can begin gathering information related to that issue. Based on the information collected, you might be able to better define the issue. Then, you hypothesize the likely causes of the issue. Evaluation of these likely causes leads to the identification of the suspected underlying root cause of an issue.

After a suspected underlying cause is identified, you next define approaches to resolve an issue and select what you consider to be the best approach. Sometimes, the best approach to resolving an issue cannot be implemented immediately. For example, a piece of equipment might need replacing. However, a business' workflow might be disrupted by implementing such an approach during working hours. In such situations, a troubleshooter might use a temporary fix until a permanent fix can be put in place.

As a personal example, when helping troubleshoot a connectivity issue for a resort hotel at a major theme park, my coworkers and I discovered that a modular Ethernet switch had an issue causing Spanning Tree Protocol (STP) to fail, resulting in a Layer 2 loop. This loop flooded the network with traffic, preventing the hotel from issuing keycards for guest rooms. The underlying cause was clear. Specifically, the

Ethernet switch had a bad module. However, the time was about 4:00 P.M., a peak time for guest registration. So, instead of immediately replacing the faulty module, we disconnected one of the redundant links, thus breaking the Layer 2 loop. The logic was that it was better to have the network function at this time without STP than for the network to experience an even longer outage while the bad module was replaced. Late that night, someone came back to the switch and swapped out the module, resolving the underlying cause while minimizing user impact.

Consider Figure 13-1, which depicts a simplified model of the troubleshooting steps previously described. This simplified model consists of three steps:

1. Problem report
2. Problem diagnosis
3. Problem resolution

Problem Report ⟩   Problem Diagnosis ⟩   Problem Resolution ⟩

Figure 13-1 Simplified Troubleshooting Flow

Of these three steps, the majority of a troubleshooter's efforts are spent in the *problem diagnosis* step. Table 13-1 describes key components of the problem diagnosis step.

Table 13-1 Steps to Diagnose a Problem

Step	Description
Collect information.	Because a typical problem report lacks sufficient information to give a troubleshooter insight into a problem's underlying cause, the troubleshooter should collect additional information, perhaps using network maintenance tools or interviewing impacted users.
Examine collected information.	After collecting sufficient information about a problem, a troubleshooter then examines that information, possibly comparing the information against previously collected baseline information.
Eliminate potential causes.	Based on a troubleshooter's knowledge of a network and his interrogation of collected information, the troubleshooter can begin to eliminate potential causes for a problem.
Hypothesize underlying cause.	After a troubleshooter eliminates multiple potential causes for the problem, he is left with one or more causes that are more likely to have resulted in the problem. The troubleshooter hypothesizes what he considers to be the most likely cause for the problem.
Verify hypothesis.	The troubleshooter then tests his hypothesis to confirm or refute his theory as to the problem's underlying cause.

Structured Troubleshooting Methodology

Troubleshooting skills vary from administrator to administrator. Therefore, although most troubleshooting approaches include the collection and analysis of information, elimination of potential causes, hypothesis of likely causes, and to test the suspected cause, different troubleshooters might spend different amounts of time performing these tasks.

If a troubleshooter does not follow a structured approach, the temptation is to move between the previously listed troubleshooting tasks in a fairly random way, often based on instinct. Although such as approach might well lead to a problem resolution, it can become confusing to remember what you have tried and what you have not tried. Also, if another administrator comes to assist you, communicating to that other administrator the steps you have already gone through could be a challenge. Therefore, following a structured troubleshooting approach not only helps prevent your trying the same thing more than once and inadvertently skipping a task, but also aids in communicating to someone else the possibilities you already eliminated.

You might encounter a variety of structured troubleshooting methodologies in networking literature. However, for the Network+ exam, the methodology shown in Figure 13-2 is what you should memorize.

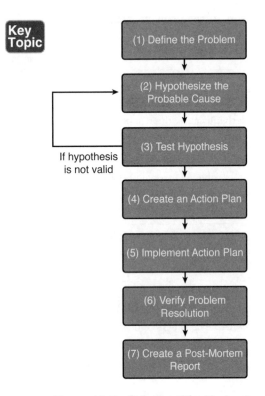

Figure 13-2 Structured Troubleshooting Approach

The following is an elaboration on this seven-step methodology:

1. **Define the problem**. Effective troubleshooting begins with a clear problem definition. This definition might include specific symptoms, such as, "User A's computer is unable to communicate with server 1 (as verified by a ping test). However, user A can communicate with all other servers. Also, no other user seems to have an issue connecting to server 1." This problem definition might come from questioning the impacted user(s) and doing your own testing (for example, seeing if you can ping from user A's computer to server 1). If possible, determine if anything has changed in the network (or in the computer) configuration. Also, find out if this is a new installation, which has never worked in the past.

2. **Hypothesize a probable cause**. This is the point in the troubleshooting process where your experience and intuition can be extremely helpful, because you are now going to brainstorm a list of possible causes. When examining your collected data (for example, output from the **ipconfig /all** command), question everything. For example, you might think that the issue described in Step 1 could result from causes such as an ACL blocking traffic to or from the PC, a connectivity issue with the PC or server, or an incorrect IP address configuration on the PC. From your list of possible causes, select the one that you consider the most likely. From the previous list, you might believe that an incorrect IP address configuration on the PC is the most likely cause of the problem. Specifically, you conclude that the issue is not related to connectivity, because other PCs can get to the server, and user A's PC can get to other servers. Also, you conclude that it is more likely that user A's PC has a bad IP-address configuration than for an ACL to have been administratively added to the router to only block traffic between user A's PC and server 1.

3. **Test hypothesis**. Before taking action on what you consider to be the most likely cause of a problem, do a *sanity check* on your theory. Would your hypothesized cause lead to the observed symptoms? In the example presented in the preceding steps, you might examine the subnet mask assigned to user A's computer and determine that it is incorrect. Specifically, the subnet mask makes user A's computer think that server 1 is on the same subnet as user A's computer. As a result, user A's computer does not forward traffic to its default gateway when attempting to reach server 1. If your hypothesis is technically sound, you can proceed to Step 4. However, if you notice a flaw in your logic, you need to formulate an alternate hypothesis. The formation of an alternate hypothesis might involve escalating the problem to someone more familiar with the device(s) in question.

4. **Create an action plan**. Now that you have confirmed that your theory makes sense technically, the time has come to develop an action plan. If time permits, you should document your action plan. The documentation of your action plan can be used as a *back-out plan* if your hypothesis is incorrect. In the example we have been building on throughout these steps, an action plan might be to change the subnet mask on user A's computer from 255.255.0.0 to 255.255.255.0.

5. **Implement action plan**. Based on your documented plan of action, you should schedule an appropriate time to implement your action plan. The selection of an appropriate time is a balance between the severity of a problem and the impact your action plan will have on other users. Sometimes, when attempting to implement your action plan, you realize that you do not have sufficient administrative privileges to perform a task in your action plan. In such cases, you should escalate the issue to someone with appropriate administrative rights. In this example, changing the subnet mask on one computer should not impact any other devices. So, you might immediately make the configuration change on user A's computer.

6. **Verify problem resolution**. After implementing your action plan, you need to verify that the symptoms listed in your original problem definition are gone. Also, attempt to determine if your action plan has caused any other issues on the network. A mistake many troubleshooters make at this point is believing the issue has been resolved, because the specific symptom, or symptoms, they were looking for is gone. However, the user who originally reported the issue might still be having a problem. Therefore, troubleshooters should live by the mantra, "A problem isn't fixed until the user believes it's fixed." So, you should always get confirmation from the person reporting an issue that, from her perspective, the reported issue has indeed been resolved. In our example, you could attempt to ping server 1 from user A. If the ping is successful, check with user A to see if she agrees that the problem is resolved.

7. **Create a post-mortem report**. A *post-mortem* report is a document that describes the reported issue, its underlying causes, and what was done to resolve the issue. This report might be useful when troubleshooting similar issues in the future.

Keep in mind when working your way through the previous steps that you might encounter an issue that you do not have sufficient information to solve. When that happens, you might need to further research the issue yourself. However, if time is of the essence, you might need to immediately escalate the issue to someone else within your organization, to an equipment vendor, or to an outside consultant.

Physical Layer Troubleshooting

Layer 1 (the physical layer) of the OSI model is foundational to all the other layers. As a result, if Layer 1 isn't functioning, none of the upper layers will function properly. Table 13-2 presents a collection of common Layer 1 issues.

NOTE   Many of these issues have been discussed in previous chapters.

Table 13-2   Common Layer 1 Troubleshooting Issues

Issue	Description
Bad cables or connectors	Faulty cables (with electrical characteristics preventing a successful transmission) or faulty connectors (which do not properly make a connection) can prevent successful data transmission at Layer 1. A *bad cable* could simply be an incorrect category of cable being used for a specific purpose. For example, perhaps you interconnected two 1000BASE-TX devices using a Cat 5 cable (instead of a Cat 6 or higher cable), resulting in corrupted data. See Chapter 4, "Understanding Ethernet," for a listing of Ethernet types and their corresponding supported cable types.
Opens and shorts	An *open* is a broken strand of copper, preventing current from flowing through a circuit. However, a *short* occurs when two copper connectors touch each other, resulting in current flowing through that short rather than the attached electrical circuit, because the short has lower resistance.
Splitting pairs in a cable	An unshielded twisted-pair (UTP) cable consists of eight separate copper leads. However, only four of those eight leads are used for data (two transmit leads and two receive leads). This results in four unused leads. Some installers use those four extra leads to support a second Ethernet connection on a single UTP cable. Although such an approach can function, nonstandard wires are being used for connecting the second Ethernet connection. Therefore, you should be aware of any nonstandard pinouts used in the network that you are troubleshooting.
dB loss	The signal power of a data transmission might be degraded to the point where the transmission is not correctly interpreted by a receiving device. This loss of signal power, called a *decibel loss* (dB loss), could result from exceeding the distance limitation of a copper or fiber cable.

Table 13-2   Common Layer 1 Troubleshooting Issues

Issue	Description
Transposed Tx/Rx leads	Some Ethernet switches support *medium dependent interface crossover* (MDIX), which allows a switch port to properly configure its leads as transmit (Tx) or receive (Rx) leads. You can interconnect such switches with a straight-through cable (as opposed to a crossover cable). However, if a network device does not support MDIX, it needs an appropriate cable (that is, a *crossover cable*) to allow its Tx leads to connect to the Rx leads on a connected device, and vice versa. Therefore, care must be taken when selecting cable types interconnecting network components. More information on crossover cables and MDIX can be found in Chapter 3, "Identifying Network Components."
Cable placement	Because copper cables are subject to *electromagnetic interference* (EMI), you should arrange cables to minimize interference. Ideally, Ethernet cables should not be placed in close proximity with high voltage cables, generators, motors, or radio transmitters. For example, when running cables between buildings via underground conduit, network cabling is ideally placed in a separate conduit than electrical cables.
Distance limitations exceeded	If Ethernet devices are interconnected using a cable that exceeds the Ethernet distance limitations for the cable type, a digital transmission between those devices can be degraded to the point where the receiving equipment is unable to correctly interpret the transmission. Therefore, network designs should consider distances between devices.
Crosstalk	Crosstalk can occur when an analog connection creates an electromagnetic field around its conductors, inducing its waveforms on a nearby analog connection. This phenomenon is most commonly experienced in an analog phone call. Crosstalk can be minimized by using a higher category of cabling, because higher categories of cables better limit the radiation of electromagnetic waves.

Physical Layer Troubleshooting: Scenario

To practice your physical layer troubleshooting skills, consider the network diagram presented in Figure 13-3.

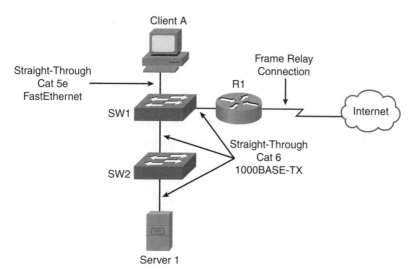

Figure 13-3 Physical Layer Troubleshooting: Sample Topology

Assume that both switches in Figure 13-3 are capable of autonegotiating Ethernet speeds of 10, 100, or 1000 Mbps. Also, assume the switches do not support MDIX. Based on the provided information, take a moment (before reading on) and identify what you believe to be a Layer 1 issue in the topology.

Physical Layer Troubleshooting: Solution

In the topology shown in Figure 13-3, notice that switches SW1 and SW2 are interconnected with a straight-through cable. Also, recall that neither switch supports MDIX. As a result, the ports interconnecting the two switches have their Tx leads interconnected with one another and their Rx leads interconnected with one another. As a result, no communication is possible. The resolution to such a scenario is to replace the straight-through Cat 6 cable between SW1 and SW2 with a crossover Cat 6 cable.

Data Link Layer Troubleshooting

Most enterprise LANs rely on some form of Ethernet technology (for example, Ethernet, Fast Ethernet, or Gigabit Ethernet). Therefore, an understanding of Ethernet switch operation, at Layer 2 (that is, the data link layer), is critical to troubleshooting many LAN issues. You might want to reference Chapter 4 for a review of Ethernet switch operation.

Table 13-3 presents a collection of common Layer 2 issues.

Table 13-3   Common Layer 2 Troubleshooting Issues

Issue	Description
Power failure	Ethernet switches are often not connected to a redundant power source (for example, an electrical outlet with a generator backup), in part due to the widely dispersed installation locations throughout a building (for example, in wiring closets or in a mechanical room). As a result, you might want to equip your Ethernet switches with an *uninterruptable power supply* (UPS). See Chapter 12, "Securing a Network," for a comparison of a UPS and a *standby power supply* (SPS).
Bad module	A modular switch gives you the flexibility to connect a variety of media types and speeds to the switch through the use of different modules. Examples of these modules include *gigabit interface converter* (GBIC) and *small form-factor pluggable* (SFP) modules. These modular interfaces can be swapped out during your troubleshooting, as opposed to swapping out an entire switch.
Layer 2 loop	Chapter 4 discussed issues resulting from Layer 2 loops, including MAC address table corruption and broadcast storms. You also read about how to mitigate these issues with *Spanning Tree Protocol* (STP). However, STP can fail (as illustrated by my personal example, which you read about at the beginning of this chapter). Or, STP might be functioning suboptimally, because a root bridge was automatically selected, rather than being specified, resulting in a suboptimal path. So, you should be able to examine your Ethernet switches, when troubleshooting, and determine the STP roles of your network's switches and switch ports.
Port configuration	Common settings for Ethernet switch ports include *speed*, *duplex*, and *MDIX*. Mismatched parameters between devices could result in slow communication (in the case of a duplex mismatch) or in no communication (in the case of a speed mismatch or incorrect MDIX settings).
VLAN configuration	In Chapter 4, you read about virtual LANs (VLAN), which were broadcast domains and represented a single subnet. Several troubleshooting issues could result from a VLAN misconfiguration on an Ethernet switch. Keep in mind that all devices belonging to the same VLAN should be assigned IP addresses in the same subnet. Also, if you want traffic to flow between VLANs, that traffic has to be routed.

Data Link Layer Troubleshooting: Scenario

Based on your knowledge of an Ethernet switch (a common example of a data link layer device), consider the following troubleshooting scenario. The network depicted in Figure 13-4 is having an issue. Specifically, client A is not able to communicate with server 1. Based on the diagram, what do you consider to be the most likely cause?

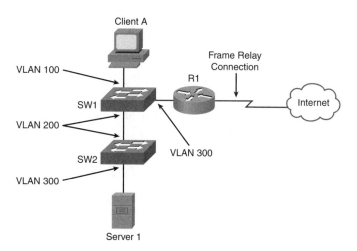

Figure 13-4   Data Link Layer Troubleshooting: Sample Topology

After determining what you believe to be the underlying cause, check your answer with the following solution.

Data Link Layer Troubleshooting: Solution

Even though client A and server 1, as shown in Figure 13-4, are on the same VLAN (VLAN 100), there is no VLAN 100 traffic flowing between switches SW1 and SW2. Specifically, the connection linking SW1 and SW2 only carries traffic for VLAN 200. A couple of solutions exist to this issue.

One solution is to change the ports on switches SW1 and SW2 to both belong to VLAN 100. Another solution is to configure an IEEE 802.1Q trunk to interconnect SW1 and SW2, because a trunk can simultaneously carry traffic for multiple VLANs.

Network Layer Troubleshooting

When troubleshooting connectivity issues for an IP-based network, the network layer (Layer 3) is often an appropriate place to begin your troubleshooting efforts. For example, if you are experiencing connectivity issues between two hosts on a network, you could check Layer 3 by pinging from one host to another. If the pings are successful, you can conclude that the issue resides above Layer 3 (Layers 4–7). However, if the pings fail, you can focus your troubleshooting efforts on Layers 1–3. The rationale for this conclusion is based on ping using *Internet Control Message Protocol* (ICMP), which is a Layer 4 protocol. If one Layer 4 protocol is functioning correctly (even though other Layer 4 protocols might be having issues), you can conclude that Layers 1–3 are operational.

Layer 3 Data Structures

As traffic is routed through a network, routers encountered along the way from the source to the destination need consistency in how they route traffic. For example, if one router selected the best path based on hop count, and another router selected the best path based on a link's bandwidth, a routing loop could conceivably occur. Fortunately, having a common routing protocol configured on all routers within a topology helps ensure consistency in routing decisions.

That is not to say that a topology could not have more than one routing protocol. You could strategically redistribute routes between different routing protocols. Also, static routes could be used in conjunction with dynamic routing protocols. However, care must be taken in environments with redundant links and multiple routing protocols to avoid potential routing loops.

To better troubleshoot specific dynamic routing protocols, let's first generically consider how dynamic routing protocols' data structures interact with a router's IP routing table.

Figure 13-5 shows the interaction between the data structures of an IP routing protocol and a router's IP routing table. Realize, however, that not all routing protocols maintain their own data structures. For example, RIP is a routing protocol that works directly with an IP routing table in a router, rather than maintaining a separate data structure.

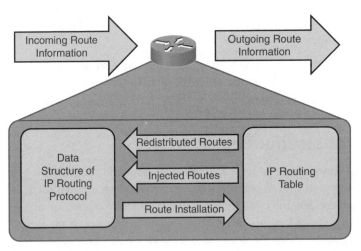

Figure 13-5   Interaction Between IP Routing Protocol Data Structures and IP Routing Tables

As a router receives route information from a neighboring router, that information is stored in the data structures of the IP routing protocol (if the IP routing protocol uses data structures). A data structure might also be populated by the local router.

For example, a router might be configured for route redistribution where route information is redistributed by a routing information source (for example, a dynamic routing protocol, a static route, or a connected route). Also, the router might be configured to have specific interfaces participate in an IP routing protocol.

The data structure analyzes all the information it receives to select the best route to certain network. This best route is determined by looking for the route with the best metric. The data structure of an IP routing protocol then injects that best route into the router's IP routing table, if that same route information has not already been learned by a more believable routing source. Specifically, different routing protocols have different *administrative distances* (AD). An administrative distance of a routing protocol can be thought of as the believability of that routing protocol. As an example, RIP has an AD of 120, while OSPF has an AD of 110. Therefore, if both RIP and OSPF had knowledge of a route to a specific network, the OSPF route would be injected into the router's IP routing table, because OSPF has a more believable AD. Therefore, the best route selected by an IP routing protocol's data structure is only a candidate to be injected into a router's IP routing table.

NOTE   Chapter 6 provides additional information about the ADs of various routing protocols.

If an IP routing protocol's data structure identifies more than one route to a destination network, multiple routes might be injected into a router's IP routing table if those multiple routes have an equal metric. In some cases, however, a routing protocol (for example, EIGRP) might support load balancing across unequal-cost paths. In such an instance, multiple routes might be injected into a router's IP routing table, even though those routes have different metrics.

Depending on the IP routing protocol in use, a router periodically advertises all of its routes, or updates to its routing information, to its neighbors. Also, be aware that some routing protocols need to establish a relationship with a neighboring router before exchanging route information with that neighbor. This relationship is called an *adjacency* or a *neighborship*.

Common Layer 3 Troubleshooting Issues

Effectively troubleshooting Layer 3 issues, as suggested by the previous discussion, largely relies on your understanding of various routing protocols. Therefore, for the real world, you must familiarize yourself with the subtle details of the routing protocol(s) running in your network.

However, the Network+ exam deemphasizes the intricacies of specific routing protocols, instead focusing on more generic Layer 3 troubleshooting issues. Examples of those issues are presented in Table 13-4.

Table 13-4   Common Layer 3 Troubleshooting Issues

Issue	Description
Mismatched MTU	Router interfaces have a parameter called the *maximum transmission unit* (MTU) that defines the largest packet size the interface will forward. For example, a 1500-byte packet could not be forwarded via a router interface with an MTU of 1470 bytes. A router attempts to fragment a packet that is too big, unless the packet has its *don't fragment* (DF) bit set. If a packet exceeds an interface's MTU and has its DF bit set, the router drops the packet. Normally, the router responds to the sender with an ICMP message indicating why the packet was dropped. However, if a router is configured to not respond to such a condition by sending an ICMP message, the packet is dropped without the sender being notified. Such a router is called a *black-hole router*. You can use the *traceroute* utility (as described in Chapter 10, "Using Command-Line Utilities") to help locate a black-hole router.
Incorrect subnet mask	When one host attempts to communicate with another host on the same subnet, the sending host sends an ARP request in an attempt to determine the MAC address of the destination host, rather than forwarding traffic to the sending host's default gateway. Therefore, if a host has an incorrect subnet mask, it could incorrectly conclude that another host is on its local subnet, when in reality, the other host is on a remote subnet. As a result, the remote host is unreachable from the perspective of the sending host.
Incorrect default gateway	If a host has an incorrect default gateway configuration, traffic from that host is not forwarded off of that host's local subnet.
Duplicate IP address	Hosts on a subnet should have unique IP addresses. If two hosts are configured with the same IP address, unpredictable traffic patterns for those hosts can occur.
Incorrect DNS configuration	Because hosts frequently use DNS to resolve domain names to IP addresses, if a host has an incorrect DNS configuration, that host will be unable to, for example, browse the Internet using domain names (as opposed to IP addresses).

Network Layer Troubleshooting: Scenario

A common network layer troubleshooting issue, as described in Chapter 5, "Working with IP Addresses," is a host with an IP address that is not valid for the subnet to which the host is physically connected. Using your subnetting skills, determine which host (*client A* or *server 1*) in Figure 13-6 is assigned an incorrect IP address, assuming the router interface's IP address is correct.

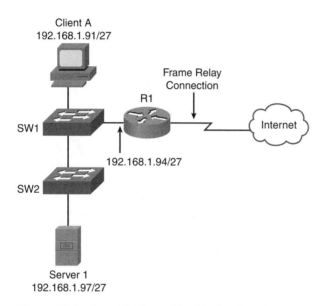

Figure 13-6   Data Link Layer Troubleshooting: Sample Topology

Network Layer Troubleshooting: Solution

The network shown in Figure 13-6 has subnetted the 192.168.1.0/24 network using a 27-bit subnet mask (255.255.255.224). To determine which client PC is assigned an IP address outside of its local VLAN, you need to determine the subnets created by the 27-bit subnet mask applied to the 192.168.1.0/24 network:

1. The *interesting octet* for a 27-bit subnet mask is the fourth octet, because the fourth octet is the last octet to contain a 1 in the 27-bit subnet mask (1111 1111.11111111.11111111.11100000, which could alternately be written as 255.255.255.224).

2. The decimal value of the third octet in the subnet mask is 224. Therefore, the block size is 32 (256 - 224 = 32).

3. The first 192.168.1.0/27 subnet is 192.168.1.0/27 (192.168.1.0/27 with the three borrowed bits in the third octet set to 0).

4. Beginning with the first subnet of 192.168.1.0/27 and counting by the block size of 32 in the interesting octet yields the following subnets:

192.168.1.0/27

192.168.1.32/27

192.168.1.64/27

192.168.1.96/27

192.168.1.128/27

192.168.1.160/27

192.168.1.192/27

192.168.1.224/27

Based on the IP address of the router interface (192.168.1.94/27) and the previous list of subnets, you can determine that the router's interface is in the 192.168.1.64/27 subnet. Similarly, you can determine the subnet of client A to be 192.168.1.64/27, and the subnet of server 1 to be 192.168.1.96/27. As a result, you can conclude that the host with an incorrect IP address is server 1, because its IP address is in a different subnet that the router interface's subnet.

Wireless Troubleshooting

Troubleshooting wireless networks can require a variety of skill sets. For example, some troubleshooting scenarios might require an understanding of antenna theory and the radio frequency spectrum. However, the Network+ exam focuses on more common wireless issues, as presented in Table 13-5.

NOTE   Chapter 8, "Connecting Wirelessly," discusses wireless networks in detail.

Table 13-5 Common Wireless Troubleshooting Issues

Issue	Description
RFI	Wireless communication can be interrupted because of *radio frequency interference* (RFI). Common RFI sources that impact wireless networks include 2.4-GHz cordless phones, microwave ovens, baby monitors, and game consoles.
Signal strength	The *Received Signal Strength Indicator* (RSSI) value measures the power of a wireless signal. An RSSI value varies based on distance from a wireless antenna and physical objects interfering with line-of-sight communication with a wireless antenna (for example, drywall, metal file cabinets, and elevator shafts). Some wireless networks automatically drop their wireless transmission rate when an RSSI value drops below a certain value.
Misconfiguration of wireless parameters	A variety of wireless parameters must match between a wireless client and a wireless *access point* (AP) in order for communication to occur. For example, the client needs to be using a wireless standard supported by the wireless AP (for example, IEEE 802.11a/b/g/n). Wireless channels must also match. However, wireless clients usually automatically set their channel based on the wireless AP's channel. Encryption standards must match. For example, a wireless client using WPA would not successfully communicate with a wireless AP using WPA2. Additionally, the *service set identifier* (SSID) of a wireless AP must be selected by the wireless client. In many cases, a wireless AP broadcasts its SSID, and a wireless client can select that SSID from a listing of visible SSIDs. In other cases, a wireless AP does not broadcast its SSID, thus requiring a wireless client to have a matching SSID manually configured.
Latency	Wireless networks can experience more delay than their wired counterparts. One reason for the increased delay is the use of *carrier sense multiple access collision avoidance* (CSMA/CA) in WLANs, which introduces a random delay before transmitting data, in an attempt to avoid collisions. Another, yet similar, reason for the increased delay is the fact that all wireless devices associated with a single wireless AP are in the same collision domain, introducing the possibility of collisions (retransmissions), which can increase delay.
Multiple paths of propagation	An electromagnetic waveform cannot pass through a perfect conductor. Admittedly, perfect conductors do not exist in most office environments. However, very good conductors, such as metal file cabinets, are commonplace in offices. As a result, if the waveform of a wireless transmission encounters one of these conductive objects, most of the signal bounces of the object creating multiple paths (*modes*) of propagation. These multiple modes of propagation can cause data (specifically, bits) to arrive at uneven intervals, possible corrupting data. This problem is similar to *multimode delay distortion*, which is seen in multimode fiber-optic cabling.

Table 13-5   Common Wireless Troubleshooting Issues

Issue	Description
Incorrect AP placement	Wireless APs should be strategically located in a building to provide sufficient coverage to all desired coverage areas. However, the coverage areas of wireless APs using overlapping channels should not overlap. To maintain coverage between coverage areas, you should have overlapping coverage areas among wireless APs using nonoverlapping channels (for example, channels 1, 6, and 11 for wireless networks using the 2.4-GHz band of frequencies). A common design recommendation is that overlapping coverage areas (using nonoverlapping channels) should have an overlap of approximately 10–15 percent.

Wireless Network Troubleshooting: Scenario

As a practice troubleshooting scenario for wireless networks, consider Figure 13-7. Based on the topology provided, can you spot a design issue with the wireless network?

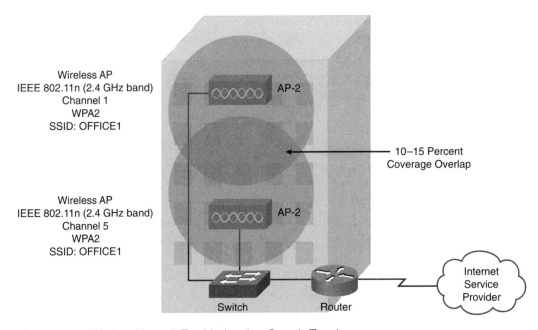

Figure 13-7   Wireless Network Troubleshooting: Sample Topology

Wireless Network Troubleshooting: Solution

The wireless network presented in Figure 13-7 has two wireless APs. Although these wireless APs have a matching wireless standard, encryption type, and SSID, the channels being used (channels 1 and 5) interfere with one another. Recall from Chapter 8 that channels in the 2.4-GHz band need at least five channels of separation (for overlapping coverage areas), while the channels used in this example only have four channels of separation. A fix for this issue is to assign AP-2 to channel 6, thus providing five channels of separation between AP-1 and AP-2.

Summary

The main topics covered in this chapter are the following:

- Troubleshooting concepts were discussed. Additionally, you were presented with a structured troubleshooting methodology.

- Common physical layer troubleshooting issues were identified, and you tested your troubleshooting skills with a Layer 1 troubleshooting exercise.

- Data link layer troubleshooting was discussed, along with a collection of common issues (for example, VLANs, port configuration, and Layer 2 loops). Again, you were challenged with another troubleshooting scenario.

- Without dealing with the unique details of individual routing protocols, this chapter overviewed network layer troubleshooting, along with a list of the common Layer 3 issues. Then, based on the subnetting skills you learned in Chapter 6, you determined the host in a given topology that had an incorrect IP address assignment.

- You reviewed common troubleshooting issues with wireless networks, including the need for wireless clients and wireless APs to have matching parameters, such as channel, encryption type, SSID, and wireless standard. Then, you examined a wireless network design and identified a design flaw.

Exam Preparation Tasks

Review All the Key Topics

Review the most important topics from inside the chapter, noted with the Key Topic icon in the outer margin of the page. Table 13-6 lists these key topics and the page numbers where each is found.

Table 13-6 Key Topics for Chapter 13

Key Topic Element	Description	Page Number
Table 13-1	Steps to diagnose a problem	439
Figure 13-2	Structured troubleshooting approach	440
Step list	Steps in the Network+ structured troubleshooting approach	441
Table 13-2	Common Layer 1 troubleshooting issues	443
Table 13-3	Common Layer 2 troubleshooting issues	446
Table 13-4	Common Layer 3 troubleshooting issues	450
Step list	Determining the subnet for a host	451
Table 13-5	Common wireless troubleshooting issues	453

Complete Tables and Lists from Memory

Print a copy of Appendix C, "Memory Tables" (found on the CD), or at least the section for this chapter, and complete the tables and lists from memory. Appendix D, "Memory Table Answer Key," also on the CD, includes the completed tables and lists so you can check your work.

Define Key Terms

Define the following key terms from this chapter, and check your answers in the Glossary:

trouble ticket, open, short, decibel loss, maximum transmission unit (MTU), black-hole router

Review Questions

The answers to these review questions are in Appendix A, "Answers to Review Questions."

1. Which of the following is most likely the first step in a structured trouble-shooting methodology?

   a. Hypothesize the probable cause.

   b. Create an action plan.

   c. Create a post-mortem report.

   d. Define the problem.

2. Which of the following comprise a simplified troubleshooting flow? (Choose three.)

   a. Problem resolution

   b. Problem monitoring

   c. Problem diagnosis

   d. Problem report

3. A broken copper strand in a circuit is known as which of the following?

   a. Short

   b. Impedance

   c. Open

   d. Split pair

4. What Ethernet switch feature allows a port to automatically determine which of its leads are used for transmitting data and which of its leads are used for receiving data?

   a. MDIX

   b. STP

   c. LAPD

   d. UTP

5. In the absence of STP, what issues might result from a Layer 2 loop in a network? (Choose two.)

   a. A router interface's MTU decrementing

   b. MAC address table corruption

   c. Broadcast storms

   d. Packet fragmentation

6. If you successfully ping from host A to host B, what can you conclude about host A?

   a. Its OSI Layers 1–4 are functional.

   b. Its OSI Layers 1–3 are functional.

   c. Its OSI Layers 1–7 are functional.

   d. You can only conclude that ICMP traffic can reach host B.

7. A router that drops a packet exceeding a router interface's MTU size, when that packet has its "do not fragment" bit set, is called which of the following?

   a. Route reflector

   b. Null hop

   c. Zero-point router

   d. Black-hole router

8. To what subnet does a host with an IP address of 172.16.155.10/18 belong?

   a. 172.16.0.0 /18

   b. 172.16.96.0 /18

   c. 172.16.128.0 /18

   d. 172.16.154.0 /18

9. Which of the following is a value measuring the power of a wireless signal?

   a. RSSI

   b. SSID

   c. RFI

   d. CSMA/CA

10. Which of the following are common sources of wireless network radio frequency interference (RFI)? (Choose three.)

   a. Game consoles

   b. 900 MHz cordless phones

   c. Microwave ovens

   d. Baby monitors

CHAPTER 14

Final Preparation

The first 13 chapters of this book cover the technologies, protocols, design concepts, and considerations required to be prepared to pass the CompTIA Network+ Exam (N10-005). Although these chapters supply all the information you need to pass the exam, most people need more preparation than simply reading the first 13 chapters of this book. This chapter details a set of tools and a study plan to help you complete your preparation for the exam.

This short chapter has two main sections. The first section lists the exam-preparation tools useful at this point in the study process. The second section lists a suggested study plan, now that you have completed all the earlier chapters in this book.

Tools for Final Preparation

This section lists some information about available study tools and how to access those tools.

Pearson Cert Practice Test Engine and Questions on the DVD

The DVD in the back of this book includes the Pearson IT Certification Practice Test engine, which is software that displays and grades a set of exam-realistic multiple-choice, drag-and-drop, fill-in-the-blank, and testlet questions. Using the Pearson IT Certification Practice Test engine, you can either study by going through the questions in study mode or take a simulated CompTIA Network+ exam that mimics real exam conditions.

Installation of the test engine is a two-step process. The DVD in the back of this book has a copy of the Pearson IT Certification Practice Test engine. However, the practice exam (that is, the database of CompTIA Network+ exam questions) is not on the DVD.

> **NOTE** The cardboard DVD case in the back of this book includes the DVD and a piece of paper. The paper lists the *activation code* for the practice exam associated with this book. Keep the activation code. Also, on the opposite side of the paper from the activation code is a unique, one-time-use coupon code for the purchase of the *CompTIA Network+ Cert Guide, Premium Edition eBook and Practice Test* product.

Install the Software from the DVD

The Pearson IT Certification Practice Test is a Windows-only desktop application. You can run it on a Mac using a Windows virtual machine, but it was built specifically for a Windows platform. The minimum system requirements are as follows:

- Windows XP (SP3), Windows Vista (SP2), or Windows 7
- Microsoft .NET Framework 4.0 Client
- Microsoft SQL Server Compact 4.0
- Pentium class 1 GHz processor (or equivalent)
- 512 MB RAM
- 650 MB disc space plus 50 MB for each downloaded practice exam

The software-installation process is similar to other wizard-based installation processes. If you have already installed the Pearson IT Certification Practice Test software from another Pearson product, there is no need for you to reinstall the software. Simply launch the software on your desktop and proceed to activate the practice exam from this book by using the activation code included in the DVD sleeve. The following steps outline the installation process:

1. Insert the DVD into your PC.

2. The software that automatically runs is the Pearson IT Certification software to access and use all DVD-based features, including the exam engine, video training, and any DVD-only appendices. From the main menu, click the option **Install the Exam Engine**.

3. Respond to the wizard-based prompts.

The installation process gives you the option to activate your exam with the activation code supplied on the paper in the DVD sleeve. This process requires that you establish a Pearson website login. You need this login to activate the exam, so please register when prompted. If you already have a Pearson website login, there is no need to register again. Just use your existing login.

Activate and Download the Practice Exam

After the exam engine is installed, you should then activate the exam associated with this book (if you did not do so during the installation process), as follows:

1. Start the *Pearson IT Certification Practice Test* (PCPT) software from the Windows *Start* menu or from your desktop shortcut icon.

2. To activate and download the exam associated with this book, from the *My Products* or *Tools* tab, select the **Activate** button.

3. At the next screen, enter the *activation key* from the paper inside the cardboard DVD sleeve in the back of the book. Once entered, click the **Activate** button.

4. The activation process will download the practice exam. Click **Next**, and then click **Finish**.

After the activation process is complete, the *My Products* tab should list your new exam. If you do not see the exam, make sure that you selected the *My Products* tab on the menu. At this point, the software and practice exam are ready to use. Simply select the exam, and click the **Open Exam** button.

To update an exam that you have already activated and downloaded, simply select the *Tools* tab and select the **Update Products** button. Updating your exams ensures that you have the latest changes and updates to the exam data.

If you want to check for updates to the Pearson Cert Practice Test exam engine software, simply select the *Tools* tab and select the **Update Application** button. This ensures that you are running the latest version of the exam engine.

Activating Other Exams

The exam-software installation process, and the registration process, only occurs once. Then, for each new exam, only a few steps are required. For example, if you buy another new Pearson IT Certification Cert Guide, extract the activation code from the DVD sleeve in the back of that book (you don't even need the DVD at this point). From there, all you have to do is start the exam engine (if not still up and running), and perform Steps 2 through 4 from the previous list.

Premium Edition

In addition to the free practice exam provided on the enclosed DVD, you can purchase additional exams with expanded functionality directly from Pearson IT Certification. The Premium Edition eBook and Practice Test for this title contains an additional two full practice exams and an eBook (in both PDF and ePub format).

Also, the Premium Edition title has remediation for each question to the specific part of the eBook that relates to that question.

Because you purchased the print version of this title, you can purchase the Premium Edition at a deep discount. There is a coupon code in the DVD sleeve that contains a one-time-use code and instructions for where you can purchase the Premium Edition.

To view the Premium Edition product page, go to the following website: `http:// www.pearsonitcertification.com/title/0132879077`.

Video Training on DVD

The DVD enclosed in this book contains ten training videos that address a couple of the most misunderstood concepts in the CompTIA Network+ curriculum, specifically the OSI Model and IP addressing. The videos, which you can access from main menu of the DVD, include the following:

- **Video #1:** Introduction to the OSI Model
- **Video #2:** Layer 1—The Physical Layer
- **Video #3:** Layer 2—The Data Link Layer
- **Video #4:** Layer 3—The Network Layer
- **Video #5:** Layer 4—The Transport Layer
- **Video #6:** Layers 5–7—The Upper Layers
- **Video #7:** IP Addressing—Part 1 (Binary Numbering Review)
- **Video #8:** IP Addressing—Part 2 (Basic Subnetting)
- **Video #9:** IP Addressing—Part 3 (Advanced Subnetting)
- **Video #10:** IP Addressing—Part 4 (Introduction to IPv6)

These training videos are presented by the author.

Memory Tables

Like most Cert Guides from Pearson IT Certification, this book purposefully organizes information into tables and lists for easier study and review. Re-reading these tables can be very useful before the exam. However, it is easy to skim over the tables without paying attention to every detail, especially when you remember having seen the table's contents when reading the chapter.

Instead of simply reading the tables in the various chapters, this book's Appendices C and D give you another review tool. Appendix C lists partially completed versions of many of the tables in this book. You can open Appendix C, which is a PDF on the accompanying DVD, and print the appendix. For review, you can attempt to complete the tables.

Appendix D, which is also a PDF on the DVD, lists the completed tables so you can check your answers. You can also just refer to the tables as printed in the book.

End-of-Chapter Review Tools

Chapters 1–13 each have several features in the "Exam Preparation Tasks" and "Review Questions" sections at the end of the chapter. You might have already worked through these in each chapter. However, it can help to use these tools again as you make your final preparations for the exam.

Suggested Plan for Final Review and Study

This section lists a suggested study plan from the point at which you finish reading this book through Chapter 13, until you take the CompTIA Network+ Exam. Certainly, you can ignore this plan, use it as is, or modify it to better meet your needs.

The plan uses five steps:

1. **Review key topics**: You can use the table at the end of each chapter that lists the key topics in each chapter, or just flip the pages looking for key topics.

2. **Complete memory tables**: Open Appendix C on the DVD and print the entire appendix. Then, complete the tables.

3. **Study "Review Questions" sections**: Go through the "Review Questions" section at the end of each chapter to identify areas in which you need more study.

4. **Subnetting practice**: Make sure that you can perform subnetting calculations quickly and correctly. You might want to review the subnetting examples and practice exercises in Chapter 5, "Working with IP Addresses." Additionally, you might want to watch videos 7, 8, and 9 on the enclosed DVD, which review binary numbering, basic subnetting, and advanced subnetting.

5. **Use the Pearson Cert Practice Test engine to practice**: The Pearson IT Certification Practice Test engine on the enclosed DVD can be used to study using a bank of unique exam-realistic questions available only with this book.

Earlier in this chapter, you read about the installation of the Pearson Cert Practice Test engine on the DVD. The database of questions used by the engine was created specifically for this book. The Pearson IT Certification Practice Test engine can be used either in *study mode* or *practice exam mode*, as follows:

- **Study mode:** Study mode is most useful when you want to use the questions for learning and practicing. In study mode, you can select options like randomizing the order of the questions and answers, automatically viewing answers to the questions as you go, testing on specific topics, and many other options.

- **Practice exam mode:** Practice exam mode presents questions in a timed environment, providing you with an exam-realistic experience. It also restricts your ability to see your score as you progress through the exam and view answers to questions as you are taking the exam. These timed exams not only allow you to study for the actual CompTIA Network+ exam, but they help you simulate the time pressure that can occur during an actual exam.

When doing your final preparation, you can use study mode, practice exam mode, or both. However, after you have seen each question a few times, you tend to remember the questions, and the usefulness of the exam database might go down. So, consider the following options when using the exam engine:

- Use the question database for review. Use study mode to study the questions by chapter, just as with the other final review steps listed in this chapter. Plan on getting another exam (possibly from the Premium Edition) if you want to take additional simulated exams.

- Save the question database, not using it for review during your review of each part of this book. Save it until the end, so you will not have seen the questions before. Then, use practice exam mode to simulate the exam.

Picking the correct mode from the exam engine's user interface is straightforward. The following steps show you how to move to the screen from which you can select study or practice exam mode:

1. Click the *My Products* tab if you are not already in that screen.

2. Select the exam you want to use from the list of available exams.

3. Click the **Use** button.

By taking these actions, the engine should display a window from which you can choose study mode or practice exam mode. When in study mode, you can further choose the book chapters, limiting the questions to those explained in the specified chapters of this book.

Summary

The tools and suggestions listed in this chapter are designed with one goal in mind: to help you develop the skills required to pass the CompTIA Network+ exam. This book has been developed from the beginning to not just present you with a collection of facts, but to help you learn how to apply those facts. Regardless of your experience level prior to reading this book, it is my hope that the broad range of preparation tools, and even the structure of the book, will help you pass the exam with ease. I wish you success in your exam and hope that our paths will cross again as you continue to grow in your networking career.

Answers to Review Questions

Chapter 1

1. C
2. C
3. D
4. C
5. C
6. A
7. B
8. A, C
9. C
10. B

Chapter 2

1. D
2. B
3. C
4. A
5. C
6. B, C, F, G
7. B
8. B
9. C
10. B, C, D

Chapter 3

1. C
2. B, C
3. B
4. B
5. D
6. A, C
7. D
8. D
9. C
10. A

Chapter 4

1. C
2. D
3. B
4. A, B
5. A
6. B
7. B
8. B
9. C
10. B

Chapter 5

1. B
2. D
3. A
4. A, B
5. A, D
6. A
7. C
8. C
9. A
10. C

Chapter 6

1. B
2. D
3. D
4. C
5. B, C
6. C
7. A
8. B
9. B
10. A

Chapter 7

1. B
2. C
3. B, C, D
4. C

5. C
6. B
7. D
8. B
9. B
10. D

Chapter 8

1. D
2. B, D, F
3. B
4. C
5. A
6. B
7. B
8. C
9. A
10. D

Chapter 9

1. B
2. C
3. A
4. A, B, D
5. D
6. B
7. C
8. C
9. B
10. A

Chapter 10

1. B
2. D
3. B, C
4. B
5. C
6. D
7. A, C, D
8. B
9. B
10. A

Chapter 11

1. C
2. B
3. D
4. A
5. B
6. D
7. B
8. D
9. A, C, D
10. A

Chapter 12

1. C
2. D
3. A
4. D
5. B, D
6. B
7. C
8. B, D
9. A
10. A, C, D

Chapter 13

1. D
2. A, C, D
3. C
4. A
5. B, C
6. B
7. D
8. C
9. A
10. A, C, D

Over time, reader feedback allows Pearson to gauge which topics give our readers the most problems when taking the exams. To assist readers with those topics, authors may create new materials clarifying and expanding upon those troublesome exam topics. As mentioned in the Introduction, this additional content about the exam is posted as a PDF document on this book's companion website at www.pearsonitcertification.com/title/9780789748218.

This appendix provides you with updated information if CompTIA makes minor modifications to the exam upon which this book is based. When CompTIA releases an entirely new exam, the changes are usually too extensive to provide in a simple updated appendix. In those cases, you need to consult the new edition of the book for the updated content.

This appendix fills the void that occurs with any print book. In particular, this appendix does the following:

- Mentions technical items that might not have been mentioned elsewhere in the book.

- Covers new topics if CompTIA adds new content to the exam over time.

- Provides a way to get up-to-the-minute current information about content for the exam.

CompTIA Network+ N10-005 Exam Updates, Version 1.0

Always Get the Latest at the Companion Website

You are reading the version of this appendix that was available when your book was printed. However, given that the main purpose of this appendix is to be a living, changing document, it is important that you look for the latest version online at this book's companion website. To do so:

1. Browse to www.pearsonitcertification.com/title/ 9780789748218.

2. Select the Updates option under the More Information box.

3. Download the latest Appendix B document.

> **NOTE** The downloaded document has a version number. Comparing the version of this print Appendix B (version 1.0) with the latest online version of this appendix, you should do the following:
>
> - **Same version:** Ignore the PDF that you downloaded from the companion website.
>
> - **Website has a later version:** Ignore this Appendix B in your book and only read the latest version that you downloaded from the companion website.

If no appendix is posted on this book's website, that simply means there are no updates to post and version 1.0 is still the latest version.

Technical Content

The current version of this appendix does not contain any additional technical coverage.

Glossary

110 block   Because 66 blocks are subject to too much crosstalk for higher speed LAN connections, 110 blocks can be used to terminate a cable (such as a Cat 5 cable) being used for those higher-speed LANs.

66 block   Traditionally used in corporate environments for cross-connecting phone-system cabling. As 10-Mbps LANs started to grow in popularity in the late 1980s and early 1990s, these termination blocks were used to cross-connect Cat 3 UTP cabling. The electrical characteristics (specifically, crosstalk) of a 66 block, however, do not support higher-speed LAN technologies, such as 100-Mbps Ethernet networks.

802.11a   Ratified in 1999, this standard supports speeds as high as 54 Mbps. Other supported data rates (which can be used if conditions are not suitable for the 54 Mbps rate) include 6, 9, 12, 18, 24, 36, and 48 Mbps. The 802.11a standard uses the 5-GHz band and the OFDM transmission method.

802.11b   Ratified in 1999, this standard supports speeds as high as 11 Mbps. However, 5.5 Mbps is another supported data rate. The 802.11b standard uses the 2.4-GHz band and the DSSS transmission method.

802.11g   Ratified in 2003, this standard supports speeds as high as 54 Mbps. Like 802.11a, other supported data rates include 6, 9, 12, 18, 24, 36, and 48 Mbps. However, like 802.11b, 802.11g operates in the 2.4-GHz band, which allows it to offer backwards compatibility to 802.11b devices. 802.11g can use either the OFDM or DSSS transmission method.

802.11n   Ratified in 2009, this standard supports a variety of speeds, depending on its implementation. Although the speed of an 802.11n network could approach 300 Mbps (through the use of channel bonding), many 802.11n devices on the market have speed ratings in the 130–150 Mbps range. Interestingly, an 802.11n WLAN can operate in the 2.4-GHz band, the 5-GHz band, or both simultaneously. 802.11n uses the OFDM transmission method.

acceptable use policy (AUP)   Identifies what users of a network are and are not allowed to do on that network. For example, retrieving sports scores during working hours via an organization's Internet connection might be deemed inappropriate by an AUP.

access control list (ACL)   Rules typically applied to router interfaces, which specify permitted and denied traffic.

Address Resolution Protocol (ARP)   An ARP request is a broadcast asking for the MAC address corresponding to a known IP address. An ARP reply contains the requested MAC address.

administrative distance (AD)   A routing protocol's index of believability. Routing protocols with a smaller AD are considered more believable that routing protocols with a higher AD.

Advanced Encryption Standard (AES)   Released in 2001, AES is typically considered the preferred symmetric encryption algorithm. AES is available in 128-bit key, 192-bit key, and 256-bit key versions.

anycast   An anycast communication flow is a one-to-nearest (from the perspective of a router's routing table) flow.

application layer (OSI model)   Layer 7 of the OSI model, it provides application services to a network. An important, and an often-misunderstood concept, is that end-user applications do not reside at the application layer. Instead, the application layer supports services used by end-user applications. Another function of the application layer is advertising available services.

application layer (TCP/IP stack)   Addresses concepts described by Layers 5, 6, and 7 (that is, the session, presentation, and application layers) of the OSI model.

arp command   Can be used in either the Microsoft Windows® or UNIX environment to see what a Layer 2 MAC address corresponds to a Layer 3 IP address.

asset management   As related to networks, this is a formalized system of tracking network components and managing the lifecycle of those components.

asymmetric encryption   With asymmetric encryption, the sender and receiver of a packet use different keys.

Asynchronous Transfer Mode (ATM)   A Layer 2 WAN technology that interconnects sites using virtual circuits. These virtual circuits are identified by a pair of numbers, called the VPI/VCI pair. A virtual path identifier (VPI) identifies a logical path, which can contain multiple virtual circuits. A virtual circuit identifier (VCI) identifies the unique logical circuit within a virtual path.

Authentication Header (AH)   An IPsec protocol that provides authentication and integrity services. However, it does not provide encryption services.

authentication server   In a network using 802.1X user authentication, an authentication server (typically, a RADIUS server) checks a supplicant's credentials. If the credentials are acceptable, the authentication server notifies the authenticator that the supplicant is allowed to communicate on a network. The authentication server also gives the authenticator a key that can be used to securely transmit data during the authenticator's session with the supplicant.

authenticator   In a network using 802.1X user authentication, an authenticator forwards a supplicant's authentication request on to an authentication server. After the authentication server authenticates the supplicant, the authenticator receives a key that is used to communicate securely during a session with the supplicant.

Automatic Private IP Addressing (APIPA)   Allows a networked device to self-assign an IP address from the 169.254.0.0/16 network. Note that this address is only usable on the device's local subnet (meaning that the IP address is not routable).

availability   The measure of a network's uptime.

baseline   A collection of data portraying the characteristics of a network under normal operating conditions. Data collected while troubleshooting can then be contrasted against baseline data.

Basic Rate Interface (BRI)   A BRI circuit contains two 64-kbps B channels and one 16-kbps D channel. Although such a circuit can carry two simultaneous voice conversations, the two B channels can be logically bonded together into a single virtual circuit (by using PPP's multilink interface feature) to offer a 128-kbps data path.

basic service set (BSS)   WLANs that have just one AP are called BSS WLANs. BSS WLANs are said to run in infrastructure mode, because wireless clients connect to an AP, which is typically connected to a wired network infrastructure. A BSS network is often used in residential and SOHO locations, where the signal strength provided by a single AP is sufficient to service all of the WLAN's wireless clients.

bit-error rate tester (BERT)   When troubleshooting a link where you suspect a high bit-error rate (BER), you can use a piece of test equipment called a bit-error rate tester (BERT), which contains both a pattern generator (which can generate a variety of bit patterns) and an error detector (which is synchronized with the pattern generator and can determine the number of bit errors) and can calculate a BER for the tested transmission link.

black-hole router   A router that drops packets that cannot be fragmented and are exceeding the MTU size of an interface without notifying the sender.

block size   The number of IP addresses in a subnet, including the subnet's address and the subnet's directed broadcast address.

Bootstrap Protocol (BOOTP)   A legacy broadcast-based protocol used by networked devices to obtain IP address information.

Border Gateway Protocol (BGP)   The only EGP in widespread use today. In fact, BGP is considered to be the routing protocol that runs the Internet, which is an interconnection of multiple autonomous systems. BGP is a path-vector routing protocol, meaning that it can use as its metric the number of autonomous system hops that must be transited to reach a destination network, as opposed to the number of required router hops.

borrowed bits   Bits added to a classful subnet mask.

buffer overflow   This attack occurs when an attacker leverages a vulnerability in an application, causing data to be written to a memory area (that is, a buffer) that's being used by a different application.

bus topology   Typically, it uses a cable running through the area requiring connectivity, and devices to be networked can tap into that cable.

butt set   A piece of test equipment typically used by telephone technicians. The clips on a butt set can connect to the tip and ring wires on a punch-down block (for example, a 66 block or a 110 block) connecting to a telephone. This allows the technician to check the line (for example, to determine if dial tone is present on the line and determine if a call can be placed from the line).

cable certifier   If you are working with existing cable and want to determine its category, or if you simply want to test the supported frequency range (and therefore data throughput) of the cable, you can use a cable certifier.

cable modem   Attaches to the same coaxial cable (typically in a residence) that provides television programming. A cable modem can use predetermined frequency ranges to transmit and receive data over that coaxial cable.

cable tester   A cable tester can test the conductors in an Ethernet cable. It contains two parts. By connecting these parts of the cable tester to each end of a cable under test, you can check the wires in the cable for continuity (that is, check to make sure there are no opens, or breaks, in a conductor). Additionally, you can verify an RJ-45 connector's pinouts (which are wires connected to the appropriate pins on an RJ-45 connector).

campus-area network (CAN)   An interconnection of networks located in nearby buildings (for example, buildings on a college campus).

carrier sense multiple access collision avoidance (CSMA/CA)   Just as CSMA/CD is needed for half-duplex Ethernet connections, CSMA/CA is needed for WLAN connections, because of their half-duplex operation. Similar to how an Ethernet device listens to an Ethernet segment to determine if a frame exists on the segment, a WLAN device listens for a transmission on a wireless channel to determine if it is safe to transmit. Additionally, the collision-avoidance part of the CSMA/CA algorithm causes wireless devices to wait for a random backoff time before transmitting.

carrier sense multiple access collision detect (CSMA/CD)   Used on an Ethernet network to help prevent a collision from occurring and to recover if a collision does occur. CSMA/CD is only needed on half-duplex connections.

central office (CO)   A building containing a telephone company's telephone-switching equipment is referred to as a central office (CO). COs are categorized into five hierarchical classes. A Class 1 CO is a long-distance office serving a regional area. A Class 2 CO is a second-level long-distance office (that is, it is subordinate to a Class 1 office). A Class 3 CO is a third-level long-distance office. A Class 4 CO is a fourth-level long-distance office, which provides telephone subscribers access to a live operator. A Class 5 CO is at the bottom of the five-layer hierarchy and physically connects to customer devices in a local area.

Challenge-Handshake Authentication Protocol (CHAP)   Like PAP, CHAP performs one-way authentication. However, authentication is performed through a three-way handshake (challenge, response, and acceptance messages) between a server and a client. The three-way handshake allows a client to be authenticated without sending credential information across a network.

Challenge-Response Authentication Mechanism Message Digest 5 (CRAM-MD5)   A common variant of HMAC frequently used in e-mail systems. Like CHAP, CRAM-MD5 only performs one-way authentication (the server authenticates the client).

channel bonding   With channel bonding, two wireless bands can be logically bonded together, forming a band with twice the bandwidth of an individual band. Some literature refers to channel bonding as *40 MHz mode*, which refers to the bonding of two adjacent 20-MHz bands into a 40-MHz band.

channel service unit/data service unit (CSU/DSU)   Acts as a digital modem, which terminates a digital circuit (for example, a T1 or an E1 circuit).

circuit-switched connection   A connection that is brought up on an as-needed basis. A circuit-switched connection is analogous to phone call, where you pick up a phone, dial a number, and a connection is established based on the number you dial.

classful mask   A classful mask is the default subnet mask applied to Class A, B, and C IPv4 networks. Specifically, Class A networks have a classful mask of 255.0.0.0. Class B networks have a classful mask of 255.255.0.0, and Class C networks have a classful mask of 255.255.255.0.

classification   Classification is the process of placing traffic into different categories.

classless interdomain routing (CIDR)   Shortens a classful subnet mask by removing right-justified 1s from a classful mask. As a result, CIDR allows contiguous classful networks to be aggregated. This process is sometimes called route aggregation.

client   Defines the device an end-user uses to access a network. This device might be a workstation, laptop, smartphone with wireless capabilities, a tablet, or a variety of other end-user terminal devices.

client-server network   In a client-server network, a dedicated server (for example, a file server or a print server) provides shared access to a resource (for example, files or a printer). Clients (for example, PCs) on the network with appropriate privilege levels can gain access to those shared resources.

client-to-site VPN   Also known as a remote access VPN, a client-to-site VPN interconnects a remote user with a site, as an alternative to dial-up or ISDN connectivity, at a reduced cost.

coaxial cable   Also known as coax, a coaxial cable is composed of two conductors. One of the conductors is an inner insulated conductor. This inner conductor is surrounded by another conductor. This second conductor is sometimes made of a metallic foil or woven wire.

collision   A collision occurs when two devices on an Ethernet network simultaneously transmit a frame. Because an Ethernet segment cannot handle more than one frame at a time, both frames become corrupted.

committed information rate (CIR)   The CIR of an interface is the average traffic rate over the period of a second.

Common Address Redundancy Protocol (CARP)   An open-standard variant of HSRP, which provides first-hop router redundancy.

congestion avoidance   If an interface's output queue fills to capacity, newly arriving packet are discarded (or *tail dropped*). Congestion avoidance can prevent this behavior. RED is an example of a congestion-avoidance mechanism.

congestion management   When a device, such as a switch or router, receives traffic faster than it can be transmitted, the device attempts to buffer (or store) the extra traffic until bandwidth becomes available. This buffering process is called *queuing* or congestion management.

content engine   A dedicated appliance whose role is to locally cache content received from a remote network (for example, a destination on the Internet). Subsequent requests for that content can be serviced locally, from the content engine, thus reducing bandwidth demand on a WAN.

content switch   Can be used to load balance requests for content across a group of servers containing that content. If one of the servers in the group needed to have maintenance performed, that server could be administratively removed from the group, as defined on the content switch. As a result, the content switch can help maximize up time when performing server maintenance. It minimizes the load on individual servers by distributing its load across multiple identical servers. A content switch also allows a network to scale, because one or more additional servers could be added to the server group defined on the content switch, if the load on existing servers increases.

crimper   Used to attach a connector (for example, an RJ-45 connector) to the end of an unshielded twisted-pair (UTP) cable.

current state modulation   One way to electrically or optically represent a binary 1 or 0 is to use current state modulation, which represents a binary 1 with the presence of voltage (on a copper cable) or the presence of light (on a fiber-optic cable). Similarly, the absence of light or voltage represents a binary 0.

customer premise equipment (CPE)   This device resides at a customer site. A router, as an example, can be a CPE that connects a customer with an MPLS service provider.

cyclic redundancy check (CRC)   A mathematical algorithm that is executed on a data string by both the sender and receiver of the data string. If the calculated CRC values match, the receiver can conclude that the data string was not corrupted during transmission.

data link layer   As Layer 2 of the OSI model, this layer is concerned with the packaging of data into frames and transmitting those frames on a network, performing error detection/correction, uniquely identifying network devices with an address, and handling flow control.

decibel (dB)   A ratio of radiated power to a reference value. In the case of dBi, the reference value is the signal strength (that is, the power) radiated from an isotropic antenna, which represents a theoretical antenna that radiates an equal amount of power in all directions (in a spherical pattern). An isotropic antenna is considered to have gain of 0 dBi.

decibel (dB) loss   A loss of signal power. If a transmission's dB loss is too great, the transmission cannot be properly interpreted by the intended recipient.

dedicated leased line   A logical connection interconnecting two sites. This logical connection might physically connect through a service provider's facility or a telephone company's central office. The expense of a dedicated leased line is typically higher than other WAN technologies offering similar data rates, because with a dedicated leased line, a customer does not have to share bandwidth with other customers.

default gateway   The IP address of a router (or multilayer switch) to which a networked device sends traffic destined for a subnet other than the device's local subnet.

default static route   A default static route is an administratively configured entry in a router's routing table that specifies where traffic for all unknown networks should be sent.

demarc   Also known as *demarcation point* or a *demarc extension*, this is the point in a telephone network where the maintenance responsibility passes from a telephone company to a subscriber (unless the subscriber purchased an inside wiring plan). This demarc is typically a box mounted to the outside of a customer's building (for example, a residence).

demilitarized zone (DMZ)   Often contains servers that should be accessible from the Internet. This approach would, for example, allow users on the Internet to initiate an e-mail or a web session coming into an organization's e-mail or web server. However, other protocols would be blocked.

denial of service (DoS)   A DoS attack floods a system with an excessive amount of traffic or requests, which consumes the system's processing resources and prevents the system from responding to many legitimate requests.

designated port   In a STP topology, every network segment has a single designated port, which is the port on that segment that is closest to the root bridge, in terms of cost. Therefore, all ports on a root bridge are designated ports.

Differentiated Services (DiffServ)   As its name suggests, DiffServ differentiates between multiple traffic flows. Specifically, packets are marked, and routers and switches can then make decisions (for example, dropping or forwarding decisions) based on those markings.

dig command   Can resolve a FQDN to an IP address on UNIX hosts.

digital subscriber line (DSL)   A group of technologies that provide high-speed data transmission over existing telephone wiring. DSL has several variants, which vary in data rates and distance limitations. Three of the more popular DSL variants include asymmetric DSL (ADSL), symmetric DSL (DSL), and very high bit-rate DSL (VDSL).

direct sequence spread spectrum (DSSS)   Modulates data over an entire range of frequencies using a series symbols called *chips*. A chip is shorter in duration than a bit, meaning that chips are transmitted at a higher rate than the actual data. These chips not only represent encoded data to be transmitted, but also what appears to be random data. Because both parties involved in a DSSS communication know which chips represent actual data and which chips do not, if a third-party intercepted a DSSS transmission, it would be difficult for that party to eavesdrop on the data, because he would not easily know which chips represented valid bits. DSSS is more subject to environmental factors, as opposed to FHSS and OFDN, because it uses of an entire frequency spectrum.

distance vector   A category of routing protocol that sends a full copy of its routing table to its directly attached neighbors.

distributed denial of service (DDoS)   These attacks can increase the amount of traffic flooded to a target system. Specifically, an attacker compromises multiple systems, and those compromised systems, called *zombies*, can be instructed by the attacker to simultaneously launch a DDoS attack against a target system.

Domain Name System (DNS) server   Performs the task of taking a domain name (for example, www.ciscopress.com) and resolving that name into a corresponding IP address (for example, 10.1.2.3).

dotted-decimal notation   A method of writing an IPv4 address or subnet mask, where groups of 8 bits (called octets) are separated by periods.

Dynamic Host Configuration Protocol (DHCP)   Dynamically assigns IP address information (for example, IP address, subnet mask, DNS server's IP address, and default gateway's IP address) to network devices.

dynamic NAT (DNAT)   A variant of NAT in which inside local addresses are automatically assigned an inside global address from a pool of available addresses.

E1   An E1 circuit contains 32 channels, in contrast to the 24 channels on a T1 circuit. Only 30 of those 32 channels, however, can transmit data (or voice or video). Specifically, the first of those 32 channels is reserved for framing and synchronization, and the 17th channel is reserved for signaling (that is, to set up, maintain, and tear down a session).

E3   A digital circuit in the same E-carrier family of standards as an E1. An E3 circuit's available bandwidth is 34.4 Mbps.

edge label switch router (ELSR)   Resides at the edge of an MPLS service provider's cloud and interconnects a service provider to one or more customers.

electromagnetic interference (EMI)   An electromagnetic waveform that can be received by network cable (possibly corrupting data traveling on the cable) or radiated from a network cable (possibly interfering with data traveling on another cable).

electrostatic discharge (ESD) wrist strap   To prevent static electricity in your body from damaging electrical components on a circuit board, you can wear an ESD wrist strap. The strap is equipped with a clip that you can attach to something with a ground potential (for example, a large metal desk). While wearing the wrist strap, if you have any static buildup in your body, the static flows to the object with a ground potential to which your strap is clipped, thus avoiding damage to any electrical components that you might touch.

Encapsulating Security Payload (ESP)   An IPsec protocol that provides authentication, integrity, and encryption services.

Enhanced Interior Gateway Routing Protocol (EIGRP)   A Cisco-proprietary protocol. So, although EIGRP is popular in Cisco-only networks, it is less popular in mixed vendor networks. Like OSPF, EIGRP is an IGP with very fast convergence and is very scalable. EIGRP is considered to be an advanced distance vector or a hybrid routing protocol.

Ethernet   Ethernet is a Layer 1 technology developed by Xerox and encompasses a variety of standards, which specify various media types, speeds, and distance limitations.

extended service set (ESS)   WLANs containing more than one AP are called ESS WLANs. Like BSS WLANs, ESS WLANs operate in infrastructure mode. When you have more than one AP, take care to prevent one AP from interfering with another. Specifically, nonoverlapping channels (that is, channels 1, 6, and 11 for the 2.4-GHz band) should be selected for adjacent wireless coverage areas.

Exterior Gateway Protocol (EGP)   A routing protocol that operates between autonomous systems, which are networks under different administrative control. Border Gateway Protocol (BGP) is the only EGP in widespread use today.

firewall   Primarily a network security appliance, a firewall can protect a trusted network (for example, a corporate LAN) from an untrusted network (for example, the Internet) by allowing the trusted network to send traffic into the untrusted network and receive the return traffic from the untrusted network, while blocking traffic for sessions that were initiated on the untrusted network.

fox and hound   See *toner probe*.

Frame Relay   A Layer 2 WAN technology that interconnects sites using virtual circuits. These virtual circuits are identified by locally significant *data-link connection identifiers* (DLCI).

frequency-hopping spread spectrum (FHSS)   Allows the participants in a communication to hop between predetermined frequencies. Security is enhanced, because the participants can predict the next frequency to be used while a third party cannot easily predict the next frequency. FHSS can also provision extra bandwidth by simultaneously using more than one frequency.

FTP bounce   An FTP bounce attack uses the FTP **PORT** command to covertly open a connection with a remote system. Specifically, an attacker connects to an FTP server and uses the **PORT** command to cause the FTP server to open a communications channel with the intended victim, which might allow a connection from the FTP server, while a connection directly from the attacker might be denied.

full duplex   This connection allows a device to simultaneously transmit and receive data.

full-mesh topology   Directly connects every site to every other site.

GNU privacy guard (GPC)   A free variant of pretty good privacy (PGP), which is an asymmetric encryption algorithm.

half duplex   A half-duplex connection allows a device to either receive or transmit data at any one time. However, a half-duplex device cannot simultaneously transmit and receive.

hardware firewall   A network appliance dedicated to the purpose of acting as a firewall. This appliance can have multiple interfaces for connecting to areas of a network requiring varying levels of security.

hold-down timers   Can speed the convergence process of a routing protocol. After a router makes a change to a route entry, the hold-down timer prevents any subsequent updates for a specified period of time. This approach can help stop *flapping routes* (which are routes that oscillate between being available and unavailable) from preventing convergence.

honey net   A network containing more than one honey pot.

honey pot   Acts as a distracter. Specifically, a system designated as a honey pot appears to be an attractive attack target. One school of thought on the use of a honey pot is to place one or more honey-pot systems in a network to entice attackers into thinking the system is real. The attackers then use their resources attacking the honey pot, resulting in their leaving the real servers alone.

host-based IPS (HIPS)   A HIPS system is a computer running intrusion prevention software for the purpose of protecting the computer from attacks.

host command   Can resolve a FQDN to an IP address on hosts.

hub   An Ethernet hub is an older technology used to interconnect network components, such as clients and servers. Hubs vary in their number of available ports. A hub does not perform any inspection of the traffic it passes. Rather, a hub simply receives traffic in a port and repeats that traffic out all of its other ports.

hub-and-spoke topology   When interconnecting multiple sites (for example, multiple corporate locations) via WAN links, a hub-and-spoke topology has a WAN link from each remote site (a spoke site) to the main site (the hub site).

independent basic service set (IBSS)   A WLAN can be created without the use of an AP. Such a configuration, called an IBSS, is said to work in an ad-hoc fashion. An ad-hoc WLAN is useful for temporary connections between wireless devices. For example, you might temporarily interconnect two laptop computers to transfer a few files.

Integrated Services (IntServ)   Often referred to as hard QoS, because IntServ can make strict bandwidth reservations. IntServ uses signaling among network devices to provide bandwidth reservations. Resource Reservation Protocol (RSVP) is an example of an IntServ approach to QoS. Because IntServ must be configured on every router along a packet's path, a primary drawback of IntServ is its lack of scalability.

Integrated Services Digital Network (ISDN)   A digital telephony technology that supports multiple 64-kbps channels (known as *bearer channels* or *B channels*) on a single connection. ISDN was popular back in the 1980s for connecting PBXs, which are telephone switches owned and operated by a company, to a telephone company's central office. ISDN has the ability to carry voice, video, or data over its B channels. ISDN also offers a robust set of signaling protocols: Q.921 for Layer 2 signaling and Q.931 for Layer 3 signaling. These signaling protocols run on a separate channel in an ISDN circuit (known as the *delta channel*, *data channel*, or *D channel*).

Interior Gateway Protocol (IGP)   An routing protocol that operates within an autonomous system, which is a network under a single administrative control. OSPF and EIGRP are popular examples of IGPs.

Intermediate System-to-Intermediate System (IS-IS)   A link-state routing protocol similar in its operation to OSPF. IS-IS uses a configurable, yet dimensionless, metric associated with an interface and runs Dijkstra's Shortest Path First algorithm. While using IS-IS as an IGP offers the scalability, fast convergence, and vendor-interoperability benefits of OSPF, it has not been deployed as widely as OSPF.

Internet Group Management Protocol (IGMP)   A multicast protocol used between clients and routers to let routers know which of their interfaces has a multicast receiver attached.

Internet Key Exchange (IKE)   A protocol used to set up an IPsec session.

Internet layer   This layer of the TCP/IP stack maps to Layer 3 (network layer) of the OSI model. Although multiple routed protocols (for example, IP, IPX, and AppleTalk) reside at the OSI model's network layer, the Internet layer of the TCP/IP stack focuses on IP as the protocol to be routed through a network.

Internet Security Association and Key Management Protocol (ISAKMP) Negotiates parameters for an IPsec session.

Intrusion Detection System (IDS)   IDS devices can recognize the signature of a well-known attack and respond to stop the attack. However, an IDS sensor does not reside in-line with the traffic flow. Therefore, one or more malicious packets might reach an intended victim before the traffic flow is stopped by an IDS sensor.

Intrusion Prevention System (IPS)   IPS devices can recognize the signature of a well-known attack and respond to stop the attack. An IPS device resides in-line with the traffic flow, unlike an IDS sensor.

IP security (IPsec)   A type of VPN that provides confidentiality, integrity, and authentication.

ipconfig command   A Microsoft Windows® command that can be used to display IP address configuration parameters on a PC. Additionally, if DHCP is used by the PC, the **ipconfig** command can be used to release and renew a DHCP lease, which is often useful during troubleshooting.

jitter   The uneven arrival of packets.

Kerberos   A client-server authentication protocol that supports mutual authentication between a client and a server. Kerberos uses the concept of a trusted third party (a *key distribution center*) that hands out tickets to be used instead of a username and password combination.

label switch router (LSR)   Resides inside a service provider's MPLS cloud and makes frame forwarding decisions based on labels applied to frames.

latency   The measure of delay in a network.

Layer 2 Forwarding (L2F)   A VPN protocol designed (by Cisco Systems®) with the intent of providing a tunneling protocol for PPP. Like L2TP, L2F lacks native security features.

Layer 2 Tunneling Protocol (L2TP)   A VPN protocol that lacks security features, such as encryption. However, L2TP can still be used for a secure VPN connection if it is combined with another protocol that provides encryption.

link aggregation   As defined by the IEEE 802.3ad standard, link aggregation allows multiple physical connections to be logically bundled into a single logical connection.

link efficiency   To make the most of the limited bandwidth available on slower speed links, you might choose to implement *compression* or link fragmentation and interleaving (LFI). These QoS mechanisms are examples of link efficiency mechanisms.

link-local IP address   A link-local IP address is a non-routable IP address usable only on a local subnet.

link state   A category of routing protocol that maintains a topology of a network and uses an algorithm to determine the shortest path to a destination network.

link-state advertisement (LSA)   Sent by routers in a network to advertise the networks the routers know how to reach. Routers use those LSAs to construct a topological map of a network. The algorithm run against this topological map is Dijkstra's Shortest Path First algorithm.

local-area network (LAN)   Interconnects network components within a local region (for example, within a building).

local loop   A connection between a customer premise and a local telephone company's central office.

logical topology   The actual traffic flow of a network determines the network's logical topology.

marking   Alters bits within a frame, cell, or packet to indicate how a network should treat that traffic. Marking alone does not change how a network treats a packet. Other tools (such as queuing tools) can, however, reference markings and make decisions (for example, forwarding decisions or dropping decisions) based on those markings.

maximum transmission unit (MTU)   The largest packet size supported on an interface.

media   Devices need to be interconnected via some sort of media. This media could be copper cabling. Alternately, it could be a fiber-optic cable. Media might not even be a cable, as is the case with wireless networks, where radio waves travel through the media of *air*.

metric   A value assigned to a route, and lower metrics are preferred over higher metrics.

metropolitan-area network (MAN)   Interconnects locations scattered throughout a metropolitan area.

Microsoft Challenge-Handshake Authentication Protocol (MS-CHAP)   A Microsoft-enhanced version of CHAP, offering a collection of additional features not present with PAP or CHAP, including two-way authentication.

Microsoft Routing and Remote Access Server (RRAS)   A Microsoft Windows Server® feature that allows Microsoft Windows® clients to remotely access a Microsoft Windows network.

multicast   A multicast communication flow is a one-to-many flow.

multifactor authentication   Similar to two-factor authentication, multifactor authentication requires two or more types of successful authentication before granting access to a network.

multilayer switch   Like a router, a multilayer switch can make traffic forwarding decisions based on Layer 3 information. Although multilayer switches more closely approach wire-speed throughput that most routers, routers tend to have a greater feature set and are capable of supporting more interface types than a multilayer switch.

multimode fiber (MMF)   Multimode fiber-optic cabling has a core with a diameter large enough to permit the injection of light into the core at multiple angles. The different paths (that is, *modes*) that light travels can lead to multimode delay distortion, which causes bits to be received out of order, because the pulses of light representing the bits traveled different paths (and therefore, different distances).

multiple input multiple output (MIMO)   MIMO uses multiple antennas for transmission and reception. These antennas do not interfere with one another, thanks to MIMO's use of spatial multiplexing, which encodes data based on the antenna from which the data will be transmitted. Both reliability and throughput can be increased with MIMO's simultaneous use of multiple antennas.

Multiprotocol Label Switching (MPLS)   A WAN technology popular among service providers. MPLS performs labels switching to forward traffic within an MPLS cloud by inserting a 32-bit header (which contains a 20-bit label) between a frame's Layer 2 and Layer 3 headers and making forwarding decisions based on the label within an MPLS header.

nbtstat command   Displays NetBIOS information for IP-based networks. The *nbt* prefix of the nbtstat command refers to NetBIOS over TCP/IP, which is called *NBT* (or *NetBT*). This command can, for example, display a listing of NetBIOS device names learned by a Microsoft Windows®-based PC.

Nessus®   A network-vulnerability scanner available from Tenable Network Security.®

netstat command   Can display a variety of information about IP-based connections on a Windows or UNIX host.

Network Address Translation (NAT)   Allows private IP addresses (as defined in RFC 1918) to be translated into Internet-routable IP addresses (public IP addresses).

Network as a Service (NaaS)   A service provider offering where clients can purchase data services (for example, e-mail, LDAP, and DNS services) traditionally hosted in a corporate data center.

network interface layer   The Network Interface Layer of the TCP/IP stack (also known as the *Network Access Layer*) encompasses the technologies addressed by Layers 1 and 2 (that is, the Physical and Data Link Layers) of the OSI model.

network layer   Layer 3 of the OSI model, it is primarily concerned with forwarding data based on logical addresses.

network-based IDS (NIDS)   A NIDS device is a network appliance dedicated to the purpose of acting as an IDS sensor.

network-based IPS (NIPS)   A NIPS device is a network appliance dedicated to the purpose of acting as an IPS sensor.

next-hop   A next-hop IP address is an IP address on the next router to which traffic should be forwarded.

Nmap   A network-vulnerability scanner.

non-designated port   In STP terms, non-designated ports block traffic to create a loop-free topology.

nslookup command   Can resolve a FQDN to an IP address on Microsoft Windows® and UNIX hosts.

octet   A grouping of 8 bits. An IPv4 address is comprised of four octets (that is, a total of 32 bits).

off-site   The term *off-site* in the context of virtualization technologies refers to hosting virtual devices on hardware physically located in a service provider's data center.

omnidirectional antenna   Radiates power at relatively equal power levels in all directions (somewhat similar to the theoretical isotropic antenna). Omnidirectional antennas are popular in residential WLANs and SOHO locations.

on-site   The term *on-site* in the context of virtualization technologies refers to hosting virtual devices on hardware physically located in a corporate data center.

open   A broken strand of copper that prevents current from flowing through a circuit.

Open Shortest Path First (OSPF)   A link-state routing protocol that uses a metric of *cost*, which is based on the link speed between two routers. OSPF is a popular IGP, because of its scalability, fast convergence, and vendor interoperability.

Open Systems Interconnection (OSI) reference model   Commonly referred to as the *OSI model* or the *OSI stack*. This seven-layer model categorizes various network technologies.

optical carrier (OC)   Optical networks often use OC levels to indicate bandwidth. As a base reference point, the speed of an OC-1 link is 51.84 Mbps. Other OC levels are multiples of an OC-1. For example, an OC-3 link has three times the bandwidth of an OC-1 link (that is, 3 * 51.84 Mbps = 155.52 Mbps).

optical time domain reflectometer (OTDR)   Detects the location of a fault in a fiber cable by sending light down the fiber-optic cable and measuring the time required for the light to bounce back from the cable fault. The OTDM can then mathematically calculate the location of the fault.

Orthogonal Frequency Division Multiplexing (OFDM)   While DSSS used a high modulation rate for the symbols it sends, OFDM uses a relatively slow modulation rate for symbols. This slower modulation rate, combined with the simultaneous transmission of data over 52 data streams, helps OFDM support high data rates while resisting crosstalk between the various data streams.

packet-switched connection   Similar to a dedicated leased line, because most packet-switched networks are always on. However, unlike a dedicated leased line, packet-switched connections allow multiple customers to share a service provider's bandwidth.

partial-mesh topology   A hybrid of a hub-and-spoke topology and a full-mesh topology. A partial-mesh topology can be designed to provide an optimal route between selected sites, while avoiding the expense of interconnecting every site to every other site.

Password Authentication Protocol (PAP)   Performs one-way authentication (that is, a client authenticates with a server). However, a significant drawback to PPP, other than its unidirectional authentication, is its clear-text transmission of credentials, which could permit an eavesdropper to learn authentication credentials.

peer-to-peer network   Allows interconnected devices (for example, PCs) to share their resources with one another. These resources could be, for example, files or printers.

personal-area network (PAN)   A network whose scale is smaller than a LAN. As an example, a connection between a PC and a digital camera via a USB cable is considered to be a PAN.

physical layer   Layer 1 of the OSI model, it is concerned with the transmission of bits on a network.

physical topology   The way a network's components are physically interconnected determines the network's physical topology.

ping command   One of the most commonly used command-line commands. It can check IP connectivity between two network devices. Multiple platforms (for example, routers, switches, and hosts) support the **ping** command.

plain old telephone service (POTS)   A POTS connection connects a customer device (such as a telephone) to the public switched telephone network (PSTN).

plenum   Plenum cabling is fire retardant and minimizes toxic fumes released by network cabling if that cable were to catch on fire. As a result, plenum cabling is often a requirement of local fire codes for cable in raised flooring or in other open air return ducts.

Point-to-Point Protocol (PPP) A common Layer 2 protocol offering features such as multilink interface, looped link detection, error detection, and authentication.

Point-to-Point Protocol over Ethernet (PPPoE) Commonly used between a DSL modem in a home (or business) and a service provider. Specifically, PPPoE encapsulates PPP frames within Ethernet frames. PPP is used to leverage its features, such as authentication.

Point-to-Point Tunneling Protocol (PPTP) An older VPN protocol (that supported the *dial-up networking* feature in older versions of Microsoft Windows®). Like L2TP and L2F, PPTP lacks native security features. However, Microsoft's versions of PPTP bundled with various versions of Microsoft Windows® were enhanced to offer security features.

poison reverse This feature of a distance-vector routing protocol causes a route received on one interface to be advertised back out of that same interface with a metric considered to be infinite.

policing Instead of making a minimum amount of bandwidth available for specific traffic types, you might want to limit available bandwidth. Both policing and traffic-shaping tools can accomplish this objective. Collectively, these tools are called *traffic conditioners*. Policing can drop exceeding traffic, as opposed to buffering it.

Port Address Translation (PAT) A variant of NAT in which multiple inside local IP addresses share a single inside global IP address. PAT can distinguish between different flows based on port numbers.

Power over Ethernet (PoE) Defined by the IEEE 802.3af and 802.3at standards, PoE allows an Ethernet switch to provide power to an attached device (for example, a wireless access point, security camera, or IP phone), by applying power to the same wires in a UTP cable that are used to transmit and receive data.

prefix notation A method of indicating how many bits are in a subnet mask. For example, */24* is prefix notation for a 24-bit subnet mask. Prefix notation is also known as *slash notation*.

presentation layer Layer 6 of the OSI model, it is responsible for the formatting of data being exchanged and securing the data with encryption.

pretty good privacy (PGP) PGP is a widely deployed asymmetric encryption algorithm and is often used to encrypt e-mail traffic.

primary rate interface (PRI) A PRI circuit is an ISDN circuit built on a T1 or E1 circuit. Recall that a T1 circuit has 24 channels. Therefore, if a PRI circuit is built on a T1 circuit, the ISDN circuit has 23 B channels and a one 64 kbps D channel. The 24th channel in the T1 circuit is used as the ISDN D channel (that is, the channel used to carry the Q.921 and Q.931 signaling protocols, which are used to set up, maintain, and tear down connections).

private IP addresses   Specific Class A, B, and C networks have been designed for private use. Although these networks are routable (with the exception of the 169.254.0.0–169.254.255.255 address range), within the organization, service providers do not route these private networks over the public Internet.

protocol data unit (PDU)   The name given to data at different layers of the OSI model. Specifically, the PDU for Layer 4 is *segment*. The Layer 3 PDU is *packet*, the Layer 2 PDU is *frame*, and the Layer 1 PDU is *bit*.

Protocol Independent Multicast (PIM)   A multicast protocol used between multicast-enabled routers to construct a multicast distribution tree.

proxy server   Intercepts requests being sent from a client and forwards those request on to their intended destination. The proxy server then sends any return traffic to the client which initiated the session. This provides address hiding for the client. Also, some proxy servers conserve WAN bandwidth by offering a content caching function. Additionally, some proxy servers offer URL filtering to, for example, block users from accessing social networking sites during working hours.

public key infrastructure (PKI)   A PKI system uses digital certificates and a certificate authority to allow secure communication across a public network.

public switched telephone network (PSTN)   The worldwide telephony network comprised of multiple telephone carriers.

punch-down tool   When terminating wires on a punch-down block (for example, a 110 block), you should use a punch-down tool, which is designed to properly insert an insulated wire between two contact blades in a punch down block, without damaging the blades.

Real-time Transport Protocol (RTP)   A Layer 4 protocol that carries voice (and interactive video).

reliability   The measure of how error-free a network transmits packets.

remote access VPN   See *client-to-site VPN*.

Remote Authentication Dial-In User Service (RADIUS)   A UDP-based protocol used to communicate with a AAA server. Unlike TACACS+, RADIUS does not encrypt an entire authentication packet, but only the password. However, RADIUS offers more robust accounting features than TACACS+. Also, RADIUS is a standards-based protocol, while TACACS+ is a Cisco-proprietary protocol.

ring topology   In a ring topology, traffic flows in a circular fashion around a closed network loop (that is, a ring). Typically, a ring topology sends data, in a single direction, to each connected device in turn, until the intended destination receives the data.

root port   In a STP topology, every non-root bridge has a single root port, which is the port on that switch that is closest to the root bridge, in terms of cost.

route command   Can add, modify, or delete routes in the IP routing table of Microsoft Windows® and UNIX hosts. Additionally, the **route** command can be used to view the IP routing table of Microsoft Windows® hosts.

route redistribution   Allows routes learned by one routing protocol to be injected into the routing process of another routing protocol.

routed protocol   A protocol with an addressing scheme (for example, IP) that defines different network addresses.

router   A router is considered a Layer 3 device, meaning that it makes its forwarding decisions based on logical network addresses. Most modern networks use IP addressing.

Routing Information Protocol (RIP)   A distance-vector routing protocol that uses a metric of *hop count*. The maximum number of hops between two routers in an RIP-based network is 15. Therefore, a hop count of 16 is considered to be infinite. RIP is considered to be an IGP.

routing protocol   A routing protocol (for example, RIP, OSPF, or EIGRP) that advertises route information between routers, which describes how to reach specified destination networks.

RSA   A popular and widely deployed asymmetric encryption algorithm.

satellite (WAN technology)   Provides WAN access to sites where terrestrial WAN solutions are unavailable. Satellite WAN connections can suffer from long round-trip delay (which can be unacceptable for latency-sensitive applications) and are susceptible to poor weather conditions.

Secure Sockets Layer (SSL)   Provides cryptography and reliability for upper layers (Layers 5–7) of the OSI model. SSL, which was introduced in 1995, has largely been replaced by Transport Layer Security (TLS). However, recent versions of SSL (for example, SSL 3.3) have been enhanced to be more comparable with TLS. Both SSL and TLS are able to provide secure web browsing via HTTPS.

security association (SA)   An agreement between the two IPsec peers about the cryptographic parameters to be used in an ISAKMP session.

security policy   A continually changing document that dictates a set of guidelines for network use. These guidelines complement organizational objectives by specifying rules for how a network is used.

server   As its name suggests, a server serves up resources to a network. These resources might include e-mail access as provided by an e-mail server, web pages as provided by a web server, or files available on a file server.

service set identifier (SSID)   A string of characters that identify a WLAN. APs participating in the same WLAN can be configured with identical SSIDs. An SSID shared among multiple APs is called an extended service set identifier (ESSID).

Session Initiation Protocol (SIP)   A VoIP signaling protocol used to set up, maintain, and tear down VoIP phone calls.

session layer   As Layer 5 of the OSI model, it's responsible for setting up, maintaining, and tearing down sessions.

shielded twisted-pair (STP) cable   STP cabling prevents wires in a cable from acting as an antenna, which might receive or transmit EMI. STP cable might have a metallic shielding, similar to the braided wire that acts as an outer conductor in a coaxial cable.

short   A short occurs when two copper connectors touch each other, resulting in current flowing through that short rather than the attached electrical circuit, because the short has lower resistance.

Simple Network Management Protocol (SNMP)   A protocol used to monitor and manage network devices, such as routers, switches, and servers.

single-mode fiber (SMF)   SMF cabling has a core with a diameter large enough to permit only a single path for light pulses (that is, only one mode of propagation). By having a single path for light to travel, SMF eliminates the concern of *multimode delay distortion*.

single sign-on (SSO)   Allows a user to authenticate once to gain access to multiple systems, without requiring the user to independently authenticate with each system.

site-to-site VPN   Interconnects two sites, as an alternative to a leased line, at a reduced cost.

slash notation   See *prefix notation*.

social engineering   Attackers sometimes use social techniques (which often leverage people's desire to be helpful) to obtain confidential information. For example, an attacker might pose as a member of an IT department and ask a company employ for their login credentials in order for the "IT staff to test the connection." This type of attack is called social engineering.

software firewall   A computer running firewall software. For example, the software firewall could protect the computer itself (for example, preventing incoming connections to the computer). Alternately, a software firewall could be a computer with more than one network interface card that runs firewall software to filter traffic flowing through the computer.

Spanning Tree Protocol (STP)   Defined by the IEEE 802.1D standard, it allows a network to have redundant Layer 2 connections, while logical preventing a loop, which could lead to symptoms such as broadcast storms and MAC address table corruption.

split horizon   This feature of a distance-vector routing protocol prevents a route learned on one interface from being advertised back out of that same interface.

star topology   In a star topology, a network has a central point (for example, a switch) from which all attached devices radiate.

state transition modulation   One way to electrically or optically represent a binary 1 or 0 is to use the transition between a voltage level (for example, going from a state of no voltage to a state of voltage, or vice versa, on a copper cable) or the transition of having light or no light on a fiber optic cable to represent a binary 1. Similarly, a binary 0 is represented by having no transition in a voltage level or light level from one time period to the next. This approach of representing binary digits is called state transition modulation.

stateful firewall   Inspects traffic leaving the inside network as it goes out to the Internet. Then, when returning traffic from the same session (as identified by source and destination IP addresses and port numbers) attempts to enter the inside network, the stateful firewall permits that traffic. The process of inspecting traffic to identify unique sessions is called *stateful inspection*.

static NAT (SNAT)   A variant of NAT in which an inside local IP address is statically mapped to an inside global IP address. SNAT is useful for servers inside a network, which need to be accessible from an outside network.

supplicant   In a network using 802.1X user authentication, a supplicant is the device that wants to gain access to a network.

switch   Like an Ethernet hub, an Ethernet switch interconnects network components. Like a hub, switches are available with a variety of port densities. However, unlike a hub, a switch doesn't simply take traffic in on one port and forward copies of that traffic out all other ports. Rather, a switch learns which devices reside off of which ports. As a result, when traffic comes in a switch port, the switch interrogates the traffic to see where it's destined. Then, based on what the switch has learned, the switch forwards the traffic out of the appropriate port, and not out all of the other ports.

symmetric encryption   With symmetric encryption, both the sender and receiver of a packet use the same key (a *shared key*) for encryption and decryption.

Synchronous Optical Network (SONET)   A Layer 1 technology that uses fiber-optic cabling as its media. Because SONET is a Layer 1 technology, it can be used to transport various Layer 2 encapsulation types, such as ATM. Also, because SONET uses fiber-optic cabling, it offers high data rates, typically in the 155 Mbps–10 Gbps range, and long-distance limitations, typically in the 20 km–250 km range.

syslog A syslog-logging solution consists of two primary components: syslog servers, which receive and store log messages sent from syslog clients, and syslog clients, which can be a variety of network devices that send logging information to a syslog server.

T1 T1 circuits were originally used in telephony networks, with the intent of one voice conversation being carried in a single channel (that is, a single DS0). A T1 circuit is comprised of 24 DS0s, and the bandwidth of a T1 circuit is 1.544 Mbps.

T3 In the same T-carrier family of standards as a T1, a T3 circuit offers an increased bandwidth capacity. Although a T1 circuit combines 24 DS0s into a single physical connection to offer 1.544 Mbps of bandwidth, a T3 circuit combines 672 DS0s into a single physical connection, with a resulting bandwidth capacity of 44.7 Mbps.

TCP/IP stack Also known as the *DoD model*, this four-layer model (as opposed to the seven-layer OSI model) targets the suite of TCP/IP protocols.

telco A telephone company. Some countries have government-maintained telcos, while other countries have multiple telcos that compete with one another.

Terminal Access Controller Access-Control System Plus (TACACS+) A TCP-based protocol used to communicate with a AAA server. Unlike RADIUS, TACACS+ encrypts an entire authentication packet rather than just the password. TACACS+ offers authentication features, but they are not as robust as the accounting features found in RADIUS. Also, unlike RADIUS, TACACS+ is a Cisco-proprietary protocol.

time-division multiplexing (TDM) Supports different communication sessions (for example, different telephone conversations in a telephony network) on the same physical medium, by allowing sessions to take turns. For a brief period of time, defined as a time slot, data from the first session is sent, followed by data from the second sessions. This continues until all sessions have had a turn, and the process repeats itself.

time domain reflectometer (TDR) Detects the location of a fault in a copper cable by sending an electric signal down the copper cable and measuring the time required for the signal to bounce back from the cable fault. A TDM can then mathematically calculate the location of the fault.

Time to Live (TTL) The TTL field in an IP header is decremented once for each router hop. Therefore, if the value in a TTL field is reduced to 0, a router discards the frame and sends a *time exceeded* ICMP message back to the source.

tip and ring   The red and green wires found in an RJ-11 wall jacks, which carry voice, ringing voltage, and signaling information between an analog device (for example, a phone or a modem) and an RJ-11 wall jack.

toner probe   Sometimes called a *fox and hound*, a toner probe allows you to place a tone generator at one end of the connection (for example, in someone's office), and use a probe on the punch-down block to audibly detect to which pair of wires the tone generator is connected.

tracert command   A Microsoft Windows®-based command that displays every router hop along the path from a source host to a destination host on an IP network. Information about a router hop can include such information as the IP address of the router hop and the round-trip delay of that router hop.

traceroute command   A UNIX command that display every router hop along the path from a source host to a destination host on an IP network. Information about the router hop can include the IP address of the router hop and the round-trip delay of that router hop.

traffic shaping   Instead of making a minimum amount of bandwidth available for specific traffic types, you might want to limit available bandwidth. Both policing and shaping tools can accomplish this objective. Collectively, these tools are called *traffic conditioners*. Traffic shaping delays excess traffic by buffering it as opposed to dropping the excess traffic.

Transmission Control Protocol (TCP)   A connection-oriented transport protocol. Connection-oriented transport protocols provide reliable transport, in that if a segment is dropped, the sender can detect that drop and retransmit that dropped segment. Specifically, a receiver acknowledges segments that it receives. Based on those acknowledgments, a sender can determine which segments were successfully received.

transport layer (OSI model)   As Layer 4 of the OSI model, it acts as a dividing line between the upper layers and lower layers. Specifically, messages are taken from the upper layers (Layers 5–7) and encapsulated into segments for transmission to the lower layers (Layers 1–3). Similarly, data streams coming from lower layers are decapsulated and sent to Layer 5 (the session layer) or some other upper layer, depending on the protocol.

transport layer (TCP/IP stack)   The transport layer of the TCP/IP stack maps to Layer 4 (transport layer) of the OSI model. The two primary protocols found at the TCP/IP stack's transport layer are TCP and UDP.

trouble ticket   A problem report explaining the details of an issue being experienced in a network.

trunk   In the context of an Ethernet network, a trunk is a single physical or logical connection that simultaneously carries traffic for multiple VLANs. However, a trunk also refers to an interconnection between telephone switches, in the context of telephony.

twisted-pair cable   Today's most popular media type is twisted-pair cable, where individually insulated copper strands are intertwined into a twisted-pair cable. Two categories of twisted-pair cable include shielded twisted pair (STP) and unshielded twisted pair (UTP).

two-factor authentication (TFA)   Requires two types of authentication from a user seeking admission to a network. For example, a user might need to know something (for example, a password) and have something (for example, a specific fingerprint that can be checked with a biometric authentication device).

unicast   A unicast communication flow is a one-to-one flow.

unidirectional antenna   Unidirectional antennas can focus their power in a specific direction, thus avoiding potential interference with other wireless devices and perhaps reaching greater distances than those possible with omnidirectional antennas. One application for unidirectional antennas is interconnecting two nearby buildings.

uninterruptable power supply (UPS)   An appliance that provides power to networking equipment in the event of a power outage.

unshielded twisted-pair (UTP) cable   Blocks EMI from the copper strands making up a twisted-pair cable by twisting the strands more tightly (that is, more twists per centimeter [cm]). By wrapping these strands around each other, the wires insulate each other from EMI.

User Datagram Protocol (UDP)   A connectionless transport protocol. Connectionless transport protocols provide unreliable transport, in that if a segment is dropped, the sender is unaware of the drop, and no retransmission occurs.

virtual desktop   A virtual desktop solution allows a user to store data in a centralized data center, as opposed to the hard drive of their local computer. Then, with appropriate authentication credentials, that user can access his data from various remote devices (for example, his smartphone or another computer).

virtual LAN (VLAN)   A single broadcast domain, representing a single subnet. Typically, a group of ports on a switch are assigned to a single VLAN. For traffic to travel between two VLANs, that traffic needs to be routed.

virtual PBX   Usually a VoIP telephony solution hosted by a service provider, which interconnects with a company's existing telephone system.

virtual private network (VPN)   Some VPNs can support secure communication between two sites over an untrusted network (for example, the Internet).

virtual server   Allows a single physical server to host multiple virtual instances of various operating systems. This allows, for example, a single physical server to simultaneously host multiple Microsoft Windows® servers and multiple Linux servers.

virtual switch   Performs Layer 2 functions (for example, VLAN separation and filtering) between various server instances running on a single physical server.

warchalking   If an open WLAN (or a WLAN whose SSID and authentication credentials are known) is found in a public place, a user might write a symbol on a wall (or some other nearby structure) to let others know the characteristics of the discovered network. This practice, which is a variant of the decades-old practice of hobos leaving symbols as messages to fellow hobos, is called warchalking.

wide-area network (WAN)   Interconnects network components that are geographically separated.

wide-area network (WAN) link   An interconnection between two devices in a WAN.

Wi-Fi Protected Access (WPA)   The Wi-Fi Alliance (a non-profit organization formed to certify interoperability of wireless devices) developed its own security standard to address the weaknesses of Wired Equivalent Privacy (WEP). This new security standard was called Wi-Fi Protected Access (WPA) version 1.

Wi-Fi Protected Access version 2 (WPA2)   Uses Counter Mode with Cipher Block Chaining Message Authentication Code Protocol (CCMP) for integrity checking and Advanced Encryption Standard (AES) for encryption. These algorithms enhance the security offered by WPA.

Wired Equivalent Privacy (WEP)   A security standard for WLANs. With WEP, an AP is configured with a static WEP key. Wireless clients needing to associate with an AP are configured with an identical key (making this a preshared key [PSK] approach to security). The IEEE 802.11 standard specifies a 40-bit WEP key, which is considered to be a relatively weak security measure.

wireless access point (AP)   A device that connects to a wired network and provides access to that wired network for clients that wirelessly attach to the AP.

wireless router   Attaches to a wired network and provides access to that wired network for wirelessly attached clients, like a wireless AP. However, a wireless router is configured such that the wired interface that connects to the rest of the network (or to the Internet) is on a different IP network than the wireless clients. Typically, a wireless router performs NATing between these two IP address spaces.

Zeroconf   A technology that performs three basic functions: assigning link-local IP addresses, resolving computer names to IP addresses, and locating network services.

Index

A

A (address) record, 89

AAA (authentication, authorization, and accounting), 412

AAAA (IPv6 address) record, 89

acceptable use policy (AUP), 403

ACL (access control lists), 410-411

action plan, 442

active hubs, 74

active-active NIC redundancy, 288

active-standby NIC redundancy, 288

AD (administrative distance), 198

Adleman, Leonard M., 388

ADSL (asymmetric DSL), 234-236

AES (Advanced Encryption Standard), 387

AH (Authentication Header) protocol, 422

AM (amplitude modulation), 34

analog phone, 100

anomaly-based detection, 428

antennas

omnidirectional, 261

orientation of, 262

overview, 260-261

unidirectional, 262

anycast transmission, 181

AP (access points)

rogue access point, 274

troubleshooting, 454

wireless access point, 259-260

APIPA (Automatic Private IP Addressing), 151, 161-162

application layer

OSI model, 46-47

TCP/IP stack, 50-53

application logs (Microsoft Windows), 376

application services, 47

ARIN (American Registry for Internet Numbers), 150

arp command

UNIX commands, 337-339

Windows commands, 316-318

asset management, 367

assigning IP addresses, 153-162

asymmetric encryption, 388-390

asynchronous transmissions, 35, 38

ATM (Asynchronous Transfer Mode), 224, 246-248

attacks

availability attacks

buffer overflow, 399

DDoS (distributed denial of service) attack, 398

DoS (denial of service) attack, 398

electrical disturbances, 400-401

environmental threats, 401-402

ICMP attacks, 399-400

B

C

F

I

O

Z